PROFESSIONAL RESPONSIBILITY

ASPEN PUBLISHERS

PROFESSIONAL RESPONSIBILITY

THIRD EDITION

James E. Moliterno
Vincent Bradford Professor of Law
Washington and Lee University School of Law

The *Emanuel Law Outlines* Series

AUSTIN   BOSTON   CHICAGO   NEW YORK   THE NETHERLANDS

© 2010 Aspen Publishers. All Rights Reserved.
http://lawschool.aspenpublishers.com

No part of this publication may be reproduced or transmitted in any form or by any means, electronic or mechanical, including photocopy, recording, or any information storage and retrieval system, without permission in writing from the publisher. Requests for permission to make copies of any part of this publication should be mailed to:

Aspen Publishers
Attn: Permissions Department
76 Ninth Avenue, 7th Floor
New York, NY 10011-5201

To contact Customer Care, e-mail customer.care@aspenpublishers.com, call 1-800-234-1660, fax 1-800-901-9075, or mail correspondence to:

Aspen Publishers
Attn: Order Department
PO Box 990
Frederick, MD 21705

Printed in the United States of America.

1 2 3 4 5 6 7 8 9 0

ISBN 978-0-7355-8994-0

Library of Congress Cataloging-in-Publication Data
Moliterno, James E., 1953-
  Professional responsibility/James E. Moliterno.—3rd ed.
    p. cm. — (The Emanuel law outlines series)
  ISBN 978-0-7355-8944-0
  1. Legal ethics — United States. 2. Lawyers — Malpractice — United States. I. Title.
  KF306.M65 2010
  174'.30973 — dc22

2009046121

This book is intended as a general review of a legal subject. It is not intended as a source of advice for the solution of legal matters or problems. For advice on legal matters, the reader should consult an attorney.

Siegel's, Emanuel, the judge logo, Law in a Flash and design, CrunchTime and design, Strategies & Tactics and design, and The Professor Series are registered trademarks of Aspen Publishers.

About Wolters Kluwer Law & Business

Wolters Kluwer Law & Business is a leading provider of research information and workflow solutions in key specialty areas. The strengths of the individual brands of Aspen Publishers, CCH, Kluwer Law International and Loislaw are aligned within Wolters Kluwer Law & Business to provide comprehensive, in-depth solutions and expert-authored content for the legal, professional and education markets.

CCH was founded in 1913 and has served more than four generations of business professionals and their clients. The CCH products in the Wolters Kluwer Law & Business group are highly regarded electronic and print resources for legal, securities, antitrust and trade regulation, government contracting, banking, pension, payroll, employment and labor, and healthcare reimbursement and compliance professionals.

Aspen Publishers is a leading information provider for attorneys, business professionals and law students. Written by preeminent authorities, Aspen products offer analytical and practical information in a range of specialty practice areas from securities law and intellectual property to mergers and acquisitions and pension/benefits. Aspen's trusted legal education resources provide professors and students with high-quality, up-to-date and effective resources for successful instruction and study in all areas of the law.

Kluwer Law International supplies the global business community with comprehensive English-language international legal information. Legal practitioners, corporate counsel and business executives around the world rely on the Kluwer Law International journals, loose-leafs, books and electronic products for authoritative information in many areas of international legal practice.

Loislaw is a premier provider of digitized legal content to small law firm practitioners of various specializations. Loislaw provides attorneys with the ability to quickly and efficiently find the necessary legal information they need, when and where they need it, by facilitating access to primary law as well as state-specific law, records, forms and treatises.

Wolters Kluwer Law & Business, a unit of Wolters Kluwer, is headquartered in New York and Riverwoods, Illinois. Wolters Kluwer is a leading multinational publisher and information services company.

To my Mother and Father, my first great teachers.
                                    JEM

Summary of Contents

Table of Contents	*xi*
Preface	*xxix*
Casebook Correlation Chart	*xxxi*
Capsule Summary	C-1
1. Introduction and the Role of Lawyer	1
2. Regulation of the Legal Profession	9
3. Controls on Lawyer Conduct	31
4. Formal Aspects of the Lawyer-Client Relationship	47
5. Confidentiality	75
6. Conflicts of Interest	99
7. Duties to Third Parties	135
8. Duties to the Legal System and Society	155
9. Special Role-Related Duties	183
10. Advertising and Solicitation	199
11. Judicial Conduct	217
Essay Exam Questions	241
Essay Exam Answers	243
Multistate-Style Exam Questions	247
Multistate-Style Exam Answers	261
Table of Cases	263
Table of Statutes, Rules, and Opinions	267
Index	271

Table of Contents

Preface	*xxix*
Casebook Correlation Chart	*xxxi*
Capsule Summary	C-1

CHAPTER 1
INTRODUCTION AND THE ROLE OF LAWYER

	ChapterScope	1
I.	**Courses Called Professional Responsibility, Legal Ethics, and Legal Profession**	1
II.	**Moral Philosophy, Right and Wrong, and the Law Governing Lawyers**	1
	A. Moral philosophy	1
	B. Right and wrong	2
	C. The law governing lawyers	2
	D. Role morality	2
	1. Lawyer's role in dispute resolution system	2
	2. Role morality v. general moral standards	2
	3. Balance of many duties	2
III.	**The Role of Lawyer**	3
	A. Differing conceptions of the lawyer's role	3
	1. The standard conception of the lawyer's role	3
	2. The lawyer as businessperson	4
	3. The moral activist lawyer	4
	B. Differences between lawyers' litigation and planning roles	4
	1. Litigation context	4
	2. Planning context	4
	3. Responsibility for client's acts	4
	C. Practice setting	5
	1. Prosecutors	5
	2. Other government lawyers	5
	3. Criminal defense	5
	4. Corporate or other organization counsel	6
	5. Legal aid	6
	D. Other roles for lawyers	6
	Quiz Yourself on INTRODUCTION AND THE ROLE OF LAWYER	6
	Exam Tips on INTRODUCTION AND THE ROLE OF LAWYER	7

Chapter 2
REGULATION OF THE LEGAL PROFESSION

	ChapterScope		9
I.	**Organization of the Bar**		10
	A.	The American Bar Association	10
		1. Beginnings	10
		2. A voluntary association	10
	B.	Alternative national bar associations	10
		1. The National Lawyers Guild	10
		2. The National Bar Association	10
		3. Organizations of women lawyers	10
		4. Others	10
	C.	State bar associations	11
		1. Voluntary state bar associations	11
		2. The integrated bar	11
II.	**Sources of Law Governing Lawyers**		11
	A.	Ethics codes	11
		1. ABA models and their organization	11
		2. State-adopted codes	13
	B.	Case authority	13
		1. Interpretation of codes	13
		2. Inherent power to regulate lawyers	13
	C.	Ethics opinions	13
	D.	Restatement	13
	E.	Constitutional restraints	13
		1. Commercial speech	13
		2. Speech rights of lawyers	13
		3. Entry to the bar	14
	F.	"Other law"	14
		1. Contracts	14
		2. Torts	14
		3. Fiduciary law	14
		4. Agency	14
		5. Criminal law	14
		6. Procedural law	14
		7. Antitrust	14
		8. Administrative regulations	15
		9. Employment law	15
III.	**Admission to Practice**		15
	A.	Policy	15
	B.	General requirements	15
		1. Education	15
		2. Knowledge	15
		3. Good character	16
		4. Misconduct in the application process	17

		5. No assistance with admission of unqualified applicant	17
	C.	Federal courts	**18**
	D.	Admission *pro hac vice*	**18**
		1. Reciprocity	18
		2. Local counsel	18
		3. Broad discretion	18
		4. No due process right to be granted *pro hac vice* admission	18
IV.	**Unauthorized Practice**		**19**
	A.	Attributes of the practice of law	**19**
		1. Court appearance	19
		2. Legal advice and counsel	19
		3. Sale of do-it-yourself forms	19
	B.	Forms of unauthorized practice	**19**
		1. Extraterritorial practice of licensed lawyers	19
		2. Multijurisdictional practice	19
		3. Practice by the unlicensed	22
V.	**Self-Governance and the Duty to Report Misconduct**		**23**
	A.	Knowledge of misconduct	**23**
	B.	Level or type of misconduct	**23**
	C.	Confidentiality limitation on duty to report	**23**
		1. A lawyer-client	23
		2. Learning from a nonlawyer client	24
	D.	Defamation privilege	**24**

Quiz Yourself on REGULATION OF THE LEGAL PROFESSION 25

Exam Tips on REGULATION OF THE LEGAL PROFESSION 28

CHAPTER 3
CONTROLS ON LAWYER CONDUCT

		CHAPTERSCOPE	31
I.	**Discipline**		**32**
	A.	Discipline v. malpractice	**32**
	B.	Grounds for discipline	**32**
		1. Violation of adopted ethics code	32
		2. Acts indicating moral turpitude	33
		3. Criminal conduct	33
		4. Dishonesty, fraud, and deceit	33
		5. Conduct prejudicial to the administration of justice	34
	C.	Forms of discipline	**34**
		1. Disbarment	34
		2. Suspension	34
		3. Reprimand	34
	D.	Disciplinary procedure	**34**
		1. Complaint	35
		2. Investigation by committee	35

		3. Hearing committee	35
		4. Review by appeal board	35
		5. State court of last resort	35
		6. Due process	35
		7. Mitigation	35
II.	**Malpractice**		**36**
	A.	Contract theories	36
	B.	Tort theories	36
		1. Duty	36
		2. Breach	37
		3. Causation	37
		4. Damages	37
	C.	Fiduciary duty	37
	D.	Necessity of expert testimony	37
	E.	Prospective limitation on malpractice liability	38
	F.	Liability to third parties for malpractice	38
III.	**Liability for Client Conduct**		**38**
IV.	**Contempt of Court**		**38**
	A.	A last resort	39
	B.	Disruption of the proceedings	39
	C.	Direct or summary contempt	39
	D.	Indirect contempt	39
	E.	Sanctions	39
V.	**Disqualification Motions and Other Litigation-Driven Controls**		**39**
	A.	Disqualification for conflicts of interest	39
		1. Substantive standards	39
		2. Other interests	39
	B.	Federal Rule of Civil Procedure 11 and its state law counterparts	40
		1. Analogous to frivolous claims ethics code provisions	40
		2. Claims that lack a basis in law or fact	40
		3. Safe harbor	40
		4. Sanctions against signer and firm	41
	C.	Other sanctions	41
	Quiz Yourself on CONTROLS ON LAWYER CONDUCT		41
	Exam Tips on CONTROLS ON LAWYER CONDUCT		44

CHAPTER 4

FORMAL ASPECTS OF THE LAWYER-CLIENT RELATIONSHIP

	CHAPTERSCOPE		47
I.	**Undertaking Representation**		**48**
	A.	Duty to undertake representation	48
		1. General	48

		2. Limited duty to accept representation	48
	B.	Duty to reject representation	**50**
		1. Representation will violate the ethics rules	50
		2. Representation will violate other law	50
		3. Lawyer's physical or mental health	50
	C.	Lawyer-client contracts and the beginning of the lawyer-client relationship	**51**
		1. When begun	51
		2. Wrongful discharge	51
II.	**Fees**		**52**
	A.	Reasonableness standard	**52**
		1. Factors	52
	B.	Writing and timing	**53**
	C.	Contingent fees	**53**
		1. Historical disapproval	53
		2. Prohibited case types	54
		3. Other restrictions	54
	D.	Fee splitting	**54**
		1. Among lawyers	54
		2. The modern rule governing lawyer fee splitting	55
		3. With former partners	55
		4. With nonlawyers	55
	E.	Court-awarded fees	**55**
	F.	Minimum fee schedules	**55**
	G.	Fee forfeiture	**55**
III.	**Fiduciary Duties**		**56**
	A.	General role of a fiduciary	**56**
	B.	Handling clients' money	**56**
		1. Violations a most serious matter	56
		2. Client trust accounts	57
		3. Commingling funds	58
		4. Prompt delivery and accounting	58
		5. Conversion	58
IV.	**Competence and Diligence**		**58**
	A.	Competence	**58**
		1. Distinct from malpractice	59
		2. Does not require possession of expertise at the beginning of representation	59
		3. Basic, cross-cutting skills and knowledge are always required	59
		4. Emergency	59
		5. Continuing competence	59
	B.	Diligence	**60**
		1. Expediting matters	60
		2. Starting and stopping	60
		3. Misleading about diligence	60
		4. Inadequate excuses	60
V.	**Communication and Shared Decision-Making**		**60**
	A.	Communication	**61**
		1. Keeping client reasonably informed	61

		2. Explaining matters to the client	61
	B.	Shared decision-making	**61**
		1. Scope of representation	61
		2. Means and ends	61
		3. Lawyer independence from client views	63
		4. Counseling crimes or frauds	63
		5. The client under a disability	64
VI.	**Terminating Representation**		**64**
	A.	Rejection of representation	64
	B.	Mandatory withdrawal	64
		1. Continued representation will violate the ethics rules	64
		2. Continued representation will violate other law	64
		3. Lawyer's physical or mental health	65
		4. Lawyer is discharged	65
	C.	Permissive withdrawal	**65**
		1. No harm to client	65
		2. Causes that will excuse some material harm to the client	65
	D.	Court order to continue	**66**
	E.	Procedural requirements for withdrawal	**67**
		1. Notice	67
		2. Court approval	67
	F.	Duties upon termination of the lawyer-client relationship	**67**
		1. Fee refund	67
		2. Client's papers and property	67
	G.	Fee liability upon termination	**67**
		1. Fixed or hourly fees	67
		2. Contingent fee	67

Quiz Yourself on FORMAL ASPECTS OF THE LAWYER-CLIENT RELATIONSHIP 68

Exam Tips on FORMAL ASPECTS OF THE LAWYER-CLIENT RELATIONSHIP 70

CHAPTER 5
CONFIDENTIALITY

		CHAPTERSCOPE	**75**
I.	**The Duty of Confidentiality and the Attorney-Client Evidentiary Privilege**		**76**
	A.	Secrets and confidences	76
	B.	Scope of the attorney-client privilege	76
	C.	Parameters of the evidentiary privilege	77
		1. Clients or prospective clients	77
		2. Desire for confidentiality required	77
		3. Communication, not knowledge	78
		4. Lawyer observations	78
		5. Physical evidence	79
		6. Exceptions	79

II.	**To Whom Is the Duty Owed?**		**80**
	A. Generally		80
		1. Former clients	80
		2. Prospective clients	80
		3. No fee necessary	80
	B. Organizational clients		81
		1. Agents of the organizational client	81
		2. Government agency client	81
	C. Client and lawyer agents		81
		1. Lawyer agents	81
		2. Client agents	81
III.	**To What Does the Duty Apply?**		**82**
	A. Duty of confidentiality or evidentiary privilege		82
	B. Duty of confidentiality broader than evidentiary privilege		82
		1. Lawyer observations	82
		2. Communications from third parties	82
		3. Work product	82
IV.	**Exceptions to the Duty of Confidentiality**		**83**
	A. Consent		83
	B. Implied authorization		83
	C. Self-defense and fees		83
		1. The three categories of self-defense permitted disclosure	84
		2. Limit disclosure to facts necessary to defend	84
		3. Limit disclosure to individuals who need to know	84
	D. Future crimes, frauds, and harms		85
		1. Distinction with past crimes or frauds	85
		2. Policy rationale	85
		3. Model Code	85
		4. Model Rules	86
		5. August 2003 amendment to Model Rule 1.6	87
		6. Organizational constituents	87
		7. State variance from Model Code and Model Rules	87
	E. Other professional responsibility rules		88
		1. Model Rule 2.4	88
		2. Model Rule 2.3	88
		3. Model Rule 3.3	88
	F. "Other law" or orders of court		88
		1. Orders of court	88
		2. Other law	88
	G. Information generally known		89
V.	**Other Professional Duties That Are Subject to the Duty of Confidentiality**		**89**
	A. Model Rule 8.3		90
	B. Model Rule 1.9(c)(2)		90
	C. Model Rule 1.13 Comment 5		90
	D. Model Rule 2.3(c)		90
	E. Model Rule 4.1		90

VI.	**Use of Confidential Information for the Lawyer's Benefit**	**90**
	A. Model Code	90
	B. Model Rules	90
	C. A meaningless distinction	90
	1. Disadvantage to client almost always potentially present	91
	2. Agency limitations	91
	Quiz Yourself on CONFIDENTIALITY	91
	Exam Tips on CONFIDENTIALITY	94

Chapter 6
CONFLICTS OF INTEREST

	CHAPTERSCOPE	**99**
I.	**Loyalty and Other General Principles**	**101**
	A. Loyalty	101
	B. Independence of professional judgment	101
	C. Implications of confidentiality	101
	D. Direct adversity	101
	E. Material limitations on representation	101
II.	**Organization of the Model Rules Provisions on Conflicts**	**101**
	A. General rule	101
	B. Specific transactions	102
	C. Special problems of former clients	102
	D. Prospective clients	102
	E. Role-relevant rules	102
	1. Regarding former government lawyers	102
	2. Regarding former judges	102
	3. Regarding lawyers for organizations	102
	F. Imputed disqualification	102
	1. Regarding former clients	102
	2. Regarding former government lawyers	102
	3. Regarding former judges	102
III.	**Waiver of Conflicts**	**102**
	A. Rationale	102
	1. The gross conflict exception	102
	2. The interest-other-than-the-client's exception	103
	B. Elements of waiver	**104**
	1. Consultation	104
	2. Client well informed	104
	3. Consent	105
	4. Enhanced waiver requirements	105
IV.	**Sources of Conflicts**	**105**
	A. Third-party interference	105
	1. Third-party payment of fees	105
	2. Other common interference settings	106

	B.	Lawyer-client conflicts	**108**
		1. General principles	108
		2. Particular transactions	108
		3. Lawyer-client conflicts and champerty, barratry, and maintenance	110
		4. Miscellaneous lawyer-client conflicts rules	111
	C.	Multiple-client conflicts	**111**
		1. Concurrent clients	112
		2. Prospective and current clients	114
		3. Former and current clients—The substantial relationship test	114
		4. Lawyer for an organization	115
		5. Sarbanes-Oxley restrictions on certain corporate lawyers	116
		6. Positional conflicts of interest	117
V.	**Imputed Conflicts**	**118**
	A.	Basic issues	**118**
	B.	Motions to disqualify	**118**
	C.	The ambulatory lawyer	**118**
	D.	Screening defenses	**118**
		1. Don't talk	118
		2. No pay	118
		3. Lock it up	118
		4. Move him out	118
	E.	Other interests at play in the motion-to-disqualify setting	**119**
		1. Client choice of lawyer	119
		2. Timing of screening procedures and motion to disqualify	119
		3. Intentional creation of conflicts by the moving party	119
		4. Judicial economy	119
	F.	Special role-related imputed disqualification rules	**119**
VI.	**Special Role-Related Conflicts Rules**	**119**
	A.	Former judge	**119**
		1. General	120
		2. Successive representation in the same matter	120
		3. Negotiating for employment	121
		4. Special imputed disqualification rules	121
	B.	Former government lawyer	**121**
		1. General	121
		2. Use of confidential government information	122
		3. Special imputed disqualification rules	123
	C.	Lawyer as witness	**123**
		1. Combining roles	123
		2. Rationale	123
		3. Exceptions	124

Quiz Yourself on CONFLICTS OF INTEREST 124

Exam Tips on CONFLICTS OF INTEREST 128

Chapter 7
DUTIES TO THIRD PARTIES

	ChapterScope	**135**
I.	**Truth-Telling Outside the Court Context**	**136**
	A. False statements of material law or fact	136
	1. False	136
	2. Material	136
	B. Fraudulent statements and silences	136
	1. Tort concepts and reliance	136
	C. The negotiation setting	137
	1. The parties to the negotiation	137
	2. What is a fact?	137
	3. Reducing agreements to writing	138
II.	**Harassment and Other Abusive Conduct**	**138**
	A. In general	139
	1. Unlawful acts by lawyers	139
	2. Assisting clients in committing unlawful or fraudulent acts	139
	3. Harassing conduct	139
	B. Opposing parties	139
	C. Witnesses	140
	1. In general	140
	2. Investigation	140
	D. Jurors	140
	1. Investigation	140
	2. Post-verdict harassing conduct	140
III.	**Threatening Criminal Prosecution**	**140**
	A. Applies to prosecutors	141
IV.	**Communicating with Represented Persons**	**141**
	A. Parties and persons	141
	B. Communicating	141
	C. Agents	141
	D. Subject matter of the dispute	141
	E. Who is an opposing party or person?	142
	1. Mere witnesses	142
	2. Organizational parties	142
	3. Class-action members	143
	F. Obtaining permission	143
	G. Authorized by law	143
	H. Authorized by court order	143
	I. Special criminal practice concerns	143
	1. Added constitutional limitations	144
	2. Investigation of crime	144
V.	**Communicating with Unrepresented Persons**	**144**
	A. Avoid misleading about the lawyer's interest	144
	1. Affirmative duty	144
	2. Clarifying duty	145

	B.	Giving advice	145
	C.	Fact gathering	145
VI.	**Civil Liability to Third Persons**	145
	A.	General	145
	B.	Intended beneficiaries of the lawyer's work for a client	145
	C.	Invited reliance	145
	D.	Assisting clients in breaching fiduciary duties	146
	E.	Preventing client harm to a third person	146

Quiz Yourself on DUTIES TO THIRD PARTIES 146

Exam Tips on DUTIES TO THIRD PARTIES 150

CHAPTER 8
DUTIES TO THE LEGAL SYSTEM AND SOCIETY

		CHAPTERSCOPE	155
I.	**Truth-Telling Inside the Court Context**	156
	A.	Statements to opposing parties	156
	B.	Fact statements to the court	156
		1. Generally	156
		2. Ex parte proceedings	157
	C.	Perjury	158
		1. General duty to refrain from offering false evidence	158
		2. Discretion to refuse to offer some evidence	158
		3. Perjury by a witness	158
		4. Perjury by a client	158
	D.	Law statements to the court	160
	E.	Disclosing adverse legal authority	160
		1. To opposing parties	161
		2. To the court	161
II.	**Suppressing Evidence and Witness Payment**	162
	A.	Suppressing witness availability	162
		1. Procuring witness unavailability	162
		2. Instructing a witness to cooperate only if subpoenaed	162
		3. Exception	162
	B.	Witness payment rules	163
		1. Lay witnesses	163
		2. Expert witnesses	163
III.	**Limitations on Presentations to a Court**	163
	A.	Frivolous claims and litigation positions	163
		1. Ethics code limits	163
		2. Federal Rule of Civil Procedure 11 and other sanctions	164
	B.	Personal opinion	164
	C.	Alluding to matters outside the record	165
		1. Reasonable lawyer standard	165
		2. Certainty not required	165

			3. Outside the lawyer's control	165
			4. Matters already ruled inadmissible	165
	D.	Obey court orders	165
	E.	Intemperate remarks	166
IV.	**Obligation to Improve the Legal System**		166
	A.	Public office	166
	B.	Support for needed legislation	166
			1. Drafting committees	166
			2. Legislative advocacy	166
	C.	Review of the judiciary	167
			1. Defending the entity	167
			2. Criticizing judges	167
			3. Judicial selection	167
V.	**Limitations on Litigation Publicity**		167
	A.	Constitutional challenge	167
	B.	General standard	168
			1. Out of court	168
			2. Likely to be disseminated by public communication	168
			3. Materially prejudice a matter	168
	C.	Permitted statements	168
			1. Nature of claim or defense	168
			2. Public records	168
			3. Investigation in process	168
			4. Scheduling	168
			5. Public assistance	168
			6. Criminal cases	168
	D.	Exception for statements that are necessary to protect the client	169
	E.	Prosecutors' supervision of subordinates' statements	169
VI.	**Ex Parte Contact with Judges and Jurors**		169
	A.	Judges	169
			1. Subject matter	169
			2. No intent requirement	170
			3. Authorized by law	170
			4. Oral or written communications covered	170
			5. Prohibited even if judge initiates	170
	B.	Jurors	170
			1. Before and during proceedings	170
			2. After proceedings end	170
			3. Reporting juror misconduct	171
VII.	**Pro Bono Publico**		171
	A.	Organized legal services for the poor	171
			1. Criminal matters	171
			2. Civil matters	171
	B.	Individual lawyer's duty	171
			1. Setting a goal	172
			2. Appropriate services	172
			3. Setting priorities	172

Quiz Yourself on DUTIES TO THE LEGAL SYSTEM AND SOCIETY 172

Exam Tips on DUTIES TO THE LEGAL SYSTEM AND SOCIETY 177

CHAPTER 9
SPECIAL ROLE-RELATED DUTIES

		CHAPTERSCOPE	**183**
I.		**Special Duties of Prosecutors**	**184**
	A.	Avoid conflicts with private interests represented	184
	B.	Dismissal of charges not supported by probable cause	184
	C.	Advising defendants of their right to counsel	184
	D.	Fair treatment of unrepresented accused	185
	E.	Disclosure of exculpatory evidence	185
	F.	Afford respect to lawyer-client relationships	185
	G.	Fairness in investigation	185
	H.	Grand jury fact fairness	185
II.		**Special Duties of Supervising and Subordinate Lawyers**	**186**
	A.	Lawyers subordinate to other lawyers	186
		1. General	186
		2. Exception	186
	B.	Lawyers supervising lawyers	**187**
		1. Providing supervision	187
		2. Responsibility for lawyer subordinates' misconduct	187
	C.	Lawyers supervising nonlawyers	**188**
		1. Providing supervision	188
		2. Responsibility for nonlawyer subordinates' misconduct	188
III.		**Lawyers as Intermediaries**	**189**
	A.	Requirements	**189**
		1. Consent after consultation	189
		2. Best interests of clients	189
		3. Impartial representation	189
	B.	Confidentiality	**189**
	C.	Withdrawal	**189**
	D.	Typical situations	**190**
		1. Buyer and seller in real estate closing	190
		2. Proposed partners setting up a business organization	190
		3. Lender and borrower	190
		4. Spouses	190
		5. Birth mother and adoptive parents in adoption document drafting ...	190
	E.	Not necessarily a mediator	**190**
	F.	A proposed set of standards for mediators	**190**
IV.		**Ancillary Businesses**	**191**
	A.	General rule	**191**
		1. Not distinct	191
		2. Failure to communicate to client	191

		B.	What are ancillary services?	191
		C.	Typical ancillary businesses	192
		D.	The ancillary business problem	192
	V.	**Multidisciplinary Practice**		192
		A.	Definition	192
		B.	Accountants	192
		C.	Lawyers and professional independence	193
		D.	Opposing arguments	193
		E.	Pro-MDP arguments	193
		F.	Other concerns	193
			1. Confidentiality	193
			2. Conflicts of interest	194
			3. Pro bono	194
		G.	Recent debacles	194

Quiz Yourself on SPECIAL ROLE-RELATED DUTIES 195

Exam Tips on SPECIAL ROLE-RELATED DUTIES 197

CHAPTER 10
ADVERTISING AND SOLICITATION

		ChapterScope		199
I.	**Traditional Distinctions Between Advertising and Solicitation**			200
	A.	Advertising		200
	B.	Solicitation		200
	C.	Blurring of the traditional distinctions		200
	D.	Model Rules		200
II.	**Constitutional Limitations on Disciplinary Authority**			201
	A.	Commercial speech		201
	B.	No broader restrictions than necessary		201
		1. Government interest in truthful advertising		201
		2. Narrowly drawn		201
		3. No accounting for matters of taste		201
	C.	Permissible regulation		201
	D.	Key Supreme Court cases		201
		1. *In re R.M.J.*		201
		2. *Zauderer*		202
		3. *Ohralik*		202
		4. *Shapero*		203
		5. *Peel*		204
		6. *Went For It, Inc.*		204
III.	**General Constraints on All Communication Regarding Services**			204
	A.	False and misleading statements, generally		204
		1. Testimonials		205
		2. Self-laudation		205
		3. Firm names		206

		4. Information about fees	206
	B.	Specialization and certification	**206**
		1. Model Code	206
		2. Model Rules	206
	C.	Post-event waiting periods	**207**
		1. General applicability	207
		2. Narrowly drawn	207
IV.	**Constraints Particular to Advertising**		**207**
	A.	Record keeping	207
	B.	Payment for advertising	207
	C.	Name of the lawyer	207
V.	**Constraints on In-Person and Live Telephone Solicitation**		**208**
	A.	Duress, coercion, and harassment	208
		1. Power of influence	208
		2. Difficult to verify content	208
	B.	Exceptions to the restrictions	208
		1. Non-live telephone	208
		2. Relationship with the prospective client	208
		3. Pecuniary gain	208
VI.	**Other Restrictions on Specific Solicitation**		**208**
	A.	"We don't want any!"	209
	B.	Disclaimer	209
VII.	**Client-Getting on the Internet**		**209**
	A.	General	209
	B.	Territorial difficulties	209
VIII.	**Client-Getting Relationship to Barratry, Maintenance, and Champerty**		**209**
	A.	Barratry	210
	B.	Maintenance	210
	C.	Champerty	210
IX.	**Lawyer Agents**		**210**
	A.	Runners and cappers	210
		1. Discipline	210
		2. Criminal violation	210
	B.	Payment for client referrals	210
	C.	Supervise employees	210

Quiz Yourself on ADVERTISING AND SOLICITATION 211

Exam Tips on ADVERTISING AND SOLICITATION 212

CHAPTER 11

JUDICIAL CONDUCT

	CHAPTERSCOPE		217
I.	**Sources of Judicial Conduct Law**		**217**
	A.	ABA Model Code of Judicial Conduct	217
		1. Not directly applicable	217

			2. Two models	217
	B.	Federal statutes		**218**
			1. 28 U.S.C. §455	218
			2. 28 U.S.C. §47	218
			3. 28 U.S.C. §144	218
			4. 28 U.S.C. §372	218
	C.	Lawyer ethics rules		**218**
			1. General	218
			2. Particular rules	218
	D.	Other sources		**218**
II.	**Who Is a Judge?**			**218**
	A.	General definition		218
			1. Need not be a lawyer	218
			2. Need not be called "Judge"	219
	B.	Part-time judge categories		219
			1. Retired judge	219
			2. Continuing part-time judge	219
			3. Periodic part-time judge	219
			4. Pro tempore judge	219
III.	**General Judicial Attributes**			**219**
	A.	Independence		219
	B.	Integrity		219
	C.	Impartiality		219
IV.	**Personal Conduct and Activity Outside the Judicial Role**			**220**
	A.	Avoid impropriety and appearance of impropriety		220
	B.	Comply with the law		220
			1. No conviction necessary	221
			2. Intentional or bad faith refusal to follow precedent and other mandatory authority	221
	C.	Preserving the prestige of the judicial office		221
	D.	Judges as witnesses		221
			1. As fact witness	221
			2. As character witness	221
	E.	Organizational membership		222
	F.	Speaking, writing, and teaching		222
			1. Pending cases	222
			2. Judicial duties take precedence	222
			3. Appearance of bias	222
	G.	Government activities		222
	H.	Civic and charitable activities		222
			1. Fundraising	222
	I.	Financial activities		222
	J.	Fiduciary activities		222
	K.	Practicing law		223
	L.	Outside income limitations and reporting requirements		223
			1. Gifts and favors	223
			2. Reporting of income	223

V.	**Judicial Duties**		**223**
	A.	Impartiality	223
	B.	Diligence	223
	C.	Competence	224
	D.	Maintain courtroom decorum	224
	E.	Patience	224
	F.	Avoid bias and prejudice	224
		1. In judicial functions	224
		2. Restraining lawyer bias	225
	G.	Ex parte communications	225
		1. Rationale	225
		2. Good faith is no excuse	225
		3. Pending matter discussion presumed	225
		4. Timing	225
		5. Exceptions	225
	H.	Public comments	226
	I.	Criticism of jurors	226
	J.	Making appointments	226
	K.	Reporting others' misconduct	227
		1. Other judges	227
		2. Lawyers	227
		3. Privilege	227
	L.	Disqualification and waiver	227
		1. Objective and subjective test	228
		2. Rule of necessity	228
		3. Grounds for disqualification	228
		4. Remittal (waiver) of disqualification	231
VI.	**Political Activities**		**231**
	A.	In general	231
	B.	Restrictions on judges and candidates of all types	232
		1. Political leadership	232
		2. Public endorsement or opposition	232
		3. Solicitation of funds	232
	C.	Restrictions on judges	232
	D.	Restrictions on candidates	232
VII.	**Liability for Civil Wrongs Committed**		**232**
	A.	Immunity for judicial action	232
	B.	Administrative actions	232

Quiz Yourself on JUDICIAL CONDUCT 233

Exam Tips on JUDICIAL CONDUCT 235

Essay Exam Questions 241

Essay Exam Answers 243

Multistate-Style Exam Questions 247

Multistate-Style Exam Answers 261

Table of Cases 263

Table of Statutes, Rules, and Opinions 267

Index 271

Preface

The Professional Responsibility course (by whatever name it is called at your school) is about the law and ethics that govern relationships lawyers have with clients, other lawyers, the profession, the justice system, and the public. It is the only law course in the typical law school curriculum that is about what lawyers do. In Torts, Contracts, and so on, you study law that affects clients' relationships with others and that lawyers interact with as an expert a step removed from the actual effect of the law. In Professional Responsibility, by contrast, the law you study is directly about the lawyer's relationships and your future role as a lawyer. In other words, Professional Responsibility is the course in which the lawyer is the "client," the one on whom the law studied actually operates. Arguably, Professional Responsibility is the most important course in the law school curriculum.

The law governing lawyers is a complicated mix of many different areas of substantive law from many different sources. Most obvious are the organized bar's self-regulations, enforced through the courts (as ethics codes adopted in the states), but other law fields have important applications to the various relationships of which lawyers are a part. Agency, contract, tort, procedure, and evidence law, among others, have specific applications to lawyers. All of these are interwoven in this outline.

In particular, the organized bar, through the American Bar Association (ABA), has promulgated model ethics codes. The ABA models have dominated the law of lawyering because these models, with some modification, have been adopted by the states as law. These models have also dominated law school courses in Professional Responsibility. They have dominated law school teaching of the subject because they are easily accessible and because they serve as simple proxies for what the law of lawyering is in the states. At some schools, you may study the ABA models and your particular state's modifications of them. At other schools, the modifications made in your state will be largely irrelevant to your course. In either event, when you study ethics codes in your course, the models will be the main focus.

Between the two models, the Model Code and the Model Rules, the Rules now dominate. The Code was originally adopted by the ABA in 1969 and was amended from time to time thereafter. When the Rules were adopted by the ABA in 1983, the ABA ceased its effort to amend and update the Model Code. The Code is now almost entirely out of date in some respects. (See Chapter 10.) States whose law reflects the Model Code as their basis have gone from a high point of nearly fifty to only one. Forty-nine states now have adopted ethics codes based on the Model Rules. In most courses the Model Rules dominate, with the Model Code being referred to occasionally and regarding particular topics (notably confidentiality; see Chapter 5) as contrast. This outline takes the approach with regard to the model that has come to be most prevalent in law school courses: The Model Rules are the basic document of study; the Model Code is used as contrast in particular areas. This trend in law school courses should continue. If your course makes more use of the Model Code than the usual, you will want to become familiar with the cross-reference charts that take you quickly back and forth between Model Code provisions and Model Rules provisions. Such charts are found in most statutory supplements that are required books for the Professional Responsibility course.

Important changes in the law governing lawyers have taken place since 2000. First, in 2000 the American Law Institute completed its work and published the Restatement of the Law Governing Lawyers, Third. The Restatement is now a critically important document of study. Second, in February 2002, the ABA adopted significant amendments to the Model Rules as a result of a report by the ABA-created Ethics 2000 Commission. In August 2003, further significant amendments were made to MR 1.6 and 1.13 in the wake of Enron and other corporate scandals. Congress adopted the Sarbanes-Oxley Act as well, which included significant new requirements for lawyers doing work on securities matters. In 2007, the ABA completed work on a new model code of judicial conduct. All these changes in the law governing lawyers are reflected in this outline.

All this talk of ethics codes must not be read to mean that law other than the ethics codes is unimportant. On the contrary, the other significant trend in Professional Responsibility courses is toward the recognition that lawyers' conduct is governed largely by law outside the ethics codes. That law is a significant part of this outline. Many of the examples in this outline come not from disciplinary matters, but from the wide variety of other areas of law that control lawyer conduct.

This outline makes use of frequent examples, some of which are drawn from decided cases. In many instances, the cases chosen as examples are leading cases in the field that are also among those excerpted in the leading casebooks.

Many Professional Responsibility courses end with exams that are at least partially multiple-choice. Bar applicants in nearly every state must pass a Multistate Professional Responsibility Exam, which is a multiple-choice exam. As a result, more teachers of Professional Responsibility than of some other subjects include multiple-choice questions on their exams. For this reason, a Multistate-Style Exam Question section is included in this book.

James E. Moliterno
September 2009

CASEBOOK CORRELATION CHART

(Note: general sections of the outline are omitted from this chart.
NC = not directly covered by this casebook.)

Emanuel's Contracts Outline *(by chapter and section heading)*	Crystal: *Professional Responsibility: Problems of Practice and the Profession* (4th edition)	Gillers: *Regulation of Lawyers* (8th edition)	Hazard, Koniak, Cramton, & Cohen: *The Law and Ethics of Lawyering* (4th edition)	Morgan & Rotunda: *Professional Responsibility* (10th edition)	Schwartz, Wydick, Perschbacher, & Bassett: *Problems in Legal Ethics* (8th edition)
CHAPTER 1 **INTRODUCTION AND THE ROLE OF LAWYER**					
I. Courses Called Professional Responsibility, Legal Ethics, and Legal Profession	xxxi	xxiii-xxvi	v-vi	v, 1-2	3
II. Moral Philosophy, Right and Wrong, and the Law Governing Lawyers	11-32	xxiv, 9-11	1-3, 13-25	14-23	3-27
III. The Role of Lawyer	1-11, 26-32, 51-55	15-20	3-20	2-11, 23-28	4-5
CHAPTER 2 **REGULATION OF THE LEGAL PROFESSION**					
I. Organization of the Bar	NC	1-2, 3-5	1136-1141	31	28-31, 36-40
II. Sources of Law Governing Lawyers	12-19	1-10	1142-1144	46-47	40-42
III. Admission to Practice	35-38	635-658	1030-1053	32-46	31-36
IV. Unauthorized Practice	477-486	690-691	909-927	614-622	157-159
CHAPTER 3 **CONTROLS ON LAWYER CONDUCT**					
I. Discipline	39-53	770-807	58-59	46-63	42-46
II. Malpractice	49-52	701-749	853-872	63-82	152-154
III. Liability for Client Conduct	523-549	NC	108-115, 632-636	280-282	146-154
IV. Contempt of Court	52-55	NC	998-999	NC	NC
V. Disqualification Motions and Other Litigation-Driven Controls	9-51, 360-369	NC	659-685	198-199	76-77
CHAPTER 4 **FORMAL ASPECTS OF THE LAWYER-CLIENT RELATIONSHIP**					
I. Undertaking Representation	236-247	23-28	754-759	84-95, 276-283	53-54
II. Fees	241-258	141-209	754-796	95-112, 120-127	54-76

Emanuel's Contracts Outline (by chapter and section heading)	Crystal: *Professional Responsibility: Problems of Practice and the Profession* (4th edition)	Gillers: *Regulation of Lawyers* (8th edition)	Hazard, Koniak, Cramton, & Cohen: *The Law and Ethics of Lawyering* (4th edition)	Morgan & Rotunda: *Professional Responsibility* (10th edition)	Schwartz, Wydick, Perschbacher, & Bassett: *Problems in Legal Ethics* (8th edition)
III. Fiduciary Duties	96-98, 258	76-78	813-816	112-127	110-114, 134-138
IV. Competence and Diligence	78-83	28-29, 78-79	848-852	276-283, 517-524	143-145, 154-157
V. Communication and Shared Decision-Making	250-255	86-102, 107-139	817-834	92-95	267-273
VI. Terminating Representation		103-106	835-846	117-120	52-53, 69-76, 146
CHAPTER 5 CONFIDENTIALITY					
I. The Duty of Confidentiality and the Attorney-Client Evidentiary Privilege	98-105, 258-261	29-68	255-261, 342-344	133-137	165-167
II. To Whom Is the Duty Owed?	265-267, 269-271	86-102	258-279	129-130, 141-142	171-179
III. To What Does the Duty Apply?	110-113, 265-269	79-84	279-302, 344-347	128, 130-134, 142-154	167-171
IV. Exceptions to the Duty of Confidentiality	105-110, 265-267	53-67	264, 302-342, 347-388	134-141, 155-157	179-181
V. Other Professional Duties That Are Subject to the Duty of Confidentiality	105-110	534-535	740-743	293-295, 155	NC
VI. Use of Confidential Information for the Lawyer's Benefit	519, 659	56-58	342-343	208-212	166
CHAPTER 6 CONFLICTS OF INTEREST					
I. Loyalty and Other General Principles	275	214-218	389	158-161, 171-172	267-269
II. Organization of the Model Rules Provisions on Conflicts	271-288, 290-298	347-350	391	NC	NC
III. Waiver of Conflicts	288-290, 310-313	278-279	410-411, 423, 429-433	161-169	NC
IV. Sources of Conflicts	273-275, 285-287, 324-334, 523, 526-534, 549-555	220-240, 241-304, 305-308, 309-327, 328-342, 343-350	392-471	173-203, 215-223	261-289, 290-304
V. Imputed Conflicts	299-305	276-277, 329-342	472-490	244-260	305-306
VI. Special Role-Related Conflicts Rules	626-629	307-308	491-514	260-274	NC

Emanuel's Contracts Outline (by chapter and section heading)	Crystal: Professional Responsibility: Problems of Practice and the Profession (4th edition)	Gillers: Regulation of Lawyers (8th edition)	Hazard, Koniak, Cramton, & Cohen: The Law and Ethics of Lawyering (4th edition)	Morgan & Rotunda: Professional Responsibility (10th edition)	Schwartz, Wydick, Perschbacher, & Bassett: Problems in Legal Ethics (8th edition)
CHAPTER 7 **DUTIES TO THIRD PARTIES**					
I. Truth-Telling Outside the Court Context	408-425	376-379	737-753	318-346	333-337
II. Harassment and Other Abusive Conduct	387-406	435-440	659-664, 706-708	377-379	NC
III. Threatening Criminal Prosecution	NC	431-433	NC	NC	NC
IV. Communicating with Represented Persons	369-385	108-126	719-733	302-310	NC
V. Communicating with Unrepresented Persons	371-372	108-126	734-735	302-303, 310-313	NC
VI. Civil Liability to Third Persons	367-369	NC	686-695	295-300, 346-350	NC
CHAPTER 8 **DUTIES TO THE LEGAL SYSTEM AND SOCIETY**					
I. Truth-Telling Inside the Court Context	3-4, 113-135	376-399	61-78, 632-658	432-453	185-206
II. Suppressing Evidence and Witness Payment	98-110, 183-186	450-453	696-701	401-432	211-219
III. Limitations on Presentations to a Court	130-131, 162-166, 168-172, 175-176	374-399	7037-7038	386-390	222-225, 227-229
IV. Obligation to Improve the Legal System	NC	763-767, 788-797	996-1014	398-401, 486-494, 643-646	54-56
V. Limitations on Litigation Publicity	162-173	475-476	NC	465-473	219-225
VI. Ex Parte Contact with Judges and Jurors	173-175, 602	NC	49, 162-163, 721-726	453-461	217-219
VII. Pro Bono Publico	481-486	194-199	968-992, 1106-1122	563-565	54-56
CHAPTER 9 **SPECIAL ROLE-RELATED DUTIES**					
I. Special Duties of Prosecutors	187-206	475-476	708-717	313-318, 464-465, 473-481	225-227
II. Special Duties of Supervising and Subordinate Lawyers	643-646	702	591-593, 1107-1108	531-534	312, 318-319
III. Lawyers as Intermediaries	504-510	NC	392-393, 455-456	NC	333-337
IV. Ancillary Businesses	659-662	755	1116-1122	NC	158-159
V. Multidisciplinary Practice	661-662	752-755	1116-1122	595	157-159

Emanuel's Contracts Outline (by chapter and section heading)	Crystal: Professional Responsibility: Problems of Practice and the Profession (4th edition)	Gillers: Regulation of Lawyers (8th edition)	Hazard, Koniak, Cramton, & Cohen: The Law and Ethics of Lawyering (4th edition)	Morgan & Rotunda: Professional Responsibility (10th edition)	Schwartz, Wydick, Perschbacher, & Bassett: Problems in Legal Ethics (8th edition)
CHAPTER 10 **ADVERTISING AND SOLICITATION**					
I. Traditional Distinctions between Advertising and Solicitation	444	911-913	928-931	519-522	82-87
II. Constitutional Limitations on Disciplinary Authority	442-448	937-939	931-932, 942-945	498-500, 508-510, 515-517	87-105
III. General Constraints on All Communication Regarding Services	442-451	921-935	946	498-506	94-95, 98
IV. Constraints Particular to Advertising	441	NC	NC	511	88
V. Constraints on In-Person and Live Telephone Solicitation	443	911-912	932-942	506-607, 512-613	NC
VI. Other Restrictions on Specific Solicitation	448-451	NC	NC	NC	NC
VII. Client-Getting on the Internet	448-451	913	945-946	507-508	NC
VIII. Client-Getting Relationship to Barratry, Maintenance, and Champerty	442-445	937-940	931	513-615	88
IX. Lawyer Agents	NC	937	946	NC	NC
CHAPTER 11 **JUDICIAL CONDUCT**					
I. Sources of Judicial Conduct Law	591-592	585-589	NC	639	342-343
II. Who Is a Judge?	609-612	NC	NC	639	NC
III. General Judicial Attributes	592-593	585-589	NC	662-664	359
IV. Personal Conduct and Activity Outside the Judicial Role	594-597, 604-608	618-627	NC	618-628, 659-662	348-355
V. Judicial Duties	592-593	589-617	NC	677-684	344
VI. Political Activities	612-616	NC	NC	684-686	355-359
VII. Liability for Civil Wrongs Committed	NC	NC	NC	656-657	NC

Capsule Summary

This Capsule Summary is intended for review at the end of the semester. Reading it is not a substitute for mastering the material in the main outline. Numbers in brackets refer to the pages in the main outline on which the topic is discussed.

CHAPTER 1
INTRODUCTION AND THE ROLE OF LAWYER

I. COURSES CALLED PROFESSIONAL RESPONSIBILITY, LEGAL ETHICS, AND LEGAL PROFESSION

The law of professional responsibility and, therefore, the course in which it is studied, are about the relationships of lawyers to their clients, their peers, the justice system, the profession, and the public. [1]

II. MORAL PHILOSOPHY, RIGHT AND WRONG, AND THE LAW GOVERNING LAWYERS

A. Moral philosophy

Moral philosophy informs the study of professional responsibility law, but moral philosophy does not replace legal analysis as the tool for determining the application of professional responsibility law. [1]

B. Right and wrong

There is a great deal more to the law governing lawyers than the difference between right and wrong. The law governing lawyers must be studied and mastered like any other law field. [2]

C. The law governing lawyers

The *law governing lawyers* is a complicated mix of many different areas of substantive law from many different sources. [2]

D. Role morality

Important to an understanding of lawyer ethics is the concept of *role morality.* Lawyers' moral decision-making involves a balancing process. Lawyers owe many duties, not all of which point in a single direction at any given moment. Lawyers owe duties to clients, the justice system, third parties generally, opposing parties, society, and the profession. [2-3]

III. THE ROLE OF LAWYER

The professional responsibility codes are an attempted expression of the limits of conduct by people acting in *the role of lawyer.* [3]

A. Differing conceptions of the lawyer's role

Different lawyers perceive themselves and the appropriate role of lawyer in differing ways. See descriptions of these alternate roles in §§IIIA.1-IIIA.3. [3-4]

B. Differences between lawyers' litigation and planning roles

1. **Litigation context:** In a litigation context, most of the lawyer's work is backward-looking. The litigation seeks to assess legal responsibility for the client's and the opposing party's past conduct. The lawyer's work involves the operation of the justice system on the client's behalf. [4]

2. **Planning context:** In the planning context, most of the lawyer's work is forward-looking. The planning seeks to predict the consequences of proposed future conduct. [4]

3. **Responsibility for clients' acts:** A lawyer bears more responsibility for a client's acts in the planning context than in the litigation context. The lawyer's planning work, advice, and assistance in execution help shape future client conduct. [4-5]

C. Practice setting

A lawyer's practice setting affects the law governing that lawyer in a variety of ways. Essentially, lawyers in different practice settings have different lawyer-client relationships. The differences in those lawyer-client relationships drive a variety of adjustments in the law governing lawyers. Aside from the private law firm representing a natural person as a client in civil matters, lawyers practice as, for example, prosecuting attorneys, other government lawyers, criminal defense lawyers including public defenders, and in-house and external corporate counsel. Some practice settings trigger the application of practice-setting-specific rules; others create adjustments by implication of attributes of the lawyer-client relationship. [5-6]

1. Prosecutors [5]
2. Other government lawyers [5]
3. Criminal defense [5]
4. Corporate or other organization counsel [6]
5. Legal aid [6]

CHAPTER 2
REGULATION OF THE LEGAL PROFESSION

The institutional framework within which lawyers and the law of lawyering exist has a significant effect on the interpretation of the law of lawyering.

I. ORGANIZATION OF THE BAR

The legal profession has organized itself in a variety of ways. Membership in some organizations is voluntary, whereas membership in others is required of those who wish to practice law in a particular jurisdiction. See §III. [10-11]

A. The American Bar Association

The *American Bar Association* (ABA) is a national, *voluntary* association of lawyers. [10]

B. Alternative national bar associations

National organizations of lawyers have been established, in some instances, to express alternative views from those held by the ABA. [10]

C. State bar associations

The ABA does not license lawyers to practice law. States, through their courts and sometimes legislatures, license lawyers to practice law within the relevant jurisdiction. [10-11]

1. **Voluntary state bar associations:** In some states, voluntary bar associations exist that licensed lawyers may or may not join at the individual lawyer's discretion. [11]

2. **The integrated bar:** In some states, membership in the state bar association is mandatory. This mandatory membership establishes what is called an "integrated bar," of which all the lawyers licensed to practice in the state are members. [11]

II. SOURCES OF LAW GOVERNING LAWYERS

The law that governs lawyers comes from a variety of sources and exists in a variety of forms. [11-15]

A. Ethics codes

Every state has an adopted code of ethics for lawyers that operates as a set of mandatory legal rules governing lawyer conduct. [11]

1. **ABA models and their organization:** Beginning in 1908, the ABA adopted a series of three model ethics codes that have served as models for state adoption. [11]

   a. **The 1908 Canons of Ethics:** The 1908 Canons of Ethics (Canons) were adopted by the ABA but were not initially expected to be routinely enforced as rules by courts and bar authorities. [11]

   b. **The 1969 Model Code of Professional Responsibility:** The Model Code was the ABA's first effort to influence the setting of mandatory, national standards for lawyer conduct. [12]

   c. **The 1983 Model Rules of Professional Conduct:** The Model Rules were drafted in the late 1970s and early 1980s and then adopted in 1983. Extensive amendments were adopted in 2002. [12]

2. **State-adopted codes:** The states have adopted ethics codes. Although all but one of the state-adopted codes are based on the ABA models, it is the state-adopted code, not the ABA model, that actually controls in the particular jurisdiction. [12-13]

B. **Case authority**

In several ways, courts make the law governing lawyers.

1. **Interpretation of codes:** Courts have interpreted the existing ethics codes and, as such, make the law of lawyering in their interpretive activities in the same way as courts make law by interpreting statutes. [13]

2. **Inherent power to regulate lawyers:** Because courts have inherent power to regulate lawyers (who are officers of the court), a common law of lawyer regulation also exists. [13]

C. **Ethics opinions**

Both the ABA and state bar associations issue nonbinding *ethics opinions* that are frequently relied on by courts in law of lawyering cases. [13]

D. **Restatement**

In 2000, in an exceedingly important development for the law of professional responsibility, the American Law Institute completed work on the Restatement of the Law Governing Lawyers. The Restatement, Third, of the Law Governing Lawyers has already been influential with courts and with the Ethics 2000 Commission revision of the Model Rules. [13]

E. **Constitutional Restraints**

Like any other area of state or federal regulation, the law governing lawyers is subject to constitutional limitations. [13-14]

F. **"Other law"**

The law of a wide variety of other substantive areas forms an essential part of the law of lawyering. [14-15]

III. ADMISSION TO PRACTICE

A license to practice law is a prerequisite to a person's lawful engagement in the activities of lawyering. [15-18]

A. **Policy**

The state has a need to protect the public from those who are incompetent or who lack integrity. [15]

B. **General requirements**

Education, knowledge, and character requirements are the chief hurdles in the path of the applicant for admission to the practice of law. [15-17]

1. **Education:** All states impose educational requirements on applicants for admission to practice law. [15]

2. **Knowledge:** An examination (the bar exam) is administered in each state. [15]

3. **Good character:** To be a successful applicant for admission to practice law, one must be found to be of good character. [15-17]

4. **Misconduct in the application process:** An applicant to the bar may not make any material false statement and must not "fail to disclose a fact necessary to correct any misapprehension known by the [applicant] to have arisen in the matter. . . ." MR 8.1(b). [17]

5. **No assistance with admission of unqualified applicant:** Licensed lawyers are duty-bound not to assist in the admission of an unqualified applicant. MR 8.1. [17]

C. **Federal courts**

Each federal court maintains a bar (a list of licensed lawyers), separate from the states in which they sit. [18]

D. **Admission pro hac vice**

When a lawyer who is licensed to practice in one state has an occasional, nonrecurring need to represent a client before the courts of another state, the lawyer requests admission before that state's courts *"pro hac vice"* ("for this turn only"). The application is made by the lawyer filing a motion with the particular court before which the lawyer wants permission to appear. [18]

IV. UNAUTHORIZED PRACTICE

By the nature of the licensing requirements, lawyers licensed to practice in a given state have a monopoly on the practice of law in that state. When a person engages in the ***unauthorized practice*** of law, civil and sometimes criminal penalties attach. [18-22]

A. **Attributes of the practice of law**

1. **Court appearance:** Court appearance constitutes the core of the practice of law for purposes of unauthorized practice analysis. [19]

2. **Legal advice and counsel:** Although giving legal advice is clearly lawyer's work, courts are understandably more reluctant to attempt to monitor and police the unauthorized practice of giving legal advice. If the advice-giving is accompanied by either a fee or document-drafting or both, the activity is seen as more clearly impinging on the lawyer monopoly. [19]

B. **Forms of unauthorized practice**

Unauthorized practice may occur when a licensed lawyer practices outside the jurisdiction in which the license was granted or when those not licensed engage in the practice of law. [19-20]

1. **Extraterritorial practice of licensed lawyers:** Lawyers licensed in one jurisdiction commit unauthorized practice violations when they practice in another jurisdiction without obtaining permission from the second jurisdiction's courts. See §III.D. [19]

2. **Multijurisdictional practice:** Transportation and communications technology have advanced since states adopted "unauthorized practice of law" (UPL) provisions in the early twentieth century. The globalization of business and finance has expanded a client's need for representation to include assistance in transactions in multiple jurisdictions and advice regarding multiple jurisdictions' laws. Lawyer regulations, particularly the UPL laws, did not effectively

respond to the evolving nature of business. As such, the ABA Commission on Multijurisdictional Practice proposed amendments to Rule 5.5 of the ABA *Model Rules for Professional Conduct*. [19-22]

3. **Practice by the unlicensed:** Professionals and others whose business borders the law may not engage in the legal work that borders their other professional duties. Real estate agents, bankers, and insurance professionals are the usual examples. [22]

V. SELF-GOVERNANCE AND THE DUTY TO REPORT MISCONDUCT

Among the chief features of the legal profession's claim to be *self-governing* is the requirement of reporting a fellow lawyer's or a judge's serious misconduct to the appropriate professional authority. MR 8.3. [23-24]

A. Knowledge of misconduct

Before a duty to report misconduct can arise, the lawyer must have "knowledge that another lawyer has committed" the *misconduct.* MR 8.3(a); Model Rules, 1.0(f). [23]

B. Level or type of misconduct

The rule requires a lawyer to report misconduct "that raises a substantial question as to that lawyer's honesty, trustworthiness or fitness as a lawyer in other respects. . . ." MR 8.3(a). "Substantial" means a "material matter of clear and weighty importance." Model Rules, 1.0(1). [23]

C. Confidentiality limitation on duty to report

The rule does not require a report of misconduct when the lawyer has learned of the misconduct through confidential communications that would be protected by the ethical duty of confidentiality under Model Rule 1.6. MR 8.3(c). See Chapter 5. But it must also be remembered that the exceptions to the duty of confidentiality (e.g., the future-crime exception) continue to apply with equal force in this setting as in any other. [23-24]

D. Defamation privilege

When a lawyer reports another lawyer's misconduct, the potential exists for a defamation action to be filed by the reported-on lawyer against the reporting lawyer. [24]

CHAPTER 3
CONTROLS ON LAWYER CONDUCT

I. DISCIPLINE

Discipline imposed at the hands of the organized bar is the most often referred to and studied, but much less often actually imposed, control on lawyer conduct. *Discipline* by the bar and then the court system operates by authority of the licensing of lawyers. See Chapter 2, §III. [27-31]

A. Discipline v. malpractice

Discipline is imposed for the protection of the public generally and for the benefit of the profession, whereas malpractice is a tort- or contract-based civil action that is meant to compensate victims of a lawyer's negligence or contract breach. Although a single act of negligence will support a malpractice action, unless that single act is sufficiently gross to indicate a substantial likelihood that the lawyer is unfit to practice, that single act will not subject the lawyer to bar discipline. [32]

B. Grounds for discipline

Discipline may be based on an incredibly wide range of conduct, both within and without the lawyer's role. It may be imposed for violations of the ethics code rules; for acts involving moral turpitude; for criminal conduct; for dishonesty, fraud, and deceit; and for acts that are prejudicial to the administration of justice. [32-33]

C. Forms of discipline

Discipline generally comes in the form of disbarment, suspension, or reprimand, either public or private. Courts may also require disciplined lawyers to engage in professional responsibility educational programs. [34]

1. **Disbarment:** Disbarment is an indefinite dismissal from the rolls of lawyers licensed to practice in the particular jurisdiction. [34]

2. **Suspension:** Suspension is a fixed-period revocation of the license to practice law. [34]

3. **Reprimand:** Reprimand is a statement of reproach issued by the bar to the disciplined lawyer. Reprimands may be either private or public. When a reprimand is public, the reprimand is published in a newspaper. [34]

D. Disciplinary procedure

The formal disciplinary procedure is designed around the goals of bar discipline. It is intended to protect the public from lawyers who have committed serious misconduct, rather than to benefit the particular complaining party, usually a client. When a complaint is dismissed, the complaining party has no right of appeal. [34-35]

II. MALPRACTICE

Malpractice is a civil claim for relief intended to remedy a wrong done by a professional (in this case, a lawyer) to an individual client or a group of clients. [36-38]

A. Contract theories

Contract theory malpractice actions have the common contract elements of agreement, breach, and damage. Damage measurement under contract theories is more limited than that under tort theories. [36]

B. Tort theories

Under tort theories, the most frequently used of the malpractice theories, the elements are the familiar negligence elements of duty, breach, causation, and damages. [36-37]

1. **Duty:** The lawyer's duty to the client is measured by the skill and knowledge of ordinary lawyers in the community, unless the lawyer is an expert in a specialized field. An expert is held to the standard of the reasonable expert in that field. [36]

2. **Breach:** Breach of the duty owed is a required element of a malpractice action. Lawyers are not guarantors of particular results. Often, a variety of reasonable strategies will be available from which to choose. When a lawyer chooses a reasonable course of action and that course later produces bad results, the lawyer has not breached the duty of care owed to the client. [36-37]

3. **Causation.** For a malpractice claim to exist, the lawyer's breach of duty must cause the client's damages. Often, this means that the client will have to prove that she would have prevailed in the matter had the lawyer not breached the duty of care. This requirement is called the *"case within a case."* The malpractice plaintiff must prove the value of the underlying case to prevail in the malpractice case. [37]

4. **Damages:** As with any tort action, the wrong is insufficient to create a claim for relief in the absence of damages. [37]

C. Fiduciary duty

As a *fiduciary,* a lawyer owes duties to clients beyond the tort and contract duties. Fiduciary duties modify contract principles. These special duties can be the basis for a malpractice action that might not otherwise lie under contract or tort theories. See Chapter 4, §III. [37]

D. Necessity of expert testimony

As with other forms of professional malpractice, expert testimony is usually needed to establish the nature of the professional duty and the existence of a breach of that duty. [37]

E. Prospective limitation on malpractice liability

The Model Code prohibited lawyers from any prospective limitation on their malpractice liability to clients. DR 6-102. The Model Rules restrict the lawyer's ability to prospectively limit malpractice liability to clients to those occasions when such agreements are permitted by law in the relevant state and a client is represented by other counsel in making the limitation of liability agreement. MR 1.8(h). [37-38]

F. Liability to third parties for malpractice

Under limited circumstances, a lawyer may be liable for malpractice to a nonclient. See Chapter 6, §VI. [38]

III. LIABILITY FOR CLIENT CONDUCT

Lawyers are prohibited under the Model Rules from "counselling a client to engage or assisting a client in conduct that the lawyer knows is criminal or fraudulent." MR 1.2(d). While this provision sets up the disciplinary exposure of a lawyer who violates the rule, a lawyer may also be criminally and civilly liable for the wrongs of the clients that the lawyer assists. [38]

IV. CONTEMPT OF COURT

Judges' *contempt* power is a considerable control on lawyer conduct in the litigation setting. The contempt power is meant to give judges reasonable control over the courtroom and to enforce standards of courtroom behavior among litigants. [38-39]

V. DISQUALIFICATION MOTIONS AND OTHER LITIGATION-DRIVEN CONTROLS

Powerful constraints on lawyer conduct exist in the form of various litigation motions. These motions, when granted, have an immediate and significant impact on the lawyer against whom they were filed. [39-40]

A. Disqualification for conflicts of interest

When a lawyer perceives that an opposing lawyer may have a conflict of interest in litigation, the lawyer may request that the court *disqualify* opposing counsel from further participation in the case. [39-40]

1. **Substantive standards:** The standards for when a disqualification motion should be granted are substantially the same as the underlying conflicts-of-interest standards, including the shield or "Chinese Wall" defense. See Chapter 6. [39]

2. **Other interests:** Because litigation consequences are at stake instead of lawyer disciplinary consequences, courts take into account interests such as delay caused by granting the motion; wrongful conduct of the moving party, especially as it relates to the timing of the motion; and the nonmoving party's legitimate interest in retaining counsel of her choice, in addition to the typical conflicts-of-interest concerns. [39-40]

B. FRCP 11 and its state law counterparts

Money sanctions are available against an offending lawyer under various *frivolous claim* prohibition rules, especially Federal Rules of Civil Procedure (FRCP) 11. See Chapter 8, §III.A. [40]

1. **Analogous to frivolous claims ethics code provisions:** Ethics code rules exist that are analogous to FRCP 11. See MR 3.1. [40]

2. **Claims that lack a basis in law or fact:** To avoid frivolous claim liability, a claim must have a basis in fact and a basis in law. [40]

3. **Safe harbor:** Under the 1993 amendments to Rule 11, a safe harbor provision exists. Before one may file a Rule 11 motion, notice must be given to the alleged offending lawyer. [40]

4. **Sanctions against signer and firm:** Under the 1993 amendments to FRCP 11, sanctions may be imposed by the court on both the lawyer who signed the frivolous court paper and the lawyer's firm. [40]

C. Other sanctions

A few other sanctions provisions that are similar to FRCP 11 exist to govern the frivolous argument conduct of lawyers, especially on appeal. See, e.g., 28 U.S.C. §1927. [40]

Chapter 4
FORMAL ASPECTS OF THE LAWYER-CLIENT RELATIONSHIP

I. UNDERTAKING REPRESENTATION

Before a lawyer has formally undertaken representation, a limited set of lawyer-to-client duties exist, including the confidentiality duty that is owed to prospective clients. See Chapter 5, §II.A.2. *Undertaking representation* signifies the beginning of the formal lawyer-client relationship. Once a lawyer has undertaken representation, the full range of duties from lawyer to client exists. [46-50]

A. Duty to undertake representation

1. **General:** In general, lawyers have no duty to undertake a particular representation. [46]

2. **Limited duty to accept representation:** Lawyers have a limited duty to undertake a fair share of pro bono work and to accept court appointments unless good cause exists to decline the appointment. For more on pro bono, see Chapter 8, §VII; for more on court appointments, see Chapter 4, §I.A.2.b. [46-48]

B. Duty to reject representation

Unlike the general rule that a lawyer has no duty to accept every client's matter, lawyers are prohibited from accepting (i.e., lawyers must reject) representation when the representation will violate ethics rules or other law. MR 1.16(a). See also §VI.B. [48]

C. Lawyer-client contracts and the beginning of the lawyer-client relationship

The lawyer-client relationship is governed by the particular contract entered into by the lawyer and client and by general contract principles, modified by the various duties that lawyers owe clients. See §§II, III. See Chapters 4-6. The lawyer-client relationship formally begins when a client reasonably believes that the lawyer has undertaken to provide the client with legal service. The relationship does not depend for its onset on the existence of a written contract or a fee payment. [49-50]

II. FEES

Although the regulation of lawyer's fees is relatively light and rarely enforced, it does exist. MR 1.5. Fees are regulated for their amount and their nature. [50-54]

A. Reasonableness standard

A lawyer's fee must be reasonable. MR 1.5. A range of factors may be considered in setting a reasonable fee. MR 1.5(a). See §§II.A.1.a-j. [50-51]

B. Writing and timing

In general, a written contract setting the fee is preferred but not required. But see §C. regarding contingent fees. [51]

C. **Contingent fees**

With a few exceptions and restrictions, a lawyer is permitted to charge a fee that is contingent on the outcome of the matter. Generally, cases that produce a *res,* a pool of recovery money from which the contingent fee may be paid, are appropriate for contingent fees. There are two exceptions: criminal cases and certain domestic relations cases. When contingent fees are permitted, additional restrictions apply. MR 1.5(c). [51-52]

1. **Writing and terms:** Although ordinarily a fee agreement need not be in writing, a contingent fee agreement must be in writing and must be signed by the client. The written agreement must explain the way in which the fee will be calculated and, in particular, the way in which deductions for expenses will be calculated. MR 1.5(c). [52]

2. **Ending statement:** The lawyer must provide an ending statement in writing to the client explaining the outcome of the matter and providing the calculation of the fee and expenses. MR 1.5(c). [52]

D. **Fee splitting**

Lawyers in the same firm routinely share fees with one another. However, when lawyers who are not members of a firm share fees or when lawyers seek to share fees with nonlawyers, special problems arise. [52-54]

1. **Among lawyers:** Fee splitting among lawyers not in the same firm, in particular the "forwarding fee," has been thought to be offensive to lawyer ethics. A forwarding fee is a fee charged by a lawyer who does no more than send a prospective client to another lawyer who actually provides the legal service. [52]

2. **The modern rule governing lawyer fee splitting:** Rather than prohibit all fee splitting among lawyers from different firms, the Model Rule drafters crafted a rule to regulate the practice. The fee splitting practice is permitted if the total fee is reasonable, the client agrees to the arrangement, and either the fee is shared in proportion to the work done or the lawyers accept joint responsibility for the representation. The agreement must be confirmed in writing. MR 1.5(e). [52-53]

3. **With former partners:** If a profit sharing, separation agreement, or retirement plan calls for it, fees may be shared with former partners and associates of the primary lawyer in the matter. [53]

4. **With nonlawyers:** Fees may not be shared with nonlawyers except under quite limited circumstances. [53]

E. **Court-awarded fees**

Lawyers receive court-awarded attorney's fees pursuant to both court appointment to representation and various statutes that allow for collection of attorney's fees. [53]

F. **Minimum fee schedules**

At one time, the organized bar typically imposed ***minimum fee schedules*** on lawyers and their clients. Such schedules are unlawful and therefore no longer enforceable. Goldfarb v. Virginia State Bar, 421 U.S. 773 (1975). [53]

G. Fee forfeiture

Modern fee forfeiture statutes provide that attorney's fees that are paid by clients from crime proceeds may be forfeited to the government. See, e.g., 21 U.S.C. §§848-853 and 12 U.S.C. §§1961-1968. [53-54]

III. FIDUCIARY DUTIES

In addition to contractual duties and tort duties, lawyers owe their clients fiduciary duties. [54-55]

A. General role of a fiduciary

A *fiduciary* is one in whom a special trust is placed. A fiduciary owes to the beneficiary scrupulous good faith, candor, and care in the management of the beneficiary's interests. [54]

B. Handling clients' money

Lawyer fiduciary duties, beyond the general care owed to client interests and confidences that the relationship implies, are usually thought of in terms of the lawyer's handling of clients' money and property. [54-56]

1. **Violations a most serious matter:** Violations of the lawyer's duty to properly handle client property have been among the most frequent grounds for lawyer discipline because such violations are easy to verify, because they present a significant opportunity for continued abuse of clients by the offending lawyer, because the rules governing property-handling are per se rules that require no intentional wrongdoing on the part of the lawyer, and because these rules involve no balancing of competing duties. [54]

2. **Client trust accounts:** Lawyers must maintain client trust accounts and safety deposit boxes for the safekeeping of client property. Lawyers must maintain the account in the state in which they practice, they must maintain records of the account for later examination, and they must keep client property and funds separate from lawyer property and funds. MR 1.15(a). [54-55]

3. **Commingling funds:** Only client money may be in the trust account. The lawyer must maintain a separate office operating account. When a lawyer commingles his funds with a client's, the lawyer is subject to discipline. MR 1.15(a). [55-56]

4. **Prompt delivery and accounting:** Unless the client agrees to another arrangement, when a lawyer receives property of another, the lawyer must promptly deliver that property and provide an accounting on request. MR 1.15(d). [56]

IV. COMPETENCE AND DILIGENCE

Competence and diligence are core lawyer duties. MR 1.1, 1.3. [56-58]

A. Competence

Competence requires that the lawyer possess and exercise on the client's behalf "the legal knowledge, skill, thoroughness, and preparation reasonably necessary for the representation." MR 1.1. [56-57]

1. **Distinct from malpractice:** Although the competence standard is similar to descriptions of the tort duty for malpractice purposes, they operate differently. [56-57]

2. **Does not require possession of expertise at the beginning of representation:** A lawyer is not required to know the law that governs the client's legal claim before undertaking representation, provided the lawyer will be able to acquire the necessary knowledge with reasonable diligence. [57]

3. **But basic, cross-cutting skills and knowledge are always required:** Virtually all practicing lawyers in all areas of expertise must have certain basic skills, such as an understanding of the use of precedent, legal research skills, ability to identify and evaluate a client's problem, and writing or drafting skill. MR 1.1 Comment. [57]

4. **Emergency:** In an emergency situation, a lawyer may provide limited assistance to a client in a matter on which the lawyer would ordinarily require further study or research before service is rendered. But the lawyer must limit this service to that which is necessary under the circumstances. MR 1.1 Comment. [57]

B. Diligence

Diligence is the timeliness aspect of competence. Lawyers are obligated to be diligent on their clients' behalf. MR 1.3. [57-58]

1. **Expediting matters:** The duty of diligence is related to the lawyer's duty to expedite matters consistent with client interests. MR 3.2. [57]

2. **Starting and stopping:** The most common pattern in a diligence duty violation involves a lawyer who begins work on a client's matter, perhaps even by filing a civil complaint, but then does little or nothing to pursue the matter to a conclusion. [57-58]

3. **Misleading about diligence:** Most of the cases that have produced lawyer discipline for diligence failures have also involved a lawyer who then misleads the client about the progress being made. [58]

4. **Inadequate excuses:** Several excuses have been offered for lack of diligence and rejected by the courts. See §§IV.B.4.a-d. [58]

V. COMMUNICATION AND SHARED DECISION-MAKING

Lawyers owe clients a duty to communicate with clients and to meaningfully share decision-making responsibilities with them. MR 1.2 and 1.4. [58-61]

A. Communication

The communication duty is critical to maintaining a quality lawyer-client relationship. It is related to the duties regarding shared decision-making, competence, and diligence and forms the underpinning of every duty that requires client consent and consultation. MR 1.4. A lawyer must keep a client informed of the status of the client's matter and must respond to a client's reasonable requests for information. MR 1.4(a). [58-59]

B. Shared decision-making

Lawyers and clients must share decision-making responsibility. [59-60]

1. **Scope of representation:** Because the scope of their relationship is generally set by contract, lawyers and their clients may negotiate and settle on the lawyer's *scope of representation.* [59]

   a. **Duration of representation:** Lawyer and client can negotiate over the lengths to which the lawyer is committed to proceed in the matter. [59]

   b. **Subject matter:** The lawyer and client may negotiate the breadth of the lawyer's service. [59]

2. **Means and ends:** As a general proposition, clients set the goals or ends of the representation, whereas lawyers are generally empowered to determine the best means to use to achieve those ends. MR 1.2(a) Comment. For particular client and lawyer decision-making responsibilities, see §§V.B.2.b.i-v. [59-61]

3. **Lawyer independence from client views:** A lawyer's representation of a client does not implicate the lawyer's sharing of or responsibility for the client's cause or views regarding matters relevant to the representation. MR 1.2(b). [61]

4. **Counseling crimes or frauds:** As an underpinning to the scope of decision-making between lawyer and client, lawyers are prohibited from counseling or assisting their clients in the commission of crimes or frauds. MR 1.2(d). [61]

   a. **In general:** When a lawyer does so advise or assist, the lawyer is not only subject to discipline but is liable criminally or civilly as the case may be. [61]

   b. **Exceptions:** This prohibition does not prevent a lawyer from either discussing proposed courses of action with a client or assisting a client in the pursuit of a test case. [61]

5. **The client under a disability:** When a lawyer represents a client whose capacity to make decisions regarding the representation is diminished, the lawyer must attempt to maintain an ordinary lawyer-client relationship to the extent possible. In seeking protective action for a client, a lawyer may reveal confidential information to the extent reasonably necessary to protect the client's interests. MR 1.14. [61]

VI. TERMINATING REPRESENTATION

The formal lawyer-client relationship ends when representation terminates. Despite termination, many lawyer duties to clients continue, such as confidentiality and a limited conflict avoidance duty. *Withdrawal* from representation is a critically important device for the lawyer who is faced with the prospect that continued representation of the client will result in a violation of the ethics code or other law. [62-65]

A. Rejection of representation

In a way, rejection of representation is a form of termination of representation. See §I.B. [62]

B. Mandatory withdrawal

Under some circumstances lawyers are required to withdraw from representation, thereby terminating the lawyer-client relationship. Failure to withdraw under these circumstances subjects the lawyer to discipline. MR 1.16(a). [62]

1. **Continued representation will violate the ethics rules:** MR 1.16(a)(1). [62]
2. **Continued representation will violate other law:** MR 1.16(a)(1). [62]
3. **Lawyer's physical or mental health is impaired:** MR 1.16(a)(2). [62]
4. **Lawyer is discharged:** MR 1.16(a)(3). [62]

C. Permissive withdrawal

In some instances lawyers are permitted but not required to withdraw. The practical effect of this rule is to allow lawyers to withdraw from representation in the enumerated circumstances without breaching a duty of continued representation to the client. MR 1.16(b). [63-64]

1. **No harm to client:** Without regard to any cause for withdrawal, a lawyer may withdraw if it can be done without material adverse effect to the client. MR 1.16(b)(1). [63]

2. **Causes that will excuse some material harm to the client:** Even if some harm may come to the client from the withdrawal, a lawyer may withdraw when any of the following causes exist. [63-64]

   a. **Lawyer's reasonable belief that client is acting criminally or fraudulently:** MR 1.16(b)(2). [63]

   b. **Past use of service for crime or fraud:** MR 1.16(b)(3). [63]

   c. **Client actions that are repugnant or imprudent:** MR 1.16(b)(4). [63]

   d. **Client failure to meet obligations:** MR 1.16(b)(5). [63-64]

   e. **Unreasonable financial burden:** MR 1.16(b)(6). See §I.A.2.b.i. [64]

   f. **Client unreasonably difficult to work with:** MR 1.16(b)(6). [64]

   g. **Other good cause:** MR 1.16(b)(7). [64]

D. Court order to continue

Even when a lawyer has good cause to withdraw, a court may order the lawyer to continue the representation. MR 1.16(c). [64]

E. Procedural requirements for withdrawal

Without regard to what cause a lawyer has for the withdrawal, certain procedural requirements must be met. [64]

1. **Notice:** Clients must be given reasonable notice before the withdrawal is effected. MR 1.16(d). [64]

2. **Court approval:** When litigation is pending, a lawyer must obtain the court's permission to withdraw from representation. MR 1.16(d) Comment. [64]

F. Duties upon termination of the lawyer-client relationship

In addition to the duties that continue beyond the end of the lawyer-client relationship, such as confidentiality and conflict avoidance, lawyers owe clients certain specific duties that arise upon termination of representation. In general, a lawyer is obliged to take reasonable measures to minimize the harm to the client upon termination of representation. MR 1.16(d). [64-65]

1. **Fee refund:** Any fees that have been paid to the lawyer but not yet earned must be refunded to the client upon withdrawal. [65]

2. **Client's papers and property:** Papers and property of the client that are in the lawyer's possession must be promptly returned upon withdrawal. The lawyer may desire to retain the client's materials in an effort to persuade the client to pay any remaining fee that is owed the lawyer. A lawyer may not do so, however, unless the law of the lawyer's jurisdiction gives the lawyer a lien that may be secured by such materials. [65]

G. Fee liability upon termination

Although a client may discharge a lawyer without cause, the client will continue to have an obligation to pay fees to the lawyer that have already been earned. MR 1.16(d). [65]

1. **Fixed or hourly fees:** When a fee is a fixed amount for a particular service or is based on hours of service, the fee upon discharge will be calculated as the value of the services rendered. Such a recovery theory is called *quantum meruit.* [65]

2. **Contingent fee:** Contingent-fee arrangements have presented a challenge to courts trying to determine the measure of compensation owed the discharged lawyer. Some courts have ruled that a contingent-fee lawyer who is discharged without cause is entitled to no fee. Others have ruled that a contingent-fee lawyer who is discharged without cause is entitled to the full benefit of the contingency if, indeed, the client eventually recovers in the matter. Still others have ruled that the discharged contingent-fee lawyer is entitled to the reasonable value of the services actually rendered (a quantum meruit theory), limited by the amount that the lawyer would have earned had the contingency occurred and the lawyer had recovered the agreed-on percentage. [65]

CHAPTER 5
CONFIDENTIALITY

I. THE DUTY OF CONFIDENTIALITY AND THE ATTORNEY-CLIENT EVIDENTIARY PRIVILEGE

This section covers the overlap between the evidentiary privilege and the duty of *confidentiality.* [74-78]

A. Secrets and confidences

The Model Code duty of confidentiality provision (DR 4-101) defines the scope of the duty as the sum of the material protected by the evidentiary *attorney-client privilege* (called *"confidences"* in DR 4-101) and the material that, although not included in the attorney-client evidentiary privilege, would be embarrassing or detrimental to the client if revealed or that the client has expressly requested be held in confidence (called *"secrets"* in DR 4-101). The Model Rules provision abandons the "confidences" + "secrets" = duty of confidentiality formula in favor of a more general and inclusive definition, "information relating to representation of a client. . . ." MR 1.6(a). [74]

B. **Scope of the attorney-client privilege**

Despite the change of terminology, the scope of the attorney-client evidentiary privilege remains critical to defining what is ultimately protected by the duty of confidentiality. When information is within the ethical duty of confidentiality, but outside the protection of the evidentiary privilege, a judge may order the lawyer to speak in the form of testimony or otherwise. See §IV.F. Thus, although the lawyer would not be free to speak absent court compulsion, the coverage of the evidentiary privilege largely determines whether compulsion will be well founded. [74-75]

C. **Parameters of the evidentiary privilege**

In general, the evidentiary privilege is created when a client or prospective client communicates in confidence to a lawyer (or a person the client reasonably believes to be a lawyer) who is being consulted as a lawyer. [75-78]

1. **Clients or prospective clients:** The privilege applies to communication from a client or a prospective client. [75]

2. **Desire for confidentiality required:** The privilege is not created when the communication is made in circumstances that do not indicate a desire for confidentiality by the client. [75-76]

   a. **Eavesdroppers:** Most modern authority indicates that if the client exercises reasonable care to avoid being overheard (or intercepted when speaking on the telephone), the court should rule an eavesdropper's testimony inadmissible upon assertion of the privilege. [76]

   b. **Multiple clients:** When multiple prospective clients consult a lawyer together, each holds a privilege that can be asserted against third parties, but none of them can prevent others among the prospective clients from testifying or otherwise waiving the privilege. Their collective communication indicates an absence of desire for confidentiality within the group. [76]

3. **Communication, not knowledge:** The privilege covers the client's communication, not the client's knowledge that was communicated. [76]

4. **Lawyer observations:** The privilege may also protect lawyer observations that result directly from the client's protected communications, as long as the lawyer does nothing to prevent other interested parties from making the same observation. [76]

5. **Physical evidence:** Although the observations of a lawyer that result directly from client communication may sometimes be privileged, items collected by the lawyer are not privileged. [76-77]

6. **Exceptions:** Many of the exceptions to the duty of confidentiality are paralleled by exceptions to the evidentiary privilege. [77-78]

   a. **Client holds privilege:** The client holds (controls the assertion of) the evidentiary privilege. Client waiver eviscerates the privilege. [77]

   b. **Future crimes and frauds:** Communications that further future crimes or frauds are excepted from protection by the evidentiary privilege. This is called the *crime-fraud exception.* [78]

II. TO WHOM IS THE DUTY OWED?

This section focuses on the ethical duty of confidentiality and, in particular, to whom the duty is owed. [78-79]

A. Generally

The duty of confidentiality is owed to current clients, former clients, and prospective clients. [78]

1. **Former clients:** Former clients are owed the duty of confidentiality. [78]

2. **Prospective clients:** Prospective clients are owed a measure of confidentiality. [78]

3. **No fee necessary:** It is not necessary for a fee to be charged for the duty of confidentiality and the evidentiary privilege to be effective. [78]

B. Organizational clients

In addition to representing people, lawyers represent organizations as clients. See MR 1.13 Comments 3, 6. [78-79]

1. **Agents of the organizational client:** Communications from agents of an *organizational client* are within the evidentiary privilege and, therefore, within the duty of confidentiality if two conditions are met: the information communicated is treated as confidential within the organization, and it is communicated to the lawyer so that the lawyer can give advice or counsel to the organization. [78-79]

2. **Government agency client:** Because of the special public responsibilities of government agencies, government lawyers may strike a confidentiality balance somewhat more toward the public interest in disclosure of government wrongdoing. [79]

C. Client and lawyer agents

Both lawyers and clients routinely use agents for communicating with each other. [79]

1. **Lawyer agents:** For purposes of the duty of confidentiality, client communication to a lawyer through a lawyer's agent is treated as if it were made directly to the lawyer. In addition, protected client information may be shared with other lawyers within the law firm or organization that represents the client. [79]

2. **Client agents:** Communications from clients through agents to lawyers are treated as if they were made directly by the client to the lawyer. [79]

III. TO WHAT DOES THE DUTY APPLY?

The duty of confidentiality applies to "information relating to representation of a client...." MR 1.6(a). The Model Code definition is the "confidences" and "secrets" formula referred to in §IA. [80]

A. Duty of confidentiality or evidentiary privilege

To be protected by the evidentiary privilege, the information must come from the client or a client's agent. Information that the lawyer learns from third parties is protected by the duty of confidentiality but not the privilege. To be protected by the duty of confidentiality, the information need merely "relat[e] to representation of a client." MR 1.6(a). [80]

B. Duty of confidentiality broader than evidentiary privilege

The duty of confidentiality applies to all information relating to the representation, not merely communications from client to lawyer. [80]

1. **Lawyer observations:** Lawyer observations are protected by the duty of confidentiality. [80]

2. **Communications from third parties:** Communications from third parties about the representation are protected by the duty of confidentiality. [80]

3. **Work product:** Lawyer thoughts and strategies about the representation are protected by the duty of confidentiality. They are also protected by the related discovery doctrine called the *work product doctrine.* [80]

IV. EXCEPTIONS TO THE DUTY OF CONFIDENTIALITY

A. Consent

A client may give informed consent to disclosure of information that would otherwise be protected by the duty of confidentiality. MR 1.6(a). [80]

B. Implied authorization

To carry out the purposes of the representation, some information that would be subject to the duty of confidentiality must be disclosed. [81]

C. Self-defense disclosures

Under certain circumstances, lawyers may reveal client confidences to defend themselves or to pursue claims against former clients. [81-82]

1. **The three categories of self-defense permitted disclosure:**

    a. **"[T]o establish a claim or defense on behalf of the lawyer in a controversy between the lawyer and the client."** This exception usually means a fee dispute between lawyer and client, but it applies beyond fee disputes to any controversy between lawyer and client, such as a lawyer malpractice claim. [81]

    b. **"[T]o establish a defense to a criminal charge or a civil claim against the lawyer based upon conduct in which the client was involved."** When a lawyer is the defendant in a criminal or civil action based on conduct of the client or is otherwise accused of misconduct that relates to a client's conduct, the lawyer may respond, using confidential information as necessary. MR 1.6 Comment 8. [81-82]

c. **"[T]o respond to allegations in any proceeding concerning the lawyer's representation of the client."** This exception extends the type of proceedings in which the lawyer may use confidential information in self-defense to include, for example, bar disciplinary proceedings, government agency investigatory proceedings, or criminal collateral review claims of ineffective assistance of counsel. [82]

2. **Limit disclosure to facts necessary to defend:** With respect to any of the three categories of permitted disclosure, the lawyer must limit disclosure to those facts necessary to self-defend. [82]

3. **Limit disclosure to individuals who need to know:** Lawyers must also limit their self-defense disclosures to those who need to know for the lawyer's self-defense or fee-collection purpose. [82]

D. **Future crimes, frauds, and harms**

In certain circumstances, lawyers may reveal confidential information to prevent *future crimes,* frauds, or harms by clients. The circumstances defined by the Model Code and Model Rules are quite different from one another. MR 1.6(b)(1), DR 4-101(C)(3). [83-85]

1. **Distinction with past crimes or frauds:** As long as all other requirements are satisfied, when a client reveals a *past* crime or fraud, that information is protected by the duty of confidentiality and the attorney-client privilege. [83]

2. **Policy rationale:** When a client has committed a crime or fraud, the lawyer's representation of the client is what the legal system expects the client to be afforded. When the lawyer knows the client intends to commit a future crime or fraud, and *the lawyer's services are used to commit the crime or fraud,* the lawyer will share both the moral and legal responsibility for the wrong. See Chapter 3, §III. [83]

3. **Model Code:** The Model Code exception for future crimes or frauds is broad but permissive. Under the Code, a lawyer "*may* reveal the intention of his client to commit a crime and the information necessary to prevent the crime." DR 4-101(C)(3). [83]

4. **Model Rules:** Before the 2002 amendments, the Model Rules' exception for future crimes had retained the permissive language of the Model Code but restricted the type of future crime that may permit revelation of confidential information. The exception before February 2002 read, "A lawyer *may* reveal . . . information [relating to representation of a client] to the extent the lawyer reasonably believes necessary to prevent the client from committing a criminal act that the lawyer believes is *likely to result in imminent death or substantial bodily harm.*" Former MR 1.6(b)(1). Model Rule 1.6 was amended in a significant way in February 2002. The new language for the future crime exception to the duty of confidentiality allows the lawyer to reveal confidences "to the extent the lawyer reasonably believes necessary to prevent reasonably certain death or substantial bodily harm." MR 1.6(b)(1). Following the amendment to MR 1.6(b)(1), this exception to the confidentiality duty might better be referred to as the "future harm" exception rather than the future-crime exception because it requires no criminal act by the client for a trigger. See also sections on perjury and noisy withdrawal, §§III.D.4.c, III.D.4.d, and Chapter 8, §I.C. [83-84]

5. August 2003 amendment to Model Rule 1.6: Before the August 2003 amendments to the Model Rules, MR 1.6 was seriously out of tune with most state ethics rules and the Restatement regarding exceptions to the duty of confidentiality. A lawyer was not permitted to reveal confidential information in situations in which the client had committed or planned to commit a fraud that caused financial injury to third persons. In August 2003, the ABA House of Delegates finally adopted a revised MR 1.6, which reflected recommendations from the 2002 ABA Task Force. Disclosure is now permissible "to the extent the lawyer reasonably believes necessary:

   a. to prevent reasonably certain death or substantial bodily harm;

   b. to prevent the client from committing a crime or fraud that is reasonably certain to result in substantial injury to the financial interests or property of another and in furtherance of which the client has used or is using the lawyer's services;

   c. to prevent, mitigate or rectify substantial injury to the financial interests or property of another that is reasonably certain to result or has resulted from the client's commission of a crime or fraud in furtherance of which the client has used the lawyer's services;

   d. to secure legal advice about the lawyer's compliance with these Rules;

   e. to establish a claim or defense on behalf of the lawyer in a controversy between the lawyer and the client, to establish a defense to a criminal charge or civil claim against the lawyer based upon conduct in which the client was involved, or to respond to allegations in any proceeding concerning the lawyer's representation of the client; or

   f. to comply with other law or a court order." MR 1.6. [84-85]

E. Other professional responsibility rules

Some ethics rules require or permit lawyers to disclose information that would otherwise be protected by the duty of confidentiality. See examples in §§IV.E.1-5. [85-86]

F. "Other law" or orders of court

Lawyers may reveal confidences when required to do so by other law or by order of court. [86]

G. Information generally known

Even when some others in addition to the lawyer and client know the protected client information, the duty of confidentiality continues to protect the information. When the information *is generally known,* however, its continued protection by the lawyer will in some cases serve little purpose, and most would say that the duty of confidentiality is lost as well. [87]

V. OTHER PROFESSIONAL DUTIES THAT ARE SUBJECT TO THE DUTY OF CONFIDENTIALITY

A wide range of lawyer duties impose requirements on lawyers only when the duty does not offend the duty of confidentiality. See examples in §§V.A.-F. [87-88]

VI. USE OF CONFIDENTIAL INFORMATION FOR THE LAWYER'S BENEFIT

As a client's agent, a lawyer is generally restricted from using confidential information of the client, either for the lawyer's benefit or to the client's detriment. [88]

A. Model Code

The Model Code expressly prohibits a lawyer from using confidential information of the client, either for the lawyer's benefit or to the client's detriment. DR 4-101(B)(2), 4-101(B)(3). [88]

B. Model Rules

The Model Rules drafters kept only the explicit restriction on using client information to the client's detriment. MR 1.8(b). [88]

C. A meaningless distinction

Technically, the distinction is important because, on its face, the Model Rules provision permits lawyer use of client confidences for the lawyer's or a third person's gain, as long as the client is not disadvantaged. As a practical matter, the distinction matters little because disadvantage to the client will almost always occur when there is advantage to the lawyer and because the law of agency prohibits the lawyer from profiting by using the client's confidences. [88]

CHAPTER 6
CONFLICTS OF INTEREST

I. LOYALTY AND OTHER GENERAL PRINCIPLES

A variety of central principles are at play in analyzing *conflicts-of-interest* questions. [97]

A. Loyalty

Basic to the lawyer-client relationship is the premise that lawyers owe clients a duty of *loyalty.* [97]

B. Independence of professional judgment

Lawyers owe clients a duty of *independent professional judgment.* When the independence is threatened by some interest other than the client's, a conflicts question is present and requires analysis. [97]

C. Implications of confidentiality

Many conflicts questions are primarily about breaches of confidentiality. See Chapter 5. [97]

D. Direct adversity

Relatively easy cases of conflicts-of-interest analysis occur when the lawyer attempts to represent directly adverse interests. See §IV.C.1.a. [97]

E. Material limitations on representation

The application of many of the conflicts rules is triggered by a determination of whether the conflict "will materially limit[] the [lawyer's representation of the client]." See, e.g., MR 1.7(b). This standard is objective. [97]

II. ORGANIZATION OF THE MODEL RULES PROVISIONS ON CONFLICTS

The Model Rules conflicts provisions are found in MR 1.7 through 1.13, and 1.18. [97-98]

A. General rule

Model Rule 1.7 sets out the general standards for conflicts-of-interest analysis. [97-98]

B. Specific transactions

Model Rule 1.8 sets out a series of specific conflicts rules that apply to particular lawyer-client transactions. See §IV.B.2. [98]

C. Special problems of former clients

Model Rule 1.9 applies to multiple client conflicts when one of the clients is a former client. See §IV.C.3. [98]

D. Prospective clients

A new rule adopted in February 2002, MR 1.18, defines and identifies duties owed to prospective clients. [98]

E. Role-relevant rules

Conflict rules that apply to lawyers in particular lawyer roles are found in MR 1.11, 1.12, and 1.13. [98]

1. Motivated by various corporate and securities defalcations, the ABA amended Mode Rule 1.13 in August 2003. The amended rule retained the actual knowledge standard—even after the amendment, the attorney must have actual knowledge of a material violation by the corporate client—but expanded the lawyer's obligation to report misconduct. The Sarbanes-Oxley Act and subsequent SEC regulations created new restrictions on certain corporate lawyers.

F. Imputed disqualification

Model Rule 1.10 provides the general imputed disqualification rules. More specific imputed disqualification rules are found in MR 1.9, 1.11, and 1.12. [98]

III. WAIVER OF CONFLICTS

A. Rationale

Because most conflicts put client interests at risk and because client autonomy and decision-making are values worthy of some respect, clients are empowered to *waive* most conflicts of interest. [98]

1. **The gross conflict exception:** The general rationale of honoring client autonomy does not apply when the conflict is sufficiently gross to make any client waiver suspect. See MR 1.7(b). [98-99]

2. **The interest-other-than-the-client's exception:** The general rationale of honoring client autonomy does not apply when the conflicts rule is less about the risk to client interests than it is about risks to justice system interests. [99-100]

B. **Elements of waiver**

At a minimum, a conflicts-of-interest waiver requires informed consent by the client. Some of the conflicts rules that allow waiver require more than informed consent. See, e.g., MR 1.8(a), MR 1.8(f), §IV.B.2.a. [100-101]

IV. SOURCES OF CONFLICTS

There are three primary sources of conflicts of interest: third-party interference, lawyer interests, and multiple client interests. [101-113]

A. **Third-party interference**

Third-party interference conflicts occur when someone who is not a party to the lawyer-client relationship seeks to affect or becomes positioned to affect the independence of the lawyer's judgment on behalf of the client. See MR 1.7(a)(2) for the general rule. Such conflicts may be waived if the client consents after consultation. [101-104]

B. **Lawyer-client conflicts**

The second major source of conflicts is lawyer interests that conflict with client interests. [104-107]

1. **General principles**

   a. **Material limitation:** As a general matter, a conflict of interest exists when a lawyer's "representation of a client will be materially limited by the lawyer's . . . personal interests." MR 1.7(a)(2). [104]

   b. **Waiver:** Waiver of this general conflict is possible if "the lawyer reasonably believes that the lawyer will be able to provide competent and diligent representation to [the client] and [the client] gives informed consent, confirmed in writing." MR 1.7(b). See §III. [104]

2. **Particular transactions:** A variety of particular transactions between lawyers and clients are governed by specific conflicts rules. [104-106]

   a. **Business transactions with clients:** Model Rule 1.8(a), which addresses business transactions between lawyer and client, requires that the client's consent be in writing, that the client be "advised in writing of the desirability of seeking and is given a reasonable opportunity to seek the advice of independent counsel," that the transaction be objectively reasonable, and that the transaction itself be in writing and in terms that can be understood by the client. The business transactions restrictions of MR 1.8(a) apply only when the client expects the lawyer to exercise legal judgment regarding the transaction. [104-105]

b. Literary rights: Lawyers are prohibited from negotiating for literary or media rights based on their clients' stories until the conclusion of representation. MR 1.8(d). No waiver of this conflict is permitted. [105-106]

c. Drafting instruments that benefit the lawyer: A lawyer is prohibited from drafting a document that makes a substantial gift to the lawyer or the lawyer's close relatives. This restriction does not apply when the donee is related to the donor. MR 1.8(c). [106]

d. Sexual or amorous relations with clients: Because of the complicated mixture of interests that can develop when a professional lawyer-client relationship is mingled with an amorous one, lawyers are well advised to avoid amorous relationships with current clients. A new Model Rule adopted in February 2002, 1.8(j), prohibits most sexual relationships between lawyers and clients. The rule does not prohibit sexual relationships that predated the beginning of the lawyer-client relationship. [106]

e. Agreements limiting the lawyer's liability: A lawyer is prohibited from entering into a contract with a client that prospectively limits the lawyer's liability for malpractice, unless state law permits and the client is represented by independent counsel with respect to the agreement. MR 1.8(h). [106]

f. Settling claims with unrepresented clients: A lawyer is prohibited from settling malpractice claims with unrepresented clients or former clients unless the lawyer first advises the client or former client that independent counsel is advisable. MR 1.8(h). [106]

3. **Lawyer-client conflicts and champerty, barratry, and maintenance:** Various restrictions on lawyer conduct, often interrelated with lawyer-client conflicts issues, are based on the doctrines of champerty, barratry, and maintenance. [106-107]

    a. Champerty, barratry, and maintenance: These three doctrines together are concerned with prohibiting the stirring up and maintaining of litigation. See definitions of champerty, barratry, and maintenance in Chapter 10, §VIII. [106]

    b. Advancing funds to clients: Lawyers are prohibited from advancing financial assistance to clients when there is pending or contemplated litigation, except that the lawyer may advance court costs. Client waiver of this "conflict" is not permitted. MR 1.8(e). [107]

    c. Acquiring an interest in the litigation or its subject matter: A lawyer is prohibited from acquiring an interest in litigation or its subject matter, whether that interest is consistent or inconsistent with the client's interests. This prohibition is not a restriction on the lawyer's contract with a client for a reasonable contingent fee. Client waiver of a violation of this rule is not permitted. MR 1.8(i). [107]

4. **Miscellaneous lawyer-client conflicts rules**

    a. Using confidential information to the client's detriment: A lawyer is prohibited from using information learned in the lawyer-client relationship to the detriment of the client. MR 1.8(b). [108]

C. Multiple client conflicts

The third major source of conflicts is the interaction of *multiple clients'* interests. Multiple client conflicts can implicate not only concurrent representation of multiple clients but also conflicts between former and current clients, prospective and current clients, or prospective and former clients. [107-113]

1. **Concurrent clients:** Even when the conflicts involve only concurrent clients, a variety of different configurations may present themselves. [108-110]

    a. **Directly adverse:** The easiest cases involve multiple representation of clients whose interests are in direct conflict. Such a direct conflict cannot be effectively waived by the clients on the theory that it is too gross a conflict. MR 1.7(a). But see exceptions in intermediary role, Chapter 9, §III. [108]

    b. **Adverse in unrelated actions:** A lawyer may also find herself representing one client against a second client in a matter unrelated to the representation of the second client. In general, such a conflict may not be waived, but when the adversity is general, waiver has been permitted. [108]

    c. **Same-side multiple-client representation:** Even multiple representation of clients who are at least initially on the same side of litigation or a transaction implicates conflicts analysis. [108-110]

2. **Prospective and current clients:** Lawyers owe prospective clients a limited loyalty duty and the duty of confidentiality. MR 1.18. Because confidentiality breaches are a primary consideration in multiple-client conflicts analysis, conflicts analysis must be done on potential conflicts between prospective and current or former clients. [110]

3. **Former and current clients—The substantial relationship test:** Because lawyers owe clients a continued measure of loyalty after representation ends and because lawyers owe clients a full measure of the duty of confidentiality after representation ends, conflicts between former and current clients arise when their interests are directly adverse or when there is a ***substantial relationship*** between the two representations. Such a conflict may be waived by both clients by informed consent. MR 1.9. [110]

4. **Lawyer for an organization:** A lawyer who represents an organization, such as a corporation, a labor union, or a public-interest organization, represents the organization, not its officers. At times, the interests of the organization and its officers may converge. Under such circumstances, a lawyer may represent both the organization and its officers, but the lawyer must withdraw if the interests of the organization and the officers diverge. MR 1.13. See §IV.A.2.a for an example. [110-112]

5. **Positional conflicts of interest:** When a lawyer represents two clients in unrelated matters for whom the lawyer must argue opposite sides of the same legal issue, a potential positional conflict of interest exists. Although "[o]rdinarily a lawyer may take inconsistent legal positions in different tribunals at different times on behalf of different clients, . . . a conflict of interest exists . . . [when] there is a significant risk that the lawyer's action on behalf of one client will materially limit the lawyer's effectiveness in representing another client in a different case. . . ." MR 1.7 Comment 24. Especially when these opposite positions are argued before the same court, however, the lawyer is effectively arguing for a precedent in one case that harms the client in the other case. This would "adversely affect" one of the clients while benefiting the other. [113]

V. IMPUTED CONFLICTS

As a general rule, when a lawyer has a conflict of interest, that conflict imputes to (transfers to, extends to) all of the lawyers in the law organization (usually a law firm) in which the lawyer works. MR 1.10. [113-115]

A. Basic issues

This *imputed disqualification* rule is mainly based on the notion that confidential information possessed by one lawyer is effectively possessed by all lawyers in the same firm. [114]

B. Motions to disqualify

Motions to disqualify counsel and entire law firms for which the disqualified lawyer works have become a favored tactical device in litigation, effectively denying an opposing party her counsel of choice and preserving the integrity of the justice system from the threat of conflicts of interest. [114]

C. The ambulatory lawyer

The increasing movement of lawyers from one practice setting to another or from one law firm to another has dramatically increased the frequency and impact of imputed disqualification rules. [114]

D. Screening defenses

An increasing number of courts, supported by Model Rules 1.10, 1.11, and 1.12, have ruled that effective *screening procedures* will prevent the application of the imputed disqualification rules. Some courts have labeled these screening procedures the "Chinese Wall" defense, because of the walling-off of the affected lawyer. Under such procedures, the conflicted lawyer is isolated from other lawyers in the organization by various devices. [114]

E. Other interests at play in the motion to disqualify setting

When a court is considering a motion to disqualify, several factors may be considered in addition to the conflicts principles that are relevant in the disciplinary context. See examples in §§V.F.1-4. [115]

F. Special role-related imputed disqualification rules

Special rules regarding imputed disqualification apply to former government lawyers and former judges. See §VI. [115]

VI. SPECIAL ROLE-RELATED CONFLICTS RULES

Lawyers who find themselves in special roles find that special conflicts rules apply. [115-120]

A. Former judge

Former judges' conflicts differ from those of lawyers who move from one practice setting to another, and they require special conflicts rules. MR 1.12. A former judge shall not engage in private representation in a matter in which the judge participated personally and substantially as a judge, unless all parties to the matter consent after consultation. MR 1.12. [115-117]

1. **Negotiating for employment:** Judges are prohibited from negotiating for employment with lawyers who are currently representing parties before the judge's court if the judge is personally and substantially participating in the matter before the court. Similar, but waivable, restrictions apply to judicial law clerks. MR 1.12(b). [117]

2. **Special imputed disqualification rules:** Special, more relaxed imputed disqualification rules apply to the law firms for which former judges work. Effective screening procedures and notice to the parties and the judge's former court permit a former judge's law firm to continue with representation in which the former judge is disqualified from participating. MR 1.12(c). [117]

B. **Former government lawyer**

Special conflicts rules apply to lawyers who move from government practice to private practice. MR 1.11. [117-119]

1. **General:** A former government "lawyer shall not represent a client in connection with a matter in which the lawyer participated personally and substantially" as a government lawyer. MR 1.11. Notice that this conflict rule applies without regard to whether the lawyer has effectively changed sides in the matter. [117-118]

2. **Exceptions:** Three exceptions allow the former government lawyer to engage in the later private representation even when his participation in the government employment was personal and substantial. [118]

    a. **Law otherwise permits:** The conflicts rule excepts from its reach cases in which the law otherwise expressly permits the private representation to occur. [118]

    b. **Not a "matter":** The rule defines what it means by a "matter." It is only later private representation in connection with a government service "matter" that triggers a conflicts-of-interest analysis. A matter includes a wide variety of instances and actions that engage the agency with a particular party or parties. The definition excludes rule drafting and other agency actions that have more general application. [118]

    c. **Consent:** The agency may waive the conflict by giving its informed consent. [118]

3. **Use of confidential government information:** Except when law otherwise expressly permits such representation, a former government lawyer is also prohibited from representing private parties who are adverse to parties about whom the lawyer has confidential information gained in the government practice that could be used against the adverse party. MR 1.11(c). The private party's interests are the ones at risk in such a case. As such, it is the private party and not the agency that must waive the conflict if the lawyer is to be permitted to proceed. [118]

4. **Special imputed disqualification rules:** Special, more relaxed imputed disqualification rules apply when former government lawyers are the law firm lawyers who have a conflict. [119]

C. **Lawyer as witness**

Special conflict problems are associated with the occasion on which a lawyer is to be called as a witness. MR 3.7. See §VI.C. [119-120]

Chapter 7
DUTIES TO THIRD PARTIES

The duties owed to third parties operate as limits on the primary duty the lawyer owes to a client. In other words, they operate to form boundaries around acceptable, client-favoring actions by lawyers.

I. TRUTH-TELLING OUTSIDE THE COURT CONTEXT

Rules governing lawyers' truth-telling duties outside the court context contrast with those that apply inside the court context. See Chapter 8, §1. The outside the court truth-telling rules apply in a lawyer's dealings with opposing lawyers, opposing parties (but also see the special communications with opposing parties rules in §§IV and V), witnesses (but also see special communication with witnesses rules in §§IV.E.1 and V), and anyone else with whom the lawyer communicates as a lawyer. [129-132]

A. False statements of material law or fact

For a statement to a third party to subject a lawyer to discipline, it must be both false and material. [130]

B. Fraudulent statements and silences

Lawyers are prohibited from making statements that are fraudulent or remaining silent when the statement or silence would amount to fraud under applicable tort principles. See MR 1.0(d). [130-131]

C. The negotiation setting

The negotiation setting presents a special circumstance within which the nature and effect of misleading statements must be analyzed. By its nature, an element of misleading is present in the negotiation process. The rules prohibit only certain forms of misleading. MR 4.1 Comment. [131-132]

1. **The parties to the negotiation:** Statements made to other lawyers in negotiations (and arguably to very sophisticated nonlawyers) are regarded much differently from statements made to nonlawyers. [131]

2. **What is a fact?** Some statements made in the negotiation setting are not regarded as statements of fact because they are simply too nebulous to be called "statements of fact," or they are accepted parts of the negotiation game that ought to be evaluated for what they are worth by the other side. [131]

3. **Reducing agreements to writing:** The process of reducing an oral agreement to writing poses special truthfulness problems. See examples in §§I.C.3.a-c. [132]

II. HARASSMENT AND OTHER ABUSIVE CONDUCT

A. In general

1. **Unlawful acts by lawyers:** Lawyers are prohibited from engaging in (or using agents to engage in) unlawful acts on behalf of clients. [132-133]

2. **Assisting clients in committing unlawful or fraudulent acts:** Although a lawyer may counsel a client about the legal consequences of a course of conduct proposed by the client, a lawyer is prohibited from counseling a client to engage (or assisting a client engaged) in criminal or fraudulent conduct. MR 1.2(d). See Chapter 4, §V.B. [133]

3. **Harassing conduct:** Model Rule 4.4(a) prohibits a lawyer from using "means that have no substantial purpose other than to embarrass, delay, or burden a third person. . . ." The rule prohibits only actions that serve no substantial, legitimate purpose but are merely done to embarrass, delay, or burden the third person. [133]

B. Opposing parties

Opposing parties are a special category of third party. Their interests are most directly contrary to those of the lawyer's client. Opposing parties are, therefore, routinely the object of a lawyer's client-favoring activities. For specific limitations, see §§I-V and Chapter 8, §II.B. [133]

C. Witnesses

A great deal of lawyer conduct toward witnesses may be perceived by the witness as harassing. (For other witness-lawyer relationship rules that affect the trial process, such as payment limitation rules, see Chapter 8.) [133-134]

1. **In general:** Conduct will violate the law of professional responsibility only when the lawyer has no "substantial purpose other than to embarrass, delay, or burden" the witness. MR 4.4(a). [134]

2. **Investigation:** Lawyers may not use unlawful means to gather evidence from witnesses. MR 4.4(a). [134]

D. Jurors

Lawyers are prohibited from engaging in live contact investigations of jurors and from other harassing conduct. (For other, "duty to the justice system" rules that relate to lawyers and jurors, (see Chapter 8, §VI.B.) [134]

1. **Investigation:** Lawyers may investigate jurors' backgrounds by means of public records such as deeds, judgments, available voting records, and so on. Lawyers may not contact jurors either in person or through agents. MR 4.4(a). [134]

2. **Post-verdict harassing conduct:** Lawyers may not engage in conduct that will cause jurors to question the justice system's use of their verdict. See Chapter 8, §VI.B. [134]

III. THREATENING CRIMINAL PROSECUTION

The Model Code includes a specific provision prohibiting threats of criminal prosecution "solely to obtain advantage in a civil matter." DR 7-105. Threatening criminal prosecution for reasons other than gaining an advantage in a civil matter is not prohibited by this rule. The Model Rules drafters did not include a specific provision on this subject in the Model Rules. Rather, they relied on the general "rights of third parties" rule to cover the use of inappropriate threats. MR 4.4. In effect, when a threat would amount to extortion, it is a prohibited threat under MR 4.4(a). [134-135]

IV. COMMUNICATING WITH REPRESENTED PERSONS

Lawyers are prohibited from communicating about the subject matter of a dispute with represented opposing parties without first obtaining permission from the opposing party's lawyer. MR 4.2. Opposing parties, however, may communicate with one another without offending MR 4.2, provided that the lawyer has not instructed the client to do so as a means of circumventing the rule. [135-138]

A. Parties and persons

The rule includes represented persons, even if they are not formally parties to active litigation. [135]

B. Who is an opposing party or person?

1. **Mere witnesses:** No matter how much a particular witness's testimony is expected to favor one side in a dispute, a mere witness is not a represented party. Model Rule 4.2 does not apply to communication with mere witnesses. [136]

2. **Organizational parties:** Organizations speak and function through individuals who are not in and of themselves the organization. When dealing with a represented organization, Model Rule 4.2 prohibits unauthorized communication between an opposing lawyer and employees with managerial responsibilities for the subject of the matter, employees whose acts or omissions may be imputed to the organization with respect to the matter, and employees whose statements may constitute an admission attributable to the organization. MR 4.2 Comment 2. [136-137]

3. **Former employees:** Whether former employees may be considered as parties for purposes of MR 4.2 has been a controversial question. Both the ABA and the majority of decisions say that former employees are not parties under MR 4.2. Other courts have ruled to the contrary. The better approach is probably to distinguish cases based on the category of employee at issue and that employee's relationship to the matter. [136-137]

4. **Class-action members:** Members of a class are treated as parties for purposes of MR 4.2. [137]

C. Obtaining permission

A lawyer may communicate with an opposing party about the subject matter of the representation if the opposing party's lawyer has given consent. [137]

D. Authorized by law

A lawyer may communicate with an opposing party about the subject matter of the representation if the lawyer is "authorized by law" to so communicate. [137]

E. Authorized by court order

The February 2002 amendments to MR 4.2 added a provision permitting unconsented contact when authorized by court order. The amendment to Model Rule 4.2 creates an unstated link to the former "Reno Rule," which replaced the former Thornburgh Memorandum on the subject of federal government lawyers' compliance with MR 4.2 and other state ethics rules. Although its effects remain murky, the McDade Amendment (28 U.S.C. sec. 530B) and Department of Justice regulations adopted pursuant to it (28 C.F.R. sec. 77.1 *et seq.*) have also affected the analysis in this area. [137]

F. Special criminal practice concerns

In criminal practice, of course, the opposing party of the prosecutor is a criminal defendant. Two different aspects of this special configuration are worthy of note. [137-138]

1. **Added constitutional limitations:** Fifth and Fourteenth Amendment due process rights and Sixth Amendment right to counsel protection restrain prosecutors' contact with criminal defendants in ways that go beyond the professional responsibility law constraints of Model Rule 4.2. [137]

2. **Investigation of crime:** Prosecutors, especially federal prosecutors invoking not only Model Rule 4.2's "authorized by law" language but also the Supremacy Clause of the United States Constitution, have argued that their crime-investigation activities are not restricted by Model Rule 4.2's requirements of consent by an opposing party's lawyer prior to communication. [138]

V. COMMUNICATING WITH UNREPRESENTED PERSONS

Although not prohibited from communicating with unrepresented persons who are involved in a client's matter, lawyers are restricted in what they may say to such a person. MR 4.3. [138-139]

A. Avoid misleading about the lawyer's interest

1. **Affirmative duty:** A lawyer is under an affirmative obligation to refrain from stalling or implying that the lawyer is disinterested in the matter about which the lawyer is communicating. Any effort to mislead an unrepresented person about the lawyer's interest subjects the lawyer to discipline. [138]

2. **Clarifying duty:** When a lawyer "reasonably should know" that an unrepresented person misunderstands the lawyer's interest in the matter, the lawyer is obliged to make reasonable efforts to clarify his role. [138]

B. Giving advice

Lawyers are prohibited from giving legal advice to the unrepresented persons with whom they inevitably come into contact, except to advise unrepresented persons to obtain counsel. [139]

C. Fact gathering

Model Rule 4.3 does not prohibit fact gathering, provided the lawyer does so without giving advice (other than advice to obtain counsel) to the unrepresented person. [139]

VI. CIVIL LIABILITY TO THIRD PERSONS

In limited circumstances, a lawyer may have civil liability for wrongful or negligent lawyering activity to those outside the lawyer-client relationship. [139-140]

A. General

As a general rule, lawyers do not owe a duty to third persons that support a negligence action. [139]

B. Intended beneficiaries of the lawyer's work for a client

When a lawyer's work for a client is intended to benefit a third person, the lawyer owes a duty of care to that third person. [140]

C. Invited reliance

When a lawyer's work for a client specifically invites the reliance of a third person, the lawyer owes a duty of care to that third person. [140]

D. Assisting clients in breaching fiduciary duties

When a lawyer does work for a client who is a fiduciary (such as a trustee of a trust for the benefit of a beneficiary), the lawyer owes a duty to the beneficiary requiring the lawyer to refrain from engaging in acts that assist the client in breaching the client's fiduciary duties. [141]

E. Preventing client harm to a third person

Lawyers who know that a client will harm a third person and fail to engage in reasonable steps to prevent the harm may have liability to the third person who is harmed by the client. This duty is highly controversial and not widely accepted. [141]

CHAPTER 8
DUTIES TO THE LEGAL SYSTEM AND SOCIETY

Many of the lawyer's duties to the legal system or the public generally conflict with duties to the client, and the discussion in this chapter covers rules that set the lines across which client-favoring actions become unacceptably harmful to the legal system or the public.

I. TRUTH-TELLING INSIDE THE COURT CONTEXT

Truth-telling inside the court context carries implications not present in out-of-court contexts, such as negotiation. When a lawyer misleads in court, the court itself is misled in addition to the opposing party. [148-153]

A. Statements to opposing parties

Lawyers' out-of-court obligations of candor to opposing parties continue in like form in the litigation context. See Chapter 7, §1. [148]

B. Fact statements to the court

A lawyer is prohibited from knowingly making false statements of material fact to the court and from otherwise engaging in acts or omissions that amount to fraud. MR 3.3(a). [148-149]

1. **Generally:** Despite the duty of candor to the court, a lawyer is under no general obligation to reveal unfavorable facts to the court. Although a lawyer is under no general obligation to reveal

unfavorable facts to the court, a lawyer must disclose material facts "when disclosure is necessary to avoid assisting a criminal or fraudulent act by the client." MR 3.3(a)(l). [148-149]

2. **Ex parte proceedings:** On those occasions when a lawyer is permitted by law to engage in ex parte communications with the court (see §VI.A), the lawyer must disclose to the court both favorable and unfavorable material facts. MR 3.3(d). [149]

C. **Perjury**

The perjury problem presents extraordinary difficulties for the lawyer, especially when the person committing the perjury is the lawyer's client. Perjury's affront to the justice system is great, as is the harm that comes to the client when the lawyer reveals the client's perjury. [150-152]

1. **General duty to refrain from offering false evidence:** A lawyer is prohibited from offering evidence the lawyer knows to be false. MR 3.3(a)(3). [150]

2. **Discretion to refuse to offer some evidence:** Further, a lawyer "may refuse to offer evidence that the lawyer reasonably believes is false." MR 3.3(a)(3). [150]

3. **Perjury by a witness:** When a lawyer knows that a witness other than the client has offered perjured testimony, the lawyer must promptly reveal the perjury to the court. MR 3.3(a)(3). [150]

4. **Perjury by a client:** Unlike the Model Code approach, which explicitly distinguished between client perjury and other witness perjury, the Model Rules' language requires the same answer to both. MR 3.3(a)(3); DR 7-102(B). [150-152]

   a. **Knowledge before the perjury:** When the lawyer knows of the client's intention to commit perjury, the lawyer must attempt to dissuade, attempt to withdraw, and, finally, if the perjury occurs, take reasonable remedial measures. The Model Rule indicates that whether the client or another witness has committed the perjury, reasonable remedial measures include disclosure of the perjury to the court. [150-151]

   b. **Knowledge gained after the perjury:** When the lawyer learns that the client's testimony was perjurious after the perjury occurs but before proceedings end, the lawyer must first attempt to persuade the client to rectify the matter by revealing the fraud and then testifying truthfully. If that effort fails, the lawyer has only the reasonable remedial measures option and, according to the Model Rules Comment, must reveal the perjury if the lawyer learns of it before the proceedings conclude. If the lawyer does not learn of the perjury until after the conclusion of the proceedings, then the lawyer has no obligation to reveal it. MR 3.3(c). [150]

   c. **Duty applies despite confidentiality:** The Model Rule duty to rectify the perjury applies even if doing so would otherwise violate the duty of confidentiality under Model Rule 1.6. MR 3.3(c). [151]

   d. **Distinctions between criminal and civil representation:** Perjury issues in criminal representation present special problems because of the criminal defendant's right to testify on his own behalf, the obligation on the state to prove the defendant guilty beyond a reasonable doubt, the privilege against self-incrimination, and the right to counsel. MR 3.3(a)(3). [151]

   e. **Other suggested options:** Although not accepted in all circles, suggested options for counsel faced with a perjurious client in a criminal case include allowing the client to give a narrative as testimony, refusing to call the client as a witness, and exempting of criminal defense counsel from the general requirement to remedy a client's perjury. [152]

D. Law statements to the court

A lawyer is prohibited from making false statements of law to the court. MR 3.3(a). As an advocate, the lawyer need not reveal his objective analysis of the law to the court but may make any nonfrivolous, client-favoring arguments regarding the law to the court. [152]

E. Disclosing adverse legal authority

Lawyers are obligated to disclose to the court controlling, directly *adverse legal authority.* MR 3.3(a)(2). [152-153]

1. **To opposing parties:** Lawyers have no obligation to disclose adverse authority to opposing parties. [152]

2. **To the court:** Lawyers are required to disclose controlling, directly adverse authority to the court. [152-153]

    a. **Controlling:** Only controlling authority, that is, mandatory authority that is controlling on the court currently making the decision, must be disclosed. [153]

    b. **Directly adverse:** Only directly adverse authority must be disclosed under this rule. Authority is directly adverse when it is applicable to the present case without extended analogy. [153]

    c. **Contesting the disclosed authority:** The requirement of disclosing the controlling, directly adverse authority does not prevent the disclosing lawyer from arguing that the authority does not apply or is wrong and should not be followed. [153]

II. SUPPRESSING EVIDENCE AND WITNESS PAYMENT

A lawyer is limited in the ways in which witnesses may be compensated and in instructing witnesses about whether to make themselves available for testimony or interview by the opposing side. [153-155]

A. Suppressing witness availability

Lawyers are prohibited generally from requesting or advising a witness to refrain from voluntarily cooperating with another litigant. MR 3.4(f). [154]

1. **Procuring witness unavailability:** Under no circumstances may a lawyer dissuade a witness from appearing at a hearing or persuade a witness to secrete himself so that the witness will be unavailable. MR 3.4(a). [154]

2. **Instructing a witness to cooperate only if subpoenaed:** In general, a lawyer may not instruct a witness to cooperate only if subpoenaed. MR 3.4(f). [154]

3. **Exception:** A lawyer is permitted to request that a witness not cooperate voluntarily if the witness is a relative, employee, or agent of the client and the lawyer reasonably believes that the request will not harm the witness. MR 3.4(f)(2). [154]

B. Witness payment rules

1. **Lay witnesses:** Lawyers may pay nonexpert witnesses only a statutory fee and reasonable expenses incurred by the witness in attending the trial or hearing. MR 3.4 Comment 3. [154]

2. **Expert witnesses:** Expert witnesses may be paid the professional fee that someone in the expert's field charges for his or her time and reasonable expenses incurred by the witness in attending the trial or hearing. However, an expert may not be paid a fee that is contingent on the outcome of the matter. MR 3.4 Comment 3. [155]

III. LIMITATIONS ON PRESENTATIONS TO A COURT

A. Frivolous claims and litigation positions

Lawyers are prohibited from bringing actions or taking positions in litigation that are frivolous. [155-158]

1. **Ethics code limits:** In several forms, the Model Rules restrict lawyers' behavior regarding frivolous litigation positions. [155]

    a. **The frivolous claims rule:** Model Rule 3.1, in most respects tracking Federal Rule of Civil Procedure 11, prohibits lawyers from bringing or defending claims on a frivolous basis. [155]

    i. **What is frivolous?** Frivolous claims or positions may be so because they lack legal or factual merit or because they are taken primarily to harass or maliciously injure a third party. [155]

    ii. **Difference between civil and criminal cases:** In a criminal case, unlike a civil case, a defendant has a due process right to plead "not guilty" and require the government to be put to its proof. Model Rule 3.1 is not intended to prevent a lawyer from assisting a criminal defendant in the process of putting the government to its proof. Prosecuting lawyers have special obligations regarding the prosecution of charges that lack merit. See Chapter 9, §I.B. [155]

    b. **Discovery and other pretrial conduct:** Frivolous discovery requests and those intended merely to delay are prohibited. MR 3.4(d). [155]

    c. **Expediting litigation:** In general, lawyers are obliged to expedite litigation to the extent that such activity is consistent with the client's interests. MR 3.2. [156]

2. **FRCP 11 and other sanctions:** Beyond the ethics code limitations that create disciplinary liability for filing frivolous claims and taking frivolous positions in litigation, Federal Rule of Civil Procedure 11 and its state law counterparts create sanctions liability for similar conduct. See also Chapter 3, §V.B. [156]

B. Personal opinion

Lawyers are prohibited from expressing their personal opinion to jurors about the justness of the client's cause, the credibility of a witness, or the culpability, guilt, or innocence of a party. MR 3.4(e). [156]

C. Alluding to matters outside the record

Lawyers are prohibited from undermining the evidence law policies by alluding to matters that are either irrelevant or will not be supported by admissible evidence. MR 3.4(e). [156-157]

1. **Reasonable lawyer standard:** Matters must not be alluded to if a reasonable lawyer would recognize that those matters will not be supported by admissible evidence. [156-157]

2. **Certainty not required:** The lawyer need not be certain that the evidence will be admitted. If the lawyer reasonably believes that the evidence will be admitted, then the lawyer may freely allude to the evidence. [157]

3. **Outside the lawyer's control:** If evidence will be admissible only on a condition over which the lawyer in question has no control, the lawyer must not allude to that matter until the evidence is admitted. [157]

4. **Matters already ruled inadmissible:** Once the court has ruled a piece of evidence inadmissible, a lawyer is prohibited from referring to it to the jury. [157]

D. Obey court orders

Lawyers must obey court orders. Even when a lawyer knows that a judge is mistaken in making an order or ruling, the lawyer must obey the order but may make reasonable efforts to preserve the record for later challenge on appeal. [157]

E. Intemperate remarks

Although the First Amendment protects most lawyer expression, lawyers are subject to discipline for intemperate remarks that serve no useful purpose. [157-158]

IV. OBLIGATION TO IMPROVE THE LEGAL SYSTEM

Lawyers have a responsibility to make efforts to improve the legal system. MR, Preamble; Model Code, Canon 8. [158-159]

V. LIMITATIONS ON LITIGATION PUBLICITY

Lawyers generally and especially prosecutors are limited in what they may say to the media regarding pending litigation and criminal investigations. MR 3.6, MR 3.8(g). [159-160]

A. Constitutional challenge

The original Model Rule 3.6 was held void for vagueness in Gentile v. State Bar of Nevada, 501 U.S. 1030 (1991). [159]

B. General standard

Because of such statements' possible effects on the judicial process, lawyers are prohibited from making out-of-court statements that a reasonable lawyer would expect to be disseminated by public communication and that the lawyer knows or should know will have a substantial likelihood of materially prejudicing the matter. MR 3.6(a). [159-160]

1. **Out of court:** Only statements made out of court are restricted by this rule. [159]

2. **Likely to be disseminated by public communication:** Only statements that a reasonable statement-maker would expect to be disseminated by means of public communication are restricted by MR 3.6. [159]

3. **Materially prejudice a matter:** Statements that subject the lawyer to discipline are those that a lawyer knows or reasonably should know will be likely to materially prejudice the matter. [160]

C. **Permitted statements**

Notwithstanding the general prohibition, statements in several distinct categories may safely be made without the risk of discipline. MR 3.6(b). For examples, see §§V.C.1-7. [160]

D. **Exception for statements that are necessary to protect the client**

When a lawyer reasonably believes that making a statement is necessary to counter the effects of a public statement made by the other side in the matter, the lawyer may make such a statement without being subject to discipline. MR 3.6(c). [160]

E. **Prosecutors' supervision of subordinates' statements**

All lawyers have a general obligation to provide reasonable supervision of subordinates in an effort to avoid their breaches of the lawyer's ethics code, but prosecutors have a specially identified duty in the case of extrajudicial statements to exercise reasonable care to prevent violative extrajudicial statements by investigators, police, and others under the supervision of the prosecutor. MR 3.8(f). [160]

VI. EX PARTE CONTACT WITH JUDGES AND JURORS

Ex parte (without the other party) *communications* seriously undermine the prospect of fair process in the justice system. As such, ex parte communication with decision-makers, both judges and jurors, is strictly regulated. [160-162]

A. **Judges**

Except in very limited circumstances, lawyers are prohibited from communicating ex parte with a judge. MR 3.5(b). [161-162]

1. **Subject matter:** Some ex parte communications are permitted because of their subject matter. [161]

    a. **Unrelated matters:** Communications between lawyers and judges about matters unrelated to pending or impending litigation are not restricted by the rule. Such communications are not truly "ex parte" because they do not involve other parties at all. [161]

    b. **Housekeeping matters:** Ex parte communications regarding so-called housekeeping matters that relate to a pending case are permitted. [161]

2. **No intent requirement:** Even innocently intended ex parte communications are prohibited. [161]

3. **Authorized by law:** When authorized by law, lawyers are permitted to engage in ex parte communications. Such authorizations are typically found in rules governing requests for emergency restraining orders, for example. When such communication is authorized, a lawyer is under heightened candor-to-the-court requirements. See §I.B.2. [161]

4. **Oral or written communications covered:** All forms of communication are covered by this rule. A lawyer who sends a letter to the judge or files a paper with the court without serving a copy on opposing counsel is engaging in prohibited ex parte communications with the judge. [161]

5. **Prohibited even if judge initiates:** A lawyer is subject to discipline if he engages in even judge-initiated ex parte communication. [161-162]

B. Jurors

Lawyers are strictly prohibited from communicating with jurors outside the courtroom before and during jurors' duties. This restriction applies to both grand jurors and trial jurors. Lawyers are prohibited from communicating with jurors after the jurors' duty ends, with some exceptions. Lawyers are prohibited from harassing jurors at any time. MR 3.5(c). See Chapter 7, §II.D. [162]

1. **Before and during proceedings:** Communication outside of open court with jurors during and prior to their duty is strictly prohibited. Even communication about matters other than the current proceedings is prohibited. Lawyers must refrain from even innocent communication with sitting jurors. [162]

2. **After proceedings end:** Once proceedings have ended, lawyers may have very limited contact with jurors for benign purposes, such as to determine whether the lawyer's presentation manner is effective. See Chapter 7, §II.D. [162]

3. **Reporting juror misconduct:** A lawyer is under an affirmative obligation to report to the court in which the proceedings are being held juror misconduct or others' misconduct with respect to jurors. Failure to do so subjects the lawyer to discipline. [162]

VII. PRO BONO PUBLICO

The ethics rules encourage lawyers to engage in pro bono activities. [162-163]

A. Organized legal services for the poor

Through the organized bar and public agencies, legal services are provided for a portion of the population that would otherwise be unable to afford to retain a lawyer. [163]

B. Individual lawyer's duty

Amendments in 1993 and 2002 to Model Rule 6.1 have come as close as the organized bar has to imposing a requirement on individual lawyers to render pro bono service. Nonetheless, even the 1993 version of MR 6.1 remains aspirational and not mandatory. A lawyer is not subject to discipline for failing to render pro bono service. [163]

CHAPTER 9
SPECIAL ROLE-RELATED DUTIES

I. SPECIAL DUTIES OF PROSECUTORS

Criminal prosecutors have ethical responsibilities in addition to those of other lawyers. Prosecutors do not represent the crime victim or a complaining witness. Charged with representing the public's interests rather than those of an individual litigant, prosecutors are required to seek justice rather than mere victory in their work. [174-176]

A. Avoid conflicts with private interests represented

Prosecutors, often part-time prosecutors, also represent private clients. Prosecutors must avoid conflicts between the representation of private clients and the prosecutor's duty to seek justice on behalf of the public. [174]

B. Dismissal of charges not supported by probable cause

Prosecutors are prohibited from prosecuting charges that the prosecutor knows are not supported by probable cause, the usual standard below which judges will not issue warrants and will dismiss charges at preliminary hearings. MR 3.8(a). [174]

C. Advising defendants of their right to counsel

Prosecutors are charged with the responsibility to make reasonable efforts to assure that defendants are advised of their right to counsel. MR 3.8(b). [174-175]

D. Fair treatment of unrepresented accused

Prosecutors must not unfairly extract waivers of important pretrial rights, such as right to a jury trial, right to counsel, and privilege against self-incrimination, from the unrepresented accused. MR 3.8(c). [175]

E. Disclosure of exculpatory evidence

Prosecutors must timely disclose **exculpatory evidence** and mitigating circumstances regarding sentencing. MR 3.8(d). [175]

F. Afford respect to lawyer-client relationships

Prosecutors are required to respect the lawyer-client relationship by refraining from unnecessarily issuing subpoenas that call on lawyers to give evidence about past or present clients. MR 3.8(e). [175]

G. Fairness in investigation

A prosecutor is obliged to pursue investigative leads evenhandedly, without regard to whether they might favor or damage her case. [175]

H. Grand jury fact fairness

All lawyers are obligated to reveal unfavorable facts in ex parte settings, such as hearings on emergency temporary restraining orders. MR 3.3(d). See Chapter 8, §I.B.2. Prosecutors are in such settings regularly in the grand jury context. Thus prosecutors have a regular duty in grand jury settings to present adverse material facts. [175-176]

II. SPECIAL DUTIES OF SUPERVISING AND SUBORDINATE LAWYERS

Under certain circumstances, *supervising lawyers* will be ethically responsible for the acts of their *subordinates,* both lawyer and nonlawyer. Under certain circumstances, subordinate lawyers will be relieved of ethical responsibility for their actions. [176-179]

A. Lawyers subordinate to other lawyers

1. **General:** Subordinate lawyers are not relieved of the duty to follow the rules of professional conduct merely because they are supervised or, for that matter, merely because the misconduct in which they might engage is ordered by the supervising lawyer. MR 5.2. [176]

2. **Exception:** A subordinate lawyer is not subject to discipline when she "acts in accordance with a supervisory lawyer's reasonable resolution of an arguable question of professional duty." MR 5.2(b). [176-177]

B. Lawyers supervising lawyers

Supervisory lawyers are responsible for providing reasonable supervision of lawyer subordinates. MR 5.1. [177-178]

1. **Providing supervision:** Separate from the acts of lawyer subordinates, supervising lawyers are subject to discipline if they fail to provide adequate supervision. [177]

2. **Responsibility for lawyer subordinates' misconduct:** Supervisory lawyers are subject to discipline for the conduct of lawyer subordinates that violates the rules of lawyer conduct when the supervisory lawyer orders the subordinate lawyer to engage in the misconduct, when the supervisory lawyer ratifies the subordinate lawyer's misconduct, or when a lawyer who is either a partner or the subordinate's direct supervisor learns of the misconduct at a time when its effect could be avoided or mitigated and yet fails to take reasonable remedial action. [177–178]

C. Lawyers supervising nonlawyers

Lawyers are responsible for providing reasonable supervision of nonlawyer subordinates on the same terms as they are responsible for supervising lawyer subordinates. [178-179]

III. LAWYERS AS INTERMEDIARIES

Contrary to the ordinary picture of the lawyer as a partisan, representing one party against the interests of another, lawyers may in limited circumstances act in the role of *intermediary.* Former MR 2.2. As an intermediary, a lawyer attempts to achieve the goals and interests of multiple parties with potentially adverse interests. Such a role is inappropriate when litigation is pending or contemplated. [179-181]

A. Requirements

To pursue a matter for multiple clients as an intermediary, the clients must consent after consultation, the intermediary form of representation must be in the clients' best interest, and the lawyer must believe that she can represent the clients impartially. [179]

B. Confidentiality

The evidentiary privilege and the duty of confidentiality do not apply as between the parties commonly represented. See Chapter 5, §I.C.2.b. [179]

C. Withdrawal

If any of the requirements ceases to be met during the representation, the lawyer must withdraw from the representation of all of the clients. Former MR 2.2(c). [179-180]

IV. ANCILLARY BUSINESSES

Some lawyers maintain *ancillary,* associated *businesses* along with their law practice. MR 5.7. [181-182]

A. General rule

Lawyers are subject to the rules of professional conduct for lawyers while providing ancillary services when either of the following two conditions is present. [181]

1. **Not distinct:** When the services provided are not distinct from the lawyer's legal services. MR 5.7(a)(1). [181]

2. **Failure to communicate to client:** When the services are provided by an entity controlled either by the lawyer or by the lawyer with others, and the lawyer fails to communicate clearly to the client that the services are not legal services and are not subject to the normal protections in the lawyer-client relationship. MR 5.7(a)(2). [181]

B. What are ancillary services?

Ancillary or "law-related" services are services that are related to legal services and are not prohibited as unauthorized practice of law when performed by a nonlawyer. MR 5.7(b). Side businesses of lawyers that are entirely unrelated to law practice are not ancillary businesses. [181]

V. MULTIDISCIPLINARY PRACTICE

A. Definition

A multidisciplinary practice is a partnership or other entity that includes lawyers and nonlawyers and has as one of its purposes the delivery of legal services to client(s) other than the multidisciplinary practice (MDP) itself or that holds itself out to the public as providing nonlegal as well as legal services. It includes an arrangement by which a law firm joins with one or more professional firms to provide services, including legal services, and there is a direct or indirect sharing of profits as part of the arrangement. [182]

B. Accountants

Associations between lawyers and accountants have been the most controversial. The Big 4 (formerly Big 5) accounting firms, as employers of vast numbers of law-trained individuals until recently, operated as de facto MDPs in which the lawyers were said to provide not legal but "consulting" services to the business's audit clients. Some European countries allow MDPs while U.S. jurisdictions do not. [182]

C. Lawyers and professional independence

The most frequently raised concern about multidisciplinary practices relates to the protection of professional independence of lawyers. The provisions of Rule 5.4 are designed to protect the lawyer's professional independence of judgment. Rule 5.4 provides as follows.

1. A lawyer or law firm shall not share legal fees with a nonlawyer (except under limited circumstances).

2. A lawyer shall not form a partnership with a nonlawyer if any of the activities of the partnership consist of the practice of law.

3. A lawyer shall not practice with or in the form of a professional corporation or association authorized to practice law for profit, if a nonlawyer owns an interest therein, or a lawyer is a corporate director thereof, or a nonlawyer has the right to direct or control the professional judgment of a lawyer. [183]

D. Opposing arguments

Those who oppose MDPs argue that practicing law in a multidisciplinary setting has the potential to unduly influence the professional independence of lawyers in the MDP. [183]

E. Pro-MDP arguments

Advocates of multidisciplinary practices argue that in today's world, many lawyers routinely work in practice settings in which they are subject to management oversight by nonlawyers. Professional independence of judgment is required of all lawyers regardless of the practice setting. Advocates of MDPs propose an added protection, recommending that a lawyer who is supervised by a nonlawyer may not use as a defense to a violation of the rules of professional conduct the fact that the lawyer acted in accordance with the nonlawyer's resolution of a question of professional duty. [183]

F. Other concerns

1. **Confidentiality**

2. **Conflicts of interest**

3. **Pro bono** [183-184]

G. Recent debacles

Recent collapses of Enron and other corporate entities may be traced in part to the work of accounting giants functioning as de facto MDPs. Regulation in the form of the Sarbanes-Oxley Act and the SEC regulations adopted pursuant to the Act, have made these de facto MDPs far more difficult and less profitable. Since 2002, the majority of lawyers working for accounting firms have migrated back into law practice. [184]

CHAPTER 10
ADVERTISING AND SOLICITATION

Warning: The Model Code advertising and solicitation provisions are misleading. DR 2-101, 2-102, 2-103, 2-104, 2-105. The Code was amended during the 1970s to reflect some of the earliest constitutional limitations on the regulation of client-getting. But because the Model Code has not been updated and amended by the ABA since the Model Rules' adoption in 1983, many of its provisions do not reflect recent court decisions that render enforcement of some of its provisions unconstitutional.

I. TRADITIONAL DISTINCTIONS BETWEEN ADVERTISING AND SOLICITATION

The ethics rules distinguish between *advertising* and *solicitation.* Categorizing a particular client-getting activity as one or the other is the first step to analyzing whether or not the activity is permitted. [190]

A. Advertising

The term *advertising* has traditionally referred to widely distributed, public statements about the services available from a particular lawyer or law organization. [190]

B. Solicitation

The term *solicitation* has traditionally referred to narrower communications directed at one or a small group of identified recipients who are known to need a particular service. [190]

C. Blurring of the traditional distinctions

Direct, personal, but form, mail to people known to have particular legal needs partakes of some of the attributes of both advertising and solicitation. [190]

D. Model Rules

The Model Rules treat advertising and solicitation in separate rules (MR 7.2 for advertising and MR 7.3 for solicitation). See §§IV and V. They also create general restrictions that apply to both advertising and solicitation in MR 7.1, 7.4, and 7.5. See §III. [190]

II. CONSTITUTIONAL LIMITATIONS ON DISCIPLINARY AUTHORITY

Advertising and solicitation are speech. As such, some First Amendment protection is provided to these activities, effectively limiting the states' authority to prohibit and regulate them. [190-194]

A. Commercial speech

Commercial speech, such as advertising, is given some protection under the First Amendment. Virginia Bd. of Pharmacy v. Virginia Citizens Consumer Council, Inc., 425 U.S. 748 (1976). [191]

B. No broader restrictions than necessary

Restrictions on commercial speech must further a substantial government interest and must be no broader than necessary. [191]

1. **Government interest in truthful advertising:** The government has a substantial interest in protecting the public from being misled or coerced by lawyer communications. [191]

2. **Narrowly drawn:** To pass constitutional muster, restrictions must be focused on the substantial government interest and must be narrowly drawn. [191]

3. **No accounting for matters of taste:** Regulating commercial speech based on its "dignity" or "taste" is constitutionally *impermissible*. [191]

C. Permissible regulation

Despite the constitutional limitations on its power to restrict lawyer commercial speech, a state may prohibit lawyer client-getting that is false or misleading, that is coercive, or that promotes transactions that are themselves illegal. In re Primus, 436 U.S. 412 (1978); Zauderer v. Office of Disciplinary Counsel of Supreme Court of Ohio, 471 U.S. 626 (1985); Bates v. State Bar of Arizona, 433 U.S. 350 (1977). [191]

III. GENERAL CONSTRAINTS ON ALL COMMUNICATION REGARDING SERVICES

Some restrictions apply equally to all forms of client-getting, whether denominated as advertising or solicitation. [194-197]

A. False and misleading statements, generally

False or misleading statements in lawyer client-getting communication are subject to discipline. MR 7.1. [194-196]

1. **Testimonials:** Courts in some states have held that lawyer ads that use client testimonials are inherently misleading by focusing the viewer's attention on selected, favorable client examples and excluding unfavorable examples. [195]

2. **Self-laudation:** Self-laudation that is either unverifiable or misleading-but-true is subject to discipline as false or misleading. [195]

    a. **Unverifiable:** Statements that are unverifiable are deemed misleading. [195]

    b. **Misleading but true:** Self-laudation is subject to discipline as being misleading-but-true when, although verifiable and true, the statement misleads the reader or viewer usually because it appears to be more important than it would be if it could be put into a full context. [195]

3. **Firm names:** Firm names may be misleading when they untruthfully imply a relationship to a government or other institution. MR 7.5. [196]

4. **Information about fees:** Since *Bates,* lawyers' statements about fees have been constitutionally protected. Like other advertising statements, they may be restricted only when they are false or misleading. [196]

B. Specialization and certification

Until the 1970s, state bars were quite restrictive in their regulation of lawyers' indications of practice concentration, specialization, or certification in areas of practice. [196-197]

1. **Areas of practice:** As long as the words used by the lawyer to designate areas in which the lawyer practices fairly communicate those areas, they will be protected commercial speech and will not subject the lawyer to discipline. [196]

2. **Certification:** An unqualified statement of certification may mislead the reader into thinking that the state has certified the lawyer in a particular area. However, a state may not impose a blanket prohibition on statements of certification. Peel v. Illinois Attorney Registration and Disciplinary Commission, 496 U.S. 91 (1990). To make Model Rule 7.4 consistent with Peel v. Attorney Registration and Disciplinary Commission of Illinois, 496 U.S. 91 (1990), the rule was amended in February 2002 to permit statements of certification by clearly identified organizations approved by the ABA or the appropriate state bar. See §II.D.5. [196-197]

C. Post-event waiting periods

In an effort to guard against the potential for lawyer overreaching of accident victims and their families, some states have imposed waiting periods before any targeted communications may be made. Narrowly drawn waiting period restrictions are constitutional. Florida Bar v. Went For It, Inc., 115 S. Ct. 2371 (1995). [197]

IV. CONSTRAINTS PARTICULAR TO ADVERTISING

Some restrictions have particular applicability to advertising. [197]

A. Record keeping

A lawyer is required to retain a copy of any advertisement, including the text of any broadcast advertisement, for two years after its last publication. Although still in effect in most states, the language requiring lawyers to maintain a two-year record of advertisements was deleted from Model Rule 7.2 in the February 2002 amendments. [197]

B. Payment for advertising

Lawyers, of course, may pay reasonable costs associated with advertising. MR 7.2(b). This rule states what may seem to be the obvious because, outside of the advertising context, lawyers may not pay others for recommending the lawyer. [197]

C. Name of the lawyer

All advertisements must include the name and address of at least one lawyer or law firm who is responsible for the advertisement's content. MR 7.2(c). [197]

V. CONSTRAINTS ON IN-PERSON AND LIVE TELEPHONE SOLICITATION

In-person and live telephone solicitation are subject to prophylactic rules that are much more restrictive than the advertising rules. [197-198]

A. Duress, coercion, and harassment

Although all client-getting communication is subject to discipline if it involves duress or coercion, restrictions on in-person and live telephone client solicitation are meant to protect prospective clients from special dangers of lawyer coercion and duress that attend such communications. [198]

B. Exceptions to the restrictions

1. **Non-live telephone:** Computer, autodial, and recorded telephone solicitations are restricted only by the advertising rules and by the general, false, and misleading and actual duress or coercion limitations. [198]

2. **Relationship with the prospective client:** Subject only to the general limitations on client-getting speech, lawyers may solicit other lawyers or people with whom the lawyer has a family, close personal, or prior professional relationship. MR 7.3(a). [198]

3. **Pecuniary gain:** The specific restrictions on in-person and live telephone solicitation apply only when a significant motive for the solicitation is pecuniary gain for the lawyer. MR 7.3(a). [198]

VI. OTHER RESTRICTIONS ON SPECIFIC SOLICITATION

There are additional restrictions on solicitation of specific prospective clients or those known to be in need of specific services. [198-199]

A. "We don't want any!"

Once a prospective client makes known her desire not to be contacted by the lawyer, the lawyer may not contact that prospective client. MR 7.3(b)(1). [198]

B. Disclaimer

Written or recorded communications to those known to be in need of specific services must include the words "Advertising Material" on the outside of any envelope used and at the beginning and end of any recorded communication. MR 7.3(c). [199]

VII. CLIENT-GETTING ON THE INTERNET

An emerging problem relates to the application of the client-getting rules to internet communications regarding lawyer services. [199]

A. General

In general, it seems likely that internet advertising ought to be treated largely as direct mail advertising is treated now. See discussions of *Shapero* and *Went For It*. [199]

B. Territorial difficulties

The Model Code restricts a lawyer's advertising to an area where the lawyer resides or maintains an office or where a significant portion of the lawyer's clients resides. DR 2-101(B). The Model Rules has no such territorial restriction. When a message is sent out on the internet, it obviously violates the Model Code provision for any lawyer or firm that does not have a truly global practice. It seems likely that these territorial restrictions will go the way of the states' failed efforts to impose residency requirements for admission to practice. See Chapter 2, §III. [199]

VIII. CLIENT-GETTING RELATIONSHIP TO BARRATRY, MAINTENANCE, AND CHAMPERTY

Lawyers have long been restrained by both ethics rules and criminal statutes from engaging in barratry, maintenance, and champerty. [199-200]

A. Barratry

Barratry is a term that refers to stirring up controversy and thereby litigation. Its relationship to client-getting activities is the connection between soliciting clients and generating the prospective clients' interest in pursuing litigation. [199]

B. Maintenance

Lawyers are limited in the ways in which they may maintain, that is, financially support, their clients. In terms of client-getting, a lawyer is prohibited from using offers of financial support of a client to induce the client to retain the lawyer. [200]

C. Champerty

Champerty law restricts lawyers from acquiring an interest in the subject matter of litigation. In terms of client-getting, champerty law restricts lawyers from buying into client claims for the purpose of attracting the client to retain the lawyer. See also Chapter 6, §IV.B.3. [200]

IX. LAWYER AGENTS

A. Runners and cappers

Runners and cappers monitor accidents and other events likely to produce legal work and then direct potential clients to the lawyer for whom the runner or capper works. [200]

1. Discipline: Lawyers who employ runners or cappers are subject to discipline. MR 5.3(c). [200]

2. Criminal violation: In many states, employment of runners or cappers is also a criminal violation. [200]

B. Payment for client referrals

In general, lawyers may not give anything of value to anyone who refers a client to the lawyer. [200]

CHAPTER 11
JUDICIAL CONDUCT

Judicial conduct law is fundamentally different from lawyer conduct law because the judge and lawyer roles are fundamentally different. For example, judges are neutrals and not partisans, so the lawyer's duty of loyalty to a client is simply not a part of a judicial conduct discussion. Likewise, judges are not confided in by either of the parties, so the lawyer confidentiality discussion drops out of judicial conduct discussions.

I. SOURCES OF JUDICIAL CONDUCT LAW

The law governing judges comes from a wide range of sources. [205-206]

A. ABA Model Code of Judicial Conduct

The American Bar Association has adopted a ***Model Code of Judicial Conduct*** (CJC). Like its lawyer conduct models, the CJC is not directly applicable to anyone. Rather, it becomes so when adopted by a state's legislature or court system as the applicable rules of judicial conduct for the particular jurisdiction. [205]

B. Federal statutes

A few federal statutes modify the CJC in federal court, particularly as it relates to judicial disqualification procedures and standards. See §V.L. See §§I.B.1-4 for examples. [206]

C. Lawyer ethics rules

Most judges are also lawyers, and to the extent they remain relevant to the judge's role, the professional ethics rules governing lawyers apply to judges as well. [206]

D. Other sources

The constitution, case law, and bar ethics opinions are also important sources of judicial conduct law. [206]

II. WHO IS A JUDGE?

The CJC defines what it means to be a judge and also expressly identifies special rules and exemptions from the rules that apply to various categories of part-time judges. CJC, Application of the CJC. Judges are officers of judicial systems who perform judicial functions, that is, decide cases. CJC, Application of CJC §I(B). [206-207]

III. GENERAL JUDICIAL ATTRIBUTES

A. Independence

Our system of justice requires that judges and the judiciary be independent of outside influences, including those of the legislative and executive branches. [207]

B. Integrity

Although a lack of integrity is rarely the sole ground for imposing judicial discipline, a fundamental expectation of judges is that they have integrity. CJC Canon 1. [207]

C. Impartiality

Most of the assumptions underlying our judicial system hinge on the impartiality of judges. See §V.A. [207]

IV. PERSONAL CONDUCT AND ACTIVITY OUTSIDE THE JUDICIAL ROLE

Public perception of judges has a significant effect on the public confidence in the justice system. As such, the notion of avoiding even the appearance of impropriety has greater force in judicial conduct law than it does in lawyer conduct law. CJC Rule 1.2 Comments. [207-211]

A. Avoid impropriety and appearance of impropriety

The CJC cautions judges about engaging in conduct that "would create in reasonable minds a perception that the judge violated this Code or engaged in other conduct that reflects adversely on the judge's honesty, impartiality, temperament, or fitness to serve as a judge." CJC Rule 1.2 Comment 5. This standard is an objective one. [208]

B. Comply with the law

Judges' misconduct that violates law violates the "comply with law" standard of the CJC. CJC Rule 1.1. [208-209]

1. **No conviction necessary:** A judge's contrary to law conduct need not result in a conviction before judicial discipline is imposed. [209]

2. **Intentional or bad faith refusal to follow precedent and other mandatory authority:** A judge can be subject to discipline for repeatedly failing to follow the law in his own decisions. [209]

C. Preserving the prestige of the judicial office

Judges are prohibited from lending the prestige of their offices to private interests. [209]

D. Judges as witnesses

Because of the judge's potentially excessive influence on a fact finder, there are some limitations on the use of judges as witnesses. The limitations in fact, however, are minimal. [209]

1. **As fact witness:** As long as the judge is not presiding over the proceeding, a judge may be called as a fact witness. [209]

2. **As character witness:** A judge is prohibited from testifying as a character witness except when duly summoned. CJC Rule 3.3. A judge must be subpoenaed to obtain her presence and testimony as a character witness. [209]

E. Organizational membership

A judge is not permitted to be a member of an organization that "practices invidious discrimination on the basis of race, sex, gender, religion, national origin, ethnicity or sexual orientation." CJC Rule 3.6(A). [209]

F. Speaking, writing, and teaching

Within certain constraints, judges are permitted to teach, speak, and write about the law, the legal profession, and the justice system. CJC Rule 3.1 Comment 1. [210]

1. **Pending cases:** Judges are required to be cautious in their discussion of pending cases. They must refrain from making either public or nonpublic comments that risk the fairness of the proceedings. [210]

2. **Judicial duties take precedence:** Speaking, teaching, and writing activities must be secondary in importance to the judge's judicial responsibilities. [210]

3. **Appearance of bias:** A judge must be careful to avoid creation of an appearance that the judge would not enforce the law or decide cases fairly. [210]

G. Government activities

Judges are permitted to engage in legislative and public hearings and to consult about legal matters with the executive or legislative branches. [210]

H. Civic and charitable activities

"Subject to the requirements of Rule 3.1, a judge may participate in activities sponsored by ..." not-for-profit organizations unless the organization would be likely to come before the judge's court or will regularly be involved in litigation in any court. CJC §4C. Judges may not engage in direct fundraising for such organizations. CJC Rule 3.7(A). [210]

I. Financial activities

Except for closely held family businesses, judges may not be director, officer, manager, partner, advisor, or employee of a business. CJC Rule 3.11(B)(1). [210]

J. Fiduciary activities

Except for such services performed for family members, a judge is prohibited from serving as executor, administrator, trustee, guardian, or other fiduciary. CJC Rule 3.8(A). [210]

K. Practicing law

Full-time judges are not permitted to practice law, except for serving interests of herself or her family members, as long as she does not serve as "the family member's lawyer in any forum." CJC Rule 3.10. [210]

L. Outside income limitations and reporting requirements

When judges are permitted to earn outside income (from teaching, writing, speaking, etc.), such income must be limited to reasonable amounts for the services rendered and must not appear to compromise the judge's integrity and impartiality. [211]

1. **Gifts and favors:** Judges may not accept gifts or favors from a person whose interests are or are likely to be before the judge. Gifts that are appropriate to special occasions (wedding or anniversary, for example) are permitted. [211]

2. **Reporting of income:** Judges must file annually as a public document a statement of the nature and amount of compensation received. CJC Rule 3.15(A). [211]

V. JUDICIAL DUTIES

The defining characteristic of the judge is the performance of judicial duties, that is, deciding cases. [211-219]

A. Impartiality

Perhaps the most central attribute of the judge's role in our justice system is impartiality. All of the other rules and assumptions flow from this central notion. See, for example, ex parte communication rules in §V.G and disqualification rules in §V.L. [211]

B. Diligence

Judges are required to be diligent in the discharge of their duties. CJC Rule 2.5(A). [211]

C. Competence

Judges must also have and maintain competence in the law and decision-making. CJC Rule 2.5(A). [211-212]

D. Maintain courtroom decorum

Judges are authorized and required to maintain courtroom decorum. CJC Rule 2.8(A). [212]

E. Patience

Even while maintaining courtroom decorum and disposing of the court's business diligently, a judge must exhibit patience. CJC Rule 2.8(B). [212]

F. Avoid bias and prejudice

To remain impartial, a judge must avoid bias and prejudice. CJC Rule 2.3(A). [212]

1. **In judicial functions:** In addition to racial, sexist, and ethnic biases, judges must avoid bias in favor of friends and associates and against particular causes or groups of lawyers. [212]

2. **Restraining lawyer bias:** In maintaining courtroom decorum and conduct, judges are required to restrain lawyer bias, though not to the extent of prohibiting legitimate argument. CJC Rule 2.3(C). [212]

G. Ex parte communications

Except in limited circumstances, judges may not engage in ex parte communications. See Chapter 8, §VI.A.

1. **Rationale:** Our adversarial justice system is undermined when some parties have opportunities to influence the judge's decision-making in the absence of other parties. [213]

2. **Good faith is no excuse:** Even when a judge engages in ex parte communications for good but not authorized-by-law reasons, the judge is subject to discipline. [213]

3. **Pending matter discussion presumed:** In the absence of evidence to the contrary, a private communication between a judge and a lawyer with a matter pending before the judge will be presumed to have been about the pending matter. [213]

4. **Timing:** A case continues to be a pending matter until its final disposition. As such, even after a trial judge has ruled, the judge is not permitted to have ex parte communications with counsel while appeals are pending. [213]

5. **Exceptions:** The CJC permits ex parte communications in a few distinct situations. [213-214]

    a. **Housekeeping matters:** Communications for scheduling or administrative purposes do not violate the ex parte communication rules, provided the judge "reasonably believes that no party will gain . . . [an] advantage [from the communication] . . . and the judge makes provision promptly to notify all other parties . . . and gives the parties an opportunity to respond." CJC Rule 2.9(A)(1). [213]

    b. Disinterested experts: Judges may consult with other judges and with disinterested experts on the law if before the consultation, the judge identifies the person to the parties and affords the parties an opportunity to respond. CJC Rule 2.9(A)(2). [213-214]

    c. Court clerks: Judges may consult with clerks about the law in the absence of the parties without restriction. Even judicial clerks, however, may not do independent fact investigation and then communicate the results to the judge. CJC Rule 2.9(A)(3). [214]

    d. Authorized by law: Other law authorizes ex parte communications in various, limited circumstances, such as requests for emergency temporary restraining orders. [214]

H. Public comments

Judges are prohibited from making public or private comments regarding pending matters that risk the fair outcome of the matter. CJC Rule 2.10(A). [214]

I. Criticism of jurors

Aside from expressing appreciation of jurors' service, judges may neither compliment nor criticize jurors' decisions. CJC Rule 2.8(C). [214]

J. Making appointments

Judges are required to make appointments that their office permits on the basis of merit and not based on nepotism or favoritism. CJC Rule 2.13(A). [214]

K. Reporting others' misconduct

Judges have duties to report misconduct of other judges and of lawyers under certain circumstances. CJC Rule 2.15. [214-215]

1. Other judges: Judges have an obligation to report other judges' misconduct under certain circumstances. CJC Rule 2.15(A) and (C). [214-215]

    a. Permissive reporting: Judges "shall take appropriate action" (which may, in the judge's discretion, mean reporting misconduct) when a judge receives information that raises a "substantial likelihood that another judge" has violated the CJC. CJC Rule 2.15(C). [214]

    b. Mandatory reporting: A judge "shall inform the appropriate authority" when the judge has "knowledge" that another judge has committed misconduct "that raises a substantial question" about that judge's fitness for office. CJC Rule 2.15(A). [215]

2. Lawyers: Judges are required to report certain lawyer misconduct as well. CJC Rule 2.15(B) & (D). [215]

    a. Permissive reporting: Judges "should take appropriate action" (which may, in the judge's discretion, mean reporting misconduct) when a judge receives information that raises a "substantial likelihood that a lawyer" has violated her state's professional ethics rules. CJC Rule 2.15(D). [215]

b. Mandatory reporting: A judge "shall inform the appropriate authority" when the judge "has knowledge" that a lawyer has committed misconduct "that raises a substantial question" about the lawyer's honesty, trustworthiness, or fitness as a lawyer in other respects. CJC Rule 2.15(B). [215]

3. Privilege: A judge's report of misconduct is absolutely privileged from civil actions for damages. [215]

L. Disqualification and waiver

Disqualification is among the most important and most litigated areas of judicial conduct. Both CJC Rule 2.11 and federal statutes govern this topic. A judge who voluntarily removes herself from hearing a matter is said to have recused herself. 28 U.S.C. §§47, 144, 455. [215-219]

1. Objective and subjective test: The basic standard for judicial disqualification is an objective one. "A judge shall disqualify himself or herself [when] the judge's impartiality might reasonably be questioned. . . ." CJC Rule 2.11(A). The central federal statute is similar. 28 U.S.C. §455. A judge must also, however, be subjectively free from bias. [215]

2. Rule of necessity: Occasionally, an issue arises that would disqualify every judge that is sitting on a court with jurisdiction to resolve the issue. When this phenomenon occurs, the "rule of necessity" says that judges are not disqualified. [215]

3. Grounds for disqualification: Beyond the general standard, a wide variety of specific categories of reasons may cause a reasonable person to question a judge's impartiality. [215-218]

a. Bias in general: Naturally, a judge's bias may be reason to question her impartiality. Bias, however, will be grounds for disqualification only when the bias is against a party, as opposed to the legal rules governing the case, and when the bias against a party arises from a source outside the present litigation. [215-216]

b. Judge's relationship to party, witness, or lawyer: A wide variety of personal and professional relationships may cause a question to be raised regarding the judge's impartiality. See examples in §§V.L.3.b.i-v. [216-217]

c. Judge's prior relationship to the matter: Judges may have prior relationships to the matter before them as well as to the parties and lawyers. [217]

i. Judge was the lawyer: When the judge was formerly a lawyer on the same or a substantially related matter, the judge is disqualified. [217]

ii. Judge formerly associated with the lawyer: When the judge was associated with one of the lawyers while the lawyer was representing the party in the same or a substantially related matter, the judge is disqualified. CJC Rule 2.11(A)(6)(a). [217]

iii. Judge is a material witness: When a judge has been a material witness in a matter, the judge is disqualified. CJC Rule 2.11(A)(6)(c). [217]

iv. Prior personal knowledge of disputed facts: When a judge has prior personal knowledge of disputed evidentiary facts regarding the matter, the judge is disqualified. CJC Rule 2.11(A)(1). [217]

d. Economic interest: A judge is disqualified from hearing the matter when she has more than a de minimis (very small) economic interest in the outcome of the matter. [217-218]

i. **Type of interest:** The disqualifying interest under this rule must be economic; it may be in either the subject matter of the controversy or a party to the proceeding. CJC Rule 2.11(A)(3). [217]

ii. **By whom and in what capacity held:** The disqualifying interest may be held by the judge personally or as a fiduciary, by a member of the judge's family residing in the judge's household, or by the judge's spouse or a person within the third degree of relationship to the judge. [218]

iii. **How affected:** The interest must be one that "could be substantially affected by the proceeding." However large the interest might be, minor or highly speculative effects on it are not disqualifying. CJC Rule 2.11(A)(2)(c). [218]

iv. **Magnitude of interest:** A de minimis (very small) interest in the subject matter or a party to the proceeding is not disqualifying. CJC Rule 2.11(A)(2)(c). [218]

v. **Knowledge:** Only those interests that are known to the judge are disqualifying, but a judge has a duty to keep informed about the judge's and his or her spouse's and minor children's economic interests. CJC Rule 2.11(A)(3), Rule 2.11(B), Rule 2.11(C). The judge also has a duty to make reasonable efforts to be informed of the economic interests of family members. [218]

4. **Remittal (waiver) of disqualification:** Most sources of disqualification can be waived by the parties, permitting the judge to continue in the matter, provided the appropriate procedures are followed. CJC Rule 2.11(C); 28 U.C.S. §455. [218-219]

   a. **CJC:** Under the CJC, parties may not waive the judge's personal bias regarding a party. They may waive any other form of disqualification. [218]

   b. **Federal law:** Under 28 U.S.C §455, the parties may waive disqualification only when it follows from the general standard, that is, when the judge's "impartiality might reasonably be questioned." They may not waive any of the more specific reasons for disqualification. [218]

   c. **Procedure:** For the waiver to be effective, the judge must disclose the nature of the disqualifying interest on the record, and the parties must all agree on the record, without the participation of the judge, that the judge should continue in the matter. CJC Rule 2.11(C). [219]

VI. POLITICAL ACTIVITIES

Judges must maintain a separation from the give and take of politics. As a result, a variety of restrictions on the political activities of judges and judicial candidates exists. CJC Canon 4. [219]

A. In general

Because states have so many varied systems for selecting judges, the CJC provisions are in some respects internally inconsistent. Some general points may be made nonetheless. [219]

B. Restrictions on judges and candidates of all types

Both judges and candidates are prohibited from political party leadership, from making public statements endorsing or opposing political candidates, and from solicitation of campaign funds. [219]

C. Restrictions on judges

A judge is required to resign from judicial office when the judge becomes a candidate for a non-judicial office. [219]

D. Restrictions on candidates

Candidates must maintain the dignity of the judicial office they seek and refrain from making promises or pledges other than to faithfully and impartially discharge the judicial function. This provision's constitutional status is in doubt. Although not specifically addressing the "pledges and promises" clause, the Supreme Court, in Republican Party of Minnesota v. White (2002), held that Minnesota's CJC violated the First Amendment by prohibiting judicial candidates from speaking publicly about their views on legal and political issues. [219]

VII. LIABILITY FOR CIVIL WRONGS COMMITTED

When judges engage in the core judicial function of deciding cases, they are absolutely immune from civil damage suits. [219-220]

A. Immunity for judicial action

Even when a judge errs in judicial decision-making, the judge is immune from damage actions. Pierson v. Ray, 386 U.S. 547 (1967). The immunity does not extend beyond the judicial function. For example, judges may be liable for negligence in driving their automobiles, for breach of contract when they fail to make the installment payments on their CD players, and so on. [220]

B. Administrative actions

Administrative actions by judges also fall outside the protection of absolute judicial immunity. [220]

CHAPTER 1
INTRODUCTION AND THE ROLE OF LAWYER

ChapterScope

- This chapter is an introduction to this outline, to the law of professional responsibility, to law school courses that focus on professional responsibility, and to the role of a lawyer.

- Law school courses on professional responsibility are required by accreditation standards, but they vary in focus. Nonetheless, all of them center on the law of professional responsibility, sometimes called the law of lawyering.

- The *lawyer's role* in its various forms is at the center of the law of professional responsibility.

- The *law of professional responsibility,* and therefore the course in which it is studied, is about the relationships of lawyers to their clients, their peers, the justice system, the profession, and the public.

- *Moral philosophy* informs the study of professional responsibility law, but moral philosophy does not replace legal analysis as the tool for determining the application of professional responsibility law.

- Important to an understanding of lawyer ethics is the concept of *role morality.* Lawyers' moral decision-making involves a balancing process. Lawyers owe many duties, not all of which point in a single direction at any given moment. Lawyers owe duties to clients, the justice system, third parties generally, opposing parties, society, and the profession.

I. COURSES CALLED PROFESSIONAL RESPONSIBILITY, LEGAL ETHICS, AND LEGAL PROFESSION

If you are reading this, you are probably enrolled in a course called *Professional Responsibility, Legal Ethics,* or *Legal Profession.* These courses may differ in nuances such as the amount of time devoted to moral philosophy, right and wrong, and the history and structure of the legal profession. Despite their differences, they all have in common as their primary material the law governing lawyers. This book focuses on that body of law.

II. MORAL PHILOSOPHY, RIGHT AND WRONG, AND THE LAW GOVERNING LAWYERS

A. Moral philosophy

Moral philosophy is the pursuit of an understanding of moral and ethical choice. Moral philosophy informs the study of professional responsibility law, but moral philosophy does not replace legal analysis as the tool for determining the application of professional responsibility law.

B. Right and wrong

Occasionally, someone will say that all you must do to be an ethical lawyer is to practice what your parents taught you, or to remember what you learned in kindergarten about golden rules: playing nicely, respecting others, and sharing belongings. No one should forget any of those good lessons, and cheating or stealing will produce predictably bad results when engaged in by lawyers. But there is a great deal more to the law governing lawyers than the difference between right and wrong. Many of the rules that govern lawyers are counterintuitive. Many are based on special role-based morality that attends the lawyer's role. Above all else, the law governing lawyers is law. It must be studied and mastered like any other law field.

C. The law governing lawyers

The *law governing lawyers* is a complicated mix of many different areas of substantive law from many different sources. Most obvious are the organized bar's self-regulations (the ethics rules as adopted in the states and enforced through the courts), but other law fields have important applications to the various relationships of which lawyers are a part. Agency, contract, tort, procedure, and evidence laws, among others, have specific applications to lawyers.

D. Role morality

Important to an understanding of lawyer ethics is the concept of *role morality.* Certain roles, although necessary to the continued existence of an ordered society, implicate moral choices for those in the particular role. Those choices, if consistent with the effective execution of the role, are by definition moral.

1. **Lawyer's role in dispute resolution system:** The lawyer occupies a critical role in the system of dispute resolution. To the extent that the dispute resolution system is thought to be moral and the lawyer's role within it essential, the lawyer who effectively carries out the lawyer's role is moral.

2. **Role morality v. general moral standards:** This role morality supplants the generally applicable moral standards where the two conflict.

    Example: A lawyer owes a duty of confidentiality to a client, and adherence to it, including its exceptions, is necessary to the system of dispute resolution. Lawyer interviews Defendant-Client and learns that Defendant-Client has committed the crime with which he is charged and that he has no valid defenses. Lawyer's continued zealous representation of the Client is moral. It comports with the lawyer's role in the dispute resolution system.

3. **Balance of many duties:** Lawyers' moral decision-making involves a balancing process. Lawyers owe many duties, not all of which point in a single direction at any given moment.

    a. **Duties owed:** Lawyers owe duties to clients, the justice system, third parties generally, opposing parties, society, and the profession.

    b. **Competing duties:** There is a hierarchy among these duties, but all difficult legal ethics questions involve an attempted balancing among these duties. The law of lawyering, at least the profession's self-regulation and rules, is essentially an attempted balance among the competing duties in given contexts.

Example: Criminal-Defendant-Client commits perjury. Lawyer owes a duty of loyalty to Client and a duty of candor to the court. Lawyer's decision-making will involve a balancing approach, according to the rules of the law of lawyering, between these two competing duties. See Chapter 8, §I.C.

Example: Lawyer is negotiating a business transaction for Client with Opposing Counsel. Opposing Counsel asks, point blank, "What is the most Client is willing to pay to make this deal?" Lawyer owes a duty of loyalty to Client and a limited duty of truthfulness to Opposing Counsel. Giving a truthful answer to this direct question will give away much of the Client's bargaining power in the negotiation. Lawyer's decision-making will involve a balancing approach, according to the rules of the law of lawyering, between these two competing duties. See Chapter 7, §I.

c. **Balanced process:** When there is talk of "higher" standards for lawyers, it usually masks the speaker's preference for one competing duty over another. The legal rules that govern lawyers are nearly all an attempted balance among competing duties: an effort to find a wise line that divides in particular contexts between devotion to one duty over another. Different standards are not really higher or lower, they merely strike the balance between the competing duties in a different place.

III. THE ROLE OF LAWYER

During a highly publicized trial, a great many media experts on the professional responsibility of lawyers were created and profusely displayed in the mass media. One of the experts described the conduct of one of the trial lawyers as follows: "Today in court, [that lawyer] was demonic, nearly unethical." The expert may think that a lawyer must be somehow worse than demonic to violate the professional responsibility rules. More likely, though, this odd comment is a reminder that being morally good or morally bad is not the primary inquiry when applying the professional responsibility codes to the conduct of lawyers. The professional responsibility codes are an attempted expression of the limits of conduct by people acting in ***the role of lawyer.***

A. **Differing conceptions of the lawyer's role**

Different lawyers perceive themselves and the appropriate role of a lawyer in differing ways. No lawyer stays at the extreme view of any one of these conceptions at all times. Rather, these conceptions mark posts along varying spectra, and lawyers often slip toward or away from one of them in the direction of another.

1. **The standard conception of the lawyer's role:** The most common standard concept of the lawyer's role sees the law as a public profession in which the lawyer operates with reference to the following basic role premises. See William H. Simon, "The Ideology of Advocacy: Procedural Justice and Professional Ethics," 1978 Wis. L. Rev. 30.

    a. **Neutrality or nonaccountability:** This premise is based on the concept that the lawyer is separated from and not responsible for the client's goals. A lawyer must have the capacity to represent people with whom the lawyer does not share common views about justice. This notion of neutrality is separate from the related premise of partisanship, which requires that the lawyer advance the client's interests even if the lawyer does not share them as permitted by the neutrality premise. See §c below.

b. **Procedural justice or role morality:** Within a moral system of justice, the lawyer must effectively carry out his role, even if that role requires actions that may produce consequences of questionable moral value.

c. **Partisanship:** The lawyer is expected to take the client's side (i.e., to be partisan).

d. **Professional, moral decision-making:** The lawyer must abide by the profession's collective judgments about the resolution of ethical questions. That is, the lawyer must follow the duly adopted rules governing lawyer behavior regardless of whether the lawyer might personally have made a different judgment about the appropriate resolution of the question.

2. **The lawyer as businessperson:** The lawyer-as-businessperson concept sees the law as a public profession only to the extent that, like some other businesses (such as public utilities), the law affects the public welfare to a greater degree than many other businesses. Lawyers from this perspective are first and foremost in a money-making trade, not unlike any other businessperson. Competence and efficiency are among the highest priorities for lawyers who adopt this perspective.

3. **The moral activist lawyer:** The moral activist lawyer shares responsibility with the client for the goals and the means of the representation. The moral activist lawyer attempts to persuade the client to do what is morally right, not merely what is legally required or permitted, and refrains from representation activities that the lawyer finds morally objectionable. See David J. Luban, Lawyers and Justice (1988).

Example: Auto Accident Victim is examined by Victim's doctor and files an insurance claim for the relatively minor injuries observed by Victim's doctor. Insurance Company requires that Victim be examined by Company Doctor. Company Doctor informs Insurance Company Lawyer that Victim actually has a subtle, not easily diagnosed, life-threatening condition that may have been caused by the auto accident, for which Company may be liable to Victim. Victim is represented by Other Counsel, both of whom are unaware of the life-threatening condition. Insurance Company Lawyer considers whether or not to reveal this information to Victim, knowing its importance to Victim and its potential to generate significant liability for Insurance Company. The moral activist lawyer would likely reveal the information after counseling her client that revelation is the morally responsible thing to do. Businessperson lawyer would balance the potential liability with the potential for damaging adverse publicity if the true facts are ever revealed to determine whether the information should be disclosed to Victim. The standard conception lawyer would be most concerned that she follow the profession's rules of conduct in making this decision. See Spaulding v. Zimmerman, 116 N.W.2d 704 (Minn. 1962).

B. **Differences between lawyers' litigation and planning roles**

1. **Litigation context:** In a litigation context, most of the lawyer's work is backward-looking. The litigation seeks to assess legal responsibility for the client's and the opposing party's past conduct. The lawyer's work involves the operation of the justice system on the client's behalf.

2. **Planning context:** In the planning context, most of the lawyer's work is forward-looking. The planning lawyer seeks to predict the consequences of proposed future conduct.

3. **Responsibility for client's acts:** A lawyer bears more responsibility for the client's acts in the planning context than in the litigation context. The lawyer's planning work, advice, and

assistance in execution help shape future client conduct. As such, a lawyer bears greater moral responsibility for a client's acts in the planning as opposed to the litigation context. See, e.g., Westlake v. Abrams, 565 F. Supp. 1330 (N.D. Ga. 1983).

Examples: Client comes to Lawyer for representation in a breach of contract matter. Client had entered into a contract with Opposing Party, and Opposing Party now claims that Client has breached the contract. Whether litigation actually results or not, Lawyer is in the litigation role in reviewing past client conduct and working to resolve the dispute over that past conduct. Lawyer bears no moral or legal responsibility for Client's past conduct.

Client and Lawyer have an ongoing relationship. Client is a businessperson who regularly consults with Lawyer about plans of action. Client proposes to breach a contract that he has previously entered. Client asks Lawyer for advice regarding this course of action. Lawyer assists Client in planning and executing a course of action and, therefore, shares the moral responsibility for those actions.

C. Practice setting

A lawyer's practice setting affects the law governing that lawyer in a variety of ways. Essentially, lawyers in different practice settings have different lawyer-client relationships. The differences in those lawyer-client relationships drive a variety of adjustments in the law governing lawyers. Aside from the private law firm representing a natural person as a client in civil matters, lawyers practice as, for example, prosecuting attorneys, other government lawyers, criminal defense lawyers including public defenders, and in-house and external corporate counsel. Some practice settings trigger the application of practice setting–specific rules; others create adjustments by implication of attributes of the lawyer-client relationship.

1. **Prosecutors:** Prosecuting attorneys represent the government or the people of their jurisdiction in the prosecution of crimes. As such, prosecutors have no individual client with whom to consult. With this lawyer-client relationship comes substantial freedom and responsibility. Prosecutors are expected to seek justice and have obligations of fairness to the opposing party (a criminal defendant) that exceed those of other lawyers. Several specific ethics rules apply to prosecutors or have substantial application to their work. See, e.g., MR 3.6, 3.8; and Chapter 9, §I.

2. **Other government lawyers:** Like prosecutors, government lawyers represent the government or the people of their jurisdiction. The government obviously has public-abiding obligations that private citizens do not, and as a representative of government as a client, government lawyers are obligated to reflect their clients' public-abiding obligations. In particular, the government is expected to be more open to public inspection than the affairs of a private client. As such, the attorney-client evidentiary privilege is far narrower in its application to government lawyers and clients. In re Grand Jury Subpoena Duces Tecum, 112 F.3d 910 (1997). Special rules apply to conflicts of former government lawyers and to imputed disqualification of their private law firms. See MR 1.11 and Chapter 6, §VI.B.

3. **Criminal defense:** Some criminal defense lawyers' fees are paid at public expense. For these lawyers, both public defenders and appointed counsel, third-party interference conflicts issues are simply a part of the job description. See MR 1.8(f) and Chapter 6, §IV.A. For all criminal defense lawyers, the special relationship with a client who faces loss of liberty and who faces the government as an opposing party creates special responsibilities for the criminal defense lawyer. In particular, the criminal defense lawyer has a client whose criminal procedure rights

create unique overlaps with the ethics rules. As well, while lawyers generally have discretion to refuse to offer testimony of their client that they believe but do not know will be false, criminal defense counsel are obliged to allow their client to testify in such circumstances. See MR 3.3(a)(3).

4. **Corporate or other organization counsel:** Corporate or other organization counsel represent the entity and not the corporate officers. Such a client cannot communicate with the lawyer, however, except through the living, breathing officers, board members, and designated individuals. Special conflicts rules result from this reality. See MR 1.13 and Chapter 6, §IV.C.4. As do special confidentiality rules. See Chapter 5, §HB, Upjohn v. United States, 449 U.S. 383 (1981).

5. **Legal aid:** Lawyers working for nonprofit corporations set up to receive government funding to represent low-income individuals must account for third-party interference conflicts. See Chapter 6, §IV.A. In such a setting, a lawyer has an individual client but is paid a salary by the nonprofit entity. Legal aid lawyers also operate under legislative restrictions on their funding, creating difficult-to-navigate constraints on their ability to effectively represent their clients. See, e.g., LSC v. Valazquez, 531 U.S. 420 (2000).

D. Other roles for lawyers

Lawyers fill a variety of roles aside from that of lawyer. The roles include, for example, those of judge (see Chapter 11) and third-party neutral (see Chapter 9, §III).

Quiz Yourself on
INTRODUCTION AND THE ROLE OF LAWYER

1. Lawyer knows that his client, Sally, has committed the crime with which she is charged. He advises her of all her options, but because the evidence against her is weak, he tells her that he thinks she should plead not guilty. Has Lawyer acted immorally? _____

2. Lawyer's client, Dr. Bob, admits to Lawyer that he made a mistake during surgery on one of his patients. His patient is unaware of the mistake and has not yet suffered any harmful side effects from the mistake. In fact, the odds are good that whatever problems the patient does develop will not be traceable to Dr. Bob's mistake. Dr. Bob wants Lawyer's advice on how to handle this situation. If Lawyer is a moral activist lawyer, what would she counsel Dr. Bob to do? _____

3. Assume that the same facts apply as in the previous question. If Lawyer were a businessperson lawyer, how would she respond? _____

Answers

1. No. Certain roles that are important to the continued existence of an ordered society implicate moral choices for those in particular roles. If these choices are consistent with the effective execution of the role, they are by definition moral. It is important to the functioning of the criminal justice system that the accused have a lawyer to zealously represent and protect the accused's interests.

2. The moral activist lawyer would counsel Dr. Bob to do what is morally right—to tell the patient of the mistake and the potential consequences. If Dr. Bob refuses to take this course of action, Lawyer, as a moral activist lawyer, would probably refuse to continue representing him.

3. The businessperson lawyer would do a cost-benefit analysis and would advise Dr. Bob to tell the patient only if it is the most efficient course of action.

Exam Tips on
INTRODUCTION AND THE ROLE OF LAWYER

The law of professional responsibility, and therefore the course in which it is studied, is about the relationships of lawyers to their clients, their peers, the justice system, the profession, and the public.

- Some essay questions may call on you to discuss moral philosophy. But remember, **moral philosophy** informs the study of professional responsibility law, but does not replace legal analysis as the tool for determining the application of professional responsibility law.

- There is a great deal more to the law governing lawyers than the difference between right and wrong. The law governing lawyers is **law.** It must be studied and mastered like any other law field.

- The concept of **role morality** plays an important role in analyzing lawyer ethics. Lawyers' moral decision-making involves a balancing process. Lawyers owe many duties, not all of which point in a single direction at any given moment. Lawyers owe duties to clients, the justice system, third parties generally, opposing parties, society, and the profession. Balancing among those competing duties is the mark of a thoughtful essay exam answer.

- Watch for the context of the lawyer's representation:

    - In a litigation context, most of the lawyer's work will be backward-looking. The litigation will seek to assess legal responsibility for the client's and the opposing party's past conduct. The lawyer's work will involve the operation of the justice system on the client's behalf.

    - In the planning context, most of the lawyer's work will be forward-looking. The planning will seek to predict the consequences of proposed future conduct. The lawyer bears more responsibility for a client's acts in the planning context than in the litigation context. The lawyer's planning work, advice, and assistance in execution will help shape future client conduct.

    - A lawyer's practice setting can have significant effects on the law governing that lawyer's conduct.

CHAPTER 2

REGULATION OF THE LEGAL PROFESSION

ChapterScope

- This chapter is about the institutional framework within which the law of lawyering, and lawyers, exists.

- The chapter relates the organizational structure of the organized bar, identifies and describes the various sources of the law of lawyering, and relates the rules governing admission to the bar and reporting fellow lawyers' misconduct, a chief feature of the profession's claim to self-regulation.

- The organizational structure of the profession is particularly important to an understanding of the sources of law that governs lawyers.

- A functional requirement of a profession with strictly enforced regulations for entry is the prohibition against the ***unauthorized practice*** of that profession.

- This chapter does not cover the particular mechanisms that are used to govern lawyer conduct. See Chapter 3.

- The ***American Bar Association*** (ABA) is a national, ***voluntary*** association of lawyers that plays a critical role in the creation of the law governing lawyers. The ABA does not license lawyers to practice law. States, through their courts and sometimes legislatures, license lawyers to practice law within the relevant jurisdiction.

- A ***license to practice law*** is a prerequisite to a person's lawful engagement in the activities of lawyering. The state has a need to protect the public from those who are incompetent or who lack integrity. To become licensed, one must satisfy education, knowledge, and character requirements.

    - An applicant to the bar may not make material false statements and must not "fail to disclose a fact necessary to correct misapprehension known by the [applicant] to have arisen in the matter. . . ." MR 8.1(b).

    - When a lawyer who is licensed to practice in one state has an occasional, nonrecurring need to represent a client before the courts of another state, the lawyer requests admission before that state's courts ***"pro hac vice,"*** "for this turn only."

- Among the chief features of the legal profession's claim to be ***self-governing*** is the requirement of reporting fellow lawyers' or a judge's serious misconduct to the appropriate professional authority. MR 8.3.

    - A lawyer's duty to report misconduct applies only to conduct "that raises a substantial question as to that lawyer's honesty, trustworthiness or fitness as a lawyer in other respects. . . ." MR 8.3(a).

    - The reporting misconduct rule does not require a report of misconduct when the lawyer has learned of the misconduct through confidential communications that would be protected by the ethical duty of confidentiality under Model Rule 1.6. MR 8.3(c).

- When a lawyer reports another lawyer's misconduct, the potential exists for a defamation action to be filed by the reported-on lawyer against the reporting lawyer.

I. ORGANIZATION OF THE BAR

The legal profession has organized itself in a variety of ways. Membership in some organizations is voluntary, whereas membership in others is required of those who wish to practice law in a particular jurisdiction. See §II below.

A. The American Bar Association

The *American Bar Association* (ABA) is a national, *voluntary* association of lawyers.

1. **Beginnings:** The ABA was created in 1888 largely to serve social functions. By the early twentieth century, it had turned its attention to efforts to speak for the legal profession with a single voice. At that time, however, it could boast of only modest membership of less than 10% of licensed lawyers. Currently, approximately 50% of licensed lawyers belong to the ABA.

2. **A voluntary association:** As a voluntary association, the ABA has no direct regulatory authority over lawyers. Nonetheless, its views on issues affecting the law of lawyering and its model ethics codes have tremendous influence. See §II.A.1.

B. Alternative national bar associations

National organizations of lawyers have been established, in some instances, to express alternative views from those held by the ABA.

1. **The National Lawyers Guild:** The National Lawyers Guild was established in 1936 as a more liberal and more progressive organization of lawyers. It continues to be active in a variety of public interest areas.

2. **The National Bar Association:** The National Bar Association (NBA) was established in 1909 as an organization for black lawyers who, until the 1940s, were denied admission to the ABA. Along with the National Conference of Black Attorneys, which was formed in 1969, the NBA plays an active role in legal and political issues.

3. **Organizations of women lawyers:** The National Association of Women Lawyers, with its roots in the Women Lawyers' Club of New York City of 1909 and the Women Lawyers' Association of 1911, exists to promote legal and political positions of its members.

4. **Others:** A wide variety of other voluntary associations of lawyers exists, organized, for example, by race or ethnicity (e.g., The Asian Bar Association), sexual preference (e.g., The National Lesbian and Gay Bar Association), religion (e.g., The Christian Legal Society), employer (e.g., The Federal Bar Association), practice subject matter (e.g., The Customs Bar), and practice activity (e.g., Association of Trial Lawyers of America and The American College of Trial Lawyers).

C. State bar associations

The ABA does not license lawyers to practice law. States, through their courts and sometimes legislatures, license lawyers to practice law within the relevant jurisdiction. In some states, voluntary bar associations exist that licensed lawyers may or may not join at the individual lawyer's discretion. In other states, membership in the bar association is mandatory, effectively a part of the licensing process.

1. **Voluntary state bar associations:** Lawyers from particular states began to organize statewide bar associations in the 1870s. At first, all of these were voluntary organizations, and in many states, they remain so.

2. **The integrated bar:** In some states, membership in the state bar association is mandatory. This mandatory membership establishes what is called an *"integrated bar,"* of which all the lawyers licensed to practice in the state are members.

   a. **State power over the bar organization:** State courts and legislatures have the power to create integrated or mandatory bars in the states.

   b. **Challenges:** Challenges to expenditure of mandatory bar dues, however, have been successful. A mandatory bar may not expend members' dues to advance political or ideological positions, such as lobbying efforts in favor of gun control, nuclear freeze initiatives, public school prayer, abortion rights, or busing. Keller v. State Bar of California, 496 U.S. 1 (1990).

II. SOURCES OF LAW GOVERNING LAWYERS

The law that governs lawyers comes from a variety of sources and exists in a variety of forms.

A. Ethics codes

Every state has an adopted code of ethics for lawyers that operates as a set of mandatory legal rules governing lawyer conduct. In some states, the *ethics code* also includes aspirational statements.

1. **ABA models and their organization:** Beginning in 1908, the ABA adopted a series of three model ethics codes that have served as models for state adoption. Because the ABA is a voluntary, non–license-granting organization, none of these three has ever been directly controlling on a lawyer's conduct. The models have, however, been the chief source of model ethics codes from which states have created their own codes. In addition, federal courts have frequently looked to both the ABA models and the code for the state in which the particular federal court sits for governing ethics rules.

   a. **The 1908 Canons of Ethics:** The 1908 Canons of Ethics was adopted by the ABA but was not initially expected to be routinely enforced as rules by courts and bar authorities.

      i. **Aspirational and mandatory terms:** The Canons are largely aspirational in tone. Only the rules on advertising and solicitation are written in mandatory terms.

      ii. **Appropriate and inappropriate conduct:** The Canons consist of 32 statements (canons) describing appropriate and inappropriate lawyer conduct.

iii. **Adopted by elite ABA:** The Canons was adopted by the ABA at a time when its membership represented less than 10% of the practicing lawyers in the United States. That 10%, furthermore, was the elite element of the bar.

iv. **Based on Alabama Code of Ethics:** The Canons was based on and, indeed, drawn almost verbatim from the 1887 Alabama Code of Ethics, which had itself been copied largely from George Sharswood, An Essay on Professional Ethics (1854).

b. **The 1969 Model Code of Professional Responsibility:** The Model Code was the ABA's first effort to influence the setting of mandatory national standards for lawyer conduct.

   i. **Basis of state codes:** The Model Code was immensely successful in terms of adoption by the states. By 1974, 49 states had adopted an ethics code based on the ABA Model Code.

   ii. **Three types of provisions:** Following its Preamble and Preliminary Statement, which includes important definitional material, the Model Code consists of three types of provisions—Canons, Disciplinary Rules, and Ethical Considerations:

   - The nine Canons are broad statements of basic norms.

   - Within each Canon are *Disciplinary Rules,* which are the mandatory prescriptions "that state a minimum level of conduct below which no lawyer can fall without being subject to disciplinary action." Model Code, Preliminary Statement.

   - The *Ethical Considerations* were meant to be aspirational rather than mandatory, but courts have at times used them as if they were mandatory.

c. **The 1983 Model Rules of Professional Conduct:** The Model Rules were drafted and then adopted during a time of serious questioning of the quality of the ABA Model Code. Much of that questioning was attributable to the large number of lawyers who were involved in the Watergate scandal.

   i. **Rule and comment" organization:** The Model Rules largely abandoned the aspirational tone of the Canons and the Ethical Considerations of the Model Code in favor of a "rule and comment," Restatement-like organizational scheme.

   ii. **Rule-of-law treatment:** The result has been a more rule-of-law treatment of the law of lawyering than was possible under the former, more aspirational, spirit-of-the-profession codes.

   iii. **Basis of state codes:** More than 45 states have replaced their Model Code–based ethics codes with Model Rules–based ethics codes.

   iv. **Basis of course studies:** The Model Rules now dominate the material studied in most Professional Responsibility courses.

   v. **February 2002 Revision of Model Rules:** In 1997, the ABA created the Ethics 2000 Commission to evaluate and revise the Model Rules. Although some believed that this revision would develop into the adoption of an entirely new code potentially with a different format from the Model Rules, the Commission confined itself to revision rather than replacement of the Model Rules. Most of the Commission's extensive proposals were adopted by the ABA in February 2002, resulting in the most wide-reaching and extensive amendments to the Model Rules since their 1983 adoption.

2. State-adopted codes: The states have adopted ethics codes. Although all but one of the state-adopted codes are based on the ABA models, it is the state-adopted code, not the ABA model, that actually controls in the particular jurisdiction. States adopt lawyer ethics codes either by legislation or by rule-making action by the state's court of last resort. Every state except for California now has ethics codes that are based on the ABA Model Rules.

B. Case authority

In several ways, courts make the law governing lawyers.

1. Interpretation of codes: Courts have interpreted the existing ethics codes and, as such, make the law of lawyering in their interpretive activities in the same way as courts make law in interpreting statutes.

2. Inherent power to regulate lawyers: Because courts have inherent power to regulate lawyers (who are officers of the court), a common law of lawyer regulation also exists.

C. Ethics opinions

Both the ABA and state bar associations issue nonbinding *ethics opinions* that are frequently relied on by courts in law of lawyering cases. These opinions are often generated by the submission of a hypothetical question (usually based on a situation currently being confronted by the questioner) to a state bar committee whose responsibility it is to answer such questions and publish the opinions.

D. Restatement

In 2000, in an exceedingly important development for the law of professional responsibility, the American Law Institute completed work on the Restatement of the Law Governing Lawyers. The Restatement, Third, of the Law Governing Lawyers has already been influential with courts and with the Ethics 2000 Commission revision of the Model Rules.

E. Constitutional constraints

Like any other area of state or federal regulation, the law governing lawyers is subject to constitutional limitations. In effect, the constitution operates as an overriding element of the law of lawyering. Prominent areas of constitutional limitation include the following.

1. Commercial speech: Lawyers' commercial speech (advertising and solicitation of clients) is afforded considerable First Amendment protection. See Chapter 10.

2. Speech rights of lawyers: Regardless of role, lawyers are sometimes called on to speak publicly for clients. In this activity, the First Amendment provides some protection from regulation. See Chapter 8, §V.

Example: Lawyer held a press conference after Client's indictment on criminal charges to counter prior adverse publicity regarding Client and to defend Client's reputation. Lawyer asserted that crooked cops were using Client as a scapegoat but refused to answer reporters' more detailed questions. After Client's acquittal six months later, the state bar disciplines Lawyer for violating an ethics rule prohibiting the making of "an extrajudicial statement that a reasonable person would expect to be disseminated by means of public communication if the lawyer knows or reasonably should know that it will have a substantial likelihood of materially prejudicing an adjudicative proceeding." Lawyer's statements constitute political speech. As interpreted by the state bar, the rule as applied is void for vagueness. It allows statements "without elaboration... [of] the general nature of the... defense" but fails to provide a sufficient explanation of the "without elaboration" safe harbor. Thus, it could result in discriminatory enforcement. First Amendment protection, then, prevents punishment of Lawyer despite the violation of a disciplinary rule. Gentile v. State Bar of Nevada, 501 U.S. 1030 (1991).

3. **Entry to the bar:** States' efforts to impose *residency requirements* for entry to practice have been held unconstitutional. See §III below.

   Example: The Rules of the State A Supreme Court limit bar admission to state residents. Lawyer lives in State B, about 400 yards from the State A border. She applied for admission to the State A bar and, except for the residency requirement, met all of the bar's entry requirements. She received word from the Board of Bar Examiners that she would have to establish a State A home address before being sworn in. A state must grant equal treatment to residents and nonresidents under the Constitution's Privileges and Immunities Clause. The Clause guarantees that residents and nonresidents can do business on substantially equal terms in any state. Further, out-of-state lawyers often represent individuals raising unpopular federal claims. State A has no reason to exclude nonresidents because it has no reason to believe that they would be less likely to keep abreast of local rules and procedures, to practice in an honest manner, to be available for court proceedings, or to do their share of volunteer and pro bono work. Finally, the state powers given to lawyers as officers of the court do not involve matters of state policy or acts of such unique responsibility that they should be entrusted only to state citizens. Supreme Court of New Hampshire v. Piper, 470 U.S. 274 (1985); Supreme Court of Virginia v. Friedman, 487 U.S. 59 (1988).

F. **"Other law"**

The law of a wide variety of other substantive areas forms an essential part of the law of lawyering.

1. **Contracts:** Contract law governs, for example, basic elements of the lawyer-client contractual relationship.

2. **Torts:** Tort law governs, for example, lawyer liability to clients for malpractice and to third parties for intentional wrongful acts and, in some cases, incompetence. Tort law also plays a major role in the law of contingent fee arrangements.

3. **Fiduciary law:** Fiduciary law governs the special relationship and duties of lawyers to clients and certain other beneficiaries of lawyer and client acts.

4. **Agency:** Agency law governs and informs much of the relationship between lawyer and client, with the lawyer acting as the client's agent. See Chapter 4, §V.

5. **Criminal law:** Criminal law governs lawyer criminal liability not only for the lawyer's individual acts, but also for possible liability as an accomplice or a conspirator with a client who is engaged in criminal conduct.

6. **Procedural law:** Criminal and civil procedural law governs lawyer conduct, particularly in litigation contexts, and includes, for example, rules that implicate the imposition of court sanctions for various lawyer conduct.

7. **Antitrust:** Antitrust law governs, for example, bar association efforts to restrain trade.

Example: State Bar A advised lawyers in State A to charge fees for listed services that were no less than a "minimum fee schedule" published by the state bar. Such a minimum fee schedule is illegal price-fixing under the antitrust laws. Goldfarb v. Virginia State Bar, 421 U.S. 773 (1975).

8. **Administrative regulations:** Administrative law in a wide range of topic areas governs lawyers in special ways. The areas include tax, banking, securities, environmental, and occupational safety regulations.

9. **Employment law:** Employment law, including employment discrimination laws, applies to law firm employment of lawyers.

Example: Female Lawyer accepted employment at Firm in reliance on representations that after five or six years, attorneys receiving satisfactory evaluations advanced to partnership as a matter of course. After six years, Firm declined to invite Lawyer to become a partner and terminated her employment. Lawyer sued Firm for gender discrimination under Title VII of the 1964 Civil Rights Act.

Lawyer stated a cognizable cause of action. Title VII applies to prohibit gender discrimination in Firm's partnership considerations if consideration for partnership constituted a term of Lawyer's employment contract or a benefit of her employment relationship with Firm. Hishon v. King & Spalding, 467 U.S. 69 (1984).

III. ADMISSION TO PRACTICE

A license to practice law is a prerequisite to a person's lawful engagement in the activities of lawyering.

A. Policy

The state has a need to protect the public from those who are incompetent or who lack integrity.

B. General requirements

Education, knowledge, and character requirements are the chief hurdles in the path of the applicant for admission to the practice of law.

1. **Education:** All states impose educational requirements on applicants for admission to practice law.

   a. **ABA accreditation:** All but a few states require graduation from an ABA-accredited law school for admission to practice.

   b. **State-accredited schools:** A few states, most notably California, permit applications from graduates of state-accredited law schools that are not ABA-accredited.

   c. **Reading the law:** A few states allow, as a substitution for law school graduation, "reading the law" in the offices of a licensed lawyer on a prescribed and approved schedule.

2. **Knowledge:** An examination (the bar exam) is administered in each state.

   a. **Bar exam:** States determine whether or not an applicant has satisfied the knowledge requirement based on the exam results.

- b. **Diploma privilege:** A few states, dwindling in number, provide for a waiver of the bar examination requirement for graduates of selected in-state law schools.

3. **Good character:** To be a successful applicant for admission to practice law, one must be found to be of *good character.*

   a. **Form of the character inquiry:** States require the completion of questionnaires from applicants and, in some states, recommendations from law school personnel or currently licensed lawyers.

   b. **The central character issue:** The issue in the bar's character examination is the same as is often present in lawyer disciplinary actions: Does this individual have the good character necessary to the practice of law? See Chapter 3, §I.

   c. **Wide range of past conduct may be considered:** A wide range of past conduct, including convictions, arrests, and civil litigation, may be considered by the admission authorities. The questions asked and the information gathered, however, must bear a relationship to the purpose of the inquiry: the applicant's fitness for the practice of law.

   Example: Applicant filed for bankruptcy to avoid payment of student loans. Admission authorities found this act to be evidence of a lack of responsibility and denied admission to Applicant. In re G.W.L., 364 So. 2d 454 (Fla. 1978).

   Example: State Bar asked applicants to disclose whether they had "within the past five years been treated or counseled for a mental, emotional, or nervous disorder." Applicant filed a Complaint claiming that the character questionnaire was too broad and intrusive and that it violated the Americans with Disabilities Act. It is legitimate for the state to inquire into applicants' mental health history, but this question is too broad. Rather, the state should ask behavioral questions (e.g., have you been disciplined for absenteeism at work or school?) or narrower mental health questions (e.g., are you currently under the care of a mental health care provider?). State Bar is enjoined from asking the mental health question as it is currently framed on the questionnaire. Clark v. Virginia Board of Bar Examiners, 880 F. Supp. 430 (E.D. Va. 1995).

   d. **Crimes involving moral turpitude:** Some crimes, because of their attributes involving intention to defraud or engage in dishonesty, are sufficient grounds, standing alone, for denial of an application for admission to the bar.

   Example: Fraud, perjury, embezzlement, bribery, theft, and robbery are crimes involving moral turpitude.

   e. **Political activity:** Political activity has been a particularly active area of inquiry by bar admission authorities. Because the lawyer must take an oath to uphold the federal and state constitutions, political activity is a legitimate area of inquiry but one that is constrained by First Amendment speech and association rights.

   Example: Among the requirements for admission to State Bar are the demonstration of the character and general fitness required of an attorney. The State Bar requires each applicant to fill out a questionnaire regarding any Communist affiliations; any involvement with groups advocating the overthrow of government by force, violence, or unlawful means; and any specific intent to overthrow the government by such methods. The State Bar also requires each applicant to take an oath to support the state and federal constitutions. A group of law students and law graduates seeking admission to practice challenge the State Bar's requirements as facially invalid and as unconstitutionally applied.

Long usage of the character and fitness requirement has defined its contours to encompass no more than an absence of dishonorable conduct relevant to the legal profession. Thus the general requirement of character and fitness is not unconstitutionally vague or overbroad and does not infringe the applicants' free exercise of their rights of speech and association. The questionnaire requirement is constitutional because Communist affiliations constitute a valid inquiry topic from the bar, involvement with organizations advocating the overthrow of the government will not necessarily bar an applicant's admission to practice law, and the legal profession's dedication to the peaceful and reasoned settlement of disputes renders inquiry into any specific intent to overthrow the government constitutionally permissible. By contrast, a question that asks merely about association with particular groups, rather than about specific intent to overthrow the government, would violate the federal constitution. Finally, the oath requirement does not violate the applicants' First and Fourteenth Amendment rights because it requires only the applicants' willingness and ability to take an oath to uphold the Constitution, and any reservations regarding the oath would not necessarily preclude admission to the bar. Law Students Civil Rights Research Council, Inc. v. Wadmond, 401 U.S. 154 (1971).

4. Misconduct in the application process

   a. Material false statements: An applicant to the bar may not make any material false statement and must not "fail to disclose a fact necessary to correct misapprehension known by the [applicant] to have arisen in the matter. . . ." MR 8.1(b).

   Example: Two years before beginning law school, Applicant was convicted of possession of marijuana. The bar application asks Applicant to state and describe any criminal convictions. Applicant concludes that the marijuana conviction is unimportant, and writes "None" in the blank provided in the questionnaire. Applicant submits the questionnaire. If Applicant is successful in obtaining admission to the bar and his misstatement is later discovered, Applicant will be subject to discipline for making a material false statement on the bar application.

   Example: Applicant to the State Bar submitted a sworn questionnaire containing inaccurate information regarding his high school education and omitting a number of his past residences. Further, the Bar found that he had falsely represented himself to others as a police officer on two occasions. Therefore, the Bar refused to certify him for admission.

   An applicant for admission to the bar must show that he possesses the good moral character and general fitness necessary for the practice of law. Applicant's failure to respond fully and accurately to the Bar's questions betrays a lack of concern for the truth. The Bar correctly refused to admit Applicant. In re DeBartolo, 488 N.E.2d 947 (Il. 1986).

   b. Frequency: Cases of denied applications based on misrepresentation in the application process outnumber cases of denied applications based on prior misconduct.

5. No assistance with admission of unqualified applicant: Licensed lawyers are duty-bound not to assist in the admission of an unqualified applicant. MR 8.1.

   Example: Two years before beginning law school, Applicant was involved in a mail-fraud scheme. Although Applicant was never charged with a criminal violation, she consulted

Lawyer about her possible liability. In this consultation, Applicant told Lawyer information about her activities that constituted mail fraud. Applicant went off to law school and is now applying for entry to the bar. The bar application asks Applicant to provide letters of reference from three current members of the bar. Applicant asks Lawyer to write her a recommendation letter, and Lawyer does so. Lawyer is subject to discipline for assisting in the admission of an unqualified applicant.

C. Federal courts

Each federal court maintains a bar (a list of licensed lawyers) separate from the states in which it sits. Typically, a lawyer who is licensed to practice and is in good standing in a state need only be introduced by a current member of the federal bar to be licensed in that federal court. Some federal courts administer their own bar examination for admission to practice in the particular federal district.

D. Admission *pro hac vice*

When a lawyer who is licensed to practice in one state has an occasional, nonrecurring need to represent a client before the courts of another state, the lawyer requests admission before that state's courts **"*pro hac vice*"** ("for this turn only"). The application is made by the lawyer filing a motion with the particular court before which the lawyer wants permission to appear.

1. **Reciprocity:** For such a motion to be granted, states typically require that the lawyer's home state have a policy of reciprocating when its lawyers have a similar need to practice in the applying lawyer's home state's courts.

2. **Local counsel:** Many states require that the applying lawyer associate, for purposes of that case, with a lawyer who is licensed in the state. This requirement is based on the expectation that the locally licensed lawyer will inform the visiting lawyer of local norms of behavior, including ethics requirements, and on the state's need to maintain some control over counsel in the instant case.

3. **Broad discretion:** A judge has broad discretion in ruling on an application to practice *pro hac vice* and may consider a broad range of factors in ruling on the application.

4. **No due process right to be granted *pro hac vice* admission:** A lawyer does not have a due process right to a particular quality of consideration of a *pro hac vice* motion.

   Example: At their arraignment, Defendants presented an entry-of-counsel form that listed Lawyers as their counsel. Lawyers were not admitted to practice law in the state prosecuting Defendants, and the form did not constitute an application for admission *pro hac vice,* nor did it alert the court that Lawyers were not admitted to practice in the state. The arraignment judge endorsed the form. When Lawyers appeared before the trial judge requesting to represent Defendants, the judge dismissed their request outright.

   The right to appear *pro hac vice* is left to the discretion of the state and is not grounded in the Constitution or in any federal statute. Absent any right to such an appearance under state law, the Constitution does not require the judge to satisfy procedural due process in denying Lawyers' request to appear *pro hac vice,* and speculative claims that Lawyers' reputations might suffer as a result of their inability to represent Defendants do not constitute injury to a constitutionally protected interest. Leis v. Flynt, 439 U.S. 438 (1979).

IV. UNAUTHORIZED PRACTICE

By the nature of the licensing requirements, lawyers licensed to practice in a given state have a monopoly on the practice of law in that state. When a person engages in the ***unauthorized practice*** of law, civil and sometimes criminal penalties attach.

A. Attributes of the practice of law

To determine which activities constitute the unauthorized practice of law, one needs to determine which activities amount to the practice of law.

1. **Court appearance:** Court appearance constitutes the core of the practice of law for purposes of unauthorized practice analysis. Nothing is more centrally and visibly lawyer's work than appearing on behalf of a client in court.

2. **Legal advice and counsel:** Although giving legal advice is clearly lawyer's work, courts are understandably more reluctant to attempt to monitor and police the unauthorized practice of giving legal advice. If the advice-giving is accompanied by either a fee or document-drafting or both, the activity is seen as more clearly impinging on the lawyer monopoly.

3. **Sale of do-it-yourself forms:** A lay person has a right to represent him- or herself. In some subject areas, such as domestic relations, real estate transactions, and the drafting of wills, do-it-yourself form kits are popular alternatives to consulting a lawyer. As long as these forms are not accompanied by advice on legal matters, most courts will not regard them as violating the unauthorized practice rules.

B. Forms of unauthorized practice

Unauthorized practice may occur when a licensed lawyer practices outside the jurisdiction in which the license was granted or when those not licensed engage in the practice of law.

1. **Extraterritorial practice of licensed lawyers:** Lawyers licensed in one jurisdiction commit unauthorized practice violations when they practice in another jurisdiction without obtaining permission from the second jurisdiction's courts. See §III.D. A lawyer who engages in the extraterritorial, unauthorized practice of law cannot state a claim for a fee.

   Example: For many years, out-of-state Lawyer advised Client and others on a variety of tax matters without holding a license to practice law in Client's state. Lawyer then helped Client sell his business. When Lawyer sued Client for payment of a bill connected with the transaction, Client claimed that Lawyer could not recover because he was not licensed to practice in Client's state.

   Because the state's statute barring the unauthorized practice of law is intended to protect the public from incompetent and unqualified attorneys, the courts must construe it liberally. If a person cannot lawfully practice law in the state, that person cannot charge a fee for such services. Therefore, Lawyer cannot recover. Ranta v. McCarney, 391 N.W.2d 161 (N.D. 1986).

2. **Multijurisdictional practice:** A wide range of simple realities of life and law practice have created a powerful impetus for the states to allow lawyers licensed in other states or countries to engage in regular but temporary practice in states in which they are not licensed as the needs of their clients dictate. More than admission to practice *pro hac vice,* the movement to create multijurisdictional practice rules addresses activities in and out of court. A report of the ABA's

Commission on Multijurisdictional Practice, proposing a relaxation on temporary admission to practice in a variety of circumstances, was adopted by the ABA in August 2002.

a. Transportation and communications technology have advanced since states adopted "unauthorized practice of law" (UPL) provisions in the early twentieth century. The globalization of business and finance has expanded a client's need for representation to include assistance in transactions in multiple jurisdictions and advice regarding multiple jurisdictions' laws. Lawyer regulations, particularly the UPL laws, did not effectively respond to the evolving nature of business. As such, the ABA Commission on Multijurisdictional Practice proposed amendments to Rule 5.5 of the ABA *Model Rules for Professional Conduct.*

b. Guiding principle: The Commission was searching "for the proper balance between the interest of a state in protecting its residents and justice system, on the one hand; and the interests of clients in a national and international economy in the ability to employ or retain counsel of choice efficiently and economically."

Example: Lawyers may go to another state in which they are not authorized to practice law to review documents, interview witnesses, enter into negotiations, or conduct other activities that are related to a pending lawsuit in their own jurisdiction or that are performed before a lawsuit is filed. Lawyers may also go to another state to conduct negotiations, gather information, or provide advice on transactional matters. Additionally, a client may want to retain a lawyer that he or she has a prior relationship with, that he or she has a particular confidence in, or that is a specialist in a particular area of the law, regardless if the lawyer is licensed in the jurisdiction his or her matter is in.

c. State UPL laws have been sporadically enforced, possibly leading to a mistaken understanding that the laws will be interpreted by courts and enforcement agencies to accommodate reasonable and conventional professional practices. Lawyers may also have mistakenly assumed they could rely on their professional understandings about the rare enforcement of UPL laws. These understandings were mistaken because of problems caused by the lack of uniformity among *pro hac vice* provisions of different states, unpredictability about how some of the provisions would be applied by the courts in individual cases, and the provisions' excessive restrictiveness. The UPL laws resulted in costs being borne by the client. For example, a client may have to forgo a skillful, efficient lawyer and hire less-capable counsel because the first lawyer is not licensed in the jurisdiction.

d. Specific changes to Model Rule 5.5:

  i. The amended Rule clarifies and strengthens 5.5(a) and (b) in its renewed commitment to jurisdictionally based law licenses.

  ii. The amendment to Rule 5.5 also added sections (c) and (d). Rule 5.5(c)(1) allows an out-of-state lawyer to work on a temporary basis in a state when that lawyer is associated in the matter with a lawyer who is admitted to practice in the jurisdiction and who actively participates in the representation. This provision also covers lawyers who assist litigation counsel, but who do not themselves appear in judicial proceedings. This provision protects the client's interest in having his or her counsel of choice, as well as the public's interest by having a local lawyer ensure the out-of-state lawyer's work is performed according to the state's standards. Rule 5.5(c)(1) is not meant to cover associates who rotate among a firm's offices for longer than temporary periods, nor is it meant to allow an in-state lawyer to associate with an out-of-state lawyer without sharing actual responsibility for the representation.

iii. Rule 5.5(c)(2) allows lawyers to provide services ancillary to pending or prospective litigation. The section's language, "is authorized by law or order to appear in such proceeding or reasonably expects to be so authorized," allows the lawyer to provide such services when the lawyer is admitted to practice in the jurisdiction or reasonably expects to gain *pro hac vice* admission. The provision does not replace *pro hac vice* requirements. This provision covers when the lawyer must travel outside the jurisdiction where the litigation takes place to interview witnesses, review documents, and conduct other necessary work. It also covers situations with prospective litigation, such as those in which the lawyer needs to perform tasks before the filing of a lawsuit in a particular jurisdiction. This provision also makes clear that jurisdictional restrictions do not apply when out-of-state lawyers are authorized by law or court order to appear before a tribunal or administrative agency in the jurisdiction.

iv. Rule 5.5(c)(3) allows a lawyer to provide services on a temporary basis in a jurisdiction in which the lawyer is not licensed to practice law in connection with the representation of clients in pending or anticipated arbitrations, mediations, or other alternative dispute resolution proceedings, where the work arises out of or is reasonably related to the lawyer's practice in a jurisdiction in which the lawyer is admitted to practice. This provision does not apply if a *pro hac vice* provision governs participation in the proceeding.

v. Rule 5.5(c)(4) permits, on a temporary basis, transactional representation, counseling, and other non-litigation work that arises out of or is reasonably related to the lawyer's practice in a jurisdiction in which the lawyer is admitted to practice. For example, this provision permits a lawyer to meet with the client or other parties to the transaction outside the lawyer's home state to conduct negotiations. This provision respects preexisting and ongoing client-lawyer relationships by permitting a client to retain a lawyer to work on multiple related matters. This provision also permits a lawyer who has, through the lawyer's regular practice, become an expert in a body of law applicable to the client's matter to provide legal services on a temporary basis outside the lawyer's home state. Under section (c)(4), the lawyer may provide services only temporarily. What is temporary and what is regular practice will become clearer as Rule 5.5 is interpreted by courts. Additionally, the services permitted under section (c)(4) must arise out of or be reasonably related to the lawyer's practice in the home state.

vi. Rule 5.5(d)(1) permits a lawyer employed by an organizational entity, admitted in another U.S. jurisdiction, to provide legal services in a jurisdiction in which the lawyer is not admitted, other than representations for which *pro hac vice* admission is required, on behalf of the employer, an affiliated entity. This provision allows the lawyer to give his organizational employer or its affiliates advice or assist in transactions on its behalf in jurisdictions in which the lawyer does not have an office. The organization's interests are served by employing a lawyer who can provide efficient, cost-effective representation, while the public's interests are served because a lawyer representing an organization on an ongoing basis poses less of a risk to the client or public than a lawyer retained on a one-time basis. This provision allows an out-of-state lawyer to permanently work from the office of a corporate, government, or other organizational employer, which is consistent with the understanding or practices in many jurisdictions.

vii. Rule 5.5(d)(2) permits a lawyer to render legal services in a jurisdiction in which the lawyer is not licensed to practice law when authorized to do so by federal or other law. Among other things, this provision makes clear that a lawyer may establish a law practice in a jurisdiction that has adopted rules permitting established practice by foreign lawyers who serve as legal consultants.

e. **Adoption:** As of August, 2005, only seven states have adopted a rule identical to Rule 5.5 as amended. Seventeen states have adopted rules similar to amended Rule 5.5. Six states have identical or similar rules pending before their highest courts. Six other states have MJP study committees that have recommended identical or similar rules be adopted. Thirteen states have created committees to study the ABA MJP recommendations. The Connecticut Bar has rejected the adoption of a rule similar to amended Rule 5.5. The Oklahoma Bar studied the issues, but took no action.

3. **Practice by the unlicensed:** Professionals and others whose business borders the law may not engage in the legal work that borders their other professional duties. Real estate agents, bankers, and insurance professionals are the usual examples.

Example: Following a fire and an unacceptable insurance settlement offer, Insureds hired Adjuster to handle their claim against Insurer. Adjuster's fee was contingent on the amount recovered. After preparing and submitting estimates of Insured's damages, Adjuster negotiated a substantially increased settlement offer. Insureds then hired Lawyer and settled their claim. Adjuster refused the $500 payment offered by Insureds and filed suit for the percentage of Insureds' recovery specified in the parties' contract. Insureds then asserted that the contract was unenforceable.

Adjuster's activities constituted the practice of law. He determined the amount of Insureds' loss, negotiated a settlement, and expected to receive remuneration contingent on the amount recovered. This process required the interpretation of contract terms. Because the State Constitution placed exclusive control of the regulation and supervision of the practice of law in the state supreme court and provided for the separation of legislative, judicial, and executive powers, the statute empowering Adjuster to engage in these activities, without being admitted to the bar or subject to the state supreme court's disciplinary rules, is unconstitutional. Thus, Adjuster failed to state a valid claim for relief. Professional Adjusters, Inc. v. Tandon, 433 N.E.2d 779 (1982).

Example: Although not admitted to the state bar, Respondent advertised a secretarial service in various local newspapers, offering to perform typing services for "do-it-yourself" divorces. Respondent charged $50 to prepare the legal documents necessary in an uncontested divorce and to advise her customers of the costs involved and the procedures required in such proceedings.

Nonlawyers may not practice law within the state. Thus, they may not advise clients regarding available remedies or assist them in preparing necessary legal forms. They may not make inquiries or answer questions regarding the presentation of evidence at a court hearing, the best method of filling out particular forms, or the proper means of filing them. Although Respondent never held herself out as an attorney, her clients relied on her to properly prepare the legal forms necessary to their divorces. Thus, she engaged in the unauthorized practice of law. Florida Bar v. Brumbaugh, 355 So. 2d 1186 (Fla. 1978).

V. SELF-GOVERNANCE AND THE DUTY TO REPORT MISCONDUCT

Among the chief features of the legal profession's claim to be *self-governing* is the requirement of reporting a fellow lawyer's or a judge's serious misconduct to the appropriate professional authority. MR 8.3.

A. Knowledge of misconduct

Before a duty to report misconduct can arise, the lawyer must "know that another lawyer has committed" the *misconduct.* MR 8.3(a). Personal knowledge of the misconduct obviously satisfies the "knowledge" requirement. While it would be counterproductive to require a lawyer to report every courthouse rumor about another lawyer's misconduct (because the lawyer in such an instance does not "know" of the misconduct), the knowledge requirement is satisfied when a lawyer has been informed of the misconduct from a credible person and there is some independent corroboration. Weber v. Cueto, 568 N.E.2d 513 (Ill. App. Ct. 1991). Put another way, "knowledge" as used in this rule means actual knowledge, but actual knowledge may be inferred from the circumstances. MR 1.0(f).

B. Level or type of misconduct

The rule does not require a lawyer to report all misconduct of which the lawyer has knowledge. It requires a lawyer to report misconduct "that raises a substantial question as to that lawyer's honesty, trustworthiness or fitness as a lawyer in other respects. . . ." MR 8.3(a). "Substantial" means a "material matter of clear and weighty importance." MR 1.0(1).

Example: Lawyer 1 and Lawyer 2 practice law in State A. State A has a rule prohibiting financial assistance to clients from lawyers when litigation is pending or contemplated. Lawyer 1 represents Client in a litigation matter. Client is indigent. Lawyer 1 gives Client $50 to help Client make an overdue rent payment, allowing Client and his family to remain in their apartment rather than be evicted. Over a casual lunch in which Lawyer 1 and Lawyer 2 were relating as friends rather than as lawyer and client, Lawyer 1 tells Lawyer 2 that he made the $50 gift without realizing that it violated the ethics rules in State A. The rule does not require intent, and Lawyer 1's conduct has violated the rule. Lawyer 2 need not report Lawyer 1's misconduct. The misconduct does not raise a "substantial question as to [Lawyer 1's] honesty, trustworthiness or fitness as a lawyer in other respects. . . ."

C. Confidentiality limitation on duty to report

The rule does not require a report of misconduct when the lawyer has learned of the misconduct through confidential communications that would be protected by the ethical duty of confidentiality under Model Rule 1.6. MR 8.3(c). See Chapter 5.

1. **A lawyer-client:** Clearly, this provision eliminates the reporting requirement when a lawyer is consulted as a lawyer by the lawyer who has engaged in the misconduct. However, it must also be remembered that the exceptions to the duty of confidentiality (e.g., the future crime exception) continue to apply with equal force in this setting as in any other.

Example: Lawyer 1 has misappropriated funds belonging to a client. Lawyer 1 consults with Lawyer 2 regarding Lawyer 1's potential liability. Lawyer 2 now knows that Lawyer 1 has committed misconduct of a substantial nature, but Lawyer 2's duty of confidentiality relieves her of the duty to report (or, viewed alternatively, prohibits her from reporting) Lawyer 1's misconduct to the bar disciplinary authorities. A benefit of this rule is the creation of an opportunity that might not otherwise exist for Lawyer 2 to counsel Lawyer 1 to rectify the misconduct.

2. **Learning from a nonlawyer client:** Less clear is whether the confidentiality aspect of Model Rule 8.3 eliminates the reporting requirement when a lawyer learns of another lawyer's misconduct from a client. The following example, drawn from the *Himmel* case, is based on the view that the reporting requirement trumps a client's desire that the misconduct of the client's former lawyer not be reported. This view is not unanimously held. Authority from other states has opined to the contrary. See, e.g., Md. Ethics Op. 89-46 (1989).

Example: Client hired Lawyer to recover settlement proceeds from Client's former attorney. Lawyer discovered that Client's former attorney had misappropriated the funds. The former attorney agreed to return the money to Client if Client and Lawyer would agree not to initiate any criminal, civil, or attorney disciplinary actions against him.

Any contact between Client and disciplinary authorities regarding former attorney's actions did not satisfy Lawyer's duty to notify the authorities of the former attorney's misconduct. Client's request that Lawyer not report the former attorney's misconduct does not relieve Lawyer of his professional duty to do so. In re Himmel, 533 N.E.2d 790 (Ill. 1988).

D. Defamation privilege

When a lawyer reports another lawyer's misconduct, the potential exists for a defamation action to be filed by the reported-on lawyer against the reporting lawyer. The policy in favor of encouraging the reporting of misconduct supports the rule that a report of misconduct to the proper authorities is absolutely privileged.

Example: Noting his professional duty to report unprivileged knowledge of ethical violations, Lawyer sent a letter to the county's chief circuit judge, the county board, and the disciplinary commission, alleging that State's Attorney and Nonattorney employed in State's Attorney's office had violated several provisions of the Code of Professional Responsibility. Lawyer admitted that he had no personal knowledge of the purportedly unethical conduct, but based his assertions on information obtained by an Employee discharged from State's Attorney's office. Nonattorney filed a defamation suit against Lawyer. Lawyer claimed an absolute privilege to reveal his suspicions to the appropriate authorities.

The class of absolutely privileged communications includes communications made in the discharge of a duty under express authority of law. Under the Disciplinary Rules promulgated by the state supreme court, lawyers have a duty to report the misconduct of other lawyers. Without reference to Nonattorney, Lawyer's report would have been incomplete and his duty to report the unethical conduct unfulfilled. Thus, Lawyer's communications regarding Nonattorney were absolutely privileged. Weber v. Cueto, 568 N.E.2d 513 (Ill. App. Ct. 1991).

Quiz Yourself on
REGULATION OF THE LEGAL PROFESSION

4. John is applying for admission to the bar in the state of Wythe. As part of the application, he is required to complete a questionnaire designed to determine whether the applicant has the good character necessary for the practice of law. The questionnaire asks the applicant to list and explain any arrests or convictions. While a 19-year-old college student, John was arrested and convicted for trespassing and theft as a result of his participation in a fraternity prank. Three years after his arrest, the incident was expunged from his record. Must John list this incident on his bar application? _____

5. Jim has come to Sally, an attorney, asking for her help in resolving his dispute with a car dealership. Sally has determined that the best course of action would be to file suit in the state of Orange. Unfortunately, Sally is licensed to practice law only in the state of Blue. Must Jim find a new lawyer in the state of Orange, or can Sally represent him? _____

6. Assume in the question above that the Judge denied Sally's *pro hac vice* petition to represent Jim in the state of Orange after giving the petition only a cursory reading. Have either Sally's or Jim's due process rights been violated? _____

7. Richard has been a real estate agent for 15 years. He is well acquainted with the steps involved in preparing the documents necessary for closing a real estate sale. He can prepare these documents for his clients for one-half the amount it costs to have an attorney do so. May Richard prepare the documents for his clients? _____

8. Bill is a licensed attorney sharing an office with Amy. He is aware that there is a dispute over a missing document in one of Amy's cases. As a result of overhearing a conversation in the lobby between Amy and one of her clients, Frank, Bill has become aware that Amy is in possession of the document requested during discovery but is claiming that it cannot be located. Bill has become close friends with Amy over the years and does not want to cause her any trouble. Must Bill report Amy to the appropriate professional authority? _____

9. In the state of Wythe, membership in the state bar association is mandatory. State bar members must pay yearly dues. The state bar association wants to pay the traveling expenses for a group of attorneys to travel to the state capital to lobby against a bill requiring more stringent application procedures for gun owners. May the state bar use the money collected from the payment of yearly dues to pay for the traveling expenses of the lobbyists? _____

10. Mary resides near the border of her state and wishes to open a solo practice upon receiving her license to practice law. She would like to have the broadest client base possible, and is considering applying to the bar in her home state as well as the neighboring state. Is it possible for Mary to be licensed in two states at once? _____

11. Alice retained an attorney, Bob, to file a medical malpractice suit against her Doctor and Hospital. Bob assured her that everything was under control, but in actuality, Bob forgot to file the suit and missed the deadline, effectively prohibiting Alice from ever filing suit. Bob has already been disciplined by the state bar. Does Alice have any further recourse? _____

12. Mary is a licensed lawyer in the state of Marshall. Marshall requires applicants to the state bar to furnish the admission authorities with recommendations from currently licensed lawyers. Mary has recently been contacted by her former college roommate, Joan, and asked if she will provide a recommendation for Joan's son, Bob, who is applying to the state bar. Mary has never met Bob and knows nothing about him other than what his mother has told her. Can Mary write the recommendation for Bob as a favor to Joan? _____

13. Sam has recently been admitted to practice law in the state of Wythe. The state of Wythe's ethics code is based on the ABA Model Rules. Sam is faced with a difficult ethical question. He is unable to find any state ethics opinions that help answer the question, but there is an ABA ethics opinion that provides guidance. As Sam is not an ABA member, must or should he give any weight to the ABA's ethics opinion? _____

14. Nathalie has come to Adnan, a lawyer, for help with recovering money from Sam, a lawyer. After investigation, Adnan concludes that Sam unlawfully converted Nathalie's funds. Adnan negotiates with Sam on Nathalie's behalf. Sam agrees to pay the stolen money to Nathalie in three installments, provided Adnan agrees not to inform the State Bar of his defalcation. Adnan consults with Nathalie, and the agreement is finalized and put into writing. Sam defaults on the installment payments, and Adnan pursues a civil action on Nathalie's behalf based on the settlement contract. The Judge files a bar complaint against Sam for stealing Nathalie's money and against Adnan for failing to report the serious misconduct of Sam. What result regarding Adnan? What result regarding Sam?

Answers

4. Yes. Any past conduct may be considered by the admission authorities, including arrests and convictions that have been expunged from records. An applicant to the bar may not make any material false statement and must not "fail to disclose a fact necessary to correct misapprehension known by the [applicant] to have arisen in the matter. . . ." MR 8.1(b). By failing to include his arrest and conviction on his application, John is leading the admissions authorities to believe that he has never been arrested or convicted, a fact he clearly knows is not true.

5. It is possible for Sally to represent Jim in the state of Orange. Before she can represent Jim in a state in which she is not licensed to practice, she must apply to the state's courts to request admission *pro hac vice*. If Sally's request is granted, she may represent Jim in the state of Orange's courts until the dispute with the car dealership is resolved.

6. No. The right to appear *pro hac vice* is within the discretion of the state. Neither Sally nor Jim has a due process right to a certain quality of consideration of their application. A number of states grant *pro hac vice* applications only to lawyers whose home state has a policy of reciprocating when its lawyers apply to practice in the applying lawyer's state. Some states require the out-of-state lawyer to associate, for purposes of the case, with a lawyer who is licensed in the state.

7. No, Richard is not an attorney and therefore cannot practice law within the state. Preparing the necessary documents in this situation is legal work that can be performed only by a licensed attorney.

8. Yes, Bill is under a duty to report Amy's misconduct, and a failure to do so is an ethical violation on Bill's part. Model Rule 8.3(a) states that "[a] lawyer who knows that another lawyer has committed a violation of the Model Rules of Professional Conduct that raises a substantial question as to that lawyer's honesty, trustworthiness, or fitness as a lawyer in other respects, shall inform the appropriate professional authority." Even though Amy has not directly informed Bill that she is withholding the

document, he has personal knowledge of her actions based on the conversation between Amy and Frank and the circumstances surrounding the case.

9. No. Although state courts and legislatures are permitted to require membership in and dues payment to the state bar association for all licensed attorneys, a mandatory bar may not expend members' dues to advance political or ideological positions. Keller v. State Bar of California, 496 U.S. 1 (1990).

10. Yes, Mary may hold licenses to practice in as many states as she wishes, provided she complies with the licensing requirements in each state. States' efforts to require in-state residency by attorneys wishing to gain a license to practice have been held unconstitutional.

11. Yes. The law of a wide variety of other areas forms an essential part of the law of lawyering. Depending on the circumstances of the case, Alice may bring suit for breach of contract or a tort suit for malpractice.

12. No. Licensed lawyers may not "knowingly make a false statement of material fact" in connection with a bar admission application. MR 8.1(a). It would be a misrepresentation of a material fact for Mary to state to the admission authorities that Bob was a qualified applicant if she did not have personal knowledge of the applicant. If Mary investigates and determines Bob to be a qualified applicant, she may write the recommendation, provided the recommendation truly represents her knowledge of Bob.

13. Yes, Sam should consider the ABA opinion even though he is not a member. The ABA's views on issues affecting the law of lawyering and its Model Rules are very influential, even though it is a voluntary organization with no direct regulatory authority over lawyers. However, even though Wythe's code is based on the ABA model, it is the state-adopted code and not the ABA model that actually controls. The best way for Sam to determine how the Wythe State Bar would resolve the question is to ask the state bar to issue an ethics opinion. Both the ABA and the state bar associations will issue nonbinding ethics opinions. These opinions are often generated by submitting a hypothetical question to a state bar committee whose responsibility it is to answer the question and publish the opinions.

14. Adnan is subject to discipline for failing to report the serious misconduct of Sam. This fact pattern closely follows that of In re Himmel, 533 N.E.2d 790 (Ill. 1988). Under Model Rule 8.3(a), a lawyer who knows that another lawyer has committed a violation of the Rules of Professional Conduct that raises a substantial question as to that lawyer's honesty, trustworthiness, or fitness as a lawyer in other respects, shall inform the appropriate professional authority. Adnan is subject to discipline even though he was protecting the interests of his client. Model Rule 8.3 does recognize that client confidentiality prevents revealing lawyer misconduct, but the mere advancing of a client's interests is insufficient to thwart the duty to report. Sam is subject to discipline for misuse of client funds. MR 1.15.

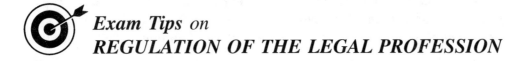

Exam Tips on
REGULATION OF THE LEGAL PROFESSION

Do not assume that every answer to an exam question will be found in the ethics codes. Some topics are simply not addressed in the ethics codes, and others require an examination of the overlap between the ethics code provisions and other law.

The institutional framework within which the law of lawyering, and lawyers, exists has a significant effect on the interpretation of the law of lawyering. Note the institutions that are involved in your exam question: Are they courts? A state bar association? The ABA?

The ***American Bar Association*** (ABA) is a national, ***voluntary*** association of lawyers that plays a critical role in the creation of the law governing lawyers. But remember, the ABA does not license lawyers to practice law, nor does it impose discipline. States, through the courts, bar associations, and sometimes legislatures, license lawyers to practice law within the relevant jurisdiction and impose discipline on lawyers who violate the adopted rules. Federal courts both admit lawyers to practice before them and impose discipline.

The law that governs lawyers comes from a variety of sources and exists in a variety of forms including state adopted ethics codes, ABA model codes, case law, lawyer ethics opinions, the Restatement of the Law Governing Lawyers, constitutional provisions, and other law. Consider a range of sources of law in your essay answers, while recognizing that the Model Rules, as adopted by particular states, still dominate analysis of most topics.

A license to practice law is a prerequisite to a person's lawful engagement in the activities of lawyering. The state has a need to protect the public from those who are incompetent or who lack integrity.

☛ To become licensed, one must satisfy education, knowledge, and character requirements.

☛ An applicant to the bar may not make any material false statement and must not "fail to disclose a fact necessary to correct misapprehension known by the [applicant] to have arisen in the matter. . . ." MR 8.1(b). The number of cases of denied applications based on misrepresentation in the application process outnumbers cases of denied applications based on prior misconduct. Particularly because of its immediate relevance to law students, misconduct in the bar application process is a fruitful area for exam questions.

☛ Licensed lawyers are duty bound not to assist in the admission of an unqualified applicant. MR 8.1.

By the nature of the licensing requirements, lawyers licensed to practice in a given state have a monopoly on the practice of law in that state. When a person engages in the ***unauthorized practice*** of law, civil and sometimes criminal penalties attach. Unauthorized practice may occur when a licensed lawyer practices outside the jurisdiction in which the license was granted or when those not licensed engage in the practice of law.

- When a lawyer who is licensed to practice in one state has an occasional, nonrecurring need to represent a client before the courts of another state, the lawyer requests admission before that state's courts *"pro hac vice,"* "for this turn only." Don't immediately conclude that a lawyer has engaged in unauthorized practice when she appears in court in a state in which she is not licensed.

Among the chief features of the legal profession's claim to be ***self-governing*** is the requirement of reporting fellow lawyers' or a judge's serious misconduct to the appropriate professional authority. MR 8.3.

- The topic of reporting misconduct makes an ideal subject area for an exam question because of the difficult mixture of competing values that is implicated. Duties to the public and the profession compete with confidentiality duties to clients when a nonlawyer client reveals the misconduct of a former lawyer to her current lawyer.

- Before a duty to report misconduct can arise, the lawyer must "know that another lawyer has committed" the ***misconduct.*** MR 8.3(a).

- The rule requires a lawyer to report misconduct "that raises a substantial question as to that lawyer's honesty, trustworthiness or fitness as a lawyer in other respects. . . ." MR 8.3(a). "Substantial" means a "material matter of clear and weighty importance." Trivial misconduct need not be reported.

- The rule does not require a report of misconduct when the lawyer has learned of the misconduct through confidential communications that would be protected by the ethical duty of confidentiality under Model Rule 1.6. MR 8.3(c). But it also must be remembered that the exceptions to the duty of confidentiality (e.g., the future-crime exception) continue to apply with equal force in this setting as in any other.

- When a lawyer reports another lawyer's misconduct, the potential exists for a defamation action to be filed by the reported-on lawyer against the reporting lawyer. A privilege applies to required reporting of another lawyer's misconduct.

Chapter 3

CONTROLS ON LAWYER CONDUCT

ChapterScope

- This chapter deals generally with the various control devices that operate to limit lawyer conduct. The specifics of the limiting rules themselves are discussed elsewhere in this outline.

- There is a strong tendency to think only of the lawyer ethics codes when thinking about limits on lawyer conduct, but such a view is too narrow. In addition to ethics codes, malpractice, criminal codes, civil liability other than malpractice, judges' in-court power, litigation sanctions, and other litigation devices all limit and control lawyer conduct.

- *Discipline* imposed at the hands of the organized bar is the most often referred to and studied, but much less often actually imposed, control on lawyer conduct. *Discipline* by the bar and then the court system operates by authority of the licensing of lawyers.

  - Discipline is imposed for the protection of the public generally and for the benefit of the profession, while malpractice is a tort or contract-based civil action that is meant to compensate victims of a lawyer's negligence or contract breach.

  - While a single act of negligence will support a malpractice action, unless that single act is sufficiently gross to indicate a substantial likelihood that the lawyer is unfit to practice, that single act will not subject the lawyer to bar discipline.

- *Malpractice* is a civil claim for relief intended to remedy a wrong done by a professional (in this case, a lawyer) to an individual client or group of clients.

- As a *fiduciary*, a lawyer owes duties to clients beyond the tort and contract duties. Fiduciary duties modify contract principles. These special duties can be the basis for a malpractice action that might not otherwise lie under contract or tort theories.

- Judges' *contempt* power is a considerable control on lawyer conduct in the litigation setting. The contempt power is meant to give judges reasonable control over the courtroom and to enforce standards of courtroom behavior among litigants.

- When a lawyer perceives that an opposing lawyer may have conflicts of interest in litigation, the lawyer may request that the court *disqualify* opposing counsel from further participation in the case.

- Money sanctions are available against an offending lawyer under various *frivolous claim* prohibition rules, especially Federal Rule of Civil Procedure 11.

I. DISCIPLINE

Discipline imposed at the hands of the organized bar is the most often referred to and studied, but much less often actually imposed, control on lawyer conduct. *Discipline* by the bar and then the court system operates by authority of the licensing of lawyers. The entity that grants the lawyer a license to practice law, the highest court in a particular state, usually through the action of the organized bar of the state, has authority to discipline lawyers who violate the ethics code of the jurisdiction. See Chapter 2, §III.

A. Discipline v. malpractice

Discipline must be contrasted with *malpractice* liability. See §II. Discipline is imposed for the protection of the public generally and for the benefit of the profession, whereas malpractice is a tort- or contract-based civil action that is meant to compensate victims of a lawyer's negligence or contract breach. Although a single act of negligence will support a malpractice action, unless that single act is sufficiently gross to indicate a substantial likelihood that the lawyer is unfit to practice, it will not subject the lawyer to bar discipline.

Example: Lawyer filed a claim after Client was bitten by a dog. Lawyer learned of the dog's history of biting only a few days before trial and moved to amend Client's Complaint. The court denied Lawyer's motion. Believing that a four-year statute of limitations applied, Lawyer withdrew the claim for subsequent refiling. Client lost the refiled suit when the defense successfully argued that the applicable three-year statute of limitations had expired. Although Lawyer's conduct is likely to support a malpractice action, his conduct does not justify any disciplinary action. Florida Bar v. Neale, 384 So. 2d 1264 (Fla. 1980).

B. Grounds for discipline

Discipline may be based on an incredibly wide range of conduct, both within and without the lawyer's role. It may be imposed for violations of the ethics code rules; acts involving moral turpitude; criminal conduct; dishonesty, fraud, and deceit; and acts that are prejudicial to the administration of justice.

1. Violation of adopted ethics code: A lawyer is subject to discipline when she violates a mandatory rule of the relevant state's adopted ethics code. All other grounds for discipline are implicitly included in this category because the adopted ethics code typically includes provisions that in one way or another require a lawyer to refrain from conduct that is criminal or fraudulent, involves moral turpitude, or prejudices the administration of justice. MR 8.4.

Example: The state Office on Attorney Ethics conducted a random compliance audit of Lawyer's trust account. The audit revealed that Lawyer had continually issued checks to his own order for fees in pending real estate matters. He had replaced these "advances" when he received the closing funds or when a closing fell through. Upon learning of the impending audit, Lawyer used personal funds to cover withdrawn fees. Lawyer knew that his conduct had violated ethical rules but felt that it could not possibly hurt anyone.

Lawyer's conduct constituted knowing misappropriation. Knowing misappropriation consists simply of a lawyer's taking a client's money entrusted to him, knowing that it is the client's money, and knowing that the client has not authorized the taking. A subjective intent to borrow rather than permanently convert, the absence of client losses, and Lawyer's prior outstanding record do not excuse the violation. To protect the public confidence in the integrity of the legal profession, Lawyer would be disbarred. In re Warhaftig, 524 A.2d 398 (N.J. 1987).

2. **Acts indicating moral turpitude:** Formerly, the standard for whether an act reflected adversely on a lawyer's fitness (and therefore subjected the lawyer to discipline) was whether the act involved *moral turpitude.* DR 1-102(A)(3). This standard, thought too broad and amorphous, is no longer the explicit standard under the Model Rule. See MR 8.4. Nonetheless, moral turpitude language, particularly in cases of lawyer sexual misconduct, finds its way into the court decisions applying Model Rule 8.4. The standard under Model Rule 8.4 is more functional. The act is disciplinable misconduct if it "reflects adversely on the lawyer's honesty, trustworthiness, or fitness as a lawyer in other respects."

   Example: Client retained Lawyer to represent her in divorce and custody proceedings. Because Client was unemployed, she had no money to pay Lawyer's retainer fee, but Lawyer agreed to represent her and began work on her case. Client then offered to engage in sexual intercourse with Lawyer for money. Lawyer told Client that he would give her money as a personal loan if she did not want to have sex, but she advised him that she had no means to pay back the money. Therefore, Client suggested that she would reimburse him with sex. Lawyer gave Client $50 and they had sexual intercourse.

   The sexual contact between Lawyer and Client in a professional context constitutes professional impropriety and an act of moral turpitude. It carried a great potential of prejudice both to Client and to her children in the pending court proceedings. Further, Lawyer's conduct reflects negatively on the integrity and honor of the legal profession. Therefore, Lawyer's license was suspended for three months. Committee on Professional Ethics & Conduct of the Iowa State Bar Ass'n v. Hill, 436 N.W.2d 57 (Iowa 1989).

3. **Criminal conduct:** A lawyer is subject to discipline when he engages in criminal conduct that reflects adversely on the lawyer's fitness as a lawyer.

   Example: Lawyer was convicted of willfully and knowingly attempting to evade income taxes. In addition to the criminal liability, Lawyer is subject to discipline. In re Colin, 442 N.Y.S.2d 66 (N.Y. App. Div. 1981).

   a. **Not all criminal conduct included:** Minor criminal conduct—such as small-amount possession of controlled substances or criminal trespass during a civil rights demonstration—that says little about the lawyer's honesty, trustworthiness, or fitness as a lawyer in other respects will not subject the lawyer to discipline. Under the Model Code rubric, such conduct amounts to a criminal act not involving moral turpitude.

   b. **Not necessarily in the role of lawyer:** Criminal conduct outside the role of lawyer that reflects adversely on the lawyer's fitness will subject the lawyer to discipline. ABA Formal Op. 336 (1974). Fraud in a lawyer's private business transactions, setting a fire in the lawyer's office or residence as insurance fraud, or engaging in drug trafficking are all examples of criminal conduct outside the role of lawyer that would subject the lawyer to discipline.

4. **Dishonesty, fraud, and deceit:** Acts, whether in or out of the lawyer's role, that involve dishonesty, fraud, and deceit, even if not rising to the level of criminal conduct, subject the lawyer to discipline. MR 8.4(c). This rule overlaps coverage with a variety of other ethics code rules that prohibit deceitful conduct of one kind or another. See, e.g., MR 3.3, 3.4, and 4.1.

   Example: Lawyer represented Client, who was converting several buildings into condominiums. Prospective Purchasers agreed to immediately close on several units on the condition that

Client deposit $10,000 in an escrow account to cover the costs of completing necessary work on the units in case Client failed to perform. If Client satisfactorily performed the work, the money would be released back to him. Lawyer agreed to act as an escrow agent even after learning that Client's check for the account was worthless. Purchasers relied on the availability of the escrow funds and paid a nonrefundable deposit.

Although a client is entitled to representation for any objective within the bounds permitted by law, he is not entitled to affirmative assistance by his attorney with conduct that the lawyer knows is illegal or fraudulent. When an attorney confronts a situation in which the client's wishes call for illegal or fraudulent conduct, the attorney is under an affirmative duty to withdraw from the representation. As an escrow agent, Lawyer owed a fiduciary duty to Purchasers to protect their investment. Lawyer is subject to discipline. In re Austern, 524 A.2d 680 (1987).

5. **Conduct prejudicial to the administration of justice:** This prohibition is a broad, catch-all category including various forms of misconduct, much of which is also prohibited by more specific rules. MR 8.4(d).

   a. **Litigation conduct:** This rule is most often invoked to discipline litigation conduct that is regarded as tactically out-of-bounds. Disregarding court orders, rude conduct in open court, being intoxicated in court, paying witnesses to engage in inappropriate conduct, and the like are the most frequent examples.

   b. **Attacks for vagueness:** The "administration of justice" rules are vague and have been used to support discipline for widely variant forms of bad behavior. These rules have been challenged as being constitutionally void for vagueness and violative of First Amendment expression rights, but they have been upheld. See Howell v. State Bar of Texas, 843 F.2d 205 (5th Cir.), *cert. den.* 488 U.S. 982 (1988). The Supreme Court may have helped to rein the rule into more reasonable boundaries by holding that a single instance of rudeness should not violate the rule. In re Snyder, 472 U.S. 634 (1985).

C. **Forms of discipline**

Discipline generally comes in the form of disbarment, suspension, or reprimand, either public or private. Courts may also require disciplined lawyers to engage in professional responsibility educational programs.

1. **Disbarment:** Disbarment is an indefinite dismissal from the rolls of lawyers licensed to practice in the particular jurisdiction. In most jurisdictions, a disbarred lawyer may petition for readmission after a designated time period has elapsed. Nonetheless, disbarment is the most serious form of discipline and often effectively ends a lawyer's legal career.

2. **Suspension:** Suspension is a fixed-period revocation of the license to practice law.

3. **Reprimand:** Reprimand is a statement of reproach issued by the bar to the disciplined lawyer. Reprimands may be either private or public. When a reprimand is public, it is published in a newspaper.

D. **Disciplinary procedure**

The formal disciplinary procedure is designed around the goals of bar discipline. It is intended to protect the public from lawyers who have committed serious misconduct. The process is not arranged for the benefit of the particular complaining party, usually a client. Each state maintains its own disciplinary process, but these processes have many features in common.

1. **Complaint:** A disciplinary proceeding is initiated by the filing of a complaint with the bar disciplinary authority.

2. **Investigation by committee:** A committee of the bar, charged with investigative responsibility, examines the complaint to determine whether, if true, the allegations constitute misconduct. Often, complaints are resolved by discussion with the complaining party at this stage, without the need for further proceedings. Complaints may also be either dismissed or sent on to the next stage of the disciplinary process.

   a. **Local in nature:** The investigating committee is usually a local committee made up of members of the bar in the county or other locality in which the complained-of lawyer practices.

   b. **No appeal from dismissal:** The process is designed for internal regulation of lawyers. When a complaint is dismissed, the complaining party has no right of appeal.

3. **Hearing committee:** Complaints that are passed on from the local investigating committee are sent to a hearing committee. A presentation of the evidence against the lawyer is made by a lawyer appointed by the state bar for that purpose.

   a. **Discovery:** Discovery procedures vary from state to state, but many states allow discovery similar to that provided for in the rules of civil procedure.

   b. **Jury:** The accused lawyer has no right to jury trial in a disciplinary proceeding.

   c. **Burden of proof:** The bar bears the burden of proving the allegations against the accused lawyer.

   d. **Right to be heard:** The accused lawyer has a right to be heard at the hearing stage.

   e. **Dismiss or impose sanctions:** At the conclusion of the hearing process, the hearing committee will either dismiss the complaint or impose sanctions. See §I.C.

4. **Review by appeal board:** If the hearing committee has imposed sanctions, the lawyer may appeal to an internal bar appeal board.

5. **State court of last resort:** If the appeal board upholds either the imposition of discipline or both the discipline and the sanctions, the lawyer may appeal to the state's court of last resort (in most places called the state supreme court). That court has the ultimate authority for regulating lawyers within its jurisdiction.

   a. **Standard of review:** Without going beyond the factual record from the hearing stage, the court may consider the matter without being bound by the hearing committee's factual findings.

   b. **Burden:** At this stage, effectively acting as an appellant, the lawyer bears the burden of showing that the bar's actions were unwarranted.

6. **Due process:** A lawyer is entitled to due process in disciplinary processes. In re Ruffalo, 390 U.S. 544 (1968).

7. **Mitigation:** At any stage at which an authority is considering sanctions, a broad range of circumstances may be considered, including the lawyer's past record of bar complaints and discipline, the lawyer's attitude during the proceedings, evidence of rehabilitation, the lawyer's personal problems (e.g., financial exigencies and substance abuse), and the state of mind of the

lawyer when the violation was committed (i.e., whether the act was intentional, negligent, done in good faith, vindictively motivated, and so on). In some states, substance abuse is considered as a mitigating factor only if the lawyer is enrolled in a treatment program.

II. MALPRACTICE

Malpractice is a civil claim for relief intended to remedy a wrong done by a professional (in this case, a lawyer) to an individual client or a group of clients.

A. Contract theories

Contract theory malpractice actions have the common contract elements of agreement, breach, and damage. Damage measurement under contract theories is more limited than that under tort theories.

B. Tort theories

Under tort theories, the most used of the malpractice theories, the elements are the familiar negligence elements of duty, breach, causation, and damages.

1. **Duty:** The lawyer's duty to the client is measured by the skill and knowledge of ordinary lawyers in the community.

    a. **No fee required:** A lawyer owes this duty to a client irrespective of whether any fee is being paid for the lawyer's service. Thus, appointed counsel and pro bono counsel, for example, owe the same duty as a lawyer who is charging a fee for service.

    b. **General knowledge and research:** Lawyers are expected to have general knowledge of the law and its fundamental principles. A lawyer is expected to be sufficiently familiar with research techniques and to use them to discover the law that applies to a client's matter. Nonetheless, a lawyer does not owe a duty to know every possible nuance in the law. See §2.a below.

    c. **Specialists:** Specialists in a particular field (e.g., tax) are held to a higher standard than that of the ordinary lawyer in the community. The standard will be set by the knowledge and skill of those specializing in the particular field.

    d. **Onset of the duty:** The duty begins when a client begins to talk with a lawyer as a lawyer. Any reasonable expectation of service that is created by the lawyer at that time creates a duty of care. The duty does not wait for a formal retainer or for payment of a fee. It begins when the client reasonably expects that the lawyer has undertaken to provide legal service.

    Example: Lawyer is attending a PTA potluck dinner. Acquaintance asks Lawyer a question about a neighbor of Acquaintance who had some years ago built a fence that encroached on Acquaintance's property. Lawyer, irritated at being asked a legal question at a social function, says, "I'll ask my partner about that." The evening goes on, and Lawyer forgets about Acquaintance's question. Lawyer owes Acquaintance a duty of care. Eight months later, after the statute of limitations has run on her possible claim, Acquaintance calls Lawyer to ask what his partner thought about her fence problem. Lawyer has breached a duty to Acquaintance. See, e.g., Togstad v. Vesely, Otto, Miller & Keefe, 291 N.W.2d 686 (Minn. 1980).

2. **Breach:** Breach of the duty owed is a required element of a malpractice action.

   a. **No liability for reasonable choices that go wrong:** Lawyers are not guarantors of particular results. Often, a variety of reasonable strategies will be available from which to choose. When a lawyer chooses a reasonable course of action and that course later produces bad results, the lawyer has not breached the duty of care owed to the client.

   Example: Lawyer represents Client at trial. Witness testifies against Client, but Opposing Lawyer forgets to draw a particularly damaging fact from Witness during direct examination. Lawyer has available impeachment material that would cast Witness's credibility in doubt, but engaging in cross-examination risks drawing out the particularly damaging fact that has not yet been admitted into evidence. Lawyer's choice between the two reasonable alternatives of engaging or not engaging in cross-examination of Witness will not breach Lawyer's duty of care to Client.

   b. **Falling below the standard of care:** Actions by a lawyer that are below the applicable standard of care breach the duty to the client. Failure to conduct legal or factual research, failure to correctly analyze straightforward legal principles, losing critical evidence, and allowing statutes of limitations to expire are examples of actions that fall below the general standard of care.

3. **Causation:** For a malpractice claim to exist, the lawyer's breach of duty must cause the client's damages. Often, this means that the client will have to prove that she would have prevailed in the matter had the lawyer not breached the duty of care. This requirement is called the *"case within a case."* The malpractice plaintiff must prove the value of the underlying case to prevail in the malpractice case.

   Example: Lawyer undertook to investigate a possible litigation matter brought to her by Client. Lawyer procrastinated and the statute of limitations for filing the action expired. Lawyer owed Client a duty, and Lawyer has breached the duty. Upon examination, however, the matter originally brought by Client to Lawyer has no merit. In other words, even if Lawyer had timely investigated and filed the action, Client could not have recovered damages in that matter. Client cannot prove the case within a case. Therefore, Lawyer's acts were not the cause of any injury to Client, and Lawyer has no liability for malpractice to Client.

4. **Damages:** As with any tort action, the wrong is insufficient to create a claim for relief in the absence of damages. Often the value of a lawyer malpractice claim's damages will be determined by the value of the client's claim that has been lost or diminished because of the lawyer's acts.

C. Fiduciary duty

As a *fiduciary,* a lawyer owes duties to clients beyond the tort and contract duties. Fiduciary duties modify contract principles when, for example, a client fails to pay a fee and a lawyer continues to have limited obligations to the client despite the client's breach of their agreement or when a lawyer holds clients' funds. These special duties can be the basis for a malpractice action that might not otherwise lie under contract or tort theories. See Chapter 4, §III.

D. Necessity of expert testimony

As with other forms of professional malpractice, expert testimony is usually needed to establish the nature of the professional duty and the existence of a breach of that duty.

E. Prospective limitation on malpractice liability

The Model Code prohibited lawyers from establishing any prospective limitation on their malpractice liability to clients. For example, a lawyer would be subject to discipline if she included a clause in her retainer agreement with clients that purported to waive the client's prospective claims for malpractice against the lawyer. DR 6-102. The Model Rules restrict the lawyer's ability to prospectively limit malpractice liability to clients to those occasions when a client is represented by other counsel in making the limitation of liability agreement and such agreements are permitted by law in the relevant state. MR 1.8(h).

F. Liability to third parties for malpractice

Under limited circumstances, a lawyer may be liable for malpractice to a nonclient. See Chapter 7, §VI.

III. LIABILITY FOR CLIENT CONDUCT

Lawyers are prohibited under the Model Rules from "counseling a client to engage or assisting a client in conduct that the lawyer knows is criminal or fraudulent." MR 1.2(d). Although this provision sets up the disciplinary exposure of a lawyer who violates the rule, a lawyer may also be criminally and civilly liable for the wrongs of their clients that the lawyer assists.

Example: Lawyer represents Drug Kingpin. Lawyer meets with Drug Kingpin once a week, at which time Drug Kingpin pays Lawyer $5,000 cash. Lawyer performs various lawyering tasks for Drug Kingpin, such as appearing in court to post bail and making initial appearances for any employees of Drug Kingpin who may be arrested, doing real estate transfers for various houses in areas well known for drug trafficking and "safe" drug house locations, and preparing the papers for Drug Kingpin's acquisition of a large boat. Although by themselves and under more ordinary circumstances all of these activities are legitimate, given the combination of these facts, Lawyer knows he is assisting Drug Kingpin with a criminal enterprise. Lawyer has criminal liability for drug trafficking.

Example: Client retains Lawyer to assist Client in a public stock offering. In the course of representation, Client generates false material to be included in Securities and Exchange Commission (SEC) submissions. Knowing the material to be false, Lawyer includes it in the SEC submission. Members of the public are deceived by the material and lose money on their investment in Client's stock. Both Client and Lawyer have civil liability to those deceived and to the SEC.

IV. CONTEMPT OF COURT

Judges' *contempt* power is a considerable control on lawyer conduct in the litigation setting. The contempt power is meant to give judges reasonable control over the courtroom and to enforce standards of courtroom behavior among litigants.

A. A last resort

The contempt power is meant to be used as a last resort to police in-court lawyer conduct when all other means of instruction, persuasion, and command by the court have failed to produce restraint in the wayward lawyer.

B. Disruption of the proceedings

The contempt power should be exercised only when the lawyer's conduct has an actual disruptive effect on the proceedings.

C. Direct or summary contempt

A direct contempt is one that relates to conduct that is within the personal knowledge of the judge. Open disruption of court or refusal to follow a judge's orders, for example, is direct contempt when the acts occur in the presence of the judge. A judge may act immediately and without further hearing to punish direct contempt.

D. Indirect contempt

Indirect contempt is contempt that occurs outside the presence of the judge. Tampering with jurors or witnesses and abusive behavior toward court clerks or other personnel are examples of indirect contempt. When the contempt is indirect, due process requires that the lawyer be given notice and an opportunity to be heard. See Taylor v. Hayes, 418 U.S. 488 (1974).

E. Sanctions

When a judge finds a lawyer to be in contempt of court, the judge may admonish the lawyer or impose fines or imprisonment.

V. DISQUALIFICATION MOTIONS AND OTHER LITIGATION-DRIVEN CONTROLS

Powerful constraints on lawyer conduct exist in the form of various litigation motions. Such motions have become much more frequently used (some say overused) during the last 20 years. These motions, when granted, have an immediate and significant impact on the lawyer against whom they were filed.

A. Disqualification for conflicts of interest

When a lawyer perceives that an opposing lawyer may have conflicts of interest in litigation, the lawyer may request that the court *disqualify* opposing counsel from further participation in the case. When such a motion is granted, counsel is no longer permitted to be employed by her client in that matter. Losing a client, at least for the particular case, and losing the associated fee are a weighty consequence.

1. **Substantive standards:** The standards for when a disqualification motion should be granted are substantially the same as the underlying conflicts of interest standards, including the shield or "Chinese Wall" defense. See Chapter 6.

2. **Other interests:** Because litigation consequences are at stake instead of lawyer disciplinary consequences, courts take into account interests in addition to the typical conflict-of-interest

concerns. The following interests, along with all of the usual conflict-of-interest policies, are considered and weighed by a court considering a disqualification motion.

> **a. Court interests:** Granting a motion to disqualify almost always means delay in the court proceedings while new counsel becomes sufficiently familiar with the matter to proceed. Courts consider the delay and court inefficiency in determining whether to grant disqualification motions.
>
> **b. Equity:** The moving party may seek a litigation advantage by filing a motion to disqualify. A court will consider the conduct of the moving party, especially as it relates to the timing of the motion. In particular, a court will consider whether the moving party has made the motion promptly after learning of the grounds for the motion or has instead waited until close to trial, when the conflicted lawyer's party would be most disadvantaged by loss of counsel. In extreme cases, the moving party may be found to have intentionally created the conflict for the opposing party's lawyers. When that occurs, courts will be reluctant to grant the motion to disqualify.
>
> **c. Client choice of counsel:** Clients who have presumably retained their counsel of choice are disadvantaged, usually without fault, when a disqualification motion is granted. Courts will take this into account when considering the motion.

B. Federal Rule of Civil Procedure 11 and its state law counterparts

Money sanctions are available against an offending lawyer under various *frivolous claim* prohibition rules, especially Federal Rule of Civil Procedure (FRCP) 11. Most states have an analogous rule of procedure that governs proceedings in state court. These motions for sanctions have become very popular litigation tools, leading, many say, to added hostility between lawyers contesting such motions. The money sanctions make Rule 11 a significant lawyer control device. What follows here is a brief summary of Rule 11's provisions. See Chapter 8, §III.A. More on these issues may also be found in a Civil Procedure book.

> **1. Analogous to frivolous claims ethics code provisions:** Ethics code rules exist that are analogous to FRCP 11. See MR 3.1. In general, when a lawyer has violated FRCP 11, that lawyer is also subject to discipline, although few instances of bar discipline for filing a frivolous claim have occurred.
>
> **2. Claims that lack a basis in law or fact:** To avoid frivolous claim liability, a claim must have a basis in fact and in law.
>
> > **a. Law basis:** A claim that lacks arguable merit under existing law and lacks a good-faith argument for an extension or modification of existing law is frivolous and exposes the filer of the claim to sanctions.
> >
> > **b. Duty to investigate:** A lawyer is obligated by FRCP 11 to make a reasonable fact investigation before filing a claim and determine that there are reasonable factual grounds to support the allegations in the complaint.
>
> **3. Safe harbor:** Under the 1993 amendments to FRCP 11, a "safe harbor" provision exists. Before one may file a Rule 11 motion, notice must be given to the alleged offending lawyer. A warning period of 21 days must pass after notice before the motion may be filed. During that 21-day period, the offending lawyer may take actions to eliminate the violation. Such actions typically involve withdrawing or amending the complained-of paper or allegation.

4. **Sanctions against signer and firm:** Under the 1993 amendments to FRCP 11, sanctions may be imposed by the court on both the lawyer who signed the frivolous court paper and the lawyer's firm.

C. **Other sanctions**

A few other sanctions' provisions that are similar to FRCP 11 exist to govern the frivolous argument conduct of lawyers, especially on appeal. See, e.g., 28 U.S.C. 1927.

Quiz Yourself on
CONTROLS ON LAWYER CONDUCT

15. Sarah retains a lawyer to represent her in a product liability case. Sarah gives her lawyer the blender that malfunctioned and caused her injury. The lawyer takes the blender home and puts it in her garage. Later, the lawyer accidently discards the blender while preparing for a yard sale. As a result of the loss of this evidence, Sarah loses her case. What course of action against the lawyer is available and what are the likely results? _____

16. Joe is one of the most successful criminal defense attorneys in the state and has always been careful to ensure that his actions as an attorney always fall well within the bounds of the ethics rules. However, Joe has had two arrests for driving under the influence in the past year and has also been arrested for spousal abuse. May the bar discipline Joe for these arrests? _____

17. In exchange for a reduced hourly rate, Jane has signed a written agreement not to sue her attorney for malpractice that may occur during the representation. Is the attorney subject to discipline? _____

18. Joan is a tax attorney with an advanced degree in tax law. One of her clients has brought a malpractice suit against her as a result of tax advice Joan gave the client. To what standard will Joan be held? _____

19. Overruling her client Joe's preference, Amy decided not to put Material Witness on the stand during Joe's civil trial. She felt that Material Witness's testimony would do more harm than good because of certain credibility problems. The jury decided against Joe. Several of the jurors said one of the influences on their decision was the fact that Material Witness did not testify. Will Joe prevail in his malpractice suit against Amy? _____

20. Tom brought a malpractice case based on a tort theory against his attorney, Bob. Tom was able to prove that but for Bob's actions he would have won the matter that Bob had undertaken for Tom. However, he would have won only nominal damages. What damages can Tom get from Bob? _____

21. During the trial of his client, Joe felt that the judge clearly misapplied the rules of evidence in refusing to let him use the written statement of the police officer to refresh the officer's memory of the license plate he saw at the scene of the crime. Joe was vigorously representing the interests of his client when Joe gave the witness the document anyway and loudly instructed the witness to use the document to refresh his memory, despite the judge's contrary ruling. The judge ordered Joe to pay a $500 fine for contempt of court. Does Joe have any immediate recourse? _____

22. Lisa's opposing counsel has made a motion to have her disqualified from the case because of a conflict of interest. In addition to the general interests meant to be furthered by the ethics rules on conflicts of interest, what interests may the judge take into consideration in deciding whether to grant the motion? _____

23. Carlos, a lawyer, was called to jury duty and reported as assigned. He was a member of the jury in an armed robbery case. Viewing all the evidence as presented, Carlos felt that the prosecution did not meet the burden of proof and therefore he would vote for acquittal. During jury deliberations, however, it became clear that Carlos was the only vote for acquittal. After repeated re-votes and discussions, Carlos said, "OK, OK, I vote to convict. I have a busy law practice that is being neglected and I have to get back to work." Is Carlos subject to discipline? _____

24. Brianna is a young lawyer in a limited-liability corporation (LLC). She has been with the firm for two years, and hopes to make partner in six more. Unfortunately, she missed a key filing deadline for her client and is now a malpractice claim defendant. Brianna claims that she should not be liable for the full damages because she works in an LLC. Is she correct? _____

25. Drinking Dan, an attorney, has been convicted of three driving-while-intoxicated violations in the past three years. The last of the three was committed after his license had been suspended as a result of the first two. He was sentenced to three days in jail following the third. Fortunately, almost miraculously, no one has yet been injured by Dan's drunken-driving conduct. Is Dan subject to discipline for the drunk driving? _____

26. Austin, an attorney, has a passion for protecting the darted snail, an endangered species in his home state of Montana. Austin sent in an op-ed piece to the local newspaper supporting his cause, and it was published in the newspaper. In reality, the piece of writing, which Austin had presented as his own, had been clipped almost verbatim from the Wikipedia entry on the darted snail. Is Austin subject to discipline for this conduct? _____

27. Ethan, a defense attorney, wears his heart on his sleeve. His facial expressions and hand motions often show what he is thinking and feeling. In court on Tuesday, Ethan had everything go against him and became frustrated. When the judge ruled against his objection, . . . again, . . . Ethan gave a sarcastic look and shook his head. The judge immediately held Ethan in contempt of court for his facial expression. Should this contempt be upheld? _____

Answers

15. Sarah could begin a malpractice action against the lawyer and file a bar disciplinary complaint. She will prevail on her malpractice claim if she can prove that she would have won her initial case had her lawyer not lost the blender, but the lawyer probably will not be disciplined by the bar if this is an isolated event.

16. Yes, discipline may be imposed for conduct outside of the lawyer's role if the conduct is criminal and reflects adversely on the lawyer's fitness to be a lawyer, as these acts do.

17. Yes, unless such agreements are permitted by law in the relevant jurisdiction and Jane was represented by impartial counsel in making the agreement.

18. Because Joan is a specialist in her field, she will be judged by the knowledge and skill of tax specialists rather than the standard of the ordinary, reasonably knowledgeable lawyer.

19. A lawyer is not liable in malpractice for reasonable strategy choices. As such, Joe will not win because Amy will not be held liable for reasonable strategy choices. Strategy choices such as these are the lawyer's to make and not the client's. Thus, Joe's preference to have Material Witness testify is irrelevant.

20. Bob's actions did not cause any actual damages, so Tom will be unable to recover anything from him.

21. No. A judge may act immediately and without a hearing to punish contempt of which he or she has personal knowledge.

22. Judges may consider a wide range of interests in ruling on conflict-based disqualification motions, including the following: court delay and inefficiency resulting from the time that new counsel would need to become sufficiently familiar with the case; timing of the motion and whether the party filed the motion merely to gain an advantage in the litigation; and the attorney preference of the party against whom the motion was filed.

23. Yes. Carlos, like all jurors, took an oath to decide the fact issues faithfully based on the evidence at trial. Changing his vote to suit his law practice is a serious act of dishonesty. Even outside the role of lawyer, a lawyer must avoid acts of dishonesty that reflect badly on the ability to practice law. MR 8.4(c). Here, Carlos has changed his vote in a very serious matter, his jury service, to suit his personal needs. He has violated his oath as a juror. This act of dishonesty is especially telling because it is in connection with the dispute resolution system and reflects very badly on the lawyer's ability to be honest in the practice of law. It is entirely appropriate for lawyers to serve as jurors, and once Carlos was called to jury duty it was his responsibility to faithfully complete his public service as a juror.

24. No. A lawyer who actually commits the act of malpractice has full liability for it despite the protections that are provided by employment or membership in an LLC. A member of an LLC has limited liability for malpractice committed by others in the organization.

25. Yes. Dan's conduct, although not in the role of lawyer, reflects badly on his fitness to practice law. His criminal conduct demonstrates a significant disregard for the law and its obligations. Continuing to drive dangerously after his license was suspended is significant. MR 8.4.

26. Yes. Austin has engaged in seriously dishonest conduct, misleading the newspaper and the public about his written product. Even though this conduct was not in his role as a lawyer, he has demonstrated a level of dishonesty that reflects on his fitness to be a lawyer. MR 8.4.

27. No. It would be unfortunate for judges to hold lawyers in contempt for their mere facial expressions. Some opportunity for actual verbal expression should precede a contempt citation.

Exam Tips on
CONTROLS ON LAWYER CONDUCT

Most exam questions ask whether the lawyer is subject to discipline. For such a purpose, you should disregard the form of discipline that you think might be appropriate to the conduct and any mitigating circumstances that might be likely to reduce the punishment. You also should disregard the likelihood that the conduct by the lawyer would be discovered and the likelihood that the bar disciplinary authorities might choose not to pursue charges against the lawyer. Such a question simply asks whether the lawyer's conduct has violated the rules (i.e., whether the lawyer is subject to discipline).

Many questions test the differences between discipline and malpractice. Usually, the discipline involved in such questions is for competence. **Discipline** by the bar and then the court system operated by the courts' authority over the licensing of lawyers.

- Discipline is imposed for the protection of the public generally and for the benefit of the profession, while malpractice is a tort- or contract-based civil action that is meant to compensate victims of a lawyer's negligence or contract breach.

- While a single act of negligence will support a malpractice action, unless that single act is sufficiently gross to indicate a substantial likelihood that the lawyer is unfit to practice, that single act will not subject the lawyer to bar discipline. Be careful with fact patterns in which the lawyer has engaged in a careless lapse that has harmed a client. Given the same conduct by the lawyer, an isolated incident will support a malpractice claim by the client, but not a disciplinary action by the bar. A repeated series of lapses will support both malpractice claims and bar discipline.

- Contract theory malpractice actions have the common contract elements of agreement, breach, and damage. Damage measurement under contract theories is more limited than that of tort theories.

- Under tort theories, the most used of the malpractice theories, the elements are the familiar negligence elements of duty, breach, causation, and damages. Watch for questions that say that the lawyer acted "reasonably" or "with due care." Such language means by definition that the lawyer has not breached the tort duty and is therefore not liable for malpractice.

- The lawyer's tort duty to the client is measured by the skill and knowledge of ordinary lawyers in the community, unless the lawyer is an expert in a specialized field. An expert is held to the standard of the reasonable expert in that field.

- Breach of the duty owed is a required element of a malpractice action. Lawyers are not guarantors of particular results. Often, a variety of reasonable strategies will be available from which to choose. When a lawyer chooses a reasonable course of action, and that course later produces bad results, the lawyer has not breached the duty of care owed to the client.

- For a malpractice claim to exist, the lawyer's breach of duty must cause the client's damages.

- Often, this means that the client will have to prove that she would have prevailed in the matter had the lawyer not breached the duty of care. This requirement is called the *"case within a case."* The malpractice plaintiff must prove the value of the underlying case to prevail in the malpractice case.

- As with any tort action, the wrong is insufficient to create a claim for relief in the absence of damages.

As a ***fiduciary,*** a lawyer owes duties to clients beyond the tort and contract duties. Fiduciary duties modify contract principles. These special duties can be the basis for a malpractice action that might not otherwise lie under contract or tort theories. Many test questions focus on lawyer-client contracts. Remember that the lawyer's fiduciary duties enhance the lawyer's obligations to the client beyond the terms of their contract.

Lawyers are prohibited under the Model Rules from "counseling a client to engage or assisting a client in conduct that the lawyer knows is criminal or fraudulent." MR 1.2(d). While this provision sets up the disciplinary exposure of a lawyer who violates the rule, a lawyer also may be criminally and civilly liable for the wrongs of clients that the lawyer assists. Watch for fact patterns that ask about lawyer criminal or civil liability for actions that further the client's crimes or civil wrongs.

When the question places the lawyer in court, remember to consider the judge's ***contempt*** power. The contempt power is a considerable control on lawyer conduct in the litigation setting. The contempt power is meant to give judges reasonable control over the courtroom and to enforce standards of courtroom behavior among litigants.

Powerful constraints on lawyer conduct exist in the form of various litigation motions. These motions, when granted, have an immediate and significant impact on the lawyer against whom they were filed.

- When a lawyer perceives that an opposing lawyer may have a conflict of interest in litigation, the lawyer may request that the court ***disqualify*** opposing counsel from further participation in the case.

- The standards for when a disqualification motion should be granted are substantially the same as the underlying conflict-of-interest standards, including the shield or "Chinese Wall" defense. Because litigation consequences are at stake instead of lawyer disciplinary consequences, courts take into account interests such as delay caused by granting the motion, wrongful conduct of the moving party, especially as it relates to the timing of the motion, and the nonmoving party's legitimate interest in retaining counsel of her choice, in addition to the typical conflict-of-interest concerns. In the disqualification setting, be sure to discuss these other interests. It is tempting to do no more than discuss the conflicts rules and their application, but such an approach would leave out significant parts of the analysis.

- Money sanctions are available against an offending lawyer under various ***frivolous claim*** prohibition rules, especially FRCP 11.

CHAPTER 4

FORMAL ASPECTS OF THE LAWYER-CLIENT RELATIONSHIP

ChapterScope

- This chapter is about a variety of formal aspects of the lawyer-client relationship, such as when the lawyer-client relationship begins and how it ends, how the lawyer functions as a fiduciary, and how the lawyer and client arrange fees.

- *Undertaking representation* signifies the beginning of the formal lawyer-client relationship. Once a lawyer has undertaken representation, the full range of duties from lawyer to client exists. When the lawyer-client relationship begins and how it ends have implications for lawyer duties such as confidentiality (see Chapter 5), the potential for liability for malpractice (see Chapter 3), and the measure of loyalty owed. The onset of those duties will in turn dictate the conflicts of interest analysis that must be done in multiple client situations (see Chapter 6).

    - Unlike the general rule that a lawyer has no duty to accept every client's matter, lawyers are prohibited from accepting (i.e., lawyers must reject) representation when the representation will violate ethics rules or other law.

    - The lawyer-client relationship formally begins when a client reasonably believes that the lawyer has undertaken to provide the client with legal service. The relationship does not depend for its onset on the existence of a written contract nor a fee payment.

- A lawyer's *fee* must be reasonable. MR 1.5. A range of factors may be considered in setting a reasonable fee. MR 1.5(a).

- With a few exceptions and restrictions, a lawyer is permitted to charge a fee that is contingent on the outcome of the matter. There are two exceptions, criminal cases and certain domestic-relations cases. When *contingent fees* are permitted, additional restrictions apply.

- *Fee splitting:* The fee splitting practice is permitted if the total fee is reasonable, the client agrees to the arrangement, and either the fee is shared in proportion to the work done or the lawyers assume joint responsibility for the representation. MR 1.5(e).

- At one time, the organized bar typically imposed **minimum fee schedules** on lawyers and their clients. Such schedules are unlawful and therefore no longer enforceable.

- The lawyer is a fiduciary, and special property-handling duties come with that role. A *fiduciary* is one in whom a special trust is placed. A fiduciary owes to the beneficiary scrupulous good faith, candor, and care in the management of the beneficiary's interests.

- Contract law dictates some aspects of the lawyer-client fee relationship, but the existence of the lawyer's fiduciary role modifies contract law to create a special body of law that governs lawyer-client fee agreements.

- *Competence* requires that the lawyer possess and exercise on the client's behalf "the legal knowledge, skill, thoroughness, and preparation reasonably necessary for the representation." MR 1.1.

- ***Diligence*** is the timeliness aspect of competence. Lawyers are obligated to be diligent on their clients' behalf. MR 1.3.

- Because the scope of their relationship is generally set by contract, lawyers and their clients may negotiate and settle on the lawyer's ***scope of representation.***

    As a general proposition, clients set the goals or ends of to the representation while lawyers generally are empowered to determine the best means to achieve those ends. MR 1.2(a) Comment.

- The formal lawyer-client relationship ends when representation terminates. Despite termination, many lawyer duties to clients continue, such as confidentiality and a limited conflict avoidance duty. ***Withdrawal*** from representation is a critically important device for the lawyer who is faced with the prospect that continued representation of the client will result in a violation of the ethics code or other law.

I. UNDERTAKING REPRESENTATION

Before a lawyer has formally undertaken representation, a limited set of lawyer-to-client duties exist, including the confidentiality duty that is owed to prospective clients. See Chapter 5, §II.A.2. ***Undertaking representation*** signifies the beginning of the formal lawyer-client relationship. When a lawyer-client relationship begins, the full range of duties from lawyer to client exists.

A. Duty to undertake representation

1. **General:** In general, lawyers have no duty to undertake a particular representation. A lawyer is not like a public utility that must accept every customer who is willing to pay the necessary fee. In general, a lawyer chooses which clients he or she will agree to represent.

    a. **Moral choice:** For some commentators, lawyers make their most significant moral choice when they determine which clients to represent. Under this view, a lawyer considers the moral worth of the representation when she chooses whether or not to undertake the particular representation. Once representation is undertaken, the lawyer largely suspends moral judgment in favor of zealous representation of the client's interests.

    b. **Financial concerns:** Obviously, a lawyer's practice situation and the attendant financial concerns also play a role in the lawyer's decision to accept or reject offers of employment from clients.

2. **Limited duty to accept representation:** Unlike an individual lawyer, the population of lawyers as a group has something in common with public utilities. Lawyers have a state-granted monopoly over the provision of legal services. See Chapter 2, §IV. Lawyers in some states take an oath when they are admitted to practice that provides, in part, that the lawyer will never reject for personal reasons the causes of the defenseless and oppressed.

    a. **Pro bono:** One may infer, from this oath and the existence of the monopoly on the provision of legal services, a very limited duty of every lawyer to accept a fair share of representation of the defenseless and oppressed. This same oath is often cited as support for the pro bono service requirements. MR 6.1. See Chapter 8, §VII.

b. Court appointments: A lawyer has a duty to accept *court appointments* to represent clients, except when good cause exists to decline. MR 6.2.

   i. Good cause: Good cause exists in the following circumstances:

   - **Violation of ethics rule or other law:** If the representation will violate an ethics rule or other law; the lawyer *must decline* the appointment. MR 6.2(a). See §§B1 and B2.

   Example: Court requests Lawyer to undertake representation on behalf of Client. Lawyer currently represents Client's Adversary in a related matter. Undertaking representation of Client would violate conflicts-of-interest rules. Lawyer must decline the representation.

   - **Unreasonable financial burden:** When the appointment would likely result in an unreasonable financial burden, the lawyer *is permitted to decline* the appointment. Simple financial loss is insufficient. The financial burden must be an unreasonable one. MR 6.2(b).

   Example: Lawyer ordinarily charges $125 per hour for her time. Court appoints Lawyer to represent Client. The court-appointed fee is $35 per hour. If Lawyer would have billed on other matters every hour she spends on the court-appointed matter, she will lose $90 per hour for the time spent on Client's matter. Lawyer estimates that she will spend approximately 30 hours on the court-appointed matter, thereby costing her $2,700 that she might otherwise earn. This is not the sort of financial burden that qualifies as an unreasonable one for purposes of Model Rule 6.2. By contrast, Lawyer is asked by Court to represent Client, who lives 250 miles from Lawyer. The matter will require Lawyer to be present at Client's location three to four days per week for a period of two months. To competently represent Client, Lawyer would be required to maintain two residences for the two-month period, and she would be absent from her practice for most of the next two months, causing significant disruption to Lawyer's current clients to the extent that she will have to withdraw from their representation and they will need to seek other counsel. This is the sort of financial burden that is deemed unreasonable under Model Rule 6.2. See, e.g., People ex rel. Conn v. Randolph, 219 N.E.2d 337 (Ill. 1966), and Brown v. Board of County Comm., 451 P.2d 708 (Nev. 1969).

   - **Repugnance for client or cause that is sufficient to threaten competence:** Mere dislike of the client by the lawyer or preference by the lawyer for areas of practice different from those involved in the client's matter are insufficient reasons to decline the appointment. On rare occasion, however, a lawyer may find the client or the client's matter so repugnant as to threaten the lawyer's ability to provide competent service. When this circumstance occurs, a lawyer *is permitted to decline,* and indeed *must decline,* the appointment. Only when the repugnance is so great as to threaten competence *may* the lawyer decline; in such cases, the lawyer *must* decline because the representation would violate the ethics rule requiring competent service. See §B.1 MR 6.2(c).

   Example: Lawyer's father was a prisoner of war during the Vietnam War. As a result, Lawyer has a powerful and genuine, even if not wholly rational, hatred for the Vietnamese. Court asks Lawyer to represent Client, a Vietnamese immigrant charged with a crime. Lawyer believes that his feelings about his father's confinement will prevent him from serving Client's interests zealously. Lawyer must request the court's permission to decline the appointment.

    ii. Duties when appointed: A lawyer who is appointed to represent a client owes the client all of the duties that any lawyer owes to any client.

    iii. Requirement of acceptance: Although the U.S. Supreme Court has held that the federal appointment statute, 28 U.S.C. §1915(d), merely authorizes federal courts to request, rather than command, that a lawyer accept an appointment (Mallard v. U.S. District Court, 490 U.S. 296 (1989)), some states have taken the position that the admission to practice in their states implies an agreement by each lawyer to accept court appointments. See, e.g., In re Amendments to the Rules Regulating the Florida Bar—1.3(a) and the Rules of Judicial Administration 2.065 (Legal Aid), 573 So. 2d 800 (Fla. 1990).

B. Duty to reject representation

Unlike the general rule that a lawyer has no duty to accept every client's matter, lawyers are prohibited from accepting (that is, lawyers must reject) representation in several different situations. MR 1.16(a). See also §VI.B.

1. Representation will violate the ethics rules: When accepting representation will violate an ethics rule, the lawyer has a duty to reject the representation.

Example: Lawyer represents Landlord-Client in a variety of matters regarding Landlord-Client's rental properties. Recently, Lawyer has drafted a form lease for Landlord-Client. Tenant-Client approaches Lawyer and requests that Lawyer represent Tenant-Client in a dispute over the interpretation of the lease that Lawyer has recently drafted for Landlord-Client. Because such representation would violate conflicts-of-interest rules, such as Model Rule 1.9(a), Lawyer has a duty to decline to represent Tenant-Client.

    a. Frivolous claims: In particular, a lawyer has a duty to decline representation when the client's claim or legal position is frivolous under Model Rule 3.1.

    b. Harassment: When the client's purpose is merely to harass someone, the lawyer must decline to represent the client. MR 3.1.

    c. Competence: When the lawyer would lack competence to represent the client, the lawyer must decline the representation. MR 1.1.

2. Representation will violate other law: When accepting representation will violate law other than an ethics rule, the lawyer has a duty to reject the representation. MR 1.16(a)(l).

Example: Client approaches Lawyer to request that Lawyer represent Client in a real estate transfer. Client asks Lawyer to do the deed work for Client's purchase of a house that Lawyer knows is to be used for Client's illegal gambling operation. Because Lawyer's representation of Client would violate the criminal aiding and abetting statute, Lawyer has a duty to decline to represent Client.

3. Lawyer's physical or mental health: When a lawyer's health will prevent the lawyer from delivering competent service to the client, the lawyer has a duty to decline the representation. MR 1.16(a)(2).

Example: Client requests that Lawyer represent him in an auto accident matter. The statute of limitations expires on Client's claim in four weeks. Lawyer has scheduled herself to enter an alcohol rehabilitation program for the next four weeks. Lawyer has a duty to decline to represent Client.

C. Lawyer-client contracts and the beginning of the lawyer-client relationship

The lawyer-client relationship is governed in the first instance by the particular contract entered into by the lawyer and client and by general contract principles. Irrespective of contract obligations, that lawyer-client contract is modified by the various duties that lawyers owe clients. These duties, such as the duty to safeguard client property and the duties of confidentiality and loyalty, are imposed by the ethics rules or by general fiduciary duty law and general agency law without regard to what the particular lawyer-client contract might say. See §§II and III; Chapters 4 and 5.

1. **When begun:** The lawyer-client relationship formally begins when a client reasonably believes that the lawyer has undertaken to provide the client with legal service. The relationship does not depend for its onset on the existence of a written contract or a fee payment.

   Example: Client consulted Lawyer about a possible medical malpractice claim. After questioning Client for 45 minutes, Lawyer advised Client that he did not believe that she had a viable claim, but that he would consult with his partner on the issue. He did not discuss any fee arrangement with Client, request medical authorizations, or advise her to see another attorney more experienced in the medical malpractice field. When Client did not hear from Lawyer for a few days, she assumed that Lawyer and his partner had concluded that she did not have a valid claim. Lawyer never billed Client for the initial interview. After the statute of limitations on any medical malpractice claim had run, Client learned that she had a valid claim. She then sued Lawyer for legal malpractice. Lawyer and Client had an attorney-client relationship under both tort and contract principles. Negligence concepts established such a relationship because Client sought and received legal advice under circumstances that made it reasonably foreseeable to Lawyer that negligent advice could cause injury to her. In contractual terms, Lawyer rendered legal advice pursuant to Client's request and Client relied on that advice. Togstad v. Vesely, Otto, Miller & Keefe, 291 N.W.2d 686 (Minn. 1980).

2. **Wrongful discharge:** In general, a lawyer has no protected expectation of continuing employment with a particular client. A client may discharge a lawyer without cause. Therefore, in general, lawyers do not have claims for *wrongful discharge* against clients. However, more and more lawyers are employees of corporations and other organizations, and more lawyers experience their work in a law firm in an employer-employee relationship. The authority is mixed on the question of whether a lawyer may have a claim for wrongful discharge against such an employer.

   Example: Corporate Client distributed medical equipment subject to Food and Drug Administration (FDA) regulation. Lawyer, employed as Client's "General Counsel," advised Client to reject a shipment that did not comply with FDA regulations. When Client insisted on accepting the shipment, Lawyer advised that he would do anything necessary to stop any sale of the defective equipment. Client then discharged Lawyer. Lawyer sought recovery against Client under a retaliatory, wrongful discharge theory.

   Lawyer does not have a cause of action against Client for wrongful discharge because the Rules of Professional Conduct requiring an attorney to report client misconduct that would result in death or serious bodily injury adequately protect the public policy otherwise safeguarded by a wrongful discharge claim. Further, the possibility of a wrongful discharge cause of action would cause employers to be less forthright and candid with their in-house counsel. In any case, an attorney has a duty to withdraw if further representation of a client would result in ethics violations, and the client should not have to bear the attorney's costs of abiding by that rationale. Balla v. Gambro, Inc., 584 N.E.2d 104 (Ill. 1991). But see Mourad v. Automobile Club Ins. Assoc., 465 N.W.2d 395 (Mich. 1991) (recognizing lawyer's claim of wrongful demotion and constructive discharge); Crews v. Buckman Laboratories, 78 S.W.Sd 852 (Tenn. 2002) (rejecting *Balla* reasoning).

Example: Lawyer was employed by Law Firm. Lawyer threatened to report the serious, disciplinable misconduct of other members of Law Firm to the state bar disciplinary authority. Law Firm discharged Lawyer. Because the ethics rules require a lawyer to report the serious, disciplinable misconduct of other lawyers to the state bar (see MR 8.3), the expectation of such reporting is an implied term in every lawyer's contract of employment with a law firm. Lawyer has a contract-based wrongful discharge claim against Law Firm. Wieder v. Skala, 609 N.E.2d 105 (N.Y. 1992).

II. FEES

Although the regulation of lawyers' fees is relatively light and rarely enforced, it does exist. MR 1.5. Fees are regulated for their amount and their nature.

A. Reasonableness standard

A lawyer's fee must be reasonable. MR 1.5. Under the Model Code, the fee regulation required that a lawyer's fee not be "clearly excessive." DR 2-106(A). Under the 1908 ABA Canons, which preceded the Model Code, a fee was subject to discipline only if it was "so exorbitant and wholly disproportionate to the services performed as to shock the conscience of those to whose attention it was called." Goldstone v. State Bar, 6 P.2d 513, 516 (Cal. 1931).

Example: Client retained Lawyer to represent him against a battery charge. Lawyer demanded a $5,000 fee, and Client paid him. Lawyer sent another attorney to appear at Client's court date. At that time, the complainant dropped all charges, but Lawyer refused to refund any part of his fee. Lawyer charged a clearly excessive fee in violation of DR 2-106. In re Kutner, 399 N.E.2d 963 (Ill. 1979).

1. **Factors:** A range of factors may be considered in setting a reasonable fee. MR 1.5(a).

    a. **Time:** The time and labor involved in the representation may be considered. MR 1.5(a)(l).

    b. **Novelty:** The commonness or, by contrast, the novelty of the legal work involved in the representation may be considered. MR 1.5(a)(l).

    c. **Skill:** The amount of skill required of the lawyer to perform the representation successfully may be considered. MR 1.5(a)(l).

    d. **Preclusion of other employment:** Some representation may preclude other employment for the lawyer, either because of the time and energy needed to represent the client, or because of conflicts that will arise that will prevent the lawyer from engaging in representation of other clients. If the client is aware of these limitations, then they may be considered. MR 1.5(a)(2).

e. **"Going rate":** The fee charged by other lawyers in the community for similar services may be considered. MR 1.5(a)(3). Note, however, that this factor is not an authorization to follow what amounts to an informal minimum fee schedule. See §F below.

f. **The amount involved and the results obtained:** The magnitude of the client's economic or other interests that are involved in the representation and the results obtained by the lawyer may be considered. MR 1.5(a)(4). These factors are chief in what is called "value billing." In value billing, the fee is a function of the value that the lawyer's services have brought the client.

g. **Time exigencies:** Time restrictions that either the client or the circumstances impose on the lawyer may be considered. MR 1.5(a)(5).

h. **The professional relationship with the client:** The way in which the particular lawyer-client relationship has developed may be considered. MR 1.5(a)(6).

i. **Lawyer quality:** The experience, ability, and reputation of the particular lawyer may be considered. MR 1.5(a)(7). The rule permits a seasoned, well-known lawyer to charge more for the same service than a lawyer fresh out of law school.

j. **The nature of the fee arrangement:** Whether the fee is fixed, hourly, contingent, prepaid with a retainer, and so on may be considered in determining whether the amount of a particular fee is reasonable. MR 1.5(a)(8).

B. Writing and timing

In general, a written contract setting the fee is preferred but not required. But see §C.3 regarding contingent fees. The terms of the agreement including the fee should be made known to the client before or soon after representation begins.

C. Contingent fees

With a few exceptions and restrictions, a lawyer is permitted to charge a fee that is contingent on the outcome of the matter. For example, a lawyer may charge a fee that is equal to 40% of the recovery on the client's claim that results from a trial verdict. The fee is contingent on the amount of the recovery. ***Contingent fee*** arrangements have traditionally been thought of as a way for a client with a meritorious claim but little money with which to pay an hourly or up-front fee to get the claim handled by a lawyer.

1. **Historical disapproval:** The organized bar has a history of suspicion and disapproval of contingent fees. Contingent fees are thought to stir up litigation that would otherwise not be pursued in the same ways as champerty, barratry, and maintenance do. See Chapter 6, §IV.B.3 and Chapter 10, §VIII. Of course, if that litigation is meritorious, the fact that contingent fee arrangements make it possible for it to be pursued ought to be regarded as a positive rather than negative effect. When, in the early twentieth century, the bar expressed its deep suspicion of contingent fees, it must be remembered that the organized bar was made up nearly exclusively of corporate practitioners whose clients were being named defendant in lawsuits brought by injured plaintiffs. The injured plaintiffs were represented on a contingent fee basis by sole practitioners.

2. **Prohibited case types:** Generally, cases that produce a *res,* a pool of recovery money from which the contingent fee may be paid, are appropriate for contingent fees. There are two exceptions.

   a. **Domestic relations:** A lawyer is prohibited from charging a contingent fee in a domestic-relations case when the fee is to be contingent on obtaining a divorce or on the amount of property, child support, or alimony recovered. MR 1.5(d)(l). The intrusion of a lawyer whose fee depends on such matters into sensitive domestic-relations matters is thought to be too risky to the sensitive and important relationships between spouses and between parent and child.

   b. **Criminal matters:** A lawyer is prohibited from charging a contingent fee to a defendant in a criminal matter in part because no res is produced from which the fee may come and in part because of the special public interest involved in criminal matters. MR 1.5(d)(2).

3. **Other restrictions:** Because of the heightened dangers of client misunderstanding and of lawyer overreaching, additional restrictions apply to contingent fee arrangements. MR 1.5(c).

   a. **Writing and terms:** Although ordinarily a fee agreement need not be in writing, a contingent fee agreement must be in writing and be signed by the client. The written agreement must explain the way in which the fee will be calculated and, in particular, the way in which deductions for expenses will be calculated. MR 1.5(c).

   b. **Ending statement:** The lawyer must provide an ending statement in writing to the client explaining the outcome of the matter and providing the calculation of the fee and expenses. MR 1.5(c).

D. Fee splitting

Lawyers in the same firm routinely share fees with one another. That process is a central part of what it means to be a partner in a firm. However, when lawyers who are not members of a firm share fees, or when lawyers seek to share fees with nonlawyers, special problems arise.

1. **Among lawyers:** Fee splitting among lawyers not in the same firm has been a controversial topic in professional responsibility law. In particular, the "forwarding fee" has been thought to be offensive to lawyer ethics. A forwarding fee is a fee charged by a lawyer who does no more than send a prospective client to another lawyer who actually provides the legal service. The forwarding fee practice raises the specter of lawyers marketing to attract large numbers of clients that they have no intention of serving but for whom they merely act as a broker. By contrast, the lawyer who interviews a prospective client, realizes that the lawyer lacks the proper expertise for the client's problem, and sends the client to a lawyer who has that expertise has done the client and the profession a service of some consequence.

   Example: Client contacted Lawyer A regarding a possible medical malpractice action. Lawyer A suggested that Client contact Lawyer B, a medical malpractice specialist. Client retained Lawyer B to represent her. Lawyer B agreed to split his fee with Lawyer A. In return, Lawyer A agreed to maintain communication with client and perform any services requested by Lawyer B. After settling Client's case, Lawyer B refused to honor the referral fee agreement.

   The referral fee agreement between Lawyer A and Lawyer B is not contrary to public policy. Thus, Lawyer A is entitled to his share of the fees collected by Lawyer B. Moran v. Harris, 131 Cal. App. 3d 913 (Cal. Ct. App. 1982).

2. **The modern rule governing lawyer fee splitting:** Rather than prohibit all fee splitting among lawyers from different firms, the Model Rule drafters crafted a rule to regulate the practice. The fee splitting practice is permitted when the following conditions are met. MR 1.5(e).

   a. **Proportion to services or joint responsibility:** The fee splitting lawyers must either share the fee in proportion to the services rendered by each lawyer or the lawyers must assume joint responsibility for the representation. MR 1.5(e)(l).

   b. **Client agreement:** The client must agree to the fee splitting arrangement by all lawyers involved and the agreement must be confirmed in writing. MR 1.5(e)(2).

   c. **Total fee must be reasonable:** The total fee charged by all lawyers involved must continue to comply with the general standard of reasonableness of the fee. MR 1.5(e)(3).

3. **With former partners:** If a profit sharing, separation agreement, or retirement plan calls for it, fees may be shared with former partners and associates of the primary lawyer in the matter.

4. **With nonlawyers:** Fees may not be shared with nonlawyers except under the following, quite-limited circumstances. Fee sharing with nonlawyers is thought to compromise the lawyer's independence and to inject into the lawyer-client relationship the interests of someone who is not bound by the ethics code.

   a. **Lawyer's estate:** Fees may be paid into a lawyer's estate or as a death benefit pursuant to an agreement governing a firm's operation and organization.

   b. **Retirement plan:** Fees may be shared with nonlawyer law firm personnel through a retirement or compensation plan for those employees.

E. Court-awarded fees

Lawyers receive court awarded attorneys' fees pursuant to both court appointment to representation and various statutes that allow for collection of attorneys' fees.

F. Minimum fee schedules

At one time, the organized bar typically imposed ***minimum fee schedules*** on lawyers and their clients. In other words, lawyers were prohibited by the state bar from charging a fee for a particular service that was less than the one set by the bar's minimum fee schedule. Such schedules are unlawful and therefore no longer enforceable. Goldfarb v. Virginia State Bar, 421 U.S. 773 (1975).

Example: Plaintiffs needed title insurance and, thus, a title examination of their home. Only members of State Bar could lawfully perform such examinations because of the unauthorized practice of law statute. No lawyers would perform this service for less than the fee recommended in the Bar's minimum fee schedule. Plaintiffs then sued Bar, stating that promulgation and enforcement of the fee schedule constituted price-fixing in violation of the Sherman Act. The fact that the Bar is a state agency for some limited purposes does not create an antitrust shield that allows it to foster anticompetitive practices for the benefit of its members. Goldfarb v. Virginia State Bar, 421 U.S. 773 (1975).

G. Fee forfeiture

Modern fee-forfeiture statutes provide that lawyers' fees that are paid by clients from crime proceeds may be forfeited to the government. See, e.g., 21 U.S.C. §§848-853 and 12 U.S.C.

§§1961-1968. Such statutes were met by challenges, but they have been upheld. United States v. Monsanto, 491 U.S. 600 (1989); Caplin & Drysdale v. United States, 491 U.S. 617 (1989).

Example: Client was indicted on racketeering, firearms, and tax evasion charges. Relying on the Comprehensive Forfeiture Act of 1984, Court issued a pretrial restraining order to freeze assets allegedly accumulated by Client as a result of drug trafficking. Client moved to reverse Court's action, so that he could use the frozen assets to retain an attorney.

Neither the forfeiture provisions nor the pretrial restraining provisions of the Act exclude assets that an individual would otherwise use to pay an attorney. Further, the restraining order issued against Client does not violate the Fifth Amendment's Due Process Clause or the right to counsel guaranteed under the Sixth Amendment because it was based on a finding of probable cause to believe that Client's assets were forfeitable. United States v. Monsanto, 491 U.S. 600 (1989).

III. FIDUCIARY DUTIES

In addition to contractual duties and tort duties, lawyers owe their clients fiduciary duties.

A. General role of a fiduciary

A *fiduciary* is one in whom a special trust is placed. A fiduciary has special obligations to care for the interests of the beneficiary (the client in the lawyer-client context), even when those interests are not aligned with the fiduciary's own interests. A fiduciary owes to the beneficiary scrupulous good faith, candor, and care in the management of the beneficiary's interests.

B. Handling clients' money

Lawyer fiduciary duties, beyond the general care owed to client interests and confidences that the relationship implies, are usually thought of in terms of the lawyer's handling of clients' money and property.

1. **Violations a most serious matter:** Violations of the lawyer's duty to properly handle client property have been among the most frequent grounds for lawyer discipline for a combination of the following reasons.

    a. **Easy verification:** Most money-handling violations are easy to verify, unlike many others that involve murky fact issues. Bank account information most often reveals the violation in a way that is beyond question. In many other lawyer disciplinary matters, fact issues develop that require witness credibility evaluations and subjective intent determinations.

    b. **Significant opportunity for continuing abuse:** Lawyers who abuse clients' property are in a position to do serious damage to future clients. The form of discipline for property-handling violations has traditionally been disbarment.

    c. **Per se rules:** The rules governing property-handling are per se rules that require no intentional wrongdoing on the part of the lawyer. Simple commingling of funds, for example, subjects the lawyer to discipline without regard to whether a client was actually harmed.

    d. **Little or no countervailing interest:** Unlike many other violations that occur when a lawyer misbalances two or more competing duties, very little in the way of a countervailing duty exists to be balanced in money-handling violations. Being disciplined for breaching a confidence in the face of significant public interest in disclosure, being in an unacceptable multiple-client conflict despite client consent, or using prohibited forms of advertising in the face of the public's interest in being made aware of lawyer services all involve a difficult balancing of competing duties and interests. Abusing client property that the lawyer holds in trust involves no such complex balance.

2. **Client trust accounts:** Lawyers must maintain *client trust accounts* and safety-deposit boxes for the safekeeping of client property. MR 1.15(a). To clarify a few technical difficulties that lawyers have had with client trust accounts, a few modest changes were made to Model Rule 1.15 in the February 2002 amendments.

   First, a new subsection (b) was added to allow lawyers to put the lawyer's own funds in a trust account for the sole purpose of covering bank service charges.

   Second, a new subsection (c) was added to make clear that when a client pays fees or expenses in advance of the lawyer earning those fees or incurring those expenses, the lawyer must place those funds in a client account, withdrawing them as the fees are earned or the expenses incurred.

   Third, old subsection (c), now subsection (e), was amended to instruct lawyers in possession of disputed funds that they must distribute the portions of those funds about which there is no dispute.

   a. **Maintained in the state:** The trust accounts must be maintained in the state in which the lawyer is licensed to practice unless the client consents to another arrangement. MR 1.15(a).

      Example: Lawyer practices in State A but lives across the border in State B. For Lawyer's convenience, she establishes her client trust account in a bank in State B. Her clients are not informed of this arrangement, and therefore have not consented to it. Lawyer is subject to discipline.

   b. **Record keeping:** Records of deposits and withdrawals from client trust accounts must be kept for a period specified by the particular state's law, usually five years. MR 1.15(a).

   c. **Separate keeping:** Client property must be kept separate from the lawyer's own property. MR 1.15(a). See §3 below.

   d. **Interest:** Traditionally, trust accounts were maintained as non–interest-bearing accounts. Lawyers are not permitted to retain the interest on a trust account (it belongs to the client). Further, interest-bearing accounts were largely impractical because the interest calculations and record keeping were unreasonably onerous due to the frequent deposits and withdrawals, often of fairly small amounts of each client's funds. Depositing funds in non–interest-bearing accounts served neither lawyers, clients, nor the public interest, but rather, served only the interests of the banks in which client trust accounts were maintained. During the 1970s and 1980s, however, bar associations began to institute *IOLTA* (Interest on Lawyer Trust Accounts) programs to help finance legal services for the poor. Such programs collect the interest earned on interest-bearing client trust accounts, and the state distributes the funds in the form of public service–oriented grants. Such programs have been challenged as a taking of client funds with mixed results. Cone v. State Bar of Florida, 819 F.2d 1002 (11th Cir.), *cert. den.*, 484 U.S. 917 (1987) (upholding Florida's IOLTA program); Washington Legal Foundation v. Texas Equal Access to Justice Foundation, 270 F.3d 180 (5th Cir. 2001) (Texas IOLTA program violates Fifth Amendment); Washington Legal Foundation v. Legal Foundation of Washington, 271 F.3d 835 (9th Cir. 2001) (en banc) (Washington state IOLTA program does not produce a taking of property).

3. **Commingling funds:** A lawyer must keep client property separate from the lawyer's property. In the trust account context, this means that only client money must be in the trust account. The lawyer must maintain a separate office operating account. When a lawyer *commingles* his funds with a client's, the lawyer is subject to discipline. MR 1.15(a). The cases of disbarment for this violation are legion.

   a. **When more than one person claims an interest:** When the lawyer and another person, usually but not always a client, each claim an interest in a fund or other property, the lawyer must keep that property separate from the lawyer's property until a settlement of the claims can be achieved. MR 1.15(d).

   Example: Lawyer represents Client in a contingent fee matter. Opposing Party agrees to a settlement and forwards a check to Lawyer that represents the settlement proceeds. Client claims to be entitled to 70% of the amount of the check, and Lawyer claims that Client is entitled to 70% of the check minus the lawyer's litigation expenses. If Lawyer deposits the check in her own account, rather than in the client trust account, Lawyer is subject to discipline.

4. **Prompt delivery and accounting:** When a lawyer receives property of another, the lawyer must promptly deliver that property and provide an accounting upon request. MR 1.15(d). A client may agree that the lawyer will maintain such property for a longer time. MR 1.15(d).

5. **Conversion:** Lawyer use of client funds, whether temporary or permanent, whether done with or without a good faith intention to return the funds, and whether harm comes to the client or not, constitutes conversion and subjects the lawyer to discipline. MR 1.15.

   Example: The state Office on Attorney Ethics conducted a random compliance audit of Lawyer's trust account. The audit revealed the Lawyer had continually issued checks to his own order for fees in pending real estate matters. He had replaced these "advances" when he received the closing funds or when a closing fell through. Upon learning of the impending audit, Lawyer had used personal funds to cover withdrawn fees. Lawyer knew that his conduct violated ethics rules, but felt that it could not possibly hurt anyone.

   Knowing misappropriation consists simply of a lawyer's taking a client's money entrusted to him, knowing that it is the client's money, and that the client has not authorized the taking. Lawyer's conduct constituted knowing misappropriation. A subjective intent to borrow, rather than permanently convert, the absence of client losses and Lawyer's prior outstanding record were insufficient to excuse the violation. To protect the public confidence in the integrity of the legal profession, Lawyer was disbarred. In re Warhaftig, 524 A.2d 398 (N.J. 1987).

IV. COMPETENCE AND DILIGENCE

Competence and diligence are core lawyer duties. MR 1.1, 1.3. Together, they form the Model Rules' analog to the Model Code's duty to provide the client with zealous representation within the bounds of the law and its basic competence standard. See Canons 6, 7; DR 6-101, 7-101, 7-102.

   A. **Competence**

   Competence requires that the lawyer possess and exercise on the client's behalf "the legal knowledge, skill, thoroughness, and preparation reasonably necessary for the representation." MR 1.1.

1. **Distinct from malpractice:** Although the competence standard is similar to descriptions of the tort duty for malpractice purposes, they operate differently. Malpractice is meant to compensate those who have been harmed by the lawyer's breach of duty; the competence standard is meant, within the general framework of the ethics code, to ensure an acceptable level of performance by lawyers generally for the public's protection. As such, a single act that breaches the malpractice duty will give rise to a malpractice claim, but will not ordinarily make the lawyer subject to discipline on competence grounds.

   Example: Following an automobile accident, Lawyer represented Client against Defendant and Insurer. Lawyer obtained a settlement from Insurer, but failed to file suit against Defendant within the statute of limitations period. Lawyer then offered Client a sum representing his estimation of the value of Client's claim, minus fees and expenses. He did not alert Client of the possibility of a legal malpractice action or advise Client to seek other counsel. When Client later brought a malpractice action against Lawyer, Lawyer tried to safeguard his assets by conveying them without consideration. Lawyer then failed to cooperate with a state bar investigation of these matters.

   An attorney's honest mistake in handling a legal matter does not ordinarily afford a basis for disciplinary action, but Lawyer's egregious conduct violated DR 6-101, DR 6-102, and DR 1-102(A). Committee on Professional Ethics & Conduct of the Iowa State Bar Ass'n v. Nadler, 467 N.W.2d 250 (Iowa 1991).

2. **Does not require possession of expertise at the beginning of representation:** A lawyer is not required to know everything about the client's legal claim before undertaking representation. It is not a breach of the competence duty for a lawyer to undertake representation without such knowledge if the lawyer will be able to acquire the necessary knowledge with reasonable diligence.

   Example: Lawyer has concentrated his practice in the area of domestic relations. Lawyer seeks to expand his practice into estate planning. Client requests Lawyer to draft his will and to work out a plan for giving regular gifts to his children to avoid the later imposition of estate tax. Lawyer reasonably believes that he can acquire the knowledge necessary to competently perform the service for Client in a reasonable time. Lawyer is not subject to discipline, even though he has undertaken representation without the current possession of the requisite knowledge to perform the service.

3. **Basic, cross-cutting skills and knowledge are always required:** Virtually all practicing lawyers in all areas of expertise must have certain basic skills to be competent. These basic skills include an understanding of the use of precedent, legal research skills, an ability to identify and evaluate a client's problem, and writing or drafting skills. MR 1.1 Comment.

4. **Emergency:** In an emergency situation, a lawyer may provide limited assistance to a client in a matter on which the lawyer would ordinarily require further study or research before service was rendered. However, the lawyer must limit this service to that which is necessary under the circumstances. MR 1.1 Comment.

5. **Continuing competence:** Lawyers must maintain competence throughout their careers. Most states have imposed continuing legal education requirements that are tied to the lawyer's permission to continue to practice in the state.

B. Diligence

Diligence is the timeliness aspect of competence. Lawyers are obligated to be diligent on their clients' behalf. Perhaps the most commonly filed complaint of lawyer conduct is that of delay and neglect. Diligence requires a persistent pursuit of the client's matter. MR 1.3.

1. **Expediting matters:** The duty of diligence is related to the lawyer's duty to expedite matters consistent with client interests. MR 3.2.

2. **Starting and stopping:** The most common pattern in a diligence duty violation involves a lawyer who begins work on a client's matter, perhaps even by filing a civil complaint, but then does little or nothing to pursue the matter to a conclusion. See, e.g., In re Hebenstreit, 764 P.2d 51 (Colo. 1988); In re Dodd, 560 N.E.2d 490 (Ind. 1990).

3. **Misleading about diligence:** Most of the cases that have produced lawyer discipline for diligence failures have also involved a lawyer who then misleads the client about the progress being made. This misleading is not actually a part of the diligence violation. Rather, the misleading is its own separate ground for discipline that merely happens to frequently coincide with a case of diligence failure.

    Example: Lawyer undertakes to represent Client in a civil matter but initially does nothing. Client calls Lawyer once per week for three months, inquiring about the status of the matter. By the time of the tenth telephone call, Lawyer tells Client that the claim has been filed; in fact, the claim has *not* been filed. Lawyer is subject to discipline for lack of diligence in pursuing the matter because he has not yet filed the complaint. Lawyer is also subject to discipline for lying to the client.

4. **Inadequate excuses:** Several excuses have been offered for lack of diligence and rejected by the courts.

    a. **Illness without remedial measures:** A lawyer who has health problems that are preventing pursuit of client matters must take action to remedy the situation, such as associating with other counsel or communicating optional courses of action to the client. Absent remedial action, illness does not excuse unreasonable delay.

    b. **Lawyer's personal feeling:** A lawyer's personal animosity for the client or the client's cause does not excuse a lack of diligence. Once the lawyer has undertaken representation, the lawyer must pursue it despite her personal feelings about the matter.

    c. **"My paralegal did it":** Blaming the delays on the lawyer's employees is inadequate to excuse the lack of diligence. The lawyer, not the lawyer's employees, bears the professional responsibility for pursuing the representation.

    d. **Overwork and other responsibilities:** Lawyers need to evaluate their workload when they accept representation responsibilities. A lawyer having too much work may not neglect any particular client's matter.

V. COMMUNICATION AND SHARED DECISION-MAKING

Lawyers owe clients a duty to communicate with clients and to meaningfully share decision-making responsibilities with them. MR 1.2, 1.4. These two duties work together, neither one being particularly meaningful without the other.

A. Communication

The communication duty is critical to maintaining a quality lawyer-client relationship. It is related to the duties regarding shared decision-making, competence, and diligence and forms the underpinning of every duty that requires client consent and consultation. MR 1.4.

1. **Keeping client reasonably informed:** A lawyer must keep a client informed of the status of the client's matter and must respond to a client's reasonable requests for information. MR 1.4(a).

2. **Explaining matters to the client:** For the client to be an effective partner of the lawyer in the decision-making process and for the client to intelligently manage his own affairs, the lawyer must explain matters to the client sufficiently to allow the client to function and make informed decisions. MR 1.4(b).

B. Shared decision-making

Lawyers and clients must share decision-making responsibility. The law governing such sharing is established generally by agency law. As the client's agent, the lawyer must abide by the client's choices with various exceptions and within various constraints. Further, the lawyer lacks authority to make and implement certain decisions on the client's behalf.

1. **Scope of representation:** Because the scope of their relationship is generally set by contract, lawyers and their clients may negotiate and settle on the lawyer's *scope of representation.*

    a. **Duration of representation:** Lawyer and client can negotiate over the lengths to which the lawyer is committed to proceed in the matter. The lawyer and client may, for example, agree that the lawyer will undertake representation short of litigation or through the first appeal.

    b. **Subject matter:** The lawyer and client may negotiate the breadth of the lawyer's service. They may agree, for example, that the lawyer will be responsible for legal matters relating to the client's sale of his ongoing business, but not the tax aspects of the transaction.

2. **Means and ends:** As a general proposition, clients set the goals or ends of the representation, whereas lawyers are generally empowered to determine the best means to use to achieve those ends. MR 1.2(a) Comment.

    a. **In general:** As a general rule, this division of decision-making responsibility serves well because it matches the relative strengths of the lawyer and client and the client's more direct relative interest in the matter. Lawyers are trained to determine and execute the means; clients have the greater interest and stake in the goals of the representation and, therefore, ought to retain decision-making authority in such matters.

        Example: Court appointed Lawyer to represent Defendant in his appeal of a robbery conviction. Defendant sent Lawyer both a letter listing several points that he wanted to raise on appeal and a pro se brief. Lawyer rejected most of Defendant's suggestions because they had no basis in the evidence on record, but he wrote to Defendant with several other potential claims of error and an invitation for Defendant's thoughts on those arguments. Lawyer then submitted both his own brief, focusing on the claims of error that he had written about in his letter to Defendant, and Defendant's pro se brief. At oral argument, however, Lawyer raised only the points presented in his own brief. The appellate court affirmed Defendant's conviction. Defendant filed a pro se petition for a writ of habeas corpus, claiming ineffective assistance of appellate counsel.

Defendant had no constitutional right to compel Lawyer to press even nonfrivolous points if Lawyer, as a matter of professional judgment, decided not to present those points. Although the accused has the ultimate authority to make certain fundamental decisions regarding the case, strategic and tactical decisions are the exclusive province of the defense counsel after consultation with the client. Jones v. Barnes, 463 U.S. 745 (1983).

b. Particular decisions: The law is fairly clear regarding who has the decision-making authority on certain matters.

i. Settlement: Clients and not lawyers have authority to settle matters. A lawyer is obliged to communicate to the client all bona-fide offers of settlement from an opposing party, and the ultimate decision about whether or not to accept an offer of settlement is the client's. Further, a lawyer is subject to discipline if the lawyer purports to settle a matter with an opposing party without the client's consent and authorization.

Example: Lawyer represents Client in a domestic-relations matter. Opposing counsel communicates an offer of settlement from her client to Lawyer. Lawyer responds by saying that "the offer is ridiculous," and does not report the offer to Client. Lawyer is subject to discipline.

Nonetheless, when a lawyer acts with ***apparent authority,*** an opposing party is entitled to rely on the lawyer's settlement agreements and may enforce an agreement that results.

Example: Plaintiff and Defendant were engaged in a patent dispute. Plaintiff worked with Defendant's Lawyer in an effort to settle the matter. After receiving copies of a draft agreement from Plaintiff, Defendant's Lawyer informed the court that the parties would soon settle the case and advised the judge to cancel the pending trial date. Defendant's Lawyer sent Plaintiff a copy of his letter to the court, never indicating that he had overstated the parties' proximity to settlement. Indeed, when a codefendant later pulled out of the proposed agreement, Defendant's Lawyer assured Plaintiff that the deal "agreed on" could proceed as soon as the codefendant's name was deleted from the settlement documents. Both Defendant's Lawyer and Plaintiff signed the final agreement, and Defendant's Lawyer indicated to Plaintiff that Defendant had finalized the agreement. When Defendant's new management later refused to proceed with the settlement, Plaintiff sued for enforcement.

Plaintiff was entitled to rely on Defendant's Lawyer's apparent authority to settle the case as long as Plaintiff had no reason to believe that Defendant's Lawyer was exceeding that authority. Plaintiff had no reason to think that Defendant's Lawyer was exceeding his authority because Defendant's Lawyer had full authority to negotiate and consummate a settlement. International Telemeter Corp. v. Teleprompter Corp., 592 F.2d 49 (2d Cir. 1979).

ii. Entry of plea: A decision to enter a particular plea in a criminal case is a decision that is exclusively within the client's province to make.

iii. Jury trial: Although most procedural aspects of litigation are the lawyer's decisions, waiving the right to a jury trial or other fundamental rights is a matter to be decided by the client.

iv. Client testimony: The decision whether the client will or will not testify in a criminal case is a matter to be decided by the client.

v. Procedural aspects of litigation: Taking advantage of the lawyer's education, training, and experience, decisions about procedural matters in litigation are questions that lawyers have authority to make. For example, lawyers make decisions regarding the manner and scope of cross-examination of a particular witness, the calling of particular witnesses, the strategy of choosing a theory of the case, and so on.

Example: During trial, Client instructs Lawyer to cross-examine Witness regarding her long-time dislike of Client. Lawyer realizes that this is excellent impeachment material, but also realizes that it may open up the reasons why Witness has long disliked Client, namely that Client has repeatedly driven his four-wheel-drive pickup truck across Witness's farm property, damaging her crops on the way to stealing her chickens. Lawyer makes a judgment and, against Client's wishes, excuses Witness without going into the line of questioning suggested by the Client. Lawyer is not subject to discipline. Such decisions are Lawyer's to make.

3. Lawyer independence from client views: A lawyer's representation of a client does not implicate the lawyer's sharing of or responsibility for the client's cause or views regarding matters relevant to the representation. Lawyers operate under the principle that they are independent of their clients' politics or moral views. MR 1.2(b).

4. Counseling crimes or frauds: As an underpinning to the scope of decision-making between lawyer and client, lawyers are prohibited from counseling or assisting their clients in the commission of crimes or frauds. MR 1.2(d).

a. In general: When a lawyer does so advise or assist, the lawyer is not only subject to discipline, but is liable criminally or civilly as the case may be.

b. Exceptions: This prohibition does not prevent a lawyer from either discussing proposed courses of action with a client or assisting a client in the pursuit of a test case.

i. Test cases: Clients may at times wish to test the application of current law. When they do so in good faith, a lawyer is permitted to assist. Indeed, without the assistance of lawyers in such cases, little would change in the law.

Example: Client rents his home in state X. Client wants to be a zoning commissioner, but state X has a statute that prohibits the application for zoning commissioner of anyone, like Client, who does not own real estate in the state. Client believes that this statute is unconstitutional and wishes to challenge it. Client consults Lawyer, who advises Client to go to the application office and submit an application, even though that conduct violates the statute. Lawyer agrees that if Client's application is denied based on the statute, then Lawyer will represent Client in his challenge of the statute. Lawyer is permitted to give this advice and assistance.

ii. Discussion of proposed conduct: Model Rule 1.2(d)'s prohibition is not intended to prevent a lawyer from discussing various proposed courses of action with a client. If a client proposes a course of action, the lawyer is permitted to investigate the lawfulness of the client's proposal and advise the client of the results of the lawyer's research and analysis. To require otherwise would prohibit the lawyer from engaging in the process of counseling a client against engaging in unlawful conduct.

5. **The client under a disability:** When a lawyer represents a client whose capacity to make decisions regarding the representation is diminished, the lawyer must attempt to maintain an ordinary lawyer-client relationship to the extent possible. MR 1.14(a).

   a. **Source of impairment:** Such an impairment may derive from minority or mental disability. MR 1.14(a).

   b. **Seeking protective action:** A lawyer should seek to have a guardian appointed to represent the interests of the client when the lawyer reasonably believes that the client cannot act in his own interest. MR 1.14(b).

   c. **Confidentiality:** In seeking protective action for a client, a lawyer may reveal confidential information to the extent reasonably necessary to protect the client's interests.

VI. TERMINATING REPRESENTATION

The formal lawyer-client relationship ends when representation terminates. Despite termination, many lawyer duties to clients continue, such as confidentiality and a limited conflict-avoidance duty. *Withdrawal* from representation is a critically important device for the lawyer who is faced with the prospect that continued representation of the client will result in a violation of the ethics code or other law.

A. Rejection of representation

In a way, rejection of representation is a form of termination of representation. Some duties are owed to prospective clients, and rejection of their representation affects their status as prospective clients. See §I.A.

B. Mandatory withdrawal

Under some circumstances, lawyers are required to withdraw from representation, thereby terminating the lawyer-client relationship. Failure to withdraw under these circumstances subjects the lawyer to discipline. MR 1.16(a).

1. **Continued representation will violate the ethics rules:** When continuing the representation will violate an ethics rule, the lawyer has a duty to withdraw. MR 1.16(a)(l).

   Example: Lawyer agrees to represent Driver and Passenger as coplaintiffs in a personal injury action. As the representation proceeds, Lawyer realizes that Passenger has a good claim against Driver and that Passenger would be ill-served by foregoing this claim. Lawyer's continued representation of either Driver or Passenger would violate conflicts-of-interest and confidentiality rules. Providing full representation for Passenger would compromise Driver; using confidences of Passenger or Driver in the continued representation of either against the other would violate confidentiality rules. Lawyer must withdraw from representation of both Passenger and Driver.

2. **Continued representation will violate other law:** When continuing representation will violate law other than an ethics rule, the lawyer has a duty to withdraw. MR 1.16(a)(l).

   Example: Client approaches Lawyer to request that Lawyer represent Client in a real-estate transfer. Lawyer agrees. Lawyer comes to realize during the representation that the Client is using Lawyer's services to further Client's illegal gambling operation. Because Lawyer's continued representation of Client would violate the criminal aiding and abetting statute, Lawyer has a duty to withdraw from representing Client.

3. **Lawyer's physical or mental health:** When a lawyer's health will prevent the lawyer from delivering competent service to the client, the lawyer has a duty to withdraw from the representation. MR 1.16(a)(2).

4. **Lawyer is discharged:** A client has an absolute right to discharge a lawyer. When the client discharges a lawyer, the lawyer must withdraw from the representation. MR 1.16(a)(3).

   Example: Lawyer represents Plaintiff-Client in a personal injury matter. Without cause, Client discharges Lawyer. Believing that she is acting in Client's best interests and wanting to prove her value to Client, Lawyer engages in settlement negotiations with Defendant's Lawyer, purporting to act on Client's behalf. Lawyer is subject to discipline for failing to promptly withdraw upon discharge by Client.

C. **Permissive withdrawal**

In some instances lawyers are permitted, but not required, to withdraw. The practical effect of this rule is to allow lawyers to withdraw from representation in the enumerated circumstances without breaching a duty of continued representation to the client. MR 1.16(b)(l).

1. **No harm to client:** Without regard to any cause for withdrawal, a lawyer may withdraw if it can be done without material adverse effect to the client. MR 1.16(b)(l).

   Example: Client retains Lawyer to pursue a personal injury action. The statute of limitations does not expire on Client's claim for another three years. After agreeing to represent Client, Lawyer decides to turn his practice away from personal injury representation and toward criminal practice. Lawyer's withdrawal will have no material adverse effect on Client: Client has sufficient time to retain new counsel and pursue his claim. Lawyer may withdraw.

2. **Causes that will excuse some material harm to the client:** Even if some harm may come to the client from the withdrawal, a lawyer may withdraw when any of the following causes exist.

   a. **Lawyer's reasonable belief that client is acting criminally or fraudulently:** A lawyer is *required* to withdraw when the lawyer *knows* that the client is using the lawyer's services to perpetrate crimes or frauds. MR 1.16(a)(2). See §B.2. When there is somewhat less certainty that the lawyer's services will result in crimes or frauds, but the lawyer nonetheless *reasonably believes* that the client is engaging in conduct that is criminal or fraudulent, the lawyer *may* withdraw. MR 1.16(b)(2).

   b. **Past use of service for crime or fraud:** When the lawyer learns that past services of the lawyer have been used by the client to perpetrate a crime or fraud, the lawyer may withdraw even if it does not appear that the lawyer's current services for the client are being so used. MR 1.16(b)(3). This rule permits a lawyer to withdraw from a client's representation and distance herself from the client's crimes or frauds at the earliest possible opportunity to do so.

   Example: Lawyer first represented Client in Client's efforts to obtain loans from Bank, and now represents Client in Client's efforts to merge her corporation with another. Lawyer learns that in the loan representation, Client used Lawyer's services to perpetrate frauds on Bank. Lawyer has no particular indication that Client is currently using Lawyer's services to perpetrate frauds. Lawyer may withdraw from the current representation.

c. **Client actions that are repugnant or imprudent:** When, after the lawyer has advised to the contrary, a client intends to continue with a course of conduct that the lawyer finds repugnant or with which the lawyer fundamentally disagrees, even though lawful, the lawyer may withdraw. MR 1.16(b)(4).

Example: Lawyer represents Insurance Company. Impecunious Plaintiff has filed a claim for benefits that is meritorious, except for the fact that it was filed one day beyond the required filing period. Lawyer advises Insurance Company to pay the claim despite its lawful authority to refuse to do so. Despite Lawyer's advice, Insurance Company determines to deny the claim. If Lawyer finds Insurance Company's action to be morally repugnant, Lawyer may withdraw.

d. **Client failure to meet obligations:** When a client has failed to meet the client's obligations, most often to pay the lawyer's reasonable fee, the lawyer must first warn the client that the lawyer intends to withdraw if the client does not meet his obligations. If the client persists in failing to meet obligations after the warning, the lawyer may withdraw. MR 1.16(b)(5).

e. **Unreasonable financial burden:** If the representation will result in unreasonable financial burden to the lawyer, the lawyer may withdraw. This financial burden is not a mere loss, but is on the same order as the sort of financial burden that would permit a lawyer to decline a court appointment. MR 1.16(b)(6). See §I.A.2.b.i.

Example: Client retained Firm to represent her in a divorce action against Husband. Client paid a retainer fee and a nominal amount for initial costs, and acknowledged her responsibility for future fees and expenses. Firm then worked extensively on client's complicated case, making court appearances on her behalf and logging more than 110 hours in office time. Client then lost her job, began receiving welfare payments, and had insufficient funds with which to pay Firm. Firm moved to withdraw from further representation of Client.

When Firm accepted Client's retainer, it impliedly agreed to prosecute her case to a conclusion. Firm did not have cause to abandon that agreement. Its duty to Client did not evaporate because the agreement was not as profitable as first imagined. Firm's motion to withdraw was denied. Kriegsman v. Kriegsman, 375 A.2d 1253 (N.J. Sup. Ct. App. Div. 1977).

f. **Client unreasonably difficult to work with:** If a client has made the representation unreasonably difficult for the lawyer, the lawyer may withdraw. MR 1.16(b)(6).

Example: Lawyer represents Client. Client has failed to appear for three appointments with Lawyer. Client has insisted on the pursuit of inconsistent courses of action. Client has rejected reasonably favorable offers of settlement from Opposing Party. Lawyer may withdraw because Client has made the representation unreasonably difficult.

g. **Other good cause:** If good cause exists of a kind not enumerated by the rule, the lawyer may withdraw. MR 1.16(b)(7).

D. Court order to continue

Even when a lawyer has good cause to withdraw, a court may order the lawyer to continue the representation. MR 1.16(c). When ordered to do so, a lawyer must continue the representation.

Such an order will often come during or on the eve of trial, and be issued by a judge who is trying to thwart a client's attempt to delay the proceedings by switching lawyers at the eleventh hour.

E. Procedural requirements for withdrawal

Without regard to what cause a lawyer has for the withdrawal, certain procedural requirements must be met.

1. **Notice:** Clients must be given reasonable notice before the withdrawal is affected. Clients need a reasonable opportunity to obtain new counsel when their lawyers are about to withdraw. MR 1.16(d).

2. **Court approval:** When litigation is pending, a lawyer must obtain the court's permission to withdraw from representation. MR 1.16(c).

F. Duties upon termination of the lawyer-client relationship

In addition to the duties that continue beyond the end of the lawyer-client relationship, such as confidentiality and conflict avoidance, lawyers owe clients certain specific duties that arise upon termination of representation. In general, a lawyer is obliged to take reasonable measures to minimize the harm to the client upon termination of representation. MR 1.16(d).

1. **Fee refund:** Any fees that have been paid to the lawyer but not yet earned must be refunded to the client upon withdrawal.

    Example: Lawyer undertakes representation for Client. Client advances $10,000 to Lawyer, out of which Lawyer's hourly charges are to be deducted. After earning $3,000 of the fee, Lawyer withdraws from representation for good cause. Lawyer must refund the remaining $7,000 to Client.

2. **Client's papers and property:** Papers and property of the client that are in the lawyer's possession must be promptly returned upon withdrawal. The lawyer may desire to retain the client's materials in an effort to persuade the client to pay any remaining fee that is owed the lawyer. A lawyer may not do so, however, unless the law of the lawyer's jurisdiction gives the lawyer a lien that may be secured by such materials.

G. Fee liability upon termination

Although a client may discharge a lawyer without cause, the client will continue to have an obligation to pay fees to the lawyer that have already been earned. MR 1.16(d).

1. **Fixed or hourly fees:** When a fee is a fixed amount for a particular service or is based on hours of service, the fee upon discharge will be calculated as the value of the services rendered. Such a recovery theory is called *quantum meruit.* An hourly fee is simply calculated as the value of the service already performed. A fixed-fee service requires a determination of the reasonable value of the service rendered toward the client's goal.

2. **Contingent fee:** Contingent-fee arrangements have presented a challenge to courts trying to determine the measure of compensation owed the discharged lawyer. Some courts have ruled that a contingent-fee lawyer who is discharged without cause is entitled to no fee, because that lawyer did not produce the contingency that would trigger the fee, and because another rule would be too great a discouragement to clients who wish to change lawyers. Others have ruled that a contingent-fee lawyer who is discharged without cause is entitled to the full benefit of the contingency if, indeed, the client eventually recovers in the matter. The lawyer in such a

case has undertaken the matter at some risk, and the lawyer has been discharged without cause. This result means that the client will have to pay double the contingent fee, one share to each of the two lawyers who worked on the matter. Still others have ruled that the discharged contingent-fee lawyer is entitled to the reasonable value of the services actually rendered (a quantum meruit theory), limited by the amount that the lawyer would have earned had the contingency occurred and the lawyer had recovered the agreed-on percentage.

Example: Client hired Lawyer to perform legal services for a $10,000 fixed fee, plus a contingent fee of 50% of any amounts recovered in excess of $600,000. Client discharged Lawyer before the resolution of the legal controversy and subsequently settled the matter for a net recovery of $500,000. Lawyer sued Client for fees based on the quantum meruit value of his services.

Lawyer's cause of action arose only on successful occurrence of the contingency. He is entitled to the reasonable value of his services on the basis of quantum meruit, but recovery is limited to the maximum fee set in the contract for those services. Clients must have the freedom to substitute attorneys without economic penalty because that freedom fosters public confidence in the legal profession. Rosenberg v. Levin, 409 So. 2d 1016 (Fla. 1982).

Quiz Yourself on
FORMAL ASPECTS OF THE LAWYER-CLIENT RELATIONSHIP

28. Rachel is on retainer to Bob. Bob comes to Rachel and asks her to represent him in a personal injury claim. After investigating, Rachel comes to believe that the potential claim is frivolous. Bob demands that the claim be filed. Is Rachel required to represent Bob because of the retainer agreement she signed agreeing to represent Bob in all of his legal affairs? _____

29. Jack's client, Sally, does not have enough money to pay Jack for representing her in her divorce. Sally suggests a fee arrangement whereby she will pay Jack an agreed-on percentage of any alimony she is awarded. Jack feels that this is a fair arrangement. Will Jack be subject to discipline if he enters into this agreement with Sally? _____

30. Jill comes to Jack, an attorney, with a legal problem in an area he has never worked on. It is not a complex problem, and Jack is aware of several sources where he can find the information he needs to represent Jill. Provided he charges Jill a reasonable rate for the time it takes him to become familiar with the law governing Jill's problem, will Jack's acceptance of this case subject him to discipline? _____

31. Larry is representing Janet in a personal injury case on a contingent-fee basis. Larry has had a number of cases against the opposing counsel in Janet's case, and he knows that they often offer settlements that turn out to be thousands of dollars lower than Janet could get if the case goes to trial. The opposing counsel makes a settlement offer. Larry knows that it would be in Janet's best interest to reject the offer. However, he knows that if Janet heard the offer, she would be so impressed by the amount she would probably want to accept it. Larry decides to reject the offer without telling Janet, and eventually he wins a much larger verdict after a trial. Will any of Larry's actions subject him to discipline? _____

32. Sam has received a court appointment to represent Joe, who has been charged with assault. Sam does not want to take the case because the amount he will be paid by the court is substantially less than the rate he normally bills, and he is trying to save money to take a vacation at the end of the year. During Sam's initial meeting with Joe, Sam realizes that Joe is the former husband of a woman that Sam represented in a divorce case 10 years ago. One of the allegations during the divorce was that Joe had assaulted his wife. Can Sam decline the court appointment? _____

33. At a party, Kelly, a lawyer, is talking to an acquaintance, Sam, who tells her that he is considering consulting a lawyer because of a problem he has been having with his landlord. He tells Kelly all the details of the problem and asks whether she thinks he has grounds for a suit. Kelly tells him that the situation poses an interesting legal question that she could not answer without doing some research and talking to her friend, a housing attorney. Has a lawyer-client relationship begun between Kelly and Sam? _____

34. What factors may be taken into consideration when determining whether an attorney's fee is reasonable? _____

35. Sarah is a solo practitioner who employs a paralegal, Joe, to help her with a variety of tasks. Joe is paid a set salary for the work he does as the office manager, but when he works on specific cases with Sarah, he receives a set percentage of any fee Sarah collects. Sarah and Joe both feel that this is a fair arrangement. Will this fee arrangement subject Sarah to discipline? _____

36. Jane has represented Harry and his family in all their legal matters for a number of years. Jane has recently become aware that Harry is using her services to commit fraud. She wants to withdraw as his counsel, but she signed a retainer agreement in which she agreed to represent him in all his legal matters. The agreement covers the next six months. Jane also knows her withdrawal will result in a material adverse effect on Harry and his family. May Jane withdraw? _____

37. Defendant Jasmine was a corporate CEO charged with major financial defalcations and frauds. She was desperate to delay the significant lawsuit pending against her, hoping that she could land a new position at another corporation before the frauds could be proven. In her answers to the plaintiff's interrogatories, she falsely swore that she has a severe, untreatable cancer and is expected to die within 3 months. Jasmine's lawyer filed the answers to interrogatories, believing them to be true. Two weeks later, Jasmine saw her lawyer at a trendy urban nightspot, and confided in him that the statements regarding cancer were entirely false, meant only to buy her time. What are permissible courses of conduct for Jasmine's lawyer to take? _____

Answers

28. Rachel is not required to represent Bob in this matter. Indeed, she has a duty to decline representation if she believes Bob's claim is frivolous.

29. Yes. Contingent fees are prohibited in most domestic-relations cases, including this type.

30. No. The duty of competence does not require Jack to possess expertise at the beginning of representation if he will be able to acquire the necessary knowledge with reasonable diligence.

31. Yes. Larry was obliged to communicate the offer to Janet and did not have the authority to reject the settlement offer without Janet's agreement.

32. No. The financial burden is not unreasonable, and the representation is unrelated to Sam's former representation of Joe's wife. As a result, Sam may not decline the appointment.

33. Yes, if Sam reasonably believes that Kelly was going to look into his legal problem. No formal agreement need be entered for a duty to arise, and it is irrelevant that there was no discussion of fee arrangements. It does not matter that Kelly never intended to take Sam as a client and was just making conversation at a party. If her actions gave rise to Sam's reasonable belief that she would research his issue and answer his question, then Kelly owes a lawyer duty to Sam.

34. Model Rule 1.5 lists a number of factors to be considered, including, for example, the following: the number of years the lawyer has been a member of the bar and the lawyer's experience in similar matters; the type of case and the legal issues raised; the time and labor involved in the representation; the nature of the professional relationship between the lawyer and client; and customary charges for such services in the locality.

35. Yes. Except in very limited circumstances outlined in Model Rule 5.4(a), fee sharing with nonlawyers is prohibited.

36. Even though Jane's withdrawal will cause a material adverse effect on the client, Jane is required to withdraw if she knows that Harry is using her services to commit fraud. If, after knowing that her services are being used to commit fraud, she does not withdraw, she will have civil liability to those whom Harry defrauds with her services.

37. Jasmine's lawyer cannot continue the litigation and protect Jasmine's confidential information, as this course of action would involve him in his client's ongoing fraudulent conduct and expose him to disciplinary, civil, and perhaps even criminal liability for the frauds.

    Jasmine's lawyer can reveal the false answers to interrogatories to the plaintiff. This is a permissible option under Model Rule 1.6. Jasmine's lawyer's services have been used to perpetrate a fraud and advance a serious financial malfeasance. The confidentiality rule permits Jasmine's lawyer to reveal his client's confidences in such circumstances.

    Alternatively, Jasmine's lawyer can seek the court's permission to withdraw from the matter and give notice to the plaintiff that he disavows responsibility for the answers to interrogatories. This is the noisy withdrawal option, which is permitted under Model Rule 1.16.

Exam Tips on
FORMAL ASPECTS OF THE LAWYER-CLIENT RELATIONSHIP

Before a lawyer has formally undertaken representation, a limited set of lawyer-to-client duties exist, including the confidentiality duty that is owed to prospective clients. ***Undertaking representation*** signifies the beginning of the formal lawyer-client relationship. Once a lawyer has undertaken representation, the full range of duties from lawyer to client exists.

In general, lawyers have no duty to undertake a particular representation. Lawyers have a limited duty to undertake a fair share of pro bono work and to accept court appointments unless good cause exists to decline the appointment. Two otherwise identical fact patterns, one with an appointment and one without, will be resolved as opposites, unlike the general rule that a lawyer has no duty to accept representation when the representation will violate ethics rules or other law. MR 1.16(a).

The lawyer-client relationship is governed by the particular contract entered into by the lawyer and client and by general contract principles, modified by the various duties that lawyers owe clients. The lawyer-client relationship formally begins when a client reasonably believes that the lawyer has undertaken to provide the client with legal service. The relationship does not depend for its onset on the existence of a written contract or a fee payment. Watch for fact patterns involving casual discussions of a prospective client's matter.

Whenever a fee is mentioned in a fact pattern, some comment is warranted. Although the regulation of lawyers' fees is relatively light and rarely enforced, it does exist. MR 1.5. Fees are regulated for their amount and their nature.

- A lawyer's fee must be reasonable. MR 1.5. A range of factors may be considered in setting a reasonable fee. MR 1.5(a).

- In general, a written contract setting the fee is preferred but not required.

- With a few exceptions and restrictions, a lawyer is permitted to charge a fee that is contingent on the outcome of the matter. There are two exceptions, criminal cases and certain domestic-relations cases. When contingent fees are permitted, additional restrictions apply. MR 1.5(c). A contingent-fee agreement must be in writing. Because these technical contingent-fee restrictions stand in sharp contrast to the lack of such restrictions on fees generally, they are popular, easy-to-isolate exam question topics.

Lawyers in the same firm routinely share fees with one another. However, when lawyers who are not members of a firm share fees, or when lawyers seek to share fees with nonlawyers, special problems arise. *Fee splitting* by lawyers not in the same firm is permitted if the total fee is reasonable, the client agrees to the arrangement in writing, and the fee is either shared in proportion to the work done by the lawyers or the lawyers accept joint responsibility for the representation. MR 1.5.

At one time, the organized bar typically imposed *minimum fee schedules* on lawyers and their clients. Such schedules are unlawful and therefore no longer enforceable. Goldfarb v. Virginia State Bar, 421 U.S. 773 (1975).

A *fiduciary* is one in whom a special trust is placed. A fiduciary owes to the beneficiary scrupulous good faith, candor, and care in the management of the beneficiary's interests.

- Lawyer fiduciary duties, beyond the general care owed to client interests and confidences that the relationship implies, are usually thought of in terms of the lawyer's handling of the client's money and property.

- Violations of the lawyer's duty to properly handle client property are per se rules that require no intentional wrongdoing on the part of the lawyer. Remember that not every violation of the lawyer ethics codes is a precise match with distinctions between right and wrong. In this area in particular, no one need be harmed by the conduct for the conduct to be subject to discipline.

- Lawyers must maintain *client trust accounts* and safety-deposit boxes for the safekeeping of client property. Lawyers must maintain the account in the state in which they practice, they must maintain records of the account for later examination, and they must keep client property and funds separate from lawyer property and funds. MR 1.15(a).

- Only client money may be in the trust account. The lawyer must maintain a separate office operating account. When a lawyer *commingles* his funds with a client's, the lawyer is subject to discipline. MR 1.15(a).

Competence and diligence are core lawyer duties. MR 1.1 and 1.3. These duties apply to all representations, and as such are appropriate for brief comment in virtually every essay exam.

- *Competence* requires that the lawyer possess and exercise on the client's behalf "the legal knowledge, skill, thoroughness, and preparation reasonably necessary for the representation." MR 1.1.

- Questions are often asked about a lawyer undertaking representation in an area that is unfamiliar to the lawyer. A lawyer is not required to know the law that governs the client's legal claim before undertaking representation, provided the lawyer will be able to acquire the necessary knowledge with reasonable diligence. But basic, cross-cutting skills such as an understanding of the use of precedent, legal research skills, the ability to identify and evaluate a client's problem, and writing or drafting skills and knowledge are always required.

- Watch for emergency situations. In an emergency, a lawyer may provide limited assistance to a client in a matter on which the lawyer would ordinarily require further study or research before service was rendered. But the lawyer must limit this service to that which is necessary under the circumstances. MR 1.1 Comment.

- *Diligence* is the timeliness aspect of competence. Lawyers are obligated to be diligent on their clients' behalf. MR 1.3. Fact patterns that involve unreasonable delay by the lawyer raise diligence issues.

Lawyers owe clients a duty to communicate with and to meaningfully share decision-making responsibilities with them. MR 1.2 and 1.4. A breach of the communication duty rarely stands alone. Such a breach is almost always combined with another breach of duty, such as a failure to explain the basis of a contingent-fee calculation or a failure to provide a client with the information necessary to obtain valid client consent to waive conflicts of interest.

As a general proposition, clients set the goals or ends of the representation whereas lawyers generally are empowered to determine the best means to use to achieve those ends. MR 1.2(a) Comment.

Lawyers are prohibited from counseling or assisting their clients in the commission of crimes or frauds. MR 1.2(d). When a lawyer does so advise or assist, the lawyer is not only subject to discipline, but is liable criminally or civilly as the case may be. This prohibition does not prevent a lawyer from either discussing proposed courses of action with a client or assisting a client in the pursuit of a test case.

- Timing is everything. When a lawyer knows that a client will use the lawyer's services to perpetrate a crime or fraud before representation has begun, the lawyer must reject the representation. When the lawyer learns the same during representation, the lawyer must withdraw from the representation. Watch for the timing of the lawyer's knowledge of client misconduct.

The formal lawyer-client relationship ends when representation terminates. Despite termination, many lawyer duties to clients continue, such as confidentiality and a limited conflict-avoidance duty. ***Withdrawal*** from representation is a critically important device for the lawyer who is faced with the prospect that continued representation of the client will result in a violation of the ethics code or other law.

Under some circumstances, lawyers are required to withdraw from representation, thereby terminating the lawyer-client relationship. Failure to withdraw under these circumstances subjects the lawyer to discipline. MR 1.16(a).

- **Continued representation will violate the ethics rules:** MR 1.16(a)(1).
- **Continued representation will violate other law:** MR 1.16(a)(1).
- **Lawyer's physical or mental health is impaired:** MR 1.16(a)(2).
- **Lawyer is discharged:** MR 1.16(a)(3).

In some instances lawyers are permitted, but not required, to withdraw. The practical effect of this rule is to allow lawyers to withdraw from representation in the enumerated circumstances without breaching a duty of continued representation to the client. MR 1.16(b).

- Without regard to any cause for withdrawal, a lawyer may withdraw if it can be done without material adverse effect to the client. MR 1.16(b)(1).

- Even if some harm may come to the client from the withdrawal, a lawyer may withdraw when any of the following causes exist.

    - **Lawyer's reasonable belief that client is acting criminally or fraudulently:** MR 1.16(b)(2).
    - **Past use of service for crime or fraud:** MR 1.16(b)(3).
    - **Client actions that are repugnant or imprudent:** MR 1.16(b)(4).
    - **Client failure to meet obligations:** MR 1.16(b)(5).
    - **Unreasonable financial burden:** MR 1.16(b)(6).
    - **Client unreasonably difficult to work with:** MR 1.16(b)(6).
    - **Other good cause:** MR 1.16(b)(7).

Even when a lawyer has good cause to withdraw, a court may order the lawyer to continue the representation. MR 1.16(c).

When litigation is pending, a lawyer must obtain the court's permission to withdraw from representation. MR 1.16(c).

Although a client may discharge a lawyer without cause, the client will continue to have an obligation to pay fees to the lawyer that have already been earned. MR 1.16(d).

When a fee is a fixed amount for a particular service or is based on hours of service, the fee upon discharge will be calculated as the value of the services rendered. Such a recovery theory is called ***quantum meruit.***

Contingent-fee arrangements and lawyer discharge is an especially tricky combination. Some courts have ruled that a contingent-fee lawyer who is discharged without cause is entitled to no fee. Others have ruled that a contingent-fee lawyer who is discharged without cause is entitled to the full benefit of the contingency if indeed the client eventually recovers in the matter. Still others have ruled that the discharged contingent-fee lawyer is entitled to the reasonable value of the services actually rendered (a quantum meruit theory) limited by the amount that the lawyer would have earned had the contingency occurred and the lawyer had recovered the agreed-on percentage.

Chapter 5
CONFIDENTIALITY

ChapterScope

- ***Confidentiality*** is among the core duties that lawyers owe clients. It is, therefore, a topic that pervades the study of professional responsibility. The applicability of the duty of confidentiality is a part of the analysis in a wide range of professional responsibility rules in addition to the central confidentiality rule, Model Rule 1.6.

- The duty of confidentiality furthers a number of important policies: By encouraging a full sharing of information from client to lawyer, it permits sounder, better representation of the client. It permits the lawyer to know enough about the client's future actions and plans to enable the lawyer to act in the role of counsel, advising the client of lawful courses of action and discouraging unlawful or immoral courses of action.

- When applicable, the duty of confidentiality prohibits the lawyer from communicating protected information at all times and in all contexts: The duty lives with the lawyer when he is at work, when he is at the PTA potluck dinner, and at all times in between.

  - The duty of confidentiality applies to "information relating to representation of a client. . . ." MR 1.6(a).

  - An informed client may consent to disclosure of information that would otherwise be protected by the duty of confidentiality. MR 1.6(a).

  - To carry out the purposes of the representation, some information that would be subject to the duty of confidentiality must be disclosed.

  - Under certain circumstances, lawyers may reveal client confidences to defend themselves or to pursue claims against former clients.

  - The lawyer must limit disclosure to those facts necessary to self-defend. Lawyers must also limit their self-defense disclosures to those who need to know for the lawyer's self-defense or fee collection purpose.

  - In certain circumstances, lawyers may reveal confidential information to prevent ***future crimes*** or harms by clients. The circumstances defined by the Model Code and Model Rules are quite different from one another. MR 1.6(b)(l) and DR 4-101(C)(3).

- The duty of confidentiality and the evidentiary ***attorney-client privilege*** overlap in important respects.

  - In general, the evidentiary privilege is created when a client or prospective client communicates in confidence to a lawyer or a person the client reasonably believes to be a lawyer who is being consulted as a lawyer.

  - The privilege applies to communication from a client or a prospective client.

  - The privilege is not created when the communication is made in circumstances that do not indicate a desire for confidentiality by the client.

- The privilege covers the client's communication, not the client's knowledge that was communicated.

- The client holds (controls the assertion of) the evidentiary privilege; client waiver eviscerates the privilege.

- Communications that further future crimes or frauds are excepted from protection by the evidentiary privilege. This is called the *crime-fraud exception.*

■ Communications from agents of an *organizational client* are within the evidentiary privilege, and therefore within the duty of confidentiality, if two conditions are met: The information communicated is treated as confidential within the organization, and it is communicated to the lawyer so that the lawyer can give advice or counsel to the organization.

■ To determine when the duty restricts the lawyer's revelation of information, these questions must be analyzed:

1. Is the information of the type that is covered by the duty?

2. Is the person or entity that communicated the information to the lawyer a client or a client's agent for the purposes of the duty?

3. Do any of the exceptions to the duty apply?

Answers to these questions will determine the applicability of the duty of confidentiality.

■ Lawyer thoughts and strategies about the representation are protected by the duty of confidentiality. They are also protected by the related discovery doctrine called the *work product* doctrine.

■ As a client's agent, a lawyer is generally restricted from using confidential information of the client either for the lawyer's benefit or to the client's detriment.

I. THE DUTY OF CONFIDENTIALITY AND THE ATTORNEY-CLIENT EVIDENTIARY PRIVILEGE

This section covers the overlap between the evidentiary privilege and the duty of *confidentiality.*

A. Secrets and confidences

The Model Code duty of confidentiality provision (DR 4-101) defines the scope of the duty as the sum of the material protected by the evidentiary *attorney-client privilege* (called *"confidences"* in DR 4-101) and the material that, although not included in the attorney-client evidentiary privilege, would be embarrassing or detrimental to the client if revealed or that the client has expressly requested be held in confidence (called *"secrets"* in DR 4-101). The Model Rules provision abandons the "confidences" and "secrets" duty of confidentiality formula in favor of a more general and inclusive definition, "information relating to the representation of a client...." MR 1.6(a).

B. Scope of the attorney-client privilege

Despite the change of terminology, the scope of the attorney-client evidentiary privilege remains critical to defining what is ultimately protected by the duty of confidentiality. When information is within the ethical duty of confidentiality but outside the protection of the evidentiary privilege, a judge may order the lawyer to speak in the form of testimony or otherwise. See §IV.F.1. Thus, although the lawyer would not be free to speak absent court compulsion, the coverage of the evidentiary privilege largely determines whether compulsion will be well founded.

C. Parameters of the evidentiary privilege

The parameters of the evidentiary privilege vary to some extent from jurisdiction to jurisdiction. It is a creature of evidence law rather than professional responsibility law. It is meant to further many of the same interests as the duty of confidentiality. In general, the evidentiary privilege is created when a client or prospective client communicates in confidence to a lawyer (or a person the client reasonably believes to be a lawyer) who is being consulted as a lawyer.

1. **Clients or prospective clients:** The privilege applies to communication from a client or a prospective client.

   Example: Prospective client walks into Lawyer's office and says, "I did it. I poisoned my boss's decaf cappuccino. Now he's dead. What should I do?" Lawyer responds, "I have no idea. My practice is confined to tax law. But here's the name of a good criminal defense lawyer I know. See her." Client leaves. The attorney-client privilege protects the communication from Client to Lawyer, and Lawyer is bound by the duty of confidentiality.

   Example: Criminal Defendant called his friend Lawyer, a civil attorney, told Lawyer that he had killed someone, and spoke of committing suicide. Lawyer and Defendant agreed that they should call a rabbi and the police. After the arrival of the police, Defendant refused to speak with them without his attorney, whom he claimed to have already contacted and identified as Lawyer. At Lawyer's suggestion, another lawyer, Criminal Defense Attorney, represented Defendant. Criminal Defense Attorney moved to suppress all evidence of the crime, asserting that Defendant's communications with Lawyer fell within the attorney-client privilege and that the authorities' knowledge of his crime resulted solely from Lawyer's breaches of that privilege. Although Lawyer never envisioned himself as Defendant's attorney, Defendant contacted him both as a friend and as an attorney. Defendant's communications with Lawyer thus fall within the attorney-client privilege. People v. Fentress, 425 N.Y.S.2d 485 (1980).

2. **Desire for confidentiality required:** The privilege is not created when the communication is made in circumstances that do not indicate a desire for confidentiality by the client.

   Example: Client, accompanied by Acquaintance, consults Lawyer at Lawyer's office regarding a possible action for divorce. Client communicates all of the private circumstances of his marital difficulties to Lawyer in the company of Acquaintance. Because Acquaintance was not necessary for Client's communication with Lawyer and because the presence of Acquaintance indicates an absence of a desire for confidentiality on the part of Client, the privilege is not created. Note that the ethical duty of confidentiality attaches nonetheless because the revelation of this information by the attorney would be embarrassing or detrimental to the client and, under the Model Rules language, is "information relating to the representation of a client. . . ." MR 1.6(a).

   Example: Client consulted Lawyer in the company of Client's Father. Client and Father have a close relationship of trust and mutual reliance. Although the privilege is usually not created when a client consults a lawyer in the presence of a third person, this situation does not indicate a lack of desire for confidentiality on the part of Client. Therefore, the privilege is created despite Father's presence during the consultation. United States v. Bigos, 459 F.2d 639 (1st Cir. 1972).

   a. **Eavesdroppers:** Although some older decisions hold that an eavesdropper may testify despite an assertion of the privilege, most modern authority indicates that if the client exercises reasonable care to avoid being overheard (or intercepted when speaking on the telephone), the court should rule an eavesdropper's testimony inadmissible upon assertion of the privilege.

   b. **Multiple clients:** When multiple prospective clients consult a lawyer together, each holds a privilege that can be asserted against third parties, but none of them can prevent others among the prospective clients from testifying or otherwise waiving the privilege. Their collective communication indicates an absence of desire for confidentiality within the group.

   Example: Driver and Passenger were involved in an automobile collision with Careless Person, who had driven her car left of the center divider, colliding with Driver and Passenger's car. Driver and Passenger consulted Lawyer together, and Lawyer undertakes their representation. As the matter develops, it becomes apparent that Passenger has a claim not only against Careless Person, but also against Driver. In an action between Careless Person and Passenger, Driver's statements to Lawyer, offered by Careless Person, are privileged. By contrast, in an action between Passenger and Driver, statements made by Driver to Lawyer in Passenger's presence, offered by Passenger, are not privileged. Simpson v. Motorists Mutual Insurance Co., 494 F.2d 850 (7th Cir. 1974).

3. **Communication, not knowledge:** The privilege covers the client's communication, not the client's knowledge that was communicated. In ordinary civil discovery, for example, clients must answer proper questions truthfully, even when the answers to those questions will reveal what the client has communicated in confidence to his lawyer.

   Example: When it applies, the privilege prevents the lawyer from being required to say "My client told me that he ran the red light," and prevents the client from being required to say "I told my lawyer that I ran the red light." It does not prevent the client from being required to say "I ran the red light" in answer to a proper question from an opposing party. Such proper questions may come, for example, in interrogatories, in a deposition, or at trial.

4. **Lawyer observations:** The privilege may also protect lawyer observations that result directly from the client's protected communications, as long as the lawyer does nothing to prevent other interested parties from making the same observation.

   Example: Criminal Defendant-Client told Lawyer that the murder victim's partially burned wallet could be found in a burn bin behind Client's house. Lawyer went to the house and retrieved the wallet. After examining it in her office, Lawyer turned the wallet over to the Prosecuting Lawyer. The wallet, as physical evidence, is ***not*** subject to the attorney-client privilege, but Client's statements to Lawyer, as communication from client to lawyer, are subject to the attorney-client privilege. The location at which the wallet was found is not subject to the attorney-client privilege because Lawyer, by her conduct of retrieving the wallet, has prevented the government from discovering by independent means the wallet's location. Had Lawyer merely observed the wallet and left it in the burn bin, Lawyer would have had no duty to submit the wallet to the Prosecuting Lawyer, and Lawyer could not be required to reveal the wallet's location. People v. Meredith, 631 P.2d 46 (Cal. 1981).

5. **Physical evidence:** Although the observations of a lawyer that result directly from client communication may sometimes be privileged, items collected by the lawyer are not privileged.

   Example: Criminal Defendant told Lawyer that the proceeds of a bank robbery could be found in a bank safe-deposit box. On his own initiative, Lawyer went to the bank, removed a bag of money and the sawed-off shotgun used in the robbery from Defendant's safe-deposit box, and placed the items in a box rented under Lawyer's own name. Lawyer's conduct and the items transferred do not fall within the attorney-client privilege. In re Ryder, 263 F. Supp. 360 (E.D. Va.), aff'd, 381 F.2d 713 (4th Cir. 1967).

   Example: Client admitted to fatally stabbing Victim and retained Lawyer. Lawyer obtained a knife possibly used in Client's crime. Invoking the attorney-client privilege, Lawyer refused to produce the knife at a coroner's inquest into Victim's death. If Lawyer obtained the knife as a result of communications with Client, the communications fall within the attorney-client privilege, and Lawyer can withhold the result of those communications (i.e., the knife) for a period of time reasonable for its use in preparing Client's defense before submitting the knife to the authorities. If, however, Lawyer obtained the knife from a third party not represented by Lawyer, the privilege would not apply to Lawyer, and the third party could also be questioned. State v. Orwell, 394 P.2d 681 (Wash. 1964).

   Example: The IRS interviewed Taxpayer-Clients regarding possible civil or criminal liability under the federal income tax laws. Taxpayer-Clients then obtained documents relating to then-tax returns from Accountants and turned these documents over to Lawyers for the purpose of obtaining legal advice. The IRS ordered production of the documents, and Lawyers refused, asserting the attorney-client privilege. The privilege does not apply, however, because preexisting documents that could have been obtained by court process when in a client's possession may also be obtained from an attorney by similar process following a client's transfer to obtain more informed legal advice. Fisher v. United States, 425 U.S. 391 (1976).

6. **Exceptions:** Many of the exceptions to the duty of confidentiality are paralleled by exceptions to the evidentiary privilege.

   a. **Client holds privilege:** The client holds (controls the assertion of) the evidentiary privilege. Client waiver eviscerates the privilege.

      Example: Criminal Defendant called Lawyer, a civil attorney, told Lawyer that he had killed someone, and spoke of committing suicide. Lawyer and Defendant agreed that they should call a rabbi and the police. Lawyer then called his Mother, who is also a friend of Defendant. Mother then called Defendant, who volunteered that he had killed someone before Mother told Defendant that Lawyer had revealed that information to her. With Defendant's permission, Mother called the police and informed them that a killing had occurred at Defendant's home. After the arrival of the police, Defendant refused to speak with them without his attorney, whom he claimed to have already contacted and identified as Lawyer. At Lawyer's suggestion, another lawyer, Criminal Defense Attorney, represented Defendant. Criminal Defense Attorney moved to suppress all evidence of the crime, asserting that Defendant's communications with Lawyer and Mother fell within the attorney-client privilege and that the authorities' knowledge of his crime resulted solely from Lawyer's and Mother's breaches of that privilege. Although a privileged relationship was created between Defendant and Lawyer, Defendant waived the right to assert the privilege when he told Mother about the crime. He again waived the privilege when he agreed with Lawyer and Mother that the police should be called. Because Defendant volunteered information about the killing to Mother without knowing that Lawyer had told her about it, Mother did not act as Lawyer's agent, and the privilege did not apply to his communications with her. People v. Fentress, 425 N.Y.S.2d 485 (Sup. Ct. 1980).

b. **Future crimes and frauds:** Communications that further future crimes or frauds are excepted from protection by the evidentiary privilege. This is called the *crime-fraud exception.*

Example: Client calls Lawyer on the telephone to tell Lawyer that he's just committed a murder and asks what to do if the police come and what to do with the murder weapon. Lawyer says, "If the police come for you, don't talk to them until I get there. In the meantime, drive across the bridge and throw the murder weapon into the deepest part of the lake." Client responds, "OK, I'm on my way." The initial client communication about the past act (the murder) is privileged. The lawyer communication about not talking to the police is privileged because the client is being advised to engage in lawful conduct. But the lawyer and client communication about hiding the evidence is not privileged; it is communication about a future crime or fraud—that of destroying evidence.

II. TO WHOM IS THE DUTY OWED?

This section focuses on the ethical duty of confidentiality and, in particular, to whom the duty is owed.

A. Generally

The duty of confidentiality is owed to current clients, former clients, and prospective clients.

1. **Former clients:** Former clients are owed the duty because the duty would be worth little and would encourage little communication if its time ran out when the representation ceased. Lawyers take the duty of confidentiality and the clients' protected information to the grave.

   Example: Lawyer interviews Client and takes notes on their conversation. Six months later, Client dies. In an investigation of Third Party, Prosecutor seeks Lawyer's notes of Client's confidential conversations with Lawyer. Even though Client is dead, Lawyer's assertion of the evidentiary privilege is effective. Absent an exception, the duty of confidentiality would also apply, prohibiting Lawyer from revealing the confidences. Swidler and Berlin v. United States, 118 S. Ct. 2018 (1998).

2. **Prospective clients:** Prospective clients are owed a measure of confidentiality. As soon as the lawyer and prospective client begin talking with each other as such, the duty of confidentiality attaches to the protected information that the client conveys. If it did not, then the client and lawyer would have to decide whether the client was going to engage the lawyer's services without the benefit of the candor that the duty of confidentiality is meant to encourage.

3. **No fee necessary:** It is not necessary for a fee to be charged for the duty of confidentiality and the evidentiary privilege to be effective.

B. Organizational clients

In addition to representing people, lawyers represent organizations as clients. The duty of confidentiality is owed to the lawyer's client, whether that client is a person or an organization such as a corporation, a labor union, a public interest group, or a government agency. See MR 1.13 Comments 3, 6.

1. **Agents of the organizational client:** Communications from agents of an organizational client are within the evidentiary privilege and, therefore, within the duty of confidentiality, if two conditions are met: the information communicated is treated as confidential within the organization, and it is communicated to the lawyer so that the lawyer can give advice or counsel to the organization.

   Example: Accountants reported to Corporate Client's in-house Lawyer that Corporate Client's foreign subsidiary had paid bribes to foreign government officials. Lawyer conducted an internal investigation of the payments, using personal interviews and questionnaires labeled "confidential." After Corporate Client filed a report with the SEC, the IRS began its own examination of the matter, requesting all files relative to Lawyer's investigation. Corporate Client refused to produce the requested documents.

   Communications fall within the attorney-client privilege when they are made to Lawyer at the direction of corporate superiors by any of Corporate Client's employees, aware that the purpose of the communications is to secure legal advice for Corporate Client, concerning matters within the scope of the employees' duties and internally described as "highly confidential." Any of Lawyer's notes and memoranda based on oral communications also receive protection from disclosure. Upjohn Co. v. United States, 449 U.S. 383 (1981).

2. **Government agency client:** A government agency–organizational client presents special problems for the duty of confidentiality. Because of the special public responsibilities of government agencies, government lawyers may strike a confidentiality balance somewhat more toward the public interest in disclosure of government wrongdoing. Arguably, government lawyers owe no duty of confidentiality to their government-client. See In re Grand Jury Subpoena Duces Tecum, 121 F.3d 910 (8th Cir. 1997).

C. Client and lawyer agents

Both lawyers and clients routinely use agents for communicating with each other.

1. **Lawyer agents:** Lawyers may employ investigators, paralegals, clerical personnel, and others. In some cases, clients may be communicating to the lawyer through the lawyer's agents. For purposes of the duty of confidentiality, such a communication is treated as if it were made directly to the lawyer. In addition, protected client information may be shared with other lawyers within the law firm or organization that represents the client. In this respect, clients hire law firms rather than individual lawyers.

2. **Client agents:** Clients may employ agents such as accountants and employees of organizational clients to communicate to lawyers. Communications from clients through agents to lawyers are treated as if they were made directly by the client to the lawyer.

   Example: Accountant prepares Client's tax documents. IRS begins to investigate, and Client hires Lawyer to protect her interests. At Client's direction, Accountant meets with Lawyer to review the documents prepared by Accountant for Client. The communications of Accountant to Lawyer during this consultation are within the duty of confidentiality.

Example: Land Developer hired Consultant to assist in a development project. Consultant's duties were to work with architects and with Lawyer and to locate tenants for the buildings to be erected. Consultant frequently consulted Lawyer on Land Developer's behalf. The communications between Consultant and Lawyer are privileged. In re Beiter Co., 16 F.3d 929 (8th Cir. 1994).

III. TO WHAT DOES THE DUTY APPLY?

The duty of confidentiality applies to "information relating to representation of a client. . . ." MR 1.6(a). The Model Code definition is the "confidences" and "secrets" formula referred to in §I.A.

A. Duty of confidentiality or evidentiary privilege

For some purposes, it is important to distinguish between what is protected by both the evidentiary privilege and the duty of confidentiality and what is protected by the duty of confidentiality alone. To be protected by the evidentiary privilege, the information must come from the client or a client's agent. Information that the lawyer learns from third parties is protected by the duty of confidentiality, but not the privilege. Remember, to be protected by the duty of confidentiality, the information need merely "relat[e] to representation of a client." MR 1.6(a).

Example: Lawyer represents Client in an auto accident case. Lawyer goes to Joe's AllStar Cafe, a bar outside Client's place of employment. Bartender Joe tells Lawyer that Client is a regular customer who consumes several shots of bourbon whiskey each day at the end of Client's shift. Joe's statement to Lawyer is protected by the duty of confidentiality, but not by the evidentiary privilege. It is not a communication from the client.

Example: Lawyer represents Client in a property dispute. Lawyer searches the property records at the county courthouse and discovers that Client does not have a sound claim to the disputed property. This information is protected by the duty of confidentiality, but not by the evidentiary privilege.

Example: Lawyer represents Client in a contract dispute. Client is a manufacturer of wingnuts. Client sold defective wingnuts to Careless Buyer. Client tells Lawyer that he intentionally defrauded Careless Buyer. This information is protected by both the evidentiary privilege and the duty of confidentiality.

B. Duty of confidentiality broader than evidentiary privilege

The duty of confidentiality applies to all information relating to the representation, not merely communications from client to lawyer.

1. **Lawyer observations:** Lawyer observations are protected by the duty of confidentiality.

2. **Communications from third parties:** Communications from third parties about the representation are protected by the duty of confidentiality.

3. **Work product:** Lawyer thoughts and strategies about the representation are protected by the duty of confidentiality. They are also protected by the related discovery doctrine called the *work product* doctrine. Although the work product doctrine works in tandem with the

evidentiary privilege to protect blocks of information from forced disclosure to opposing parties, the work product doctrine does not have the same symbiotic relationship with the duty of confidentiality as does the evidentiary privilege. (For more on work product, consult civil procedure reference materials.)

IV. EXCEPTIONS TO THE DUTY OF CONFIDENTIALITY

A. Consent

The client is the holder of the evidentiary privilege and the party whose communication is being protected. A client may give informed consent to disclosure of information that would otherwise be protected by the duty of confidentiality. MR 1.6(a).

B. Implied authorization

To carry out the purposes of the representation, some information that would be subject to the duty of confidentiality must be disclosed.

Example: Lawyer represents Client, who wants to purchase Art's art collection. Client has told Lawyer various facts about Client's creditworthiness, his cash reserves, his interest in the collection, and so on. Client authorizes Lawyer to approach Art and engage in negotiations for the purchase of the collection. In carrying out Client's instructions, Lawyer may need to reveal some information relating to the representation that would otherwise be protected by the duty of confidentiality.

C. Self-defense and fees

A lawyer is permitted to reveal (and use for her own benefit) information that would be protected by the duty of confidentiality in three self-defense type situations. The three self-defense type situations are "to establish a claim or defense on behalf of the lawyer in a controversy between the lawyer and the client, to establish a defense to a criminal charge or a civil claim against the lawyer based upon conduct in which the client was involved, or to respond to allegations in any proceeding concerning the lawyer's representation of the client." MR 1.6(b)(3).

Example: After sustaining substantial losses on stock purchased in an initial public offering, Plaintiffs brought an action against Corporation, Firm, and certain Firm Partners for willful violations of securities law. Plaintiffs claimed that Corporation's Securities and Exchange Commission registration statement and prospectus had provided materially false and misleading information. They alleged that the defendants did not disclose payments due to and a compensation arrangement made with Firm in connection with the offering. Asserting that Corporation and Firm had concealed the fee arrangement from him, one Partner met with Lawyers representing Plaintiffs and convinced them to drop the claims against him. The remaining defendants then moved to disqualify Lawyers from further involvement in the litigation, alleging that Partner had revealed confidential information obtained from Corporation while discussing the case with Lawyers. A lawyer may reveal confidences or secrets necessary to defend himself against accusations of wrongful conduct. Partner had the right to make appropriate disclosures with respect to his role in the public offering and the right to support his version of the facts with suitable evidence. Further, Partner's duty of confidentiality applied only to information gained from Corporation, not information regarding events at Firm. Because Partner's conduct did not violate his professional responsibilities, his contacts with Lawyers did not disqualify them from representing Plaintiffs. Meyerhofer v. Empire Fire & Marine Ins. Co., 497 F.2d 1190 (2d Cir.), *cert. den.,* 419 U.S. 998 (1974).

1. **The three categories of self-defense permitted disclosure**

    a. **"[T]o establish a claim or defense on behalf of the lawyer in a controversy between the lawyer and the client":** This exception usually means a fee dispute between lawyer and client. Through this exception, the lawyer is permitted to use confidential information to collect his fee from the client or to defend a claim by the client to recover a portion of the fee already paid to the lawyer. This exception would apply beyond fee disputes to any controversy between lawyer and client, such as a lawyer malpractice claim.

    b. **"[T]o establish a defense to a criminal charge or a civil claim against the lawyer based upon conduct in which the client was involved":** Sometimes, a lawyer is the defendant in a criminal or civil action based on conduct of the client. This occurs in at least two ways.

    First, a lawyer may be a defendant based on joint activity with a client, such as when a client is accused of being a drug dealer and the lawyer is accused of doing lawyer activities that assisted the drug enterprise. Second, a defendant-client may assert, formally or informally, that the lawyer and not the client is the wrongdoer. When such an assertion is made, the lawyer may respond, using confidential information as necessary, without waiting for charges or claims to be filed. MR 1.6 Comment 8. Some would argue that this exception also permits proactive disclosures when the lawyer reasonably believes it is necessary to distance herself from potential charges or claims. If so, then a lawyer could use this exception to reveal confidential information when the lawyer discovers that her services have been used by the client to perpetrate a crime or fraud. See Hazard & Modes, The Law of Lawyering §1.6, at 312 (2d ed. 1990).

    c. **"[T]o respond to allegations in any proceeding concerning the lawyer's representation of the client":** This exception extends the type of proceedings in which the lawyer may use confidential information in self-defense to include, for example, bar disciplinary proceedings, government agency investigatory proceedings, or criminal collateral review claims of ineffective assistance of counsel.

2. **Limit disclosure to facts necessary to defend:** With respect to any of the three categories of permitted disclosure, the lawyer must limit disclosure to those facts necessary to self-defend.

    Example: Lawyer was discharged by Client. Client sued Lawyer for malpractice. In his Answer to Client's Complaint, Lawyer included the following allegation: "Client constantly worried about everything, including an affair her husband supposedly had with Client's sister eight years ago." The allegation bore no relationship to the Complaint's allegations. A lawyer may reveal those confidences that are necessary to self-defend, but revelation of confidences beyond those necessary to defend is subject to discipline. Dixon v. State Bar of California, 187 Cal. Rptr. 30 (Cal. 1982).

3. **Limit disclosure to individuals who need to know:** Lawyers must also limit their self-defense disclosures to those who need to know for the lawyer's self-defense or fee collection purpose.

    Example: Lawyer represents Client. Client willfully refuses to pay Lawyer's fee without cause. Lawyer is angry. Lawyer tells Hairstylist that Client has "stiffed me on my last three billings even though she has loads of readily available cash." Lawyer is subject to discipline because Hairstylist does not need to know the confidences of Client for Lawyer to collect his fee.

Example: Prospective Adoptive Parents retained Lawyer to assist with adoption procedures. During representation, a fee dispute arose. Lawyer contacted Social Worker, whose job it was to determine the parental fitness of Prospective Adoptive Parents, and informed Social Worker of the fee dispute. This act was subject to discipline. A lawyer may reveal confidences to affect collection of a fee but, in this instance, Lawyer has revealed the confidences to individuals who have no need to know with respect to his efforts to collect his fee. In addition, before confidences are revealed, a lawyer must reasonably believe that disclosure is necessary. Here, Lawyer's belief that disclosure was necessary is unreasonable and is formed and acted upon prematurely. Florida Bar v. Ball, 406 So. 2d 459 (Fla. 1981).

D. Future crimes, frauds, and harms

In certain circumstances, lawyers may reveal confidential information to prevent *future crimes,* frauds, or harms caused by clients. The circumstances defined by the Model Code and Model Rules are quite different from one another. MR 1.6(b)(l); DR 4-101(C)(3).

1. **Distinction with past crimes or frauds:** As long as all other requirements are satisfied, when a client reveals a *past* crime or fraud, that information is protected by the duty of confidentiality and the attorney-client privilege. Indeed, protecting such communications is central to the policies that support the evidentiary privilege and the duty of confidentiality, and the lawyer is duty-bound to protect such information. This exception refers to *future* crimes, frauds, and harms only.

   Example: Defendant is charged with murder. He tells Lawyer where to find the as-yet-undiscovered body of another victim. Lawyer does not reveal the location of the body. Lawyer has complied with the duty of confidentiality. The client's communication related to a past, not future, crime. People v. Belge, 372 N.Y.S.2d 798, *aff'd* 376 N.Y.S.2d 771 (A.D. 1975).

2. **Policy rationale:** When a client has committed a crime or fraud, the lawyer's representation of the client is what the legal system expects the client to be afforded. The lawyer bears no moral responsibility for the client's past acts. When, in contrast, a lawyer becomes aware that a client intends to commit a crime or fraud, a shift occurs. The lawyer, if he does nothing to prevent the crime or fraud, shares the moral if not the legal responsibility for the client's future wrongful acts that the lawyer could have prevented. When the lawyer knows the client intends to commit a future crime or fraud, and *the lawyer's services are used to commit the crime or fraud,* the lawyer will share both the moral and legal responsibility for the wrong. See Chapter 3, §III.

3. **Model Code:** The Model Code exception for future crimes or frauds is broad but permissive. Under the Code, a lawyer "*may* reveal the intention of his client to commit a crime and the information necessary to prevent the crime." DR 4-101(C)(3).

   a. **May reveal:** The rule is cast in permissive language, allowing a lawyer some discretion in determining whether or not a particular situation warrants revelation of a client confidence and the diminished sense of trust between lawyer and client that comes with such revelation. But see ABA Opinion 314 (1965) (indicating that when the lawyer is certain about the client's intention to commit a crime, the lawyer must reveal it).

b. **Any crime, but discretion:** working with the permissive, "may" language, the Code exception applies to any crime. A lawyer must use discretion in determining whether or not to reveal a particular future crime intention of a client.

   Example: Client walks into Lawyer's office wearing a fishing cap pinned with innumerable lures and announces, "I'm going out to fish without a license!" Lawyer should use discretion and determine not to call the authorities to prevent Client's future crime.

4. **Model Rules:** Before the February 2002 amendments, the Model Rules' exception for future crimes had retained the permissive language of the Model Code, but restricted the type of future crime that may permit revelation of confidential information. The language before February 2002 read: "A lawyer *may* reveal . . . information [relating to representation of a client] to the extent the lawyer reasonably believes necessary to prevent the client from committing a criminal act that the lawyer believes is ***likely to result in imminent death or substantial bodily harm.***" Former MR 1.6(b)(l).

   Model Rule 1.6 was amended in a significant way in February 2002. The new language for the future-crime exception to the duty of confidentiality allows the lawyer to reveal confidences "to the extent the lawyer reasonably believes necessary to prevent reasonably certain death or substantial bodily harm." MR 1.6(b)(l). Following the amendment to Model Rule 1.6(b)(l), this exception to the confidentiality duty might better be referred to as the "future harm" exception rather than the future-crime exception.

   The new exception does not require as a trigger any criminal act by the client. It is focused on preventing serious, imminent harms, and authorizes the revelation of client information when necessary to accomplish its ends. The example chosen by the drafters involves a negligent, not necessarily criminal, discharge of pollutants into a water supply that presents a "substantial risk" of "life-threatening or debilitating disease" to the water drinkers. In such an instance, the lawyer is permitted to reveal the information necessary to prevent the harm. See MR 1.6 Comment 6.

   a. **Still "may":** The Model Rules future-crime exception retains the permissive "may" language of the Model Code.

   b. **The special case of fraud on the court:** In general, future frauds are not within the Model Rules' future crimes exception to the duty of confidentiality. However, preventing a future fraud on the court (perjury) presents a special case of the future-crime or frauds exception to the duty of confidentiality. In some cases, Model Rule 3.3 overrides Model Rule 1.6 and requires revelation of confidential information. See §E.3 and Chapter 8, §I.

   c. **"Noisy withdrawal":** Although a lawyer is prohibited from explicitly disclosing protected client information, the Model Rules permit a form of withdrawal from representation that will often implicitly reveal protected client information. When a client intends to use a lawyer's services to further a crime or fraud, the lawyer must withdraw from the representation. See Chapter 4, §VI. When a lawyer withdraws, she may inform interested parties of the fact of her withdrawal. When giving notice of withdrawal, the lawyer "may also withdraw or disaffirm any opinion, document, affirmation, or the like." MR 1.6 Comment 14. The reason is clear enough; the lawyer may need to distance her services from any connection to wrongful conduct those services may have furthered. Nonetheless, an implicit revelation of confidences has occurred and is authorized by the Comment.

Example: Lawyer represents Client in Client's efforts to obtain loans from Bank. In so doing, lawyer gathers information from Client regarding collateral that may form the security for the loans. Lawyer then sends Bank a series of letters listing the items that Client offers as collateral. Lawyer discovers that Client has been falsifying the lists of collateral items. Lawyer withdraws from the representation. In withdrawing, Lawyer sends a letter to Bank informing Bank that Lawyer no longer represents Client and disavowing the previous letters from Lawyer to Bank that had included the false collateral lists. Lawyer has made a "noisy withdrawal" and is not subject to discipline, even if Bank infers from the letter that Client has defrauded Bank.

5. **August 2003 amendment to Model Rule 1.6:** Before the August 2003 amendments, Model Rule 1.6 was seriously out of tune with most state ethics rules and the Restatement regarding exceptions to the duty of confidentiality. A lawyer was not permitted to reveal confidential information in situations in which the client had committed or planned to commit a fraud that caused financial injury to third persons. In August 2003, the ABA House of Delegates finally adopted a revised Model Rule 1.6 that reflected recommendations from the 2002 ABA Task Force. Disclosure is now permissible "to the extent the lawyer reasonably believes necessary:

   a. to prevent reasonably certain death or substantial bodily harm;

   b. to prevent the client from committing a crime or fraud that is reasonably certain to result in substantial injury to the financial interests or property of another and in furtherance of which the client has used or is using the lawyer's services;

   c. to prevent, mitigate or rectify substantial injury to the financial interests or property of another that is reasonably certain to result or has resulted from the client's commission of a crime or fraud in furtherance of which the client has used the lawyer's services;

   d. to secure legal advice about the lawyer's compliance with these Rules;

   e. to establish a claim or defense on behalf of the lawyer in a controversy between the lawyer and the client, to establish a defense to a criminal charge or civil claim against the lawyer based upon conduct in which the client was involved, or to respond to allegations in any proceeding concerning the lawyer's representation of the client; or

   f. to comply with other law or a court order." MR 1.6.

6. **Organizational constituents:** The lawyer's duty not to violate Model Rule 1.6 when the lawyer is representing an organization does not prohibit disclosing information imparted to the lawyer from an organizational constituent to another organizational constituent.

7. **State variance from Model Code and Model Rules:** The future-crime exception is an area in which several states have departed from the ABA models when drafting their own professional responsibility codes.

   a. Must for may: Some states have made disclosure mandatory by changing the Model Rule and Model Code's "may reveal" language to "must reveal." See, e.g., Texas Rule 1.05, Illinois Rule 1.6, Florida Rule 1.6, Virginia DR 4-101.

   b. Expand crimes category: Some have expanded the restrictive Model Rules' "criminal act that the lawyer believes is likely to result in imminent death or substantial bodily harm" language to include other kinds of crimes or frauds. See, e.g., Michigan Rule 1.6, Minnesota Rule 1.6, Texas Rule 1.05.

c. **Rectify past crimes or frauds:** Some have permitted disclosure of confidential facts necessary to rectify past crimes or frauds *when the lawyer's services have been used* to further those past crimes or frauds. See, e.g., Michigan Rule 1.6, Minnesota Rule 1.6, Texas Rule 1.05.

E. **Other professional responsibility rules**

A number of ethics rules requires or permits lawyers to disclose information that would otherwise be protected by the duty of confidentiality.

1. **Model Rule 2.4:** With the adoption of new Rule 2.4 in February 2002, the ABA deleted the little-used Rule 2.2. Model Rule 2.4 defines a role other than that of lawyer, in which a lawyer may serve. The third-party-neutral role, such as arbitrator or mediator, is now a common, reasonably well-understood role in various alternative dispute resolution systems. Lawyers sometimes serve in such roles, and new Rule 2.4 makes clear that the third-party-neutral role is distinct from that of lawyer. The rule defines the third-party-neutral role, distinguishes it from that of lawyer, then requires that lawyers serving in the third-party-neutral role inform the parties to the process that the lawyer does not represent the parties and inform them of the role's distinctions with that of lawyer.

2. **Model Rule 2.3:** Some disclosures of otherwise protected client information are inevitable when a lawyer properly evaluates a matter for a client for the use of a third party.

3. **Model Rule 3.3:** Duties imposed by Model Rule 3.3(c) (candor to the court) "apply even if compliance requires disclosure of information otherwise protected by Model Rule 1.6." See Chapter 8, §I.

F. **"Other law" or orders of court**

Lawyers may reveal confidences when required to do so by other law or by order of court.

1. **Orders of court:** When a court orders a lawyer to speak about matters that will reveal protected client information, usually after an unsuccessful assertion of the attorney-client evidentiary privilege, the lawyer may reveal the information without risking disciplinary liability. MR 1.6 Comment 11.

2. **Other law:** Despite a presumption against other provisions of law superseding the duty of confidentiality (see MR 1.6 Comment 10), in several circumstances, provisions of law outside the professional responsibility rules require or permit lawyers to disclose information that would otherwise be protected by the duty of confidentiality. A few common examples follow.

a. **SEC:** Securities law requires clients and their lawyers to make certain disclosures, regardless of their confidential nature.

Example: Corporations A and B decided to merge. However, the corporations conditioned the deal on an exchange of satisfactory "comfort letters" from their independent accountants confirming that there was no reason to believe that the parties' financial reports required any material adjustments to fairly represent the results of their operations. Corporation A's accountants determined that the company's financial reports required adjustments that would transform an apparent $700,000 profit into a $200,000 loss. On the day of the deal's closing, Corporation A's comfort letter reflecting these adjustments had not yet arrived at the office of Corporation A's Lawyer, where representatives of both corporations had gathered to complete the transaction. Thus, Lawyer telephoned the accountants and had them dictate the letter to his secretary. The typed copy provided to Corporation B's Attorneys detailed substantial adjustments made by Corporation A's accountants. However, Lawyer omitted sections of the letter that showed that Corporation A's properly adjusted financial reports would reflect a net loss rather than a profit. Despite even the substantial adjustments reflected in the edited comfort letter, Attorneys allowed Corporation B to proceed with the merger. When Attorneys received the accountants' unedited letter several days after the closing, they did not disclose its contents to the SEC or the public. The price of the companies' combined stock increased dramatically until the press learned of the new corporation's questionable financial situation. Investors then experienced serious financial losses.

Attorneys violated the SEC's antifraud provisions by acquiescing in the merger after reading the edited comfort letter and by failing to disclose the true contents when they later received it. On the basis of the edited letter, they should have withdrawn their approval of the merger and demanded resolicitation of Corporation B's shareholders. If Corporation B's representatives had refused, Attorneys should have withdrawn from the representation. After receiving the unedited letter, they should have revealed its contents. SEC v. National Student Marketing Corp., 457 F. Supp. 682 (D.D.C. 1978).

   b. IRS: An attorney may not mislead the IRS deliberately through misstatements, omissions, or misrepresentations of a client. ABA Formal Op. 85-352 (1985).

G. Information generally known

Even when some others in addition to the lawyer and client know the protected client information, the duty of confidentiality continues to protect the information. If the client has shared the information with even a few others, the evidentiary privilege will be lost, but not the duty of confidentiality. When the information *is generally known,* however, its continued protection by the lawyer will in some cases serve little purpose, and most would say that the duty of confidentiality is lost as well. Nonetheless, the lawyer's general duty of loyalty to the client counsels for the lawyer's exercise of discretion; if the client's lawyer speaks about information, even information that is generally known, there may be harm to the client's interests that the lawyer is duty-bound to refrain from causing. A lawyer is specifically permitted to use, to the disadvantage of a *former client,* information that is generally known. MR 1.9(c)(1).

Example: Lawyer represents Client, who is attempting to purchase a piece of property for development purposes. Newspaper prints a story indicating that Client is about to make this purchase. The confidence is now generally known, and the duty of confidentiality may be of diminished importance. Nonetheless, Lawyer should refrain from speaking about Client's plans. Revelations by a client's lawyer will in many instances be more meaningful than revelations of the same facts by newspapers or other sources that have no duty of loyalty to the client.

V. OTHER PROFESSIONAL DUTIES THAT ARE SUBJECT TO THE DUTY OF CONFIDENTIALITY

A wide range of lawyer duties impose requirements on lawyers only when the duty does not offend the duty of confidentiality. Typically, a Model Rule in this category will require a lawyer to comply with it "subject to the duty of confidentiality" or "unless the information is subject to Model Rule 1.6" (the confidentiality rule).

A. Model Rule 8.3

This rule requires a lawyer to report certain misconduct of other lawyers, but not if such reporting would "require disclosure of information otherwise protected by Rule 1.6." MR 8.3(c). See Chapter 3, §V.

B. Model Rule 1.9(c)(2)

This rule defines the nature of conflict of interests with former clients and restricts the use of information from the former client's representation "except as [Rule 1.6] . . . would permit or require."

C. Model Rule 1.13 Comment 5

This rule sets out the special duties and roles of lawyers whose clients are organizations. See Chapter 6, §IV.A.2.a. The Comment indicates that Rule 1.13 "does not limit or expand the lawyer's responsibilities under Rule 1.6. . . ."

D. Model Rule 2.3(c)

This rule permits lawyers to prepare materials on a client's behalf for the evaluation by third parties. In doing so, "[except as authorized in connection with a report of an evaluation, information relating to the evaluation is otherwise protected by Rule 1.6."

E. Model Rule 4.1

This rule requires lawyers to disclose certain facts to "avoid assisting a criminal or fraudulent act by a client, unless disclosure is prohibited by Rule 1.6."

VI. USE OF CONFIDENTIAL INFORMATION FOR THE LAWYER'S BENEFIT

As a client's agent, a lawyer is generally restricted from using confidential information of the client, either for the lawyer's benefit or to the client's detriment.

A. Model Code

The Model Code expressly prohibits a lawyer from using confidential information of the client, either for the lawyer's benefit or to the client's detriment. DR 4-101(B)(2), 4-101(B)(3).

B. Model Rules

The Model Rules drafters kept only the explicit restriction on using client information to the client's detriment. MR 1.8(b).

C. A meaningless distinction

Technically, the distinction is important because, on its face, the Model Rules provision permits lawyer use of client confidences for the lawyer's or a third person's gain, as long as the client is not disadvantaged. As a practical matter, two points make the distinction little more than a technical oddity.

1. **Disadvantage to client almost always potentially present:** In virtually every scenario imaginable, the lawyer's gain from the use of information will represent a lost opportunity for the client's gain.

   Example: Client tells Lawyer that Client intends to purchase Plot 1 for a significant development. Client's purchase will increase the value of surrounding pieces of property. Client does not intend to purchase any other neighboring pieces of property. Lawyer believes that it will cause no harm to Client if Lawyer purchases a piece of property that borders on Plot 1, thereby making a profit on its later resale after Client's purchase of Plot 1. Lawyer's actions, however, create risk for Client. Other potential suitors of Plot 1's current owner may notice Lawyer's purchase and bid on Plot 1; Plot 1's owners may notice Lawyer's purchase and increase their asking price to Client.

2. **Agency imitations:** Even if some scenario of lawyer gain without client opportunity loss is imaginable, as a matter of general agency law, a lawyer's (agent's) gain that is attributable to his duty to a client (principal) is the property of the client and not the lawyer. See Restatement of Agency §§388, 395. Although the client may, of course, consent to the lawyer's use and retention of the gain, in such a case, the lawyer would no longer be making use of protected client confidences.

Quiz Yourself on CONFIDENTIALITY

38. Henry met his lawyer for lunch at a popular local restaurant. At the salad bar, Henry discussed his role in the crime for which he has recently been indicted. Does the attorney-client privilege protect the information that Henry told his lawyer during lunch? _____

39. Bob and Sue are charged with committing a crime together. Bob confesses everything to his lawyer and waives the attorney-client privilege. Sue doesn't want Bob's lawyer to be able to reveal the communication because it would implicate her in the crime, and she plans to argue that she didn't take part. Can Sue prevent the revelation of the communication by invoking the attorney-client privilege? _____

40. Joe told his attorney that he was outside of the building acting as a lookout when the crime was committed. Joe has chosen to testify during his trial. While on the witness stand, the Prosecutor asks Joe if he was outside of the building at the time the crime was committed. Can Joe invoke the attorney-client privilege to avoid answering the question? _____

41. Jim told his attorney that he committed the crime and threw the gun in the woods. Lawyer goes to the woods and sees the gun, but he does not touch it or disturb it in any way. The prosecutor asks the lawyer if he knows where the gun is. Does the lawyer have to reveal the location of the gun without revealing how he knows where it is located? _____

42. Assume that the same situation exists as in the above question, except that the lawyer picked up the gun and took it back to his office. What would be protected by the attorney-client privilege in this situation? _____

43. Joe and Sam go to Lawyer to ask him to help them reach an agreement on a business deal they are considering entering. What effect does this arrangement have on the creation of the attorney-client privilege? _____

44. Attorney is investigating the circumstance surrounding the crime with which his client, Bill, has been charged. During the investigation, Bill's friend tells the attorney where Bill was on the night the crime occurred. Is the communication between the client's friend and the attorney protected by the attorney-client privilege? _____

45. Four years ago, Nick came to Lawyer and confessed that he had committed a murder and asked Lawyer to represent him if he was ever charged with the crime. Nick was never arrested for the murder, and Lawyer's unrelated representation of Nick ended three years ago. John has recently asked Lawyer to represent him. John has been charged with committing the murder that Nick confessed to Lawyer four years ago. What should Lawyer do? _____

46. Lawyer represented Jack and, in the course of the representation, he learned that Jack had saved a substantial amount of money. Lawyer has been unable to collect his fee from Jack and has filed suit against him to collect the fee. During the trial, Jack claims that he has no money with which to pay the rest of the fee. Revealing the information would certainly help Lawyer's case, but would be detrimental to Jack. Must Lawyer keep quiet? _____

47. Lawyer represents a corporation that is considering building a large park in an area that is currently rural. If the park is built, the property near the park will rapidly increase in value. Lawyer is considering buying property near the proposed park site. Is the Lawyer violating any ethics rules by buying this property? _____

48. Sarah storms into Lawyer's office and says, "When I leave your office I'm going to find Joe and shoot him." Lawyer believes Sarah is telling the truth. Is this communication protected by the attorney-client privilege or the duty of confidentiality, and does Lawyer have any responsibility to warn Joe? _____

49. An attorney working for a government agency becomes aware that agency personnel have illegally accepted thousands of dollars in trips and gifts from assorted lobbying groups. Is Lawyer bound by the attorney-client privilege not to reveal the violations? _____

50. Sally is a middle manager who works at VeryCorp. She is involved in a dispute over her pay with VeryCorp. From her office computer, she sent an email to her private lawyer who is representing her in that dispute. Litigation has begun, and VeryCorp has located Sally's email on its IT system. Is her message to her private lawyer privileged? _____

Answers

38. No. The evidentiary privilege is not created when the communication is made in circumstances that do not indicate a desire for confidentiality by the client. Keep in mind that the duty of confidentiality still protects the information. The lawyer should have warned Client that the communication would not be protected by the attorney-client privilege.

39. No. The attorney-client privilege between Bob and his lawyer belongs to Bob, and he has chosen to waive it.

40. No. Joe must answer the question truthfully. The attorney-client privilege would allow Joe to refuse to answer a question about whether he told his attorney that he was outside of the building, but the privilege does not work to shield all information that a client reveals to his attorney.

41. No. The lawyer's observation of the gun's location was a direct result of the communication with the client and, therefore, it is protected by the attorney-client privilege. Requiring a lawyer to reveal the location of the gun in this situation without revealing the source of the information would undermine the purpose of the privilege. Clients would not be able to speak freely with their lawyers. Keep in mind that if Jim chose to testify, waiving his Fifth Amendment privilege against self-incrimination, and he was asked where the gun was, he would have to answer truthfully under penalty of perjury.

42. The lawyer would have to turn the gun over to the authorities. It is not privileged. The gun's location would also not be privileged because the lawyer has disrupted the opposing party's (here the government's) opportunity to discover the location. Effectively, the lawyer has destroyed the evidence of location. The client's communication to the lawyer would remain subject to the privilege. The lawyer could not be required to reveal how he found the gun because that would reveal the privileged communication.

43. When acting as an intermediary between clients, the lawyer must disclose to both that the attorney-client privilege is not available to either client for purposes of restricting the other's testimony regarding client communications to the lawyer.

44. No, unless the friend is an agent of the client. However, the friend's communication and the information he conveyed are covered by the duty of confidentiality.

45. The Lawyer is bound by the attorney-client privilege and the duty of confidentiality not to reveal Nick's confession to either John or the police. Lawyer may not accept representation of John. To do so would require Lawyer to either breach Nick's confidences or fail to serve John's interests fully.

46. No. A lawyer is permitted to reveal and use for her own benefit information that would be protected by the duty of confidentiality "to establish a claim or defense on behalf of the lawyer in a controversy between the lawyer and the client." Model Rule 1.6(b)(3). The lawyer is permitted to reveal only those facts necessary to present her claim.

47. Yes. The Model Code expressly prohibits a lawyer from using confidential information of the client, either to the client's detriment or to the lawyer's gain. DR 4-101(B)(2), 4-101(B)(3). The Model Rules prohibit a lawyer from using confidential information to a client's detriment. MR 1.8(b). Lawyer's act creates too great a risk of detriment to the client. If the client consents to Lawyer's acts, Lawyer may go forward with his purchase.

48. The attorney-client privilege in evidence law does not protect communications that further future crimes or frauds. Sarah's communication is not protected by the privilege. Further, both the Model Code and the Model Rules provide an exception to the duty of confidentiality for future crimes. Under the Code, a lawyer may reveal the intention of his client to commit a crime and the information necessary to prevent it. However, an ABA opinion indicates that "may" in this case means "must" if a lawyer is certain about the client's intention to commit a serious crime. The Model Rules use the word "may," but restrict the type of future crime that permits the revelation of confidential information to prevent future harms that the lawyer reasonably believes are likely to result in imminent death or substantial bodily harm. MR 1.6(b)(1). Therefore, if Lawyer believes that Sarah is telling the truth, this communication is not protected by the duty of confidentiality and Lawyer should take steps to prevent Sarah from carrying out her threat.

49. Although the attorney technically represents the interests of agency, the attorney, as a public employee, also represents the interests of the public. The special public responsibilities of government agencies require lawyers to strike a confidentiality balance more toward the public interest in disclosure of government wrongdoing. In this case, the attorney would not be disciplined for revealing the violations.

50. Several recent courts have held such communications to be privileged, but the question remains open because several courts have ruled otherwise. The issue involved the reasonableness of Sally's conduct in communicating with her lawyer in this manner. A client, for example, who speaks with her lawyer in a loud voice at the local McDonald's destroys the privilege because the communication is not made in a way that shows an expectation that it will be private.

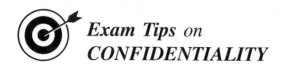

Exam Tips on CONFIDENTIALITY

To determine when the duty of confidentiality restricts the lawyer's revelation of information, the following questions must be analyzed.

- Is the information of the type that is covered by the duty?
- Is the person or entity that communicated the information to the lawyer a client or a client's agent for the purposes of the duty?
- Do any of the exceptions to the duty apply?

Answers to these questions will determine the applicability of the duty of confidentiality.

Before analyzing any exception, first make sure the information is protected by the duty of confidentiality (or the communication protected by the attorney-client privilege).

- The Model Code duty of confidentiality provision (DR 4-101) defines the scope of the duty as the sum of the material protected by the ***evidentiary attorney-client privilege*** (called **"confidences"** in DR 4-101) and material that, while not included in the attorney-client evidentiary privilege, would be embarrassing or detrimental to the client if revealed or that the client has expressly requested be held in confidence (called **"*secrets*"** in DR 4-101). The Model Rules provision abandons the "confidences" and "secrets" duty of confidentiality formula in favor of a more general and inclusive definition, "information relating to representation of a client. . . ." MR 1.6(a).

- In general, the evidentiary privilege is created when a client or prospective client communicates in confidence to a lawyer or a person the client reasonably believes to be a lawyer who is being consulted as a lawyer. It is not necessary for a fee to be charged for the duty of confidentiality and the evidentiary privilege to be effective.

- The privilege applies to communication from a client or a prospective client and continues beyond the end of the lawyer-client relationship even beyond the client's death.

- The privilege is not created when the communication is made in circumstances that do not indicate a desire for confidentiality by the client.

- The privilege covers the client's communication, not the client's knowledge that was communicated.

- The privilege also may protect lawyer observations that result directly from the client's protected communications, as long as the lawyer does nothing to prevent other interested parties from making the same observation.

- Although the observations of a lawyer that result directly from client communication may sometimes be privileged, physical items collected by the lawyer are not privileged.

- Many of the exceptions to the duty of confidentiality are paralleled by exceptions to the evidentiary privilege.

- The client holds (controls the assertion of) the evidentiary privilege; informed client consent to disclosure eviscerates the privilege and waives the duty of confidentiality.

- To carry out the purposes of the representation, some information that would be subject to the duty of confidentiality must be disclosed.

- Under certain circumstances, lawyers may reveal client confidences to defend themselves or to pursue claims against former clients.

- The lawyer must limit disclosure to those facts necessary to self-defend. Lawyers must also limit their self-defense disclosures to those who need to know for the lawyer's self-defense or fee collection purpose.

Communications that further future crimes or frauds are excepted from protection by the evidentiary privilege. This is called the ***crime-fraud exception.***

In certain circumstances, lawyers may reveal confidential information to prevent ***future crimes*** or harms by clients. The circumstances defined by the Model Code and Model Rules are quite different from one another. MR 1.6(b)(l) and DR 4-101(C)(3). The Model Rules' exception for future crimes retains the permissive language of the Model Code, but restricts the type of future crime that may permit revelation of confidential information. A lawyer ***may*** reveal information [relating to representation of a client] to the extent the lawyer reasonably believes necessary to prevent future harm that the lawyer believes is ***likely to result in imminent death or substantial bodily harm.*** MR 1.6(b)(1). This distinction between the Code and Rules is a significant one. If your course emphasizes distinctions between the Code and the Rules, this one is certain to be prominent.

- The crime-fraud exception to the attorney-client privilege is much broader than the future-crime exception to the duty of confidentiality. When a communication is within the crime-fraud exception to the attorney-client privilege but is not within the future-crime exception to the duty of confidentiality, the attorney-client privilege does not protect the communication, but the lawyer continues to have an ethical duty to maintain the confidence. If eventually a court rejects the assertion of the attorney-client privilege and orders the lawyer to testify, the "orders of court" exception to the duty of confidentiality will permit the lawyer to reveal the confidence.

- As long as all other requirements are satisfied, when a client reveals a *past* crime or fraud, that information is protected by the duty of confidentiality and the attorney-client privilege.

- When a client has committed a past crime or fraud, the lawyer's representation of the client is what the legal system expects the client to be afforded. When the lawyer knows the client intends to commit a future crime or fraud, and *the lawyer's services are used to commit the crime or fraud,* the lawyer will share both the moral and legal responsibility for the wrong.

- Lawyers may reveal confidences when required to do so by other law or by order of the court.

- Even when some others in addition to the lawyer and client know the protected client information, the duty of confidentiality continues to protect the information. When the information *is generally known,* however, its continued protection by the lawyer will in some cases serve little purpose, and most would say that the duty of confidentiality is lost as well.

- A wide range of lawyer duties impose requirements on lawyers only when the duty does not offend the duty of confidentiality. A number of ethics rules require or permit lawyers to disclose information that would otherwise be protected by the duty of confidentiality. Notice the frequent interconnectedness of the confidentiality duty with other rules and topics. Failure to account for the application of Model Rule 1.6 when analyzing any of these other rules will produce errors.

Communications from agents of an *organizational client* are within the evidentiary privilege, and therefore within the duty of confidentiality, if two conditions are met: the information communicated is treated as confidential within the organization, and it is communicated to the lawyer so that the lawyer can give advice or counsel to the organization.

Because of the special public responsibilities of government agencies, government lawyers may strike a confidentiality balance somewhat more toward the public interest in disclosure of government wrongdoing.

Both lawyers and clients routinely use agents for communicating with each other. For purposes of the duty of confidentiality, client communication to a lawyer through a lawyer's agent is treated as if it were made directly to the lawyer. In addition, protected client information may be shared with other lawyers within the law firm, or an organization that represents the client. Communications from clients through agents to lawyers are treated as if they were made directly by the client to the lawyer.

Watch for the distinctions between the duty of confidentiality and the evidentiary privilege. It is critical that you watch the terminology in this area. Focus on the distinctions between the duty of confidentiality and the evidentiary attorney-client privilege. Carelessly mixing those two in reading a question or writing an answer will produce error after error.

- To be protected by the evidentiary privilege, the information must come from the client or a client's agent. Information that the lawyer learns from third parties is protected by the duty of confidentiality but not the privilege. To be protected by the duty of confidentiality, the information need merely "relat[e] to representation of a client." MR 1.6(a).

- The duty of confidentiality applies to all information relating to the representation, not merely communications from client to lawyer.

- Lawyer observations are protected by the duty of confidentiality.

- Communications from third parties about the representation are protected by the duty of confidentiality.

☛ Lawyer thoughts and strategies about the representation are protected by the duty of confidentiality. They are also protected by the related discovery doctrine called the ***work product*** doctrine.

As a client's agent, a lawyer is generally restricted from using confidential information of the client either for the lawyer's benefit or to the client's detriment. Notice that the Model Rules' drafters placed this rule with the conflicts-of-interest rules rather than with the confidentiality rule. Because of the overlap between these two areas, you need to discuss both when faced with a fact pattern that involves lawyer abuse of client information.

CHAPTER 6
CONFLICTS OF INTEREST

ChapterScope

- Conflicts of interest is among the most central, most pervasive, most complex, most important to practicing lawyers, and most-tested topics in the professional responsibility field.

- Conflicts of interest concepts have become increasingly important for several reasons:
    1. Lawyers change jobs during a career with much greater frequency today than lawyers of even 20 years ago. Because conflicts between former clients and current clients must be analyzed, the moving lawyer carries potential conflicts with all of his former clients with him into the new job.
    2. Corporate mergers, acquisitions, dissolutions, and divestitures occur at a much greater pace today than they did even 20 years ago. When corporate clients and opponents buy each other, sell off parts, and split up, potential conflicts occur.
    3. Law firms are bigger today than they were 20 years ago. Because many kinds of conflicts are presumed to affect the entire firm rather than the individual conflicted lawyer in the firm, conflicts affecting a 200-lawyer firm are far more numerous and likely than conflicts affecting a 20-lawyer firm.
    4. The job-changing's effect on conflicts is magnified by the reality that many large-firm lawyers move to other large firms and move to do work within their particular specialties. The result is that when lawyers change jobs, they are likely to move from one firm that works on a matter to another firm working on the same or a substantially related matter for a different client.

- When you analyze conflicts problems, ask yourself these questions:
    1. What is the source of the conflict? (third-party interference? multiple-client conflict? lawyer interests?)
    2. Does the conflict meet its particular rule's threshold requirements?
    3. Is the conflict one that imputes to the entire law organization?
    4. If so, can the affected lawyer be effectively screened or isolated from the organization?
    5. Is the conflict of a type that allows client waiver?
    6. If so, what has to occur for the waiver to be effective?

- Basic to the lawyer-client relationship is the premise that lawyers owe clients a duty of *loyalty*.

- Lawyers owe clients a duty of *independent professional judgment*. When the independence is threatened by some interest other than the client's, a conflicts question is present and requires analysis.

- Many conflicts questions are primarily about breaches of confidentiality.

- Because most conflicts put client interests at risk and because *client autonomy* and decision-making are values worthy of some respect, clients are empowered to *waive* most conflicts of interest.
    - The general rationale of honoring client autonomy does not apply when the conflict is sufficiently gross to make any client waiver suspect. See MR 1.7(a) and (b).

- The general rationale of honoring client autonomy does not apply when the conflicts rule is less about the risk to client interests than it is about risks to justice system interests.

- At a minimum, conflicts of interest waiver requires *informed consent* of the affected client. Some of the conflicts rules that allow waiver require more.

■ *Third-party interference* conflicts occur when someone who is not a party to the lawyer-client relationship seeks to affect or becomes positioned to affect the independence of the lawyer's judgment on behalf of the client.

■ In part because of the increased frequency of conflicts issues, lawyers now *move to disqualify* opposing counsel when they believe that a conflict exists. Filing a motion gets the matter before a court and affects strategies and outcomes of pending litigation. Therefore, conflicts issues are analyzed with much greater frequency than other professional responsibility issues that are chiefly raised through the infrequently operative bar disciplinary machinery.

■ Conflicts discovered after representation begins often require a lawyer to withdraw from the representation.

■ *Multiple-client conflicts* can implicate not only concurrent representation of multiple clients but also conflicts between former and current clients, or prospective and current clients, or prospective and former clients.

- Multiple-client conflicts discovered after representation begins often require a lawyer to withdraw from representation of all the affected clients.

- Because lawyers owe clients a continued measure of loyalty and a full measure of the duty of confidentiality after representation ends, conflicts between former and current clients arise when their interests are directly adverse or when there is a *substantial relationship* between the two representations.

■ A lawyer who represents an organization, such as a corporation, a labor union, or a public-interest organization, represents the organization, not its officers. At times, the interests of the organization and its officers may converge. Under such circumstances, a lawyer may represent both the organization and its officers, but the lawyer must withdraw if the interests of the organization and the officers diverge. MR 1.13.

■ When a lawyer represents two clients in unrelated matters for whom the lawyer must argue opposite sides of the same legal issue, a potential *positional conflict of interest* exists.

■ As a general rule, when a lawyer has a conflict of interest, that conflict imputes to (transfers to, extends to) all of the lawyers in the law organization (usually a law firm) in which the lawyer works. MR 1.10.

This *imputed disqualification* rule is mainly based on the notion that confidential information possessed by one lawyer is effectively possessed by all lawyers in the same firm.

- Effective *screening procedures* will prevent the application of the imputed disqualification rules. Some courts have labeled these screening procedures the "Chinese Wall" defense, because of the walling off of the affected lawyer. Under such procedures, the conflicted lawyer is isolated from other lawyers in the organization by various devices.

- When a court is considering a motion to disqualify, several factors may be considered in addition to the conflicts principles that are relevant in the disciplinary context.

- Special rules regarding imputed disqualification apply to former government lawyers and former judges.
- Various restrictions on lawyer conduct, often interrelated with lawyer-client conflicts issues, are based on the doctrines of *champerty, barratry,* and *maintenance.*

I. LOYALTY AND OTHER GENERAL PRINCIPLES

A variety of central principles is at play in analyzing *conflicts-of-interest* questions.

A. Loyalty

Basic to the lawyer-client relationship is the premise that lawyers owe clients a duty of *loyalty.*

B. Independence of professional judgment

Lawyers owe clients a duty of *independent professional judgment.* When the independence is threatened by some interest other than the client's, a conflicts question is present and requires analysis.

C. Implications of confidentiality

Many conflicts questions are primarily about breaches of confidentiality. See Chapter 5. When a lawyer who is serving multiple clients has confidences of one that would benefit the other, a conflicts-of-interest problem exists. Such a lawyer must either breach the confidences of one client or serve the other's interests less well than would be possible through the breach of the first client's confidence. Either choice is a breach of lawyer duty.

D. Direct adversity

Relatively easy cases of conflicts-of-interest analysis occur when the lawyer attempts to represent directly adverse interests. See §IV.C.1.a.

E. Material limitations on representation

The application of many of the conflicts rules is triggered by a determination of whether the conflict "will materially limit[] the [lawyer's representation of the client]." See, e.g., MR 1.7(b). This standard is objective. It requires an examination to determine whether the lawyer's options on behalf of the client will be limited in ways of consequence by interests other than the client's.

II. ORGANIZATION OF THE MODEL RULES PROVISIONS ON CONFLICTS

The Model Rules conflicts provisions are found in Model Rules 1.7 through 1.13 and 1.18.

A. General rule

Model Rule 1.7 sets out the general standards for conflicts-of-interest analysis. Those general standards are divided into those that apply to directly adverse representation of multiple clients

(MR 1.7(a)(1)) and limitations on representation from third parties, lawyer interest, and multiple clients (MR 1.7(a)(2)).

B. Specific transactions

Model Rule 1.8 sets out a series of specific conflicts rules that apply to particular lawyer-client transactions. See §IV.B.2.

C. Special problems of former clients

Model Rule 1.9 applies to multiple-client conflicts when one of the clients is a former client. See §IV.C.3.

D. Prospective clients

A new rule adopted in February 2002, Model Rule 1.18, defines and identifies duties owed to prospective clients.

E. Role-relevant rules

Conflict rules that apply to lawyers in particular lawyer roles are found as follows.

1. **Regarding former government lawyers:** MR 1.11.

2. **Regarding former judges:** MR 1.12.

3. **Regarding lawyers for organizations:** MR 1.13.

F. Imputed disqualification

Model Rule 1.10 provides the general imputed disqualification rules. More specific imputed disqualification rules are found in the following rules.

1. **Regarding former clients:** MR 1.9(b), 1.9(c).

2. **Regarding former government lawyers:** MR 1.11(a), 1.11(b).

3. **Regarding former judges:** MR 1.12(c).

III. WAIVER OF CONFLICTS

A. Rationale

Because most conflicts put client interests at risk and because client autonomy and decision-making are values worthy of some respect, clients are empowered to *waive* most conflicts of interest. By doing so, a client may then be represented by counsel of the client's choice in spite of the existence of a conflicts-of-interest concern. Two important exceptions to this general rationale exist.

1. **The gross conflict exception:** The general rationale of honoring client autonomy does not apply when the conflict is sufficiently gross to make any client waiver suspect. Some conflicts rules that allow for client waiver include an element that is independent of the client's preferences, requiring that the lawyer "reasonably believe that the lawyer will be able to provide competent and diligent representation to each affected client." MR 1.7(b). This test implicates both objective and subjective standards. The lawyer must in fact believe that the

representation will not be adversely affected. In addition, the lawyer's belief must be one that would be shared by a disinterested, reasonable lawyer.

Example: Client is a tenant, renting an apartment at Awful Arms Apartments. Client approaches Lawyer with Client's interest in pursuing a claim against Awful Arms based on breach of the warranty of habitability. Lawyer's spouse is the sole owner of Awful Arms Apartments, Inc. In effect, if Lawyer undertakes this representation, Lawyer would be filing a claim on Client's behalf against Lawyer's spouse. Even if Client asked that Lawyer engage in the representation despite the conflict, Lawyer cannot "reasonably believe that the representation will not be adversely affected [by the conflict]" and must, therefore, decline to undertake this representation.

Example: Client was represented by Law Firm A. Some time after her representation was concluded, Client determined to file a malpractice action against Firm A. In the interim, two of Firm A's partners, Pat and Pete, left Firm A and joined Firm B. Pat and Pete have continued liability for negligence that occurred at Firm A during their association with it. Client sought counsel from Firm B to represent her in her malpractice action against her former counsel, Firm A. If Client is successful, Pat and Pete will be liable for their pro rata share of the damages, along with the other Firm A partners. Client wishes to waive the conflict represented by Pat and Pete's joint status as partners in Firm B and potentially liable parties in her lawsuit. Her attempted waiver should be ineffective. No reasonable lawyer could conclude that representation would not be adversely affected when a plaintiff's lawyers are effectively the defendants in plaintiff's claim. Greene v. Greene, 391 N.E.2d 1355 (N.Y. 1979).

2. **The interest-other-than-the-client's exception:** The general rationale of honoring client autonomy does not apply when the conflicts rule is less about the risk to client interests than it is about risks to justice system interests. When it is not the client's interest that is primarily at risk, the client should not be permitted to waive the effect of the conflict. See, e.g., MR 1.8(d), 1.8(e), 1.8(i).

   a. **In particular:** All three of these particular rules, none of which allows for client waiver, implicate the lawyer's interests mixing with the client's interests in ways that may adversely affect the general interests of the justice system.

      i. **Model Rule 1.8(d):** This rule involves a lawyer's taking of literary rights in a client's story. See §IV.B.2.b. Waiver of such a conflict is not permitted in part because a lawyer interested in enhancing the drama of the client's matter may abuse the justice system, and the client's interests may lead him or her to enhance that drama.

      ii. **Model Rule 1.8(e):** This rule involves a lawyer's providing financial assistance to a client when litigation is pending or contemplated. See §IV.B.3.b. Waiver of such a conflict is not permitted in part because of the natural tendency for clients to freely give it (they may accept the financial assistance if they could waive the conflict) and because of the danger of lawyers' abusing the justice system by stirring up litigation with promises of financial support to prospective clients.

      iii. **Model Rule 1.8(i):** This rule involves a lawyer's acquiring an interest in the subject matter of litigation. See §IV.B.3.c. Waiver of such a conflict is not permitted in part because of the fear that lawyers will be too greatly interested in the litigation and that they will abuse the litigation process because of the extent of their personal interests.

b. **Another view:** Another way to view these aberrant conflicts rules is to regard them as not conflicts rules at all, but rather as remaining vestiges of restrictions on maintenance, champerty, and barratry. See §IV.B.3 and Chapter 10, §VIII. Nonetheless, they are mingled with the conflicts rules, and they do implicate possible impairment of lawyer's independent judgment potentially, but not always, to client detriment.

B. Elements of waiver

The February 2002 amendments changed the language from "consent after consultation" to "informed consent." By adding new definitions and using the newly defined terms throughout the Model Rules, the drafters have changed the terminology for client waiver from the former "consent after consultation," to "informed consent." In some instances, the amended rules require the informed consent to be "confirmed in writing." And in some, the writing must be signed by the client.

These changes are largely consistent with the provisions of Restatement of the Law Governing Lawyers (Third) sec. 122, and will probably not work any fundamental change in the law except for details of particular waiver rules requiring writings and in some cases client signature. Writings and client signatures have always been marks of the better practice when obtaining a waiver, but some rules for the first time will require that better level of practice.

1. **Consultation:** The original Model Rules had required "consent after consultation." The original Model Rules drafters had intentionally and carefully chosen the word *"consultation"* to describe the interaction between lawyer and client that must precede an effective waiver. The Model Code language for the same concept had been "full disclosure." See, e.g., DR 5-101. Full disclosure has a connotation of revelation rather than discussion. The Model Rules drafters wanted the language to indicate the necessity of both revelation and discussion with the client regarding the conflicts. They chose "consultation" for that reason.

   Example: Lawyer has agreed to represent Client at a reduced fee. Client's Mother approaches Lawyer and offers to pay the balance of Lawyer's normal fee. If Lawyer simply tells Client that Mother will pay the balance of Lawyer's fee, it might be said that Lawyer has "disclosed" the conflict. "Consultation" would require more than mere revelation. For consultation to occur, Lawyer must explain the possible ramifications of the conflict to Client. For example, Mother may seek to interpose herself between Lawyer and Client when strategic decisions are to be made in Client's case; Mother may expect Client or Lawyer to conduct the representation according to her wishes; Mother may have her own agenda in the representation. Despite Lawyer's assurances that Client is Lawyer's client and that Lawyer will protect Client's confidences from disclosure to Mother, these potential problems are issues that Client is better positioned to evaluate than Lawyer. Therefore, these possible ramifications should be discussed with Client in the context of "consultation."

2. **Client well informed:** The changes eliminate the absolute requirement of consultation in favor of a requirement that the client be well-informed, from whatever source that information might come. Sophisticated clients may need less information from the lawyer regarding the implications of a conflict.

   Some confusion yet to be resolved: Some confusion will be obtained on one question, however. The definitions and various comments to particular rules are not entirely consistent with respect to the source of client information upon which the waiver decision is to be based. The former term, "consent after consultation," carried the clear implication of the lawyer providing information and engaging in a discussion of that information with the client. Model Rule 1.0(e)'s definition of "informed consent" seems to carry that notion forward when it states that the client consent occurs "after the lawyer has communicated adequate information and explanation about the material risks and reasonably available alternatives to the proposed course of conduct." The new term itself, "informed consent," has its focus on the client's state of mind and not on the source of information. Comment 6 to Rule 1.0 opens the possibility that the information could acceptably come from sources other than the lawyer, stating that "a lawyer need not inform a client . . . of facts or implications already known to the client, . . . but a lawyer who does not personally inform the client . . . assumes the risk that the client . . . is inadequately informed and the consent is invalid." The sophistication of the client and the nature of the lawyer-client relationship will have a significant effect on how much if any information the lawyer needs to personally convey about the conflict and its implications. Comment 18 to Model Rule 1.7, also a new comment, adds to the uncertainty about the lawyer as a required source of information regarding waiver. It says that "informed consent requires that each affected client be aware of the relevant circumstances. . . ." It makes no mention of sources of information, but rather focuses attention on the client's state of mind with the "be aware" language.

3. **Consent:** After consultation, a client must consent if waiver is to be effective. The client consent must be freely given and not coerced. It may be partial or conditional, consenting to some but not all potential conflicts. See Restatement of the Law Governing Lawyers, Third, §122 (ALI 2000).

4. **Enhanced waiver requirements:** Some of the conflicts rules that allow waiver require more than informed consent. See, e.g., MR 1.8(a), MR 1.8(f).

IV. SOURCES OF CONFLICTS

There are three primary sources of conflicts of interest: third-party interference, lawyer interests, and multiple-client interests. Identifying the conflict's source tracks the lawyer into the applicable rules and analytical modes.

A. Third-party interference

Third-party interference conflicts occur when someone who is not a party to the lawyer-client relationship seeks to affect or becomes positioned to affect the independence of the lawyer's judgment on behalf of the client. See MR 1.7(a)(2) for the general rule. Such conflicts may be waived if the client gives informed consent.

1. **Third-party payment of fees:** The most common third-party interference example occurs when a third party pays the lawyer's fee for the lawyer's representation of a client. MR 1.8(f).

   Example: Harry has retained Lawyer to represent him in a divorce proceeding. Lawyer has agreed to represent Harry at a reduced fee. Harry's Mother approaches Lawyer and offers to pay lawyer's full fee on Harry's behalf. Lawyer may not agree to this proposal unless Harry gives informed consent. Even then, Lawyer must instruct Harry's Mother that Lawyer represents Harry and not Harry's Mother, and that Lawyer owes the lawyer's professional duties, including confidentiality, to Harry alone. MR 1.8(f).

2. **Other common interference settings:** Many practice settings place the lawyer in a position of guarding against inappropriate third-party influence as a regular, daily part of practice.

   a. **Lawyer for an organization:** The lawyer who represents an organization (e.g., a corporation, a labor union) represents the organization, not the individual directors or managers of the organization. MR 1.13. Nonetheless, the organization's lawyer talks and interacts with the directors and managers; indeed, the primary way in which the organization's legal needs and interests can be made known to the lawyer is through the communications of the directors and managers. To the extent that the managers and directors articulate the organization's interests, the lawyer is hearing from her client. But when the directors and managers interpose their personal interests between the lawyer and the organization-client, a third-party interference conflict of interest occurs.

   Example: Lawyer is in-house counsel to Corporation. CEO confides in Lawyer that CEO has been engaged in an ongoing series of frauds on behalf of Corporation, and instructs Lawyer to maintain this as a confidence. CEO has an interest in not being discovered and in continuing the frauds. Corporation has an interest in discontinuing CEO's actions and in distancing itself from the unauthorized and wrongful actions of CEO. CEO is a third party attempting to interfere with Lawyer's lawyer-client relationship with Corporation. Even though CEO ordinarily speaks for Corporation, Lawyer's duty is to Corporation, the entity that is Lawyer's client.

   b. **Legal services practice:** Lawyers who provide legal services to the poor through an organized legal services or legal aid office represent the clients, but are paid to do so by the organization for which they work. The legal aid organization is typically a not-for-profit corporation with a board of directors that obtains grants from the government and employs lawyers to represent people who meet low-income and asset eligibility requirements. Two sources of third-party interference are present and must be guarded against.

      i. **Board of directors:** The organization, usually through its board of directors, will typically establish case acceptance priority guidelines that restrict the lawyer's freedom to accept the cases that the lawyer might prefer to accept. Members of the board of directors of a legal services organization are not lawyers for the purpose of the lawyer-client relationship with the organization's clients. MR 6.3. Therefore, board members may represent clients who are adverse to the organization's clients, but may not participate in decisions of the organization that materially affect the interests of the organization's clients when the board member represents a client adverse to the organization's client. MR 6.3.

      ii. **Government restrictions:** Government regulations, especially those of the federal Legal Services Corporation, restrict the type of services that may be provided by organizations that receive the applicable category of funding. For example, a Legal Services Corporation grantee legal aid lawyer is prohibited from engaging in legislative lobbying services for clients. These restrictions are interferences by third parties with the lawyer-client relationship.

   c. **Insurance defense:** In some insurance contexts, a lawyer is hired and paid by an insurance company to represent the insured. When the insurance company is not also a party to the matter, the company is a potential third-party interference with the lawyer-client relationship between the lawyer and the insured.

Example: Defendant assaulted Plaintiffs. Plaintiffs filed suit against Defendant. Defendant's insurance policy would cover the incident unless Defendant acted intentionally. Despite representation of Defendant by Insurer's Lawyer, Insurer specifically reserved the right to assert this exclusionary clause against Defendant. While representing Defendant, Lawyer obtained confidential information that Defendant had acted intentionally. He then shared this information with Insurer. When the trial court found in favor of Plaintiffs, Plaintiffs attempted to recover against Insurer. Asserting that Defendant acted intentionally and invoking the intentional-act exclusion, Insurer successfully defended the Plaintiffs' attempt to execute the judgment against Insurer, thus leaving Defendant exposed to pay the judgment.

Although compensated by Insurer, Lawyer owed Defendant undivided loyalty. After obtaining the confidential information detrimental to Defendant's interests in relation to Insurer, Lawyer should not have revealed this information to Insurer. Parsons v. Continental Nat'l Am. Group, 550 P.2d 94 (Ariz. 1976).

Example: These are the sorts of restrictions that insurance companies place on insurance defense lawyers who are representing insureds:

GUIDELINE 1:

Preliminary workup should be restricted to a review of the Summons and Complaint, Appearance, investigative material, Answer, Demands for Answers to Interrogatories, requests for admission, requests for production of documents, and filing of Cross-Complaints, if applicable. No further workup is to be done without express authorization from the Company.

GUIDELINE 2:

Attorneys should not engage in investigation or lengthy and repeated interviews with witnesses or insureds if those procedures can be properly performed by independent adjusters or investigators. If extenuating circumstances cause a deviation from this instruction, authorization must be obtained from the Company.

GUIDELINE 3:

Legal research requirements should be promptly reported to the Company. You are requested to provide a summary of the reasons necessitating research requiring more than two hours, and not undertake same without authorization from the Company.

GUIDELINE 4:

Six-month interim billing is encouraged; however, other arrangements will be entertained. In no case will billing be considered on less than a quarterly basis. Time sheets and details of the services performed are required.

GUIDELINE 5:

If depositions are authorized, we request a "brief" narrative report covering the highlights of the testimony as they refer to the liability and damages. If the testimony simply confirms our prior knowledge of the claim, it is not necessary to highlight that testimony. In no case do we require copies of depositions unless specifically requested.

GUIDELINE 6:

The Company must be promptly advised of court appearances, settlement conferences, pre-trial depositions, and trial. It is required that counsel report twice daily when on trial. If reporting should have to take place after Company local hours, arrangements may be made to report to the handling examiner at home.

GUIDELINE 7:

The Company requests that attorney reports be concise and brief.

GUIDELINE 8:

Reports are to be forwarded directly to the examiner in charge of the file, addressing your correspondence to their individual attention. Single copies of your reports are all that is needed.

Pfeifer v. Sentry Insurance, 745 F. Supp. 1434 (E.D. Wis. 1990).

   d. **Military lawyers:** Military lawyers, not unlike legal aid lawyers, are paid by an entity to represent particular categories of individuals.

B. **Lawyer-client conflicts:**

The second major source of conflicts are lawyer interests that conflict with client interests.

   1. **General principles**

      a. **Material limitation:** As a general matter, a conflict of interest exists when a lawyer's "representation of a client will be materially limited by the lawyer's . . . personal interests." MR 1.7(a)(2).

      b. **Waiver:** Waiver of this general conflict is possible if "the lawyer reasonably believes that the lawyer will be able to provide competent and diligent representation to [the client] and [the client] gives informed consent, confirmed in writing." MR 1.7(b). See §III.

      Example: Client comes to Lawyer for assistance in drafting a lease for a building in which Client intends to establish a Mexican restaurant. Lawyer owns a one-half interest in the town's only other Mexican restaurant. Lawyer's financial interests will be harmed by the successful completion of work for Client. Lawyer's own interests may "materially limit" Lawyer's representation of Client. Nonetheless, if Lawyer reasonably believes that his representation of Client will not be adversely affected and if Client consents after consultation, Lawyer may accept the representation.

   2. **Particular transactions:** A variety of particular transactions between lawyers and clients is governed by specific conflicts rules.

      a. **Business transactions with clients:** Model Rule 1.8(a), which addresses business transactions between lawyer and client, requires that the client's consent be in writing, that the client be "advised in writing of the desirability of seeking and is given a reasonable opportunity to seek the advice of independent counsel," that the transaction be objectively reasonable, that the transaction itself be in writing and in terms that can be understood by the client, and that the client give informed consent in writing.

Example: Firm drafted a trust agreement for Client, designating Client and Lawyer of Firm as co-trustees. Lawyer had power to invest up to $100,000 of the trust's funds without Client's approval, limited only by liability for willful misconduct or gross neglect. Lawyer received a fee for his services and 10% of the profits from any sale of trust assets.

Lawyer may contract with Client, but Lawyer may not take advantage of his superior knowledge and position and must provide Client with full disclosure. Greene v. Greene, 436 N.E.2d 496 (N.Y. 1982).

Example: For several years, Lawyer advised Client on a number of business and personal matters. Client then decided to replace his small boat with a larger model, paying a deposit and requesting Lawyer to arrange for the financing of a $30,000 balance. Lawyer was unable to obtain sufficient funds for payment of the balance. Insisting that he did not want to lose his deposit, Client agreed to borrow $30,000 from Lawyer, with title to the new boat as security. Further, Client conveyed a parcel of real estate and all of the personal property on it and his small boat to Lawyer. Client also signed an agreement indicating his awareness of the drawbacks of the deal and containing his acknowledgement that Lawyer had advised against the transaction. When Client defaulted on the first payment on the note, Lawyer took possession of the new boat without notice to Client, as permitted by their agreement.

The transaction between Lawyer and Client was fundamentally unfair. At a minimum, Lawyer should not have proceeded with the transaction until Client had an opportunity to receive independent advice on the matter. Lawyer breached his fiduciary duty to Client. Lawyer must return the fair market value of the assets transferred plus interest. Goldman v. Kane, 329 N.E.2d 770 (Mass. App. Ct. 1975).

   i. **Exception:** The business transactions restrictions of Model Rule 1.8(a) apply only when the client expects the lawyer to exercise legal judgment regarding the transaction. As such, lawyer and client may enter ordinary business transactions with one another without restriction.

   Example: Lawyer and Client live in the same neighborhood. Lawyer attends Client's garage sale and purchases Client's used lawn mower at a very reasonable price. Because Lawyer was not expected to exercise legal judgment regarding the transaction, the business transaction restrictions do not apply.

   Example: Lawyer represents Sears, Roebuck and Co. in a variety of legal matters. Lawyer buys a Sears furnace to replace his at home. Because Lawyer was not expected to exercise legal judgment regarding the transaction, the business transaction restrictions do not apply.

b. **Literary rights:** Lawyers are prohibited from negotiating for literary or media rights based on their clients' stories until the conclusion of representation. A lawyer's judgment may be compromised if the lawyer has an interest in the client's matters being handled in a dramatic fashion. MR 1.8(d). No waiver of this conflict is permitted.

   Example: Murder Defendant is the son of a famous movie star. Lawyer agrees to represent Murder Defendant in exchange for Murder Defendant's agreement to cooperate only with Lawyer and with no other writer working on books or movie projects based on his story. Without more, Lawyer is subject to discipline. Government offers Murder Defendant a very favorable plea agreement. Lawyer's interests are furthered by rejection of the plea agreement. (Who wants to watch a movie-of-the-week with a negotiation session as the climactic scene?) Lawyer's independent judgment on behalf of Murder Defendant has been impaired.

    i. Ineffective assistance of counsel: The existence of a literary contract agreement does not in and of itself demonstrate that a criminal defendant has received ineffective assistance of counsel in violation of the Sixth Amendment. The lawyer is subject to discipline, but the defendant may not get appellate relief from a conviction based on the literary contract arrangement. See Maxwell v. Superior Court, 639 P.2d 248 (Cal. 1982).

c. Drafting instruments that benefit the lawyer: A lawyer is prohibited from drafting a document that makes a substantial gift to the lawyer or the lawyer's close relatives. This restriction does not apply when the donee is related to the donor. MR 1.8(c).

d. Sexual or amorous relations with clients: Because of the complicated mixture of interests that can develop when a professional lawyer-client relationship is mingled with an amorous one, lawyers are well advised to avoid amorous relationships with current clients. Some states have used a conflicts rationale to prohibit such relationships, whereas others have used a moral turpitude rationale.

    i. Specific rules: A new Model Rule adopted in February 2002, 1.8(j), prohibits most sexual relationships between lawyers and clients. The rule does not prohibit sexual relationships that predated the beginning of the lawyer-client relationship; however, some states have adopted specific rules that prohibit such relationships. See, e.g., Iowa DR 5-101. In such states, sexual relations with current clients are prohibited unless the lawyer and client had a consensual sexual relationship prior to the representation.

    ii. Rejection of specific rule: In at least one state, a proposed specific rule has been rejected on the ground that its restrictions are already adequately covered by the more general conflicts rules, such as the general lawyer-interests rule in Model Rule 1.7(a)(2). See Washington Bar News 27 (Feb. 1994) (regarding proposed amendment to RFC 8.4).

e. Agreements limiting the lawyer's liability: A lawyer is prohibited from entering into a contract with a client that prospectively limits the lawyer's liability for malpractice, unless state law permits and the client is represented by independent counsel with respect to the agreement. MR 1.8(h).

f. Settling claims with unrepresented clients: A lawyer is prohibited from settling malpractice claims with unrepresented clients or former clients, unless the lawyer first advises the client or former client that independent counsel is advisable. MR 1.8(h).

3. Lawyer-client conflicts and champerty, barratry, and maintenance: Various restrictions on lawyer conduct, often interrelated with lawyer-client conflicts issues, are based on the doctrines of champerty, barratry, and maintenance.

    a. Champerty, barratry, and maintenance: These three doctrines together are concerned with prohibiting the stirring-up and maintaining of litigation. They also, however, have an unfavorable history. Especially in the late nineteenth and early twentieth centuries, these rules were used to exclude and persecute ethnic lawyers, many of whom represented injured people in actions against the corporate clients of the powerful lawyers of the time who controlled the ABA, many state bar associations, and their disciplinary mechanisms. See definitions of champerty, barratry, and maintenance in Chapter 10, §VIII.

b. **Advancing funds to clients:** Lawyers are prohibited from advancing financial assistance to clients when there is pending or contemplated litigation, except that the lawyer may advance court costs. Client waiver of this "conflict" is not permitted. MR 1.8(e).

Example: Lawyer advanced money to three clients for purposes other than the cost of litigation (e.g., to help pay the clients' rent or grocery bills). He did not aim to obtain legal business or collect interest, but merely to provide charitable and humanitarian assistance to clients in extremely dire financial need.

The rule proscribing Lawyer's conduct makes no exceptions. It is intended to prevent an attorney from procuring an interest in a legal matter, but does not require proof of such intent or effect. Lawyer's conduct is subject to discipline. Committee on Professional Ethics & Conduct of the Iowa State Bar Ass'n v. Bitter, 279 N.W.2d 521 (Iowa 1979).

i. **State variation:** In some states, this restriction is relaxed when the client is indigent. These variations permit very limited financial assistance without the requirement that the assistance be repaid. See, e.g., Minnesota Rule 1.8(e)(3).

c. **Acquiring an interest in the litigation or its subject matter:** A lawyer is prohibited from acquiring an interest in litigation or its subject matter, whether that interest is consistent or inconsistent with the client's interests. This prohibition is not a restriction on the lawyer's contract with a client for a reasonable contingent fee. Client waiver of a violation of this rule is not permitted. MR 1.8(i).

Example: Client is engaged in a dispute over ownership of 22 acres of prime commercial property. Lawyer agrees to represent Client in this dispute in exchange for a 5% interest in the property conveyed to Lawyer from Client. Lawyer's interest is worth nothing unless Client prevails in the dispute. Lawyer is subject to discipline because the lawyer's interest may impair the lawyer's independent judgment, and because the lawyer's purchase of an interest in the subject matter of litigation is thought to violate the champerty policy against stirring up litigation. The same would be true if Lawyer had purchased a 5% interest in the property from Client's Opponent, but for different reasons. In this instance, Lawyer's interests would be adverse to Client's interests. By contrast, however, Client could pay Lawyer's fee by conveying a 5% interest in some other property of client's that was not the subject matter of the dispute.

4. **Miscellaneous lawyer-client conflicts rules**

    a. **Using confidential information to the client's detriment:** A lawyer is prohibited from using information learned in the lawyer-client relationship to the detriment of the client. In most instances, a lawyer is also prohibited from using such information to the lawyer's benefit on the theory that such use is also detrimental to the client. MR 1.8(b).

C. **Multiple-client conflicts**

The third major source of conflicts is the interaction of *multiple clients'* interests. Largely because lawyers owe a duty of confidentiality (and to a limited extent, loyalty) to both prospective and former clients, multiple-client conflicts can implicate not only concurrent representation of multiple clients, but also conflicts between former and current clients, prospective and current clients, or prospective and former clients.

1. **Concurrent clients:** Even when the conflicts involve only concurrent clients, a variety of different configurations may present themselves.

   a. **Directly adverse:** The easiest cases involve representation of multiple clients whose interests are in direct conflict. Simply put, lawyers may not represent clients on opposite sides of the same matter, especially when litigation is involved. Such a direct conflict cannot be effectively waived by the clients on the theory that it is too gross a conflict. MR 1.7(a). But see exceptions in intermediary role, Chapter 9, §III.

      Example: Firm has offices in City A and City B. Lawyer is a partner in Firm. Firm's City A office represents corporate Defendant in antitrust actions in two markets, and sought to represent Defendant against claims of Plaintiff that Defendant had conspired to create a monopoly in a third market. Firm's City B office represented Plaintiff in the "third market" suit. Lawyer owes a duty of undivided loyalty to each of his clients. Because such adverse representation is improper, Firm is disqualified from representing Plaintiff. Cinema 5 Ltd. v. Cinerama, Inc., 528 F.2d 1384 (2d Cir. 1976).

      Example: Plaintiff retained Firm A to represent her against Defendant. Lawyer X appeared on her behalf. Without making an official appearance on behalf of Defendant, Lawyer Y of Firm B did work on Defendant's case and spoke with Lawyer X about a dismissal of the claims against Defendant. However, an attorney for Firm C later appeared on behalf of Defendant. Lawyer Y then left Firm B to join Firm A, but did not participate in any way in representing Plaintiff. Firm B then replaced Firm C in representing Defendant.

      A presumption arises that Lawyer Y received confidential information regarding the representation of Defendant while at Firm B. Firm A did not rebut this presumption with evidence of any institutional mechanisms insulating Lawyer B from participation in and information about the litigation between Plaintiff and Defendant. Thus, Firm A is disqualified from continued representation of Plaintiff. Schiessle v. Stephens, 717 F.2d 417 (7th Cir. 1983).

   b. **Adverse in unrelated actions:** A lawyer may also find herself representing one client against a second client in a matter unrelated to the representation of the second client. The authority is mixed on whether such a conflict may be waived. It may depend on the context of the lawyer-client relationships involved and on the magnitude of the adversity. Both loyalty interests and the appearance of impropriety are offended by such representation. In general such a conflict may not be waived, but when the adversity is general, waiver has been permitted.

      Example: Lawyer represents Criminal Defendant against burglary charges. Lawyer also represents Grocery Store Owner as a regular matter in filing small claims to collect on bad checks and unpaid credit charges. Grocery Store Owner has such a claim against Criminal Defendant and wants Lawyer to file it. Lawyer should be subject to discipline for engaging in the representation against Criminal Defendant, unless both clients consent after consultation. MR 1.7 Comment.

      Example: Lawyer regularly represents Bank 1 and Bank 2 in a variety of matters. Bank 1 and Bank 2 are generally competitors. This generally adverse simultaneous representation should be permitted without the necessity of client waiver. MR 1.7 Comment.

c. **Same-side multiple-client representation:** Even representation of multiple clients who are at least initially on the same side of litigation or a transaction implicates conflicts analysis.

   i. **General:** Joint representation on civil claims brought simultaneously by multiple clients is permitted if the clients consent after consultation and if both the objective and subjective elements of the waiver test are met. See §III. When such representation is permissible, withdrawal from all representation may be the only adequate remedy if nonwaivable conflicts later develop. When that is the case, the lawyer may represent none of the multiple clients.

   Example: Driver and Passenger approach Lawyer with a potential claim against Careless Driver, who went left-of-center and collided with Driver's car. Lawyer interviews both Driver and Passenger and files a Complaint on their behalf against Careless Driver. Later in the litigation, Lawyer learns that Driver had been drinking before the collision. Under these circumstances, Passenger has a claim against Driver as well as the claim against Careless Driver. To continue to represent Passenger, Lawyer must advise the filing of a claim against Lawyer's client (or former client), Driver, and would have to use the information Lawyer learned in the representation of Driver (i.e., Driver's drinking) against Driver. To continue to represent Driver, Lawyer would have to refrain from revealing the confidences of Driver to Passenger. In either instance, Lawyer will have to breach duties to a client. Therefore, Lawyer must withdraw from representing both Driver and Passenger.

   Example: Husband, Wife, and Daughter retained Firm to represent them in a personal-injury claim against Driver and Owner and in an uninsured-motorist claim against Insurer that arose out of an automobile accident. After Firm determined that Husband's negligence had contributed to the accident, Husband discharged Firm as his counsel in the personal-injury action, and Wife and Daughter amended complaint, adding Husband as a defendant. Despite Husband's express waiver of the attorney-client privilege regarding his communications with Firm, and despite Wife and Daughter's explicit desire for representation by Firm, Insurer objected to Firm's continued involvement in the case.

   Insurer has standing to move for Firm's disqualification because it would be injured by Firm's use of any information obtained from Husband. Firm's representation of Husband raises the presumption that Firm received confidential information from him. Firm's continued representation of Wife and Daughter against Husband in the same matter in which it formerly represented Husband violates Model Rule 1.7. Firm is disqualified from representing Wife and Daughter. State Farm Mut. Auto. Ins. Co. v. K.A.W., 575 So. 2d 630 (Fla. 1991).

   ii. **Aggregate settlements:** In both civil and criminal matters, a lawyer is prohibited from engaging in aggregate settlements of multiple clients' claims or charges unless all clients give informed consent in a writing signed by the client. MR 1.8(g).

   Example: Lawyer represents Codefendant 1 and Codefendant 2. Prosecutor approaches Lawyer with a plea-bargain proposal. Prosecutor proposes that he will dismiss charges against Codefendant 1 if Codefendant 2 pleads guilty to a reduced charge. Lawyer may not participate in this aggregate settlement of claims against his two clients.

    iii. Special problems of joint representation in criminal cases: Representation of multiple criminal defendants implicates ineffective assistance of counsel principles as well as the conflicts principles and their disciplinary implications.

    Example: Criminal Defendant accepted representation from Lawyers retained by Codefendants. Defendant's trial occurred before those of Codefendants. Although the case against him consisted of entirely circumstantial evidence, Lawyers rested Defendant's case without presenting any evidence and Defendant was convicted. Subsequent trials resulted in acquittals of Codefendants. On appeal, one of the Lawyers admitted that concern for Codefendants affected his decision that Defendant would not present a defense.

    The possibility of a conflict of interest is insufficient to impugn a criminal conviction. However, if Defendant can demonstrate that an actual conflict adversely affected Lawyer's performance (i.e., show a connection between the lawyer's actions and the harm suffered by Defendant), his Sixth Amendment right to adequate legal assistance has been violated and Defendant is entitled to a new trial. Cuyler v. Sullivan, 446 U.S. 335 (1980).

2. Prospective and current clients: Lawyers owe prospective clients a limited loyalty duty and the duty of confidentiality. MR 1.18. Because confidentiality breaches are a primary consideration in multiple-client conflicts analysis, conflicts analysis must be done on potential conflicts between prospective and current or former clients.

    Example: Lawyer drafted a consumer contract for Local Audio Store. Local Audio Store uses the form contract for sales of audio equipment to consumers. Audio Consumer buys equipment at Local Audio Store pursuant to the form contract agreement. Audio Consumer later wants to avoid liability on the contract and consults Lawyer about ways in which he might avoid payment under the contract's terms. After the consultation, Lawyer concludes that he is prohibited from representing Audio Consumer because of his prior representation of Local Audio Store, and in particular his drafting of the agreement in question. Audio Consumer stops making installment payments under the contract, and Local Audio Store requests that Lawyer represent it in a civil action against Audio Consumer. Lawyer is prohibited from representing Local Audio Store in this matter because of his duty of confidentiality to his prospective client Audio Consumer. Even though Lawyer and Audio Consumer never formed a lawyer-client relationship, Lawyer owes Audio Consumer a duty of confidentiality and is prohibited from using Audio Consumer's confidences for Local Audio Store's benefit against Audio Consumer.

3. Former and current clients—The substantial relationship test: Because lawyers owe clients a continued measure of loyalty and a full measure of the duty of confidentiality after representation ends, conflicts between former and current clients arise when their interests are directly adverse or when there is a ***substantial relationship*** between the two representations. Such a conflict may be waived by both clients by informed consent. MR 1.9.

    Example: Lawyer worked as in-house counsel for Corporation before joining Firm A. After Lawyer joined Firm A, Firm A represented Plaintiff in a suit against Corporation. While employed by Corporation, Lawyer had access to confidential information relating to Corporation's business practices relevant to the litigation between Plaintiff and Corporation. While working for Firm A, Lawyer had personal involvement in the litigation between Plaintiff and Corporation. Whether or not Lawyer *actually* shared information about Corporation with Firm A, Lawyer is disqualified from the case. Haagen-Dazs Co. v. Perche No! Gelato, Inc., 639 F. Supp. 282 (N.D. Cal. 1986).

4. **Lawyer for an organization:** A lawyer who represents an organization, such as a corporation, a labor union, or a public-interest organization, represents the organization, not its officers. At times, the interests of the organization and its officers may converge. Under such circumstances, a lawyer may represent both the organization and its officers, but the lawyer must withdraw if the interests of the organization and the officers diverge. MR 1.13. See §IV.A.2.a for an example.

   Motivated by various corporate and securities defalcations, the ABA amended Model Rule 1.13 in August 2003. The amended rule retained the actual knowledge standard—even after the amendment, the attorney must have actual knowledge of a material violation by the corporate client.

   a. Model Rule 1.13 continues to require a corporate lawyer to act in the best interests of the corporation he or she represents. Before the 2003 amendments, the tone of Model Rule 1.13 tended to discourage action by the lawyer to prevent or rectify corporate misconduct.

   b. Before the 2003 amendments, Model Rule 1.13(b) required that any measure taken by the lawyer "be designed to minimize disruption of the organization and the risk of revealing information relating to the representation to persons outside the organization."

   c. Despite calls to change, the new rule continues to narrow the scope of any reporting duty to matters that relate to the lawyer's representation of the corporate client. Unlike the former 1.13, the amended rule presumes that reporting of misconduct within the rule's scope will occur. The old rule tended to discourage the reporting by articulating various interests that might justify a lawyer's decision to not report. The new rule allows the lawyer to decline to report only when the lawyer reasonably believes that reporting is not necessary in the organization's best interests.

      Example: Corporate Lawyer learns of serious misconduct occurring in another department of the corporation, one that does not rely on Corporate Lawyer's work in any way. Corporate Lawyer has no duty to report this misconduct under Model Rule 1.13. If Corporate Lawyer practices before the SEC, however, Sarbanes-Oxley regulations may require Corporate Lawyer to report this misconduct.

   d. Sometimes reporting "up the ladder" within the organization may not be enough. MR 1.13(c), a new provision, permits, but does not require, a lawyer for an organization "to communicate with persons outside the organization in order to prevent substantial injury to the organization."

      i. Model Rule 1.13(c) permits the lawyer to do so when the lawyer has already "reported up" in accordance with Model Rule 1.13(b), but the highest authority that can act on behalf of the organization does not act in an appropriate fashion and is clearly in violation of a law *and* the lawyer reasonably believes the violation is reasonably certain to result in substantial injury to the organization.

ii. When the lawyer does report outside the organization, the lawyer may only report to the extent the lawyer reasonably believes necessary to prevent substantial injury to the organization. In this circumstance, the lawyer may reveal information relating to the representation whether or not Rule 1.6 permits such disclosure.

iii. The 2003 Amendments also added provision Model Rule 1.13(d) to limit the scope of information that may be revealed through Model Rule 1.13(c). Model Rule 1.13(d) prohibits the lawyer from revealing information related to the lawyer's representation when the lawyer was engaged to investigate an alleged violation of law or to defend the organization or person associated with the organization against a claim arising out of an alleged violation of law.

e. In the 2003 amendments, Model Rule 1.13(e) was also added, giving discharged counsel additional options. "A lawyer who reasonably believes that he or she has been discharged because of the lawyer's actions taken pursuant to (b) or (c), or who withdraws in circumstances that require or permit the lawyer to take action under either of those, shall proceed as the lawyer reasonably believes necessary to assure that the organization's highest authority is informed of the lawyer's discharge or withdrawal."

f. In-house counsel have particular problems under Model Rule 1.13. An in-house lawyer may comply with Model Rule 1.13, but despite the lawyer's efforts, the officers or directors of the organization may not follow the lawyer's advice. The lawyer's last alternative under Model Rule 1.13 is to withdraw from representing the client. Unlike a lawyer in a private firm who has many clients, the in-house lawyer only has one client, the organization. If the lawyer withdraws from representation, he or she no longer has *any* client, nor a job or monthly income.

5. **Sarbanes-Oxley restrictions on certain corporate lawyers**

    a. Corporate counsel represent the entity and not the individual constituents of an organization. Recent corporate scandals, such as Enron, revealed the failure of the then-current system to properly communicate that counsel's loyalty is to the entity. In response, the Sarbanes-Oxley Act was enacted July 30, 2002, "to protect investors by improving the accuracy and reliability of corporate disclosures made pursuant to the securities laws." Pub. L. 107-204.

    b. Included within the Act is section 307, which includes rules of professional responsibility for attorneys. Section 307 gives the SEC broad power to establish rules of professional conduct for securities lawyers. The new rules were meant to require lawyers for a public company to climb the ladder of authority within the company, to the board of directors, if necessary "to report evidence of a material violation of securities law or breach of fiduciary duty or similar violation by the company or any agent thereof . . . if the [chief legal] counsel or [chief executive] officer does not appropriately respond to the evidence [by] adopting, as necessary, appropriate remedial measures or sanctions with respect to the violation." 17 CFR §§205.1-205.7.

    c. This SEC action represents a significant shift in the power to regulate lawyers from the profession itself to a government agency. Section 307 clearly requires a lawyer to report up the ladder of authority in an organization when the lawyer knows that the organization's managers are harming the organization by engaging in criminal or fraudulent conduct. The ABA and state bar organizations initially objected to the new rule on this basis.

d. The new rule requires lawyers to report up the ladder evidence of material violations of securities laws. Evidence of a material violation means "credible evidence, based upon which it would be unreasonable, under the circumstances, for a . . . [lawyer] not to conclude that it is reasonably likely that a material violation has occurred, is occurring, or is about to occur." Note that the SEC rule requires it be only "reasonably likely" that a violation has occurred, while Model Rule 1.13 requires actual knowledge of a material violation.

e. If evidence of a material violation is present, the lawyer, whether in-house or outside counsel, must report the violation to the chief legal officer, CEO, or a qualified legal compliance committee if one was created for the organization.

f. The chief legal officer is required to conduct an investigation and, unless he or she reasonably believes that no material violation has occurred, is ongoing, or is about to occur, the chief legal officer must take action to cause the company to adopt measures to stop the wrongdoing or prevent any material violations that have not yet occurred.

g. Section 307, however, provides some uncertainties.

  i. How much evidence must exist of the violation to trigger the report?

  ii. How much time can pass between the discovery of evidence and its disclosure?

  iii. What are the characteristics of appropriate and inappropriate responses to this disclosure by the CEO or senior company counsel?

  iv. How much time may pass between disclosure to the appropriate official and response?

  v. How does this new reporting requirement relate to state rules of professional conduct and malpractice liability?

6. Positional conflicts of interest: Lawyers are trained to be able to argue either side of a legal issue. When a lawyer represents two clients in unrelated matters for whom the lawyer must argue opposite sides of the same legal issue, a potential ***positional conflict of interest*** exists. Although "[o]rdinarily a lawyer may take inconsistent legal positions in different tribunals at different times on behalf of different clients, . . . a conflict of interest exists . . . [when] there is a significant risk that the lawyer's action on behalf of one client will materially limit the lawyer's effectiveness in representing another client in a different case. . . ." MR 1.7 Comment 24. Especially when these opposite positions are argued before the same court, however, the lawyer is effectively arguing for a precedent in one case that harms the client in the other case. This would "adversely affect" one of the clients while benefitting the other. This situation ought to be regarded as a multiple-client conflict under Model Rule 1.7 that requires that affected clients give informed consent for the lawyer to continue with both representations.

Example: Lawyer represents Client Art in Trial Court in the case of Art v. Millie. Lawyer represents Client Bart in Trial Court in the case of Willie v. Bart. Both cases are landlord-tenant disputes involving interpretation of a form lease. Millie and Bart are landlords; Art and Willie are tenants. Both Millie and Bart use the same form lease. Both Art and Willie are arguing that the lease fails to comply with a "Plain English" law in the jurisdiction. Lawyer argues this issue for Art (the lease violates the "Plain English" law); Lawyer argues the opposite side of the issue for Bart (the lease complies with the "Plain English" law). Winning the issue for one of his clients harms the other. A positional conflict of interest exists, and Lawyer needs informed consent from both clients for the representation to proceed.

V. IMPUTED CONFLICTS

As a general rule, when a lawyer has a conflict of interest, that conflict imputes to (transfers to, extends to) all of the lawyers in the law organization (usually a law firm) in which the lawyer works. MR 1.10.

A. Basic issues

This *imputed disqualification* rule is mainly based on the notion that confidential information possessed by one lawyer is effectively possessed by all lawyers in the same firm. In addition, loyalty and appearance of impropriety concerns arise when one lawyer in a firm engages in representation from which another lawyer in the firm would be disqualified for conflicts-of-interest reasons.

B. Motions to disqualify

Motions to disqualify counsel and entire law firms for which the disqualified lawyer works have become a favored tactical device in litigation, effectively denying an opposing party her counsel of choice and preserving the integrity of the justice system from the threat of conflicts of interest.

C. The ambulatory lawyer

The increasing movement of lawyers from one practice setting to another or from one law firm to another has dramatically increased the frequency and impact of imputed disqualification rules.

D. Screening defenses

An increasing number of courts, supported by Model Rules 1.10, 1.11, and 1.12, have ruled that effective *screening procedures* will prevent the application of the imputed disqualification rules. Some courts have labeled these screening procedures the "Chinese Wall" defense because of the walling-off of the affected lawyer. Under such procedures, the conflicted lawyer is isolated from other lawyers in the organization by various devices including, for example, the following.

1. **Don't talk:** The firm's lawyers are prohibited from speaking with the conflicted lawyer about the particular matter.

2. **No pay:** The conflicted lawyer is denied any remuneration from the firm's profits that are attributable to the particular matter.

3. **Lock it up:** The files from the particular matter are kept in locked file cabinets to which the conflicted lawyer has no access.

4. **Move him out:** When the matter is significant and long-term, the conflicted lawyer's office may be moved to a location away from the lawyers working on the matter.

Example: Lawyer worked as in-house counsel for Corporation before joining Firm A. After Lawyer joined Firm A, Firm A represented Plaintiff in a suit against Corporation. While employed by Corporation, Lawyer had access to confidential information relating to Corporation's business practices relevant to the litigation between Plaintiff and Corporation. While working for Firm A, Lawyer had personal involvement in the litigation between Plaintiff and Corporation. Whether or not Lawyer *actually* shared information about Corporation with Firm A, Lawyer is disqualified from the case. Because Firm A did not institute a screening procedure to isolate Lawyer from matters involving Plaintiff until after litigation between Plaintiff and Corporation had commenced, Firm A is disqualified from the case. Haagen-Dazs Co. v. Perche No! Gelato, Inc., 639 F. Supp. 282 (N.D. Cal. 1986).

Example: In previous employment, Lawyer represented X in an action to enforce certain contract rights against Y. Lawyer's New Firm is approached to represent Z in a contract claim against X. New Firm recognizes the potential conflict that Lawyer would have with this representation, and isolates Lawyer from the matter. New Firm issues a memorandum to all personnel prohibiting them from discussing the Z v. X matter with Lawyer. It restricts Lawyer's access to the area in which files on the matter will be kept, and it issues a memo to Lawyer indicating that his partnership share will be calculated without any remuneration for work New Firm does for Z. New Firm may go forward with its representation of Z. Its screening defense should be effective against a motion to disqualify it from the representation filed by X.

E. Other interests at play in the motion-to-disqualify setting

When a court is considering a motion to disqualify, several factors may be considered in addition to the conflicts principles that are relevant in the disciplinary context.

1. **Client choice of lawyer:** Clients have a limited interest in having their lawyer of choice. This interest weighs against granting of motions to disqualify.

2. **Timing of screening procedures and motion to disqualify:** Effective screening procedures instituted *after* the conflicted lawyer has been in the law firm for some time, or, worse yet, *after* the motion to disqualify is filed, make the screening procedures less likely to excuse imputed disqualification. By contrast, a motion to disqualify filed well after the moving party had reason to know of the presence of the conflicted lawyer, or, worse yet, close to the date of trial when the presence of the conflicted lawyer had been known to the moving party for some time, make the motion to disqualify less likely to be successful.

3. **Intentional creation of conflicts by the moving party:** Some institutional clients (banks, hospitals, insurance companies, etc.) have spread their legal work among a variety of law firms so that all such firms will be arguably disqualified from representing clients against the institution. At least one court has indicated that such tactics will make such an institution's motions to disqualify less likely to be successful. SWS Financial Fund A v. Salomon Brothers, Inc., 790 F. Supp. 1392 (N.D. Ill. 1992).

4. **Judicial economy:** When a motion to disqualify is granted, litigation is set back while replacement counsel becomes familiar with the matter. Notions of judicial economy favor the denial of motions to disqualify.

F. Special role-related imputed disqualification rules

Special rules regarding imputed disqualification apply to former government lawyers and former judges. See §VI.

VI. SPECIAL ROLE-RELATED CONFLICTS RULES

Lawyers who find themselves in special roles find that special conflicts rules apply.

A. Former judge

Former judges' conflicts differ from those of lawyers who move from one practice setting to another, and they require special conflicts rules. MR 1.12.

1. **General:** In their judicial role, judges do not represent parties and thus have little of the loyalty transfer concerns of lawyers representing multiple clients. In addition, judges are not the confidants of clients and thus carry forward into private practice no former client confidences. Nonetheless, the appearance-of-impropriety considerations are stronger in the case of certain former judge conflicts situations than are the like concerns with lawyers' similar conflicts. See Chapter 11.

2. **Successive representation in the same matter:** A former judge shall not engage in private representation in a matter in which the judge participated personally and substantially as a judge, unless all parties to the matter consent after consultation. MR 1.12.

    a. **Personal and substantial participation:** Judges in most courts are members of a group of judges who individually hear cases brought before their court. The mere fact that a judge was a member of a group of judges that variously hear cases brought to a particular court does not disqualify the judge from all matters that were in the court while the judge was there. Only when the judge has participated personally and substantially will the conflicts rule apply.

    i. **Personally:** Personal participation is just that: The rule does not apply if the judge's court, but not the particular judge, heard the matter.

    Example: Judge is a member of the Common Pleas Court for Harsh County. The case of A v. B is pending in the court during Judge's tenure there, but Judge does not preside over it, Fellow Judge does. Judge has not participated personally in this matter and is therefore not later disqualified if she enters private practice and is approached by A or B for representation.

    Example: Judge is a member of a three-judge court of appeals panel hearing the intermediate appeal in X v. Y. The judge is a voting member of a unanimous decision affirming a trial court judgment for X. After the decision, Judge's term on the intermediate appellate court expires, and Judge takes a position in Law Firm. Y appeals from the decision of the intermediate appellate court to the state supreme court. X approaches Judge in her new law firm employment to ask that Judge represent X on appeal to the state supreme court. Judge is disqualified from doing so because Judge participated both personally and substantially in the matter while a judge.

    ii. **Substantially:** Even personal participation does not implicate the conflicts rule when the participation is insubstantial. If the judge's personal participation in the matter is limited to noncontroversial, non-merits matters, that personal participation will not disqualify the judge under the conflicts rule.

    Example: Judge is a member of the Trial Court bench. There are ten judges who hear on a rotating basis cases brought to Trial Court. The matter of X v. Y was tried in Trial Court. Early in the pendency of X v. Y, Y filed a motion, agreed to by X, for an extension of time to respond to X's Interrogatories. As the judge on call at the time, Judge signed the Order based on Y's motion for an extension of time. Judge's participation in X v. Y is personal, but not substantial.

    Example: Judge is a member of the Trial Court bench. There are ten judges who hear on a rotating basis cases brought to Trial Court. The matter of X v. Y was tried in Trial Court. During the pendency of X v. Y, Y filed a motion for discovery sanctions against X. The motion was hotly contested by the parties, involving crucial discovery disputes. Judge presided over this motion proceeding, but did not preside over the later trial. Judge's participation in X v. Y is both personal and substantial, even though Judge did not preside over the trial or any merits issues. The motion proceeding was a substantial part of the litigation.

3. **Negotiating for employment:** Judges are prohibited from negotiating for employment with lawyers who are currently representing parties before the judge's court if the judge is personally and substantially participating in the matter before the court. Similar, but waivable, restrictions apply to judicial law clerks. MR 1.12(b).

4. **Special imputed disqualification rules:** To prevent a handcuffing of former judges' efforts to obtain private-law-firm employment after judicial service, and because former judge conflicts do not implicate the same sort of loyalty and confidentiality abuse as do multiple client-lawyer conflicts, special, more relaxed imputed disqualification rules apply to the law firms for which former judges work. Effective screening procedures and notice to the parties and the judge's former court permit a former judge's law firm to continue with representation in which the former judge is disqualified from participating. MR 1.12(c).

B. Former government lawyer

Special conflicts rules apply to lawyers who move from government practice to private practice. MR 1.11. At least two facts distinguish former government lawyers who move into private practice from private-practice lawyers who have moved from employment in one law firm to employment in another law firm. First, government lawyers represent the government (or the public or the particular agency within which they worked). As a result, in later private practice, any representation of private parties against the government might be seen as former-client conflicts. Because of the breadth of the potential disqualification from representation, this result must be ameliorated. Second, as a government lawyer, the stakes of the appearance of impropriety are raised. The possibility of abuses of either relationships with former colleagues still in government practice or of confidential government information creates greater concern regarding private practice subsequent to government practice. Both of these facts have effects on the formulation of the special conflicts rules that apply to former government lawyers.

1. **General:** A former government "lawyer shall not represent a client in connection with a matter in which the lawyer participated personally and substantially" as a government lawyer. MR 1.11.

    a. **Without regard to changing sides:** Notice that this conflict rule applies without regard to whether the lawyer has effectively changed sides in the matter.

   Example: The SEC investigated and prosecuted Defendants for misappropriating money and property from a group of investment companies. Following a default judgment against Defendants, Judge appointed Receiver to recover the judgment from Defendant. Receiver retained Firm to assist in litigation against Defendants. However, Firm employed Lawyer, a former SEC official who had had supervisory authority over the original prosecution of Defendants. Although Lawyer had not participated on a daily basis, he was generally aware of the facts of the case and the status of the litigation. Lawyer may not participate in the representation of the Receiver absent agency consent. Armstrong v. McAlpin, 625 F.2d 433 (2d Cir. 1980), *vacated on other grounds,* 449 U.S. 1106 (1981).

b. **Personal and substantial participation:** Similar to the treatment of former judges, the mere fact that a lawyer was employed in a particular agency while that agency was involved in a matter does not disqualify the lawyer under the conflicts rules. Only when the lawyer has participated personally and substantially will the conflicts rule's disqualification threshold issues be satisfied.

   i. **Personally:** Personal participation is just that: The rule does not apply if the lawyer's agency or department was involved in a matter, only when the lawyer was involved.

   ii. **Substantially:** Even personal participation does not implicate the conflicts rule when the participation is insubstantial. Mere presence, for example, at a staff meeting at which a matter was discussed or participation in a minor, tangential aspect of a matter will not implicate the conflicts rule.

c. **Exceptions:** Three exceptions allow the former government lawyer to engage in the later private representation, even when his participation in the government employment was personal and substantial.

   i. **Law otherwise permits:** The conflicts rule excepts from its reach cases in which the law otherwise expressly permits the private representation to occur. If, for example, the agency for which the lawyer formerly worked has within its regulations a provision authorizing later private practice in various instances, the conflict rule does not restrict the lawyer.

   ii. **Not a "matter":** The rule defines what it means by a "matter." It is only later private representation in connection with a government service "matter" that triggers a conflicts-of-interest analysis. A matter includes a wide variety of instances and actions that engage the agency with a particular party or parties. The definition excludes rule drafting and other agency actions that have more general application.

   Example: Lawyer worked in the IRS policy office. Lawyer's primary task was to draft a new set of regulations for determining the deductibility of business travel expenses. The regulations that Lawyer drafted became law through normal agency procedures. Later, Lawyer leaves the IRS and goes into private practice. Client hires Lawyer to defend an action being brought by the IRS. At issue is the interpretation of the business travel regulation that Lawyer had written. Lawyer may represent Client because the regulation drafting activity is not a "matter." MR 1.11(e).

   iii. **Consent:** The agency may waive the conflict by giving its informed consent. In the absence of a specific statute that applies to the specific agency to the contrary, an agency may waive all future conflicts for its departing lawyers.

2. **Use of confidential government information:** Except when law otherwise expressly permits such representation, a former government lawyer is also prohibited from representing private parties who are adverse to parties about whom the lawyer has confidential information gained in the government practice that could be used against the adverse party. MR 1.11(c).

   Example: Lawyer formerly worked for the IRS. In that capacity, Lawyer was privy to confidential information about Taxpayer's finances and assets. In private practice, Client approaches Lawyer requesting representation against Taxpayer in a complex matter that involves the finances and assets of Taxpayer. Lawyer has a conflict of interest and may not represent Client against Taxpayer unless Taxpayer consents.

a. **Private party, not agency waiver:** The private party's interests are the ones at risk in such a case. As such, it is the private party and not the agency that must waive the conflict if the lawyer is to be permitted to proceed. Such a waiver is, of course, highly unlikely in such an instance.

3. **Special imputed disqualification rules:** Special, more relaxed imputed disqualification rules apply when former government lawyers are the law firm lawyers who have a conflict. The government would have a difficult time recruiting qualified lawyers if those lawyers knew that their firms would be disqualified from doing virtually all of the type of work they did in government practice.

Example: Lawyer was employed at the IRS. During that time, Lawyer represented the IRS, or, more generally, the federal government as a client. Lawyer left government service for private practice. If the conflict rules applied strictly in this instance, Lawyer could not represent anyone against the IRS (a former client) without IRS consent. Further, as a general proposition, Lawyer's disqualification would be imputed to Lawyer's law firm, thus preventing both Lawyer and her law firm from doing federal tax practice. The conflict rules relax slightly for former government lawyers. MR 1.11.

The imputed disqualification rules relax with respect to former government lawyers' law firms.

Example: The SEC investigated and prosecuted Defendants for misappropriating money and property from a group of investment companies. Following a default judgment against Defendants, Judge appointed Receiver to recover the judgment from Defendant. Receiver retained Firm to assist in litigation against Defendants. However, Firm employed Lawyer, a former SEC official who had had supervisory authority over the original prosecution of Defendants. Although Lawyer had not participated on a daily basis, he was generally aware of the facts of the case and the status of the litigation. Receiver learned of Lawyer's employment with Firm during his initial meetings with Firm, and Receiver and Firm agreed to screen Lawyer from the litigation against Defendants. Both the SEC and Judge authorized this plan.

Although Lawyer may not participate in the representation of the Receiver absent agency consent, Firm is not disqualified because (1) the SEC had turned over its files to Receiver before he retained Firm, (2) Lawyer was properly screened from the case, (3) disqualification would hamper government efforts to recruit qualified attorneys by limiting their future employment opportunities, and (4) disqualification would delay and perhaps thwart Receiver's attempts to redress the wrongs committed by Defendants. Armstrong v. McAlpin, 625 F.2d 433 (2d Cir. 1980), *vacated,* 449 U.S. 1106 (1981).

C. Lawyer as witness

Special conflict problems are associated with the occasion on which a lawyer is to be called as a witness. MR 3.7.

1. **Combining roles:** The lawyer-as-witness problem is a conflict problem in the sense that the lawyer as witness has a mixture of roles that may compromise the lawyer's independence of judgment on behalf of the client. The compromising aspects are complex, and the lawyer may be disqualified from representing the client when the combination of interests dictates.

2. **Rationale:** Like every witness, a lawyer as a witness has an interest in simply testifying truthfully. That interest mixes with the lawyer's advocacy interest in presenting her client's

case favorably to the fact-finder. When a lawyer is to be advocate for both a client and a witness, one of several unfortunate things may happen.

   a. **Unfavorable testimony:** The lawyer may be testifying to facts that are unfavorable to her client, creating a conflict in their interests. A fact-finder, recognizing the lawyer's advocacy role, may give even greater than ordinary credence to the unfavorable testimony, thus harming the client.

   b. **Favorable testimony:** The lawyer may be testifying to facts that are favorable to the client. A fact-finder, recognizing the lawyer's advocacy role, may discount the favorable testimony, thus diminishing its favorable effect for the client.

   c. **Mixed testimony:** Because a single witness's testimony is most often a mixture of the favorable and unfavorable, most instances of lawyer as witness implicate a combination of the harms referred to in a and b.

   d. **Unfair cross-examination:** Viewed from the opposing party's perspective, opposing counsel may regard as unfair the prospect of cross-examining the lawyer-witness. Indeed, despite the potentially harmful effects of lawyer testimony on the lawyer-witness's client (see a and b), most often such testimony is challenged before a court by motion of the opposing party. In re American Cable Productions, Inc., 768 F.2d 1194 (10th Cir. 1985).

3. **Exceptions**

   a. **Uncontested matters:** When the lawyer's testimony relates merely to uncontested matters, the harms are diminished greatly and the rules do not require the lawyer to withdraw from the representation. MR 3.7(a)(1).

   b. **"As an advocate at trial":** The rule requiring disqualification applies only to trial lawyers. Trial preparation activities of lawyers who are likely to be called as a witness are permitted.

   c. **Nature and value of legal services:** A lawyer may testify regarding the nature and value of services the lawyer has rendered even when he acts as his own trial counsel in a case regarding the collection of the lawyer's fee. MR 3.7(a)(2).

   d. **Substantial hardship from disqualification:** When the disqualification would work a substantial hardship to the client, the disqualification rule does not apply. This analysis requires a balancing of the client's special need for the particular lawyer's representation, the cost of replacing counsel, the timing of the motion, and the potential harm to the moving party. MR 3.7(a)(3).

Quiz Yourself on
CONFLICTS OF INTEREST

51. Alan and Bill were car-pooling to work one morning when they were involved in a car accident. Alan was driving. Alan and Bill both believe the other driver to be primarily at fault, but Alan was fumbling with his seat-belt at the time—an issue that the fact-finder may find relevant, especially in their comparative negligence state.

Alan and Bill approach you, seeking joint legal representation. Are there any circumstances under which you may represent both Alan and Bill, rather than advising one of them to seek other counsel? _____

52. Assume that the facts are the same as those given in the above question. Alan and Bill seek joint representation for their suit against the other driver in a car accident. However, in this case, interviews with the prospective clients and two different witnesses reveal that Alan had been drinking before the incident and may have been largely at fault for the collision. After a full consultation, Alan and Bill still insist that they wish to be jointly represented, and they waive any possible conflicts. Can you represent them? _____

53. Judge Bennett recently moved from the bench to private practice with XYZ law firm. XYZ is approached by Chemical Corp. for legal representation. While still acting as a judge, a motion came before Judge Bennett involving the same case against Chemical Corp. The Judge ruled that Chemical Corp. had not complied with discovery request deadlines and ordered the Corporation to either turn over the requested materials or face contempt charges. Is Judge Bennett disqualified from this representation? _____

54. Ann approaches Lawyer Fred concerning a possible lawsuit against a local real estate agency. In fact, the agency is owned and managed by Fred's wife, and some of the couple's personal funds were invested to start the business. Fred is confident, however, that he can remain neutral and, after a complete consultation with Ann, Ann voluntarily agrees to waive the conflict of interest. Is Fred's representation of Ann against the agency a violation of the ethics rules? _____

55. Brian, an attorney in private practice, takes a pro bono tort case for an indigent client. Because his client is poor, Brian offers to cover the expenses involved in taking several depositions, including a very expensive expert-witness doctor. One of Brian's friends questions whether Brian can do this under the rules, but Brian assures his friend that he had the client sign a waiver of the conflict of interest. Does Brian's paying for the depositions violate the ethics rules? _____

56. Sandra, a one-time attorney with the Environmental Protection Agency (EPA), has recently moved to a private environmental law practice. While with the EPA, Sandra participated in a case against CleanCo. for its violations of several major environmental laws. Her participation in the case allowed her access to confidential business information about the company, as well as a lot of information about its system of environmental compliance and the difficulties it has had in implementing and maintaining the system. Now, Sandra is approached by a citizens group that wishes to bring suit against CleanCo. for violations of a completely different environmental statute. Can Sandra act as their attorney? _____

57. An attorney with the Labor Department learns of a case in which the Circus Workers' Union has figured out a loophole to one of the Department's regulations. In response to the Union's activity, the attorney launches an initiative that results in an amended regulation preventing further Union activity. Now that she is in private practice, may the attorney represent the Union in defending an agency-brought action based on the regulation? _____

58. As you attempted to cross the street in the safe haven of a crosswalk one afternoon, a driver ran a stop sign and hit you. You receive severe injuries and incur sizable medical bills. Seeking redress, you go to Lawyer Jill. You give her all of the basic details about the accident, your insurance coverage, and your medical history and problems. Lawyer Jill believes you have a claim, but regretfully declines to represent you when she discovers a potential conflict of interest. If you discover that Jill later agreed to represent the driver in the accident, is Jill subject to discipline? _____

59. You are injured in a car wreck in which your friend was driving. You and your friend both believe the other driver was at fault. You decide to join together to sue the other driver and go see Attorney Paul.

Paul listens to the details of the accident and tells you that you two could have conflicting interests in the case. However, Paul says he can still represent you both if you sign waivers. Is Paul subject to discipline? _____

60. You have a casual attorney friend named Alex. You like Alex, but recently you have learned of some disturbing activity in which Alex was involved. You know that lawyers are prohibited from drafting instruments in which they are personal beneficiaries. However, you have discovered that Alex recently drafted his aunt's will, in which he is named as one of the beneficiaries. Do you have a duty to report Alex? _____

61. You are planning to defend Denise against criminal charges. Denise is suffering financial difficulties in addition to her criminal problems, and you agree to do the work pro bono. Later in the week, however, her brother calls and offers to pay your fee. What must occur for you to accept her brother's proposal? _____

62. The state of Robbins is governed by a statute allowing uncontested divorce parties to "share" the same attorney when it is reasonable to do so. Attorney Julie has, in the course of her divorce practice, represented several such couples, acting as a successful intermediary. Today, Paul and Alison enter her office, and they seem perfect for the same situation. They have no children, no hard feelings, and have already divided the assets. In light of their situation, Julie has them sign a contract for services without any further discussion. They begin to discuss the specific details of the divorce. Has Julie violated any rules? _____

63. Leslie works for a law firm doing securities work for various clients. From several passing comments by colleagues, Leslie hears of fraudulent conduct being committed by a securities client in a matter for which Leslie has no responsibility. Based on these comments, Leslie believes the misconduct may have occurred, but does not know that it has. How should Leslie determine her obligations to report this possible misconduct? _____

64. Ned represents his neighbor Bob in various routine business matters relating to Bob's barber shop. They have had a long-time personal friendship as well, as they live in the same neighborhood. Bob stages an impressive yard sale. While walking his Shih Tzu, Ned walks by Bob's and notices his sale. Ned is in the market for a new lawnmower, and stops to buy Bob's used Toro mower. The price seems fair, and they make the deal. Ned and the Shih Tzu walk home with his new possession.

Later that year, Bob decides to sell part of his barbershop business to Ned. Ned writes the contract for the selling of part of the business, but before Bob signs it, he asks Ned if he should get an opinion of another lawyer. Ned tells him this is nonsense, because they are such good friends and that this is just a simple matter. Bob later finds out that Ned bought part of the barber shop for far below the price he could have gotten at the time.

Was the selling of the lawnmower between lawyer and client appropriate? Was the selling of part of the barber shop between lawyer and client appropriate? _____

Answers

51. Yes, provided that you receive each client's informed consent. In this case, the clients should be informed of how comparative negligence works and the fact that Bill will have to give up any of his possible claims against Alan, which could preclude Bill's full recovery. However, as long as no "gross conflict" exists, you may represent them with consent. Nonetheless, if conflicts develop during representation, you will likely have to withdraw from representing both Alan and Bill.

52. No. Joint representation requires both consent AND a reasonable belief that representation will not be adversely affected (MR 1.7(a), MR 1.7(b)). You must not only personally believe that the representation will not be adversely affected, but the belief must be one that would be shared by an objective, reasonable attorney.

53. Yes. A judge who has participated personally and substantially in a matter is disqualified from later representation of either party. Ruling on a pretrial motion of significance should be considered such a personal and substantial involvement. MR 1.12.

54. Yes. When competing interests are at stake, a lawyer must not only get client consent, but also hold a reasonable belief that the representation will not be adversely affected. Here, such a belief is not reasonable.

55. No. An attorney is permitted to advance the costs of litigation to his client, even without an assurance that they will be paid regardless of the outcome. Moreover, no waiver was necessary in this situation because advancing litigation costs created no conflict. However, Brian could not advance any other financial assistance to his client (e.g., living expenses while the case is pending), and no waiver of this rule is allowed.

56. No, unless CleanCo. consents, an unlikely prospect. Sandra is not permitted to represent a private party with interests adverse to a party about whom she gained confidential information while still in government practice. Here, although the environmental statutes are different, the confidential information Sandra gained about CleanCo. while with the EPA could be used unfairly and to CleanCo.'s disadvantage.

57. Yes. Even though the government attorney's participation in this was personal and substantial, an exception is made when her participation did not involve a "matter." A matter generally involves instances and actions that engage that agency with a particular party or parties. Drafting regulations does not fit under this category.

58. Yes. Lawyers owe a duty of confidentiality even to prospective clients. Although Jill did not represent you, she also owes you a limited loyalty duty and must avoid a conflict of interest in your case. No formal lawyer-client relationship need be formed to implicate these duties.

59. Yes. An informed client waiving a conflict of interest should know not only of the existence of the conflict, but also the possible consequences that may result from the waiver. Here, Paul should have explained issues such as a possible inability to get a full recovery if your friend is found partially at fault and any possible claims against your friend you would be waiving.

60. No, because Alex has not violated any professional conduct rules. Lawyers cannot draft documents that make a substantial gift to the lawyer or close relative. However, an exception is made when, as here, the donee is related to the donor. MR 1.8(c).

61. You must cover several bases to accept payment from a third party for Denise's legal expenses. First, Denise must consent to the arrangement after consultation. Then, you must make clear to Denise's brother that Denise is still your client, regardless of who is paying the fees. Denise will still get to call the shots, and you will owe your lawyer duties such as confidentiality to Denise alone.

62. Yes. To represent both parties in a divorce, both a consultation on the common risks and effect on confidentiality and the consent of the clients are needed. Even with these safeguards, the potential for an escalated conflict still exists, and if this happens Julie will have to withdraw as counsel.

63. If Leslie were not doing securities work, Sarbanes-Oxley would be irrelevant and only the possible reporting requirements of Model Rule 1.13 would apply. Because she is doing securities work, the MR 1.13 and Sarbanes-Oxley reporting requirements may overlap and must both be examined. Unlike the Model Rule 1.13 requirements, the Sarbanes-Oxley reporting requirements apply even when a lawyer learns of activities that are not within his or her scope of representation activities. This misconduct is outside Leslie's scope, so only Sarbanes-Oxley applies and Model Rule 1.13 is irrelevant. Another reason exists for Model Rule 1.13 to be inapplicable: Leslie does not "know" of the misconduct, as is required to trigger the Model Rule 1.13 reporting requirements. But she does have "evidence" of the misconduct, and as such, she must report as Sarbanes-Oxley requires.

64. The business transaction involving the lawnmower was appropriate because in this transaction, Bob had no expectation that Ned would exercise lawyer judgment on Bob's behalf. The rule that regulates lawyer-client business transactions (MR 1.8(a)) is not triggered unless the client is relying in some measure on the lawyer's legal judgment. There seems to be no reason why Bob would rely on any legal judgment by Ned in the purchase of his used lawnmower.

The business transaction involving the barbershop was not appropriate, however. Although a lawyer is not prohibited from entering into a business transaction with a client, the transaction must be fair and reasonable to the client and fully disclosed and transmitted in writing in a manner that can be reasonably understood by the client. The client must also be advised in writing of the desirability of seeking and given a reasonable opportunity to seek the advice of independent legal counsel on the transaction. The client must also give informed consent. MR 1.8(a).

In this case, the terms of the transaction were not fair and reasonable to Bob. Ned also did not give Bob the opportunity to seek advice of independent legal counsel. Therefore, the business transaction involving the selling of part of the barbershop business was not appropriate.

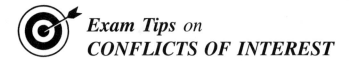

Exam Tips on
CONFLICTS OF INTEREST

Conflicts of interest is the most central, pervasive, complex, and important issue in the law governing lawyers. Consequently, it is also the most-tested topic in the professional responsibility field. It is not unusual for a multiple-choice professional responsibility exam to include 30 to 50% of its questions in the form of conflicts questions of one variety or another.

When you analyze conflicts problems, ask yourself these questions:

1. What is the source of the conflict (third-party interference, multiple-client conflict, lawyer interests)?
2. Does the conflict meet its particular rule's threshold requirements, i.e., is there a conflict within the meaning of the appropriate rule?
3. Is the conflict one that imputes to the entire law organization?
4. If so, can the affected lawyer be effectively screened or isolated from the organization?
5. Is the conflict of a type that allows client waiver?
6. If so, what must occur for the waiver to be effective?

As you study, notice that some of the conflicts rules are like "nested dolls" that live inside one another. Take a fact pattern in which the lawyer has loaned the client money. You might first look at the financial assistance rule and conclude that it does not restrict the lawyer because there is no pending or contemplated litigation. MR 1.8(e). You might then notice that a loan of money is a business transaction and examine the business transaction rule. MR 1.8(a). If for some reason it does not restrict the lawyer either, you should then examine the general lawyer versus client interest rule (MR 1.7) and apply it. Treating each possible rule will add points to your score.

Always focus on the setting in which a question places you. The policies in the motion to disqualify setting will differ from those in the disciplinary setting, which will differ from those in the malpractice setting, and so on.

Basic to the lawyer-client relationship is the premise that lawyers owe clients a duty of **loyalty**. Lawyers owe clients a duty of *independent professional judgment.* When loyalty or independent judgment is threatened by some interest other than the client's, a conflicts question is present and requires analysis.

Many conflicts questions are primarily about breaches of confidentiality. When a question involves the potential for a confidentiality breach, you must analyze both the confidentiality issues and the conflicts issues. See Chapter 5.

Relatively easy cases of conflict of interest analysis occur when the lawyer attempts to represent directly adverse interests.

The application of many of the conflicts rules is triggered by a determination of whether there is a "significant risk" that the conflict "will materially limit[] the [lawyer's representation of the client]."

See, e.g., MR 1.7(b). This standard is objective.

Because true conflicts put client interests at risk and because client autonomy and decision-making are values worthy of some respect, clients are empowered to **waive** most but not all conflicts of interest.

☞ The general rationale of honoring client autonomy does not apply when the conflict is sufficiently gross to make any client waiver suspect.

☞ The general rationale of honoring client autonomy does not apply when the conflicts rule is less about the risk to client interests than it is about risks to justice system interests.

☞ At a minimum, a conflict-of-interest waiver requires informed consent of the affected client. Some of the conflicts rules that allow waiver require more, such as confirmation of the waiver in writing, sometimes signed by the client.

☞ Whether a conflict is waivable is often the critical deciding point. Be careful to distinguish between the conflicts that may be waived and those that may not. Recognize that when a conflict exists and is waivable, a lawyer will be subject to discipline if she goes forward with anything less than informed client consent. Many questions will have the lawyer giving notice to the client, or merely disclosing but not discussing the conflict with the client, neither of which satisfies the waiver requirements. Recognize that when the rule does not permit waiver, even when a question describes what would be an effective waiver, the conflict persists.

There are three primary sources of conflicts of interest: third-party interference, lawyer interests, and multiple-client interests. Identify the source of the conflict to locate the applicable Model Rule provision.

- ☞ *Third-party interference* conflicts occur when someone who is not a party to the lawyer-client relationship seeks to affect or becomes positioned to affect the independence of the lawyer's judgment on behalf of the client. See MR 1.7(a)(2) for the general rule. Such conflicts may be waived if the client gives informed consent. A frequent third-party interference fact pattern on exams involves a third-party payer of a lawyer's fee. See MR 1.8(f) for the specific rule.

- ☞ The second major source of conflicts is *lawyer interests that conflict* with client interests.
    - ☞ Waiver of such a general conflict is possible if "the lawyer reasonably believes that the lawyer will be able to provide competent and diligent representation [despite the conflict] and the affected client gives informed consent." MR 1.7(b).
    - ☞ A variety of particular transactions between lawyers and clients are governed by specific conflicts rules.
    - ☞ *Business transactions with clients,* Model Rule 1.8(a). This rule has enhanced waiver requirements.
    - ☞ *Literary rights,* MR 1.8(d). No waiver of this conflict is permitted.
    - ☞ *Drafting instruments that benefit the lawyer,* MR 1.8(c).
    - ☞ *Sexual or amorous relations with clients,* MR 1.8(j).
    - ☞ *Agreements limiting the lawyer's liability,* MR 1.8(h).
    - ☞ *Settling claims with unrepresented clients,* MR 1.8(h).

- ☞ Various restrictions on lawyer conduct, often interrelated with lawyer-client conflicts issues, are based on the doctrines of *champerty, barratry,* and *maintenance.*
    - ☞ Lawyers are prohibited from advancing financial assistance to clients when there is pending or contemplated litigation, except that the lawyer may advance court costs. Client waiver of this "conflict" is not permitted. MR 1.8(e).
    - ☞ A lawyer is prohibited from acquiring an interest in litigation or its subject matter, whether that interest is consistent or inconsistent with the client's interests. This prohibition is not a restriction on the lawyer's contract with a client for a reasonable contingent fee. Client waiver of a violation of this rule is not permitted. MR 1.8(i).
    - ☞ A lawyer is prohibited from using information learned in the lawyer-client relationship to the detriment of the client. MR 1.8(b).

☛ The third major source of conflicts is the interaction of *multiple clients'* interests. Multiple-client conflicts can implicate not only concurrent representation of multiple clients, but also conflicts between former and current clients, or prospective and current clients, or prospective and former clients.

☞ The easiest cases involve representation of multiple clients whose interests are in direct conflict. Such a direct conflict cannot be effectively waived by the clients on the theory that it is too gross a conflict.

☞ A lawyer may also find herself representing one client against a second client in a matter unrelated to the representation of the second client. In general, such a conflict may not be waived, but when the adversity is merely general, waiver has been permitted.

☞ Even representation of multiple clients who are at least initially on the same side of litigation or a transaction implicates conflicts analysis.

☞ Lawyers owe prospective clients a limited loyalty duty and the duty of confidentiality.

Because confidentiality breaches are a primary consideration in multiple-client conflicts analysis, conflicts analysis must be done on potential conflicts between prospective and current or former clients. Watch for fact patterns involving a prospective client who reveals information to a lawyer, but then does not retain the lawyer's services.

☞ Because lawyers owe clients a continued measure of loyalty and a full measure of the duty of confidentiality after representation ends, conflicts between former and current clients arise when interests are directly adverse or when there is a *substantial relationship* between the two representations. Such a conflict may be waived by both clients by consent after consultation. MR 1.9.

☞ A lawyer who represents an organization, such as a corporation, a labor union, or a public-interest organization, represents the organization, not its officers. At times, the interests of the organization and its officers may converge. Under such circumstances, a lawyer may represent both the organization and its officers, but the lawyer must withdraw if the interests of the organization and the officers diverge. MR 1.13.

☞ The perceived importance of multidisciplinary practices (MDPs) has risen and fallen dramatically. A key marker was the Enron crisis, after which, with the adoption of the Sarbanes-Oxley Act, many have come to regard the MDP phenomenon as over. It is more likely sleeping than dead, however, and you should be alert to the importance placed on the topic in your course.

As a general rule, when a lawyer has a conflict of interest, that conflict imputes to (transfers to, extends to) all of the lawyers in the law organization (usually a law firm) in which the lawyer works. MR 1.10. This *imputed disqualification* rule is mainly based on the notion that confidential information possessed by one lawyer is effectively possessed by all lawyers in the same firm.

☛ *Motions to disqualify* counsel, and entire law firms for which the disqualified lawyer works, have become a favored tactical device in litigation, effectively denying an opposing party her counsel of choice and preserving the integrity of the justice system from the threat of conflicts of interest. Such fact patterns allow an instructor to examine students in a way that goes beyond the Model Rules. When a court is considering a motion to disqualify, several factors may be considered in addition to the conflicts principles that are relevant in the disciplinary context. Expand your answer accordingly in a motion to disqualify situation.

☛ The increasing movement of lawyers from one practice setting to another, from one law firm to another, has dramatically increased the frequency and impact of imputed disqualification rules. Lawyers changing firms or moving from government to private practice are especially popular exam fact patterns.

☛ An increasing number of courts, supported by Model Rules 1.10, 1.11, and 1.12, have ruled that effective *screening procedures* will prevent the application of the imputed disqualification rules. Under such procedures, the conflicted lawyer is isolated from other lawyers in the organization by various devices.

☛ Special rules regarding imputed disqualification apply to former government lawyers and former judges.

Former judges' conflicts differ from those of lawyers who move from one practice setting to another, and they require special conflicts rules. MR 1.12. A former judge shall not engage in private representation in a matter in which the judge participated personally and substantially as a judge, unless all parties to the matter consent after consultation. MR 1.12.

☛ Judges are prohibited from negotiating for employment with lawyers who are currently representing parties before the judge's court if the judge is personally and substantially participating in the matter before the court. Similar, but waivable, restrictions apply to judicial law clerks. MR 1.12(b).

☛ Special, more relaxed imputed disqualification rules apply to the law firms for which former judges work. Effective screening procedures and notice to the judge's former court permit a former judge's law firm to continue with representation in which the former judge is disqualified from participating. MR 1.12(c).

Special conflicts rules apply to lawyers who move from government practice to private practice. MR 1.11.

☛ A former government "lawyer shall not represent a private client in connection with a matter in which the lawyer participated personally and substantially" as a government lawyer. MR 1.11. Notice that this conflict rule applies without regard to whether the lawyer has effectively changed sides in the matter.

☛ Three exceptions allow the former government lawyer to engage in the later private representation even when his participation in the government employment was personal and substantial.

  ☞ The conflicts rule excepts from its reach cases in which the law otherwise expressly permits the private representation to occur.

  ☞ The rule defines what it means by a "matter." It is only later private representation in connection with a government service "matter" that triggers a conflict of interest analysis. A matter includes a wide variety of instances and actions that engage the agency with a particular party or parties. The definition excludes rule drafting and other agency actions that have more general application.

  ☞ The agency may waive the conflict by giving its consent after consultation.

☛ Except when law otherwise expressly permits such representation, a former government lawyer is also prohibited from representing private parties who are adverse to parties about whom the lawyer has confidential information gained in the government practice that could be used against the adverse party. MR 1.11(c). The private party's interests are the ones at risk in such a case. As such, it is the private party and not the agency that must waive the conflict if the lawyer is to be permitted to proceed.

☛ Special, more relaxed imputed disqualification rules apply when former government lawyers are the law firm lawyers who have a conflict.

Special conflict problems are associated with the occasion on which a lawyer is to be called as a witness. MR 3.7.

CHAPTER 7
DUTIES TO THIRD PARTIES

ChapterScope

- Lawyers owe their primary duties to their clients. See Chapters 4 through 6. Lawyers also owe duties to the court, the justice system, the profession, and the public generally. See Chapter 8. This chapter is about the limited duties lawyers owe to specific categories of third parties, as opposed to the client, the court, the profession, or the public generally.

- *Third parties* are strangers to the lawyer-client relationship. They may or may not be represented by another lawyer. Such third parties are, for example, opposing parties, witnesses, jurors, and unrepresented interested parties.

- The duties owed to third parties operate as limits on the primary duty the lawyer owes to a client.

  In other words, they operate to form boundaries around acceptable, client-favoring actions by lawyers.

- For a statement to a third party to subject a lawyer to discipline, it must be both *false and material.*

- Lawyers are prohibited from making statements that are fraudulent or remaining silent when the statement or silence would amount to fraud under applicable tort principles.

  - The negotiation setting presents a special circumstance within which the nature and effect of misleading statements must be analyzed. By its nature, an element of misleading is present in the negotiation process. The rules prohibit only certain forms of misleading.

- The process of reducing an oral agreement to writing poses special truthfulness problems.

- Model Rule 4.4 prohibits a lawyer from using "means that have no substantial purpose other than to embarrass, delay, or burden a third person. . . ." The rule prohibits only actions that serve no substantial, legitimate purpose, but are merely done to embarrass, delay, or burden the third person.

- Lawyers are prohibited from communicating about the subject matter of a dispute with represented opposing parties without first obtaining permission from the opposing party's lawyer. MR 4.2.

- While not prohibited from communicating with unrepresented persons who are involved in a client's matter, lawyers are restricted in what they may say to such a person. MR 4.3.

  - A lawyer is under an affirmative obligation to refrain from stating or implying that the lawyer is disinterested in the matter about which the lawyer is communicating. Any effort to mislead an unrepresented person about the lawyer's interest subjects the lawyer to discipline.

- In limited circumstances, a lawyer may have civil liability for wrongful or negligent lawyering activity to those outside the lawyer-client relationship.

I. TRUTH-TELLING OUTSIDE THE COURT CONTEXT

Rules governing lawyers' truth-telling duties outside the court context contrast with those that apply inside the court context. See Chapter 8, §I. The outside-the-court truth-telling rules apply in a lawyer's dealings with opposing lawyers, opposing parties (but also see the special communications with opposing parties rules in §§IV and V), witnesses (but also see special communication with witnesses rules in §§IV.E.1 and V), and anyone else with whom the lawyer communicates as a lawyer. These rules apply in a variety of contexts including investigation, negotiation, intermediary activities, and so on.

A. False statements of material law or fact

For a statement to a third party to subject a lawyer to discipline, it must be both false and material.

1. **False:** A false statement is one that does not subjectively conform to the lawyer's knowledge of the facts. (See §C for the nuances of the negotiation setting.)

2. **Material:** A statement is material if it bears on the merits of the discussion or is one upon which the recipient's further action of consequence may be based.

   Example: Lawyer tells Witness that Lawyer will meet Witness for an interview at Witness's convenience. Witness suggests they meet at 2:00 P.M. Thursday. Lawyer prefers not to meet at that time because Lawyer regularly plays roller hockey on Thursday afternoons. Instead of saying so, Lawyer says, "I can't meet on Thursday afternoon because I have to be in court. How about Friday morning?" Witness agrees. Lawyer's statement is unquestionably false (and despicable), but it is not material, and thus Lawyer is not subject to discipline under Model Rule 4.1.

B. Fraudulent statements and silences

Lawyers are prohibited from making statements that are fraudulent or remaining silent when the statement or silence would amount to fraud under applicable tort principles. For Model Rules purposes, fraud "denotes conduct having a purpose to deceive and not merely negligent misrepresentation or failure to apprise another of relevant information." MR 1.0(d).

Example: Plaintiff sued Defendant for injuries sustained in an automobile accident. Plaintiff's Doctor diagnosed his condition as a series of fractures and a concussion. Defendant's Doctor examined Plaintiff and found an aortic aneurysm that may have resulted from the accident. Defendant's Doctor informed Defendant's Lawyer of her discovery. Plaintiff settled his claims against Defendant with the Court's approval. Two years later, a physical revealed Plaintiff's aneurysm and linked it to the accident. Defendant's Lawyer's failure to disclose Defendant's Doctor's diagnosis constituted a defect in the settlement agreement, and Plaintiff was permitted to rescind the settlement agreement. Spaulding v. Zimmerman, 116 N.W.2d 704 (Minn. 1962).

1. **Tort concepts and reliance:** Inevitably, some reliance on general tort concepts must be had in interpreting the Model Rules' definition of fraud. For example, fraud generally requires a reasonableness of reliance on the part of the recipient of the fraudulent statement. The same statement made once to a lawyer and another time to an unrepresented witness may be regarded differently.

   Example: Lawyer sends a State 1 subpoena purporting to command attendance at a hearing in State 1 to Unrepresented Witness, who lives in State 2. Lawyer knows that the subpoena is wholly unenforceable outside the boundaries of State 1. Lawyer intends and expects that

Unrepresented Witness will be misled by the unenforceable subpoena and attend the hearing. Witness, seeing the official-looking document and its commands, sent to her by Lawyer, would be reasonable in relying on the misleading statement of Lawyer. Such an action is fraudulent, and Lawyer is subject to discipline. The same unenforceable subpoena, sent instead to Represented Witness's Lawyer, could not be reasonably relied on, but rather, would be interpreted as an unenforceable request for the attendance of Witness. Such an action would not be fraudulent under general tort principles and should not be so for disciplinary purposes.

C. The negotiation setting

The negotiation setting presents a special circumstance within which the nature and effect of misleading statements must be analyzed. By its nature, an element of misleading is present in the negotiation process. Negotiators legitimately mislead other negotiators about their resolve, estimates of value, options available to the negotiator's client, their time constraints, and a variety of other aspects of the negotiation "dance." Some misleading is inevitable in negotiating. The rules prohibit only certain forms of misleading. MR 4.1 Comment.

1. **The parties to the negotiation:** Statements made to other lawyers in negotiations (and arguably to very sophisticated nonlawyers) are regarded much differently from statements made to nonlawyers. Lawyers may not legitimately rely on vague, misleading statements to the same extent as may nonlawyers.

   Example: In a lawyer-to-lawyer negotiation session regarding a claim of Lawyer 1's client against Lawyer 2's client, Lawyer 1 says, "This claim is worth $50,000." Lawyer 1's ***objective*** analysis of the matter leads her to estimate privately that trial is likely to produce a $25,000 verdict. In some sense, Lawyer 1's statement is false; it is certainly meant to mislead Lawyer 2 about the estimated value of the claim. If Lawyer 2 takes Lawyer 1's assertion as absolute truth and without further analysis agrees to settle the claim for $50,000, Lawyer 1 is not subject to discipline, even though Lawyer 1's statement has misled Lawyer 2. Lawyer 2 is not entitled to rely on vague assertions of value by Lawyer 1. If the same statement were made by Lawyer 1 in a negotiation with Unrepresented NonLawyer, Lawyer 1 would be subject to discipline because, unlike Lawyer 2, Unrepresented NonLawyer may reasonably rely on Lawyer 1's statement.

2. **What is a fact?** Some statements made in the negotiation setting are not regarded as statements of fact. These statements are simply too nebulous to be called "statements of fact," or they are accepted parts of the negotiation game that ought to be evaluated for what they are worth by the other side.

   Example: Statements of estimated value of the thing or claim being traded ("My client's claim is worth at least $50,000"), statements of resolve ("My client intends to make full use of his legal remedies," or "My client is intent on pursuing this matter in court"), and statements about time and similar constraints ("My client does not need the money so quickly that she will compromise without a full airing of the issues, no matter how long that might take") generally are not considered "statements of fact."

   By contrast, statements of verifiable, basic fact are subject to this rule, and false statements of such facts make the lawyer subject to discipline.

   Example: "My client has only one policy of insurance that could cover such a loss as your client has suffered" (when in fact two such are known to be in force) and "My client was driving his blue Dodge Dart on the date in question" (when in fact the client has told his lawyer that he was driving the green Dodge Dart on the date in question) are statements of verifiable facts.

3. **Reducing agreements to writing:** The process of reducing an oral agreement to writing poses special truthfulness problems.

   a. **Alterations:** The intentional alteration of the agreed-to terms in the process of reducing the agreement to writing is fraud, subjecting the lawyer to discipline as well as civil liability.

   Example: Lawyer 1 and Lawyer 2 negotiate on behalf of their clients and reach an agreement. The agreement reached during their discussions calls for Lawyer 1's Client to pay Lawyer 2's Client $50,000, spread out in payments extending over the next four years. Lawyer 1 is to draft the agreement. Lawyer 1 thinks that Lawyer 2 may be careless in reading the written agreement, and writes in it that his client agrees to pay $50,000 to Lawyer 2's Client spread out as payments extending over the next six years. Lawyer 1 has perpetrated a fraud and is subject to discipline. Further, if Lawyer 2 carelessly advises her client to sign the document without reading it, the agreement will be voidable on Lawyer 2's Client's request.

   b. **Matters not expressly covered:** Except in the most detailed, thorough discussions, some matters are inevitably not discussed and agreed on. Here, the document preparer has some latitude in inserting what amounts to reasonable terms, particularly when they are standard in the particular trade. Inclusion of a new term of significance without disclosing its inclusion to the opposing party that effectively alters the agreed-on core terms, however, is fraud.

   Example: Through their lawyers, Budgee Buyer and Budgee Seller have agreed to terms for the sale and shipment of 20,000 Budgees. The parties agree that Budgee Seller's Lawyer will draft the agreement. The parties did not discuss a "choice of law" term for the contract. (This term determines which state's law applies in case of default on the contract.) If it is standard practice for the home state of a seller to be included as the choice-of-law term, Seller's Lawyer may do so and forward the agreement for examination to Buyer's Lawyer without comment or risk of fraud. If, however, Seller's Lawyer inserts the very-favorable-to-Sellers State of Chaos choice-of-law-term, in contravention of standard practice, Seller's Lawyer must inform Buyer's Lawyer of this insertion when forwarding the document for examination or risk fraud liability.

   c. **Disclosing a drafter's scrivener's error:** When a non-drafting lawyer's examination of a document reveals an error in the recording of the parties' agreement, the non-drafting lawyer is obligated to reveal this error to the drafting lawyer. ABA Informal Op. 86-1518 (1986).

II. HARASSMENT AND OTHER ABUSIVE CONDUCT

Lawyers may not use unlawful means to achieve a client's goals. Lawyers also may not use lawful but harassing conduct to achieve a client's goals if there is no legitimate, substantial purpose served by the harassing conduct. Several special harassment rules apply in the context of specific categories of third parties. Third parties are those outside the lawyer-client relationship, such as opposing parties, witnesses, jurors, and court personnel.

A. In general

1. **Unlawful acts by lawyers:** Lawyers are prohibited from engaging in or using agents to engage in unlawful acts on behalf of clients.

    Example: Client wants to acquire Prime Property and asks Lawyer's assistance in doing so. Lawyer sends a group of thugs to threaten harm to Prime Property Owner unless Owner sells Prime Property to Client at a fair price. Lawyer is subject to discipline for using unlawful means to assist Client.

    Example: Lawyer represents Client in a divorce action. Client believes that Spouse is engaged in extramarital sexual conduct, but has no evidence of it. Lawyer hires Prostitute to solicit Spouse. Solicitation is a crime. Lawyer is subject to discipline for procuring a criminal act. See, e.g., In re Knight, 281 A.2d 46 (Vt. 1971).

2. **Assisting clients in committing unlawful or fraudulent acts:** Although a lawyer may counsel a client about the legal consequences of a course of conduct proposed by the client, a lawyer is prohibited from counseling a client to engage (or assisting a client already engaged) in criminal or fraudulent conduct. MR 1.2(d). See Chapter 4, §V.B.

    Example: Client retains Lawyer to assist Client in obtaining secured loans from Bank. Client proposes to generate false inventory reports for the purpose of inducing Bank to make loans to Client. Client requests that Lawyer forward the false inventory reports to Bank in conjunction with Client's loan application process. Lawyer may counsel Client about the consequences of such action, but Lawyer may not forward the false reports or otherwise assist Client in engaging in this fraud.

3. **Harassing conduct:** Model Rule 4.4(a) prohibits a lawyer from using "means that have no substantial purpose other than to embarrass, delay, or burden a third person...." At first reaction, one might guess that the prohibition should be absolute, but reflection says otherwise. Lawyers legitimately engage in a wide variety of acts that embarrass, delay, and burden others. Merely noticing a deposition creates a possibility of embarrassment, delay, and burden to a third person who is commanded to attend and be a witness. Cross-examination, filing a complaint, sending a demand letter, and so on all create possibilities for third parties to be delayed and burdened. Thus, the rule prohibits only actions that serve no substantial, legitimate purpose, but are merely done to embarrass, delay, or burden the third person.

    Example: Witness-Seller testifies on direct examination that he read a warranty waiver document to Lawyer's Client-Buyer. Lawyer cross-examines Witness, bringing out the fact that Witness is unable to read or write. Although such an act by Lawyer is undoubtedly embarrassing and burdensome to Witness, Lawyer has a substantial, legitimate purpose for the cross-examination.

B. Opposing parties

Opposing parties are a special category of third party. Their interests are most directly contrary to those of the lawyer's client. Opposing parties are, therefore, routinely the object of a lawyer's client-favoring activities. Specific limits on those client-favoring activities directed toward opposing parties are found in the assisting client misconduct rule (see §II.A.2), the statements to others rule (see §I), the communications limits rules (see §§IV and V), the threatening criminal prosecution rule (see §III), and various in-litigation rules (see Chapter 8, §III).

C. Witnesses

A great deal of lawyer conduct toward witnesses may be perceived by the witness as harassing. (For other witness-lawyer relationship rules that affect the trial process, such as payment limitation rules, see Chapter 8, §II.B.)

1. **In general:** Cross-examination, being commanded by subpoena to attend a trial or deposition, and being made to wait in court for hours or even days to be called to the stand are all potentially quite unpleasant. Such conduct will violate the law of professional responsibility, however, only when the lawyer has no "substantial purpose other than to embarrass, delay, or burden" the witness. MR 4.4(a).

2. **Investigation:** Lawyers may not use unlawful means to gather evidence from witnesses. MR 4.4(a).

   Example: Lawyer represents Domestic Relations Client. In an effort to gather evidence of Client's spouse's infidelity, Lawyer unlawfully places a recording device on Paramour's telephone. Lawyer is subject to discipline for using unlawful means to gather evidence.

D. Jurors

Lawyers are prohibited from engaging in live contact investigations of jurors and from other harassing conduct. (For other "duty to the justice system" rules that relate to lawyers and jurors, see Chapter 8, §VI.B.)

1. **Investigation:** Lawyers may investigate jurors' backgrounds by means of public records such as deeds, judgments, available voting records, and so on. Lawyers may not contact jurors either in person or through agents. MR 4.4(a).

2. **Post-verdict harassing conduct:** Lawyers may not engage in conduct that will cause jurors to question the justice system's use of their verdict. Lawyers may contact jurors when the sole purpose is to inquire about the lawyer's trial performance, provided the lawyer refrains from harassing conduct. See, e.g., In re Hanson, 318 N.W.2d 856 (Minn. 1982). See Chapter 8, §VI.B.

   Example: Lawyer is upset that Judge excluded crucial evidence (X) at trial. After an unfavorable verdict, Lawyer telephones several jurors to ask whether they think their verdict would have been different if the judge had let them hear X. Lawyer is subject to discipline. She has undermined the jurors' confidence in the justice system by suggesting that the evidentiary ruling prevented them from doing justice.

III. THREATENING CRIMINAL PROSECUTION

The Model Code includes a specific provision prohibiting threats of criminal prosecution "solely to obtain advantage in a civil matter." DR 7-105. Threatening criminal prosecution for reasons other than gaining an advantage in a civil matter is not prohibited by this rule. The Model Rule drafters did not include a specific provision on this subject in the Model Rules. Rather, they relied on the general "rights of third parties" rule to cover the use of inappropriate threats. MR 4. In effect, when a threat would amount to extortion, it is a prohibited threat under Model Rule 4.4.(a). See, e.g., Fla. Bar Op. 89-3 (1989); N.J. Ethics Op. 595 (1986).

A. Applies to prosecutors

Although prosecuting lawyers must sometimes threaten individuals with criminal prosecution, this prohibition against using such threats to gain advantage in a civil matter applies to them as well as it does to other lawyers.

Example: During a police drug raid, Jack is severely beaten by police who are using excessive force. Jack is not arrested because the police fail to find any evidence that Jack has committed any criminal act. Nonetheless, the police believe that Jack is a significant player in a local drug distribution operation. Jack files a civil rights action against police. Prosecutor contacts Jack through Jack's lawyer and says that he will pursue criminal charges against Jack unless Jack settles the civil rights claim for a relatively small amount of damages. Prosecutor is subject to discipline.

IV. COMMUNICATING WITH REPRESENTED PERSONS

Lawyers are prohibited from communicating about the subject matter of a dispute with represented opposing persons without first obtaining permission from the opposing person's lawyer. MR 4.2.

A. Parties and persons

The original version of Model Rule 4.2 adopted by the ABA prohibited unauthorized contact with opposing "parties." The rule was intended to include represented persons, even if they were not formally parties to active litigation. See, e.g., United States v. Jamil, 546 F. Supp. 646 (E.D.N.Y. 1982). The rule has been amended to change "parties" to "persons" to make clear that there need not be pending litigation for the rule to have effect.

B. Communicating

In the context of this rule, all forms of communication are prohibited, including in-person, telephone, and written or electronic forms of communication.

C. Agents

Lawyers may not avoid the application of this rule by communicating with opposing parties through a lawyer's agent. MR 5.3(c). Opposing parties, however, may communicate with one another without offending Model Rule 4.2, provided that the lawyer has not instructed the client to do so as a means of circumventing the rule.

Example: Lawyer believes that Opposing Lawyer is being obstructive. Lawyer believes that if the parties themselves could get together, they could resolve the dispute. Lawyer instructs his Client to contact Opposing Party and attempt to negotiate the dispute. Lawyer is subject to discipline under Model Rules 4.2 and 8.4(a). See In re Marietta, 569 P.2d 921 (Kan. 1977).

D. Subject matter of the dispute

Model Rule 4.2's restriction applies only to communication regarding the subject matter of the representation. Lawyers may communicate with individuals who happen to be opposing parties of the lawyer's clients on matters unrelated to the representation.

Example: Lawyer represents Client against Opposing Party in a commercial dispute. Lawyer lives in the same neighborhood as Opposing Party. A Neighborhood Watch meeting is called, and both Lawyer and Opposing Party attend. Lawyer communicates with Opposing Party about the wisdom of various proposed refinements in the Neighborhood Watch's policies. Lawyer is not subject to discipline for this unrelated communication with an opposing party.

E. Who is an opposing party or person?

Especially in cases involving organizational parties, identifying who will be regarded as a represented opposing person or party for purposes of Model Rule 4.2 becomes crucial to determining with whom a lawyer may have unauthorized communication.

1. **Mere witnesses:** No matter how much a particular witness's testimony is expected to favor one side in a dispute, a mere witness is not a represented party. Model Rule 4.2 does not prohibit communication between a lawyer and an opposing party's witnesses and does not require a lawyer to obtain an opposing party's lawyer's permission to so communicate.

2. **Organizational parties:** Organizations speak through and function through individuals who are not in and of themselves the organization. When dealing with a represented organization, Model Rule 4.2 prohibits unauthorized communication between an opposing lawyer and employees with managerial responsibilities for the subject of the matter, employees whose acts or omissions may be imputed to the organization with respect to the matter, and employees whose statements may constitute an admission attributable to the organization. MR 4.2 Comment 7.

   Example: Plaintiff suffered injuries when he fell from a construction-site scaffold. Plaintiff sued the Corporation that employed him and moved for permission to have his Lawyer conduct ex parte interviews of Corporation employees on the site at the time of the accident.

   Current employees whose acts or omissions in the matter under inquiry are binding on or imputed to their employer are parties to a suit for purposes of Model Rule 4.2. Employees who implement the advice of counsel also qualify as parties. Other employees are not parties. Neisig v. Team I, 558 N.E.2d 1030 (N.Y. 1990).

   a. **Managerial employees:** Employees who are managers relative to the subject of the matter and those who are in the control group of the organization are parties for purposes of Model Rule 4.2.

   b. **Acts or omissions:** Any employee, whether management or not, may have engaged in acts or omissions that are the subject of the matter and that may be the basis under contract, tort, and agency law for the liability of the organization. Such employees are considered the party for purposes of Model Rule 4.2.

   c. **Statements as admissions:** Under Federal Rule of Evidence 801(d)(2)(D) and analogous state evidence rules and decisions, certain employees may make statements that will be admissible over a hearsay objection as an admission of the organization. Such employees are parties for purposes of Model Rule 4.2.

   d. **Former employees:** Whether former employees may be considered as parties for purposes of MR 4.2 has been a controversial question. Both the ABA and the majority of decisions say that former employees are not parties under Model Rule 4.2. ABA Formal Op. 91-359 (1991). A new, February 2002 Comment to Model Rule 4.2 suggests that consent of an organization's lawyer is not required for contact with former employees of the organization, by implication leaving the communicating lawyer to comply with Model Rule 4.3 in such circumstances. See Comment 5. See, e.g., Amarin Plastics v. Maryland Cup Corp., 116 F.R.D. 36 (D. Mass. 1987). Other courts have ruled to the contrary. See, e.g., Public

Services Electric and Gas Co. v. Associated Electric and Gas Ins. Services Ltd., 745 F. Supp. 1037 (D. N.J. 1990). The better approach is probably to distinguish cases based on the category of employee at issue and that employee's relationship to the matter. Under Federal Rule of Evidence 801(d)(2)(D), when a former employee makes a statement, that statement is not attributable to the former organizational employer as an admission of a party opponent. When a former employee's statement about a matter is the former employee's only relationship to the matter, Model Rule 4.2 should not be interpreted to bar unauthorized communication; such a former employee ought to be treated as a mere witness. By contrast, when it is the former employee's act or omission that is the subject of the matter, that former employee ought to continue to be treated as a party and communication must be authorized by counsel.

e. **Attorney-client privilege:** Under Upjohn v. United States, 449 U.S. 383 (1981), communications that have occurred between the organization's counsel and a wide variety of employees may be protected by the attorney-client evidentiary privilege. See Chapter 5. Such protection exists both during and after the employee's employ. When a former or current employee is not a party under Model Rule 4.2 but is a "client" for purposes of the evidentiary privilege with respect to communications relating to the matter, courts will grant protective discovery orders to guard against abuse of the evidentiary privilege.

3. **Class-action members:** Members of a class are treated as parties for purposes of Model Rule 4.2.

F. Obtaining permission

A lawyer may communicate with an opposing party about the subject matter of the representation if the opposing party's lawyer has given consent.

G. Authorized by law

A lawyer may communicate with an opposing party about the subject matter of the representation if the lawyer is "authorized by law" to so communicate.

Example: Lawyer represents Client in a dispute with the Internal Revenue Service (IRS). Lawyer may communicate directly with Agents of the IRS, even though they speak for an Opposing Party, the IRS, because such communications with a government agency are authorized by law.

H. Authorized by court order

The February 2002 amendments to Model Rule 4.2 added a provision permitting unconsented contact when authorized by court order. The amendment to Model Rule 4.2 creates an unstated link to the former "Reno Rule," which replaced the former Thornburgh Memorandum on the subject of federal government lawyers' compliance with Model Rule 4.2 and other state ethics rules. Although its effects remain murky, the McDade Amendment (28 U.S.C. §530B) and Department of Justice regulations adopted pursuant to it [28 C.F.R §77.1 *et seq.*] have also affected the analysis in this area.

I. Special criminal practice concerns

In criminal practice, of course, the opposing party of the prosecutor is a criminal defendant. Two different aspects of this special configuration are worthy of note.

1. **Added constitutional limitations:** Fifth and Fourteenth Amendment due process rights and the Sixth Amendment right to counsel protection restrain prosecutors' contact with criminal defendants in ways that go beyond the professional responsibility law constraints of Model Rule 4.2. Although the details of the constitutional constraints are beyond the scope of this outline, when a prosecutor intentionally violates the constitutional constraints, the prosecutor is subject to discipline for engaging in conduct that is prejudicial to the administration of justice. MR 8.4(d).

2. **Investigation of crime:** Prosecutors, especially federal prosecutors invoking not only Model Rule 4.2's "authorized by law" language, but also the Supremacy Clause of the U.S. Constitution, have argued that their crime-investigation activities are not restricted by Model Rule 4.2's requirements of consent by an opposing party's lawyer before communication. In essence, the prosecutors have argued that crime investigation, particularly surreptitious crime investigation, would be unreasonably diminished by a rule that required a prosecutor to contact a criminal investigation target's lawyer before any contact by the prosecutor's agents, police investigators. Two particular situations are prominent.

    a. **Undercover agents:** When prosecutors, through police undercover agents, seek to infiltrate the ranks of organized crime, the prosecutors know as a general matter that some of the investigation's targets are represented by counsel. Strict compliance with Model Rule 4.2 would require the prosecutor to obtain the target's counsel's permission before the investigation proceeding to the stage at which the undercover investigators communicate with the target. Such strict compliance is not required by the rule. See, e.g., United States v. Sutton, 801 F.2d 1346 (D.C. Cir. 1986); United States v. Schwimmer, 882 F.2d 22 (2d Cir. 1989).

    b. **Plea bargains:** Defendants sometimes wish to negotiate for a plea arrangement with prosecutors without their lawyer's knowledge. Strict compliance with 4.2 would prohibit this direct communication even when the defendant waives his right to counsel. In such a fact scenario, the result is questionable. See United States v. Lopez, 765 F. Supp. 1433 (N.D. Cal. 1991) (court dismissed indictment against defendant because of prosecutor's unauthorized plea negotiations with defendant). On appeal, the Ninth Circuit upheld the district court's ruling that the prosecutor had committed misconduct, but reversed the dismissal of the indictment as an inappropriate remedy for the prosecutor's violation. United States v. Lopez, 4 F.3d 1455 (9th Cir. 1993).

V. COMMUNICATING WITH UNREPRESENTED PERSONS

Although not prohibited from communicating with unrepresented persons who are involved in a client's matter, lawyers are restricted in what they may say to such a person. MR 4.3.

A. Avoid misleading about the lawyer's interest

Lawyers have both affirmative and clarifying duties with respect to the lawyer's role in communicating with an unrepresented person.

1. **Affirmative duty:** A lawyer is under an affirmative obligation to refrain from stating or implying that the lawyer is disinterested in the matter about which the lawyer is communicating. Any effort to mislead an unrepresented person about the lawyer's interest subjects the lawyer to discipline.

Example: Lawyer represents Client in a workplace sexual harassment matter. Lawyer wants to investigate workplace practices by questioning various company employees. To enhance the candor of these persons, Lawyer initially tells them that he is a writer working on a novel about workplace sexual harassment and that he wants to get background information on the environment in a variety of workplaces. Lawyer is subject to discipline.

2. **Clarifying duty:** When a lawyer "reasonably should know" that an unrepresented person misunderstands the lawyer's interest in the matter, the lawyer is obliged to make reasonable efforts to clarify his role.

B. Giving advice

Lawyers are prohibited from giving legal advice to unrepresented persons with whom they inevitably come into contact, with one exception. Lawyers are permitted to advise unrepresented persons to obtain counsel.

C. Fact gathering

Lawyers must be permitted to gather information from unrepresented persons. Otherwise, witnesses to an event, as well as opposing parties who choose to proceed without counsel, could never be contacted for the purpose of fact investigation. Model Rule 4.3 does not prohibit fact gathering, provided the lawyer does so without giving advice (other than advice to obtain counsel) to the unrepresented person.

VI. CIVIL LIABILITY TO THIRD PERSONS

In limited circumstances, a lawyer may have civil liability for wrongful or negligent lawyering activity to those outside the lawyer-client relationship.

A. General

As a general rule, lawyers do not owe a duty that supports a negligence action to third persons. When a lawyer error on behalf of a client harms a third person, that third person's action against the lawyer will fail because the lawyer generally owes neither a contract nor a tort duty to exercise care on behalf of the third person. In particular, lawyer conduct that harms an opposing party will not support a claim against the lawyer on behalf of the opposing party. Lawyers do not owe a duty of care to opposing parties.

B. Intended beneficiaries of the lawyer's work for a client

When a lawyer's work for a client is intended to benefit a third person, the lawyer owes a duty of care to that third person.

Example: Lawyer is retained by Client to draft a will leaving all of Client's assets to Beneficiary. Lawyer negligently drafts the will and, following Client's death, the will is successfully challenged by Left-Out-Son-of-Client. As a result of Lawyer's negligence, Beneficiary does not receive the benefits that Client intended to result from Lawyer's work for Client. Lawyer is liable for malpractice to Beneficiary.

C. Invited reliance

When a lawyer's work for a client specifically invites the reliance of a third person, the lawyer owes a duty of care to that third person.

Example: Lawyer represents Client in Client's ongoing business concern. Client has a regular need to borrow money from Bank. Bank secures its loans to Client by acquiring a security interest in Client's inventory. Bank requires as a condition of making the loans that Lawyer issue a letter to Bank stating that Lawyer has investigated and determined that no prior security interests exist on Client's inventory. Lawyer issues such letters to Bank on Client's behalf, and Client obtains loans from Bank. Lawyer negligently engaged in the investigation and, in fact, prior security interests do exist on Client's inventory. Client defaults on the Bank's loans and on others. The holder of the prior security interest takes possession of Client's inventory, and Bank is left without security for the loans. Lawyer is liable to Bank for malpractice.

D. Assisting clients in breaching fiduciary duties

When a lawyer does work for a client who is a fiduciary (such as a trustee of a trust for the benefit of a beneficiary), the lawyer owes a duty to the beneficiary requiring the lawyer to refrain from engaging in acts that assist the client in breaching the client's fiduciary duties.

Example: Lawyer represents Client. Client is a Trustee responsible for the management of funds that are held in trust for Beneficiary. Client misappropriates $10,000 of those funds, and Lawyer assists Client in placing the misappropriated funds in an off-shore bank account that will be difficult to reach when Beneficiary discovers the misappropriation and seeks to recover the funds from Client. Lawyer is liable to Beneficiary for assisting Client in Client's breach of fiduciary duties.

E. Preventing client harm to a third person

Lawyers who know that a client will harm a third person and fail to engage in reasonable steps to prevent the harm may have liability to the third person who is harmed by the client. This duty is highly controversial and not widely accepted. It has support in cases decided against therapists, such as Tarasoff v. Regents of the University of California, 551 P.2d 334 (Cal. 1976). No such reported cases against lawyers have been successful. This duty to a third person, if it exists, would create friction with the confidentiality rules that generally permit, but do not require, a lawyer to reveal information that the lawyer believes is reasonably necessary to prevent harms from client conduct that are likely to result in death or substantial bodily harm. MR 1.6. See Chapter 5, §IV.D. Some states have amended their versions of Model Rule 1.6 to make such disclosures mandatory, however, and in those states an argument that the lawyer owes a duty to such third persons is stronger than it is elsewhere.

Quiz Yourself on
DUTIES TO THIRD PARTIES

65. Lawyer Anne represents a man accused of murder. Several days before trial, the prosecutor and Anne sit down and negotiate in an attempt to reach a plea bargain. The prosecutor tells Anne that he believes the evidence against Anne's client is so strong that the jury will not only convict him, but also impose the death penalty. The prosecutor convinces Anne that his case is unbeatable, so she tentatively agrees to a deal that will leave her client in prison for a large portion of his life. Later, before meeting with her client to discuss his reaction to the tentative deal, she goes over the prosecutor's case again and finds large holes in the prosecutor's theory. Is the prosecutor subject to discipline for misleading Anne regarding the strength of his case? _____

66. During negotiations, Attorney Carl is sometimes prone to slight exaggeration. He believes it makes things more interesting, and that other lawyers not only expect such puffery, but are doing the same thing. During a recent negotiation conference concerning a car wreck, Carl stretched the truth in several respects. He said that his client had sought the advice of seven doctors who all concurred on the severity of his client's injuries, and he said he didn't think his client would accept less than $75,000. In reality, Carl's client has consulted only two doctors, and he knows perfectly well that his client would be extremely happy to receive $50,000. Are Carl's negotiating tactics subject to discipline? _____

67. Lawyer's Client wishes to buy an expensive piece of beachfront property, but would like to get a lower price than the seller is willing to give. Lawyer has a friend pose as an Environmental Protection Agency (EPA) inspector and tell the seller that the adjacent property is contaminated and that his own property may decline in value as a result. The seller acts quickly but, rather than sell to lawyer's Client, seller finds a third party to pay full price. The seller, therefore, was apparently not harmed by the false EPA report. Should the lawyer be subject to discipline? _____

68. Lawyer is sorting through jury forms, trying to decide which potential jurors seem likely to be sympathetic to his arguments. She notices that one of the jurors lives next door to an old college friend. She calls her friend, asking about the potential juror's views on many topics. Her friend even asks the potential juror some of the lawyer's questions and reports back. Is lawyer subject to discipline? _____

69. Husband and Wife are involved in protracted divorce proceedings with no end in sight. Wife's Attorney discusses the proceedings with her client. Wife's Attorney is concerned that Husband would be more willing to reach settlement without constant pressure from his lawyer not to "give in on anything." Wife's Attorney remarks that she thinks sometimes people would reach agreements more easily without such acrimonious influences. After considering her attorney's statements, Wife contacts Husband to attempt to reach a settlement without their attorneys present. Is Wife's Attorney subject to discipline? _____

70. Following an even more bitter divorce, a custody battle rages between Ex-Husband and Ex-Wife. Ex-Husband plans to have his girlfriend as his main witness, who will testify about all the bad behavior she has witnessed Ex-Wife display in the past. Following Girlfriend's deposition, Ex-Wife's attorney notices a couple of confusing things and calls Girlfriend to clear them up. Is Ex-Wife's attorney subject to discipline? _____

71. You represent an injured employee of Corporation. The employee worked in the chemistry laboratory, under the Products Development Division. Not knowing much about the Corporation generally, you wish to get a little background information. To that end, you interview a neighbor of yours who is a midlevel manager in a department of Corporation that is unrelated to the subject matter of your representation. Before conducting the interview, you notify Corporation's lawyer of your intentions. You tell the neighbor who you represent and the nature of your interest in talking with him about Corporation. Assuming that the employee you chose may not make a statement that could be admissible as an admission of Corporation, have you violated any disciplinary rules? _____

72. Lawyer is hired to sue a drunk driver in a car accident in which a single mother was injured. Lawyer does a poor job and gets the mother a very limited damage recovery. Several years later, the mother dies of an un-

related cause. Her children come to you seeking to sue Lawyer for malpractice, because his poor lawyering served to decrease their possible inheritance. What is your advice for them? _____

73. During negotiations, a rental car company agrees to buy 2,000 new cars from a car manufacturer. The two parties orally agree to some of the terms. At the end of the meeting, the car manufacturer's attorney (Attorney A) offers to draw up the agreement. The rental car company attorney (Attorney B) agrees, and asks that while drawing up the agreement, Attorney A refers to the notes that Attorney B had taken during the meeting; essentially, Attorney B had already drawn up a draft agreement. Attorney A takes the notes, and notices that in B's draft, the car rental company agreed to buy 200, rather than 2,000 cars. A changes this figure to 2,000. In making this alteration, can A be subject to discipline? _____

74. Lawyer is representing a man in a slip-and-fall incident that occurred at a local bar. One evening, Lawyer goes to the bar and sits with a few of the regulars, the waitresses, and the bartender. They talk for a while, and Lawyer asks them questions like whether the waitresses often spill beer and make the floor slippery, etc. He does not identify himself as an attorney, nor does he affirmatively lie and give another reason for his curiosity. Is the lawyer subject to discipline? _____

75. Lawyer represented Client in a medical malpractice action against Doctor. After a flurry of pretrial discovery, Lawyer and Client concluded that there was little or no chance of proving Doctor's liability. They therefore agreed to let the case lie dormant for a time, to see if Doctor's insurance carrier might offer a modest sum in settlement. Ultimately, Doctor moved for summary judgment, won the motion, and had the case dismissed. Then he sued Lawyer for malpractice, claiming that Lawyer had brought a baseless lawsuit against him, thereby injuring his reputation in the community and among members of the medical profession. Is Lawyer liable to Doctor for malpractice? _____

76. Randy Recipient is in the middle of a product-liability dispute. Millions of dollars are at stake, and Randy has been having trouble gaining access to documents during the discovery process. Opposing Counsel has been generally unresponsive, and at times hostile, to Randy's requests.

Days before the trial is set to begin, Randy opens his email and sees a message from Opposing Counsel. Randy knows that Opposing Counsel did not intend to disclose the information contained in the email. However, he also realizes that it could help him advance the interests of his client, and could provide him with information that he has been unable to gain through normal methods of discovery. Should Randy read the email? _____

Answers

65. No. The prosecutor may have put his case in its most favorable light to convince her to negotiate, but unless the prosecutor has made material, false statements of fact, he will not be subject to discipline. Anne is presumed to be a competent attorney. This should have enabled her to make her own professional judgment, and she was not entitled to rely on the prosecutor's mere puffery.

66. Yes. Statements about the estimated value of a case are not considered facts, but rather, parts of negotiation strategy that each side is expected to take into account. However, specific factual statements, when false and material, such as Carl's lie about the number of doctors consulted, subject a lawyer to discipline under Model Rule 4.1.

67. Yes. Lawyers are prohibited from engaging in unlawful acts on behalf of their clients, and his actions through his friend were intended to fraudulently induce the seller to lower his price. The prohibitions on using unlawful means and on making material false statements exist regardless of whether any actual harm results from the actions, so the lawyer should still be subject to discipline.

68. Yes. It does not matter that Lawyer had a legitimate contact in the juror's next-door neighbor; by initiating the contact between her friend and the juror, her friend became an agent. Model Rules 3.5 and 4.4 prohibit the lawyer from contacting any jurors or potential jurors in this manner.

69. No. Wife's Attorney only expressed her view that opposing counsel was making negotiations difficult, and that divorces in general might sometimes go easier without outside influences of this type. Had Wife's Attorney directed Wife to contact Husband to work out an agreement, then a violation would have occurred. Here, Wife's Attorney did not direct the meeting, so no improper communication with the represented Husband occurred.

70. No. Even though Girlfriend is Ex-Husband's prime witness, she is still an unrepresented party. As such, Model Rule 4.2 does not prohibit communication between Girlfriend and the opposing counsel. A violation would occur, however, if Ex-Wife's attorney attempted to use Girlfriend as an intermediary in an attempt to communicate with Ex-Husband.

71. No. Attorneys are prohibited from having contact only with employees who are managers relative to the subject of the matter, who may make statements that would be attributable to the organizational party, or whose acts or omissions may be attributable to the organizational party. Here, the neighbor's department is not involved in the subject of the matter. Had the neighbor fallen into any of the above categories, however, mere notice to the Corporation's lawyer would have been insufficient. To avoid discipline, the attorney would need to receive actual approval from Corporation's lawyer, rather than merely give notice. (The need to get consent to communicate with an opposing party is always present and not limited only to the organizational party context.)

72. The children will not be permitted to sue because they are third parties, and Lawyer did not owe them a duty to exercise care. The mother was the direct beneficiary of the lawsuit. Even though the outcome affected them adversely, they were not intended beneficiaries of Lawyer's work, such as would be the case if Lawyer had drafted a shoddy will, poorly carrying out the mother's intention to leave them her estate. (In the will-drafting case, Lawyer would owe a duty of care to the children, as the ones intended to benefit.)

73. No. The question states that 2,000 cars was the actual figure that the parties had already agreed on. As long as Attorney A is confident of this fact, he has not intentionally altered agreed-to terms. Therefore, Attorney A should not be disciplined.

74. Although the lawyer did not affirmatively lie to the people in the bar, he failed in his duty to unrepresented persons to notify them of his interest in the matter. MR 4.3. By sitting and drinking with the others in the bar, he implied that his purpose was not an investigative one. (The easier questions are those in which lawyers actually lie about their motives.) In this instance, the lawyer would be subject to discipline under Model Rule 4.3.

75. No, Lawyer is not *liable for malpractice* to Doctor because Doctor was not Lawyer's client and was not a third party intended to benefit from Lawyer's legal services to Client. For a lawyer to be liable for malpractice there must first be some duty that the lawyer owes to the malpractice plaintiff. Here,

Lawyer owed no such duty to Doctor. As an opposing party to Lawyer's client, Lawyer owed no duty to prevent harm such as this to Doctor. Under certain circumstances, however, a lawyer may be liable for malicious prosecution.

76. This question raises the difficult problem of inadvertent disclosures. Use of electronic communication has increased the occurrence of such disclosures. The courts have been struggling with what to do about this thorny problem. Some say that the disclosure waives the attorney-client privilege. Others disagree, noting that the client owns the privilege, and careless acts by the lawyer should not disadvantage the client. The ABA adopted Model Rule 4.4(b) to create a duty on the recipient lawyer to contact the sender of an inadvertently disclosed privileged communication. There are also recent amendments to the Federal Rules of Evidence (FRE 502) that limit the circumstances in which an inadvertent disclosure will waive the privilege.

Under Model Rule 4.4(b), if Randy reads the email he will be subject to discipline. The recipient of inadvertently disclosed confidential information has a duty to inform the sender and await instructions before reading further. Opposing counsel might also be subject to discipline or liable for malpractice. However, that does not affect the recipient lawyer's duty under Model Rule 4.4(b).

Exam Tips on
DUTIES TO THIRD PARTIES

- The duties owed to third parties operate as limits on the primary duty the lawyer owes to a client. In other words, they operate to form boundaries around acceptable, client-favoring actions by lawyers.

- Rules governing lawyers' truth-telling duties outside the court context contrast with those that apply inside the court context. The outside-the-court truth-telling rules apply in a lawyer's dealings with opposing lawyers, opposing parties, witnesses, and anyone else with whom the lawyer communicates as a lawyer.

- For a statement to a third party to subject a lawyer to discipline, it must both be false and material. Lawyers are prohibited from making statements that are fraudulent or remaining silent when the statement or silence would amount to fraud under applicable tort principles.

    - The negotiation setting presents a special circumstance within which the nature and effect of misleading statements must be analyzed. By its nature, an element of misleading is present in the negotiation process. The rules prohibit only certain forms of misleading.

    - Statements made to other lawyers in negotiations (and arguably to very sophisticated nonlawyers) are regarded much differently from statements made to nonlawyers.

    - Some statements made in the negotiation setting are not regarded as statements of fact because they are simply too nebulous to be called as such, or they are accepted parts of the negotiation game that ought to be evaluated for what they are worth by the other side.

- ☞ The process of reducing an oral agreement to writing poses special truthfulness problems.

☛ Model Rule 4.4 prohibits a lawyer from using "means that have no substantial purpose other than to embarrass, delay, or burden a third person. . . ." The rule prohibits only actions that serve no substantial, legitimate purpose, but are merely done to embarrass, delay, or burden the third person.

- ☞ Opposing parties are a special category of third party. Their interests are most directly contrary to those of the lawyer's client. Opposing parties are, therefore, routinely the object of a lawyer's client-favoring activities.

- ☞ A great deal of lawyer conduct toward witnesses may be perceived by the witness as harassing.

- ☞ Lawyers may not use unlawful means to gather evidence from witnesses. MR 4.4.

☛ Lawyers may investigate jurors' backgrounds by means of public records such as deeds, judgments, available voting records, and so on. Lawyers may not contact jurors either in person or through agents. MR 4.4.

☛ Remember that the language here is "merely to harass." Many client claims might be deemed to be harassing actions, but if the action has a substantial, legitimate purpose and both factual and legal merit, the claim will not be harassment.

☛ The Model Code includes a specific provision prohibiting threats of criminal prosecution "solely to obtain advantage in a civil matter." DR 7-105. Threatening criminal prosecution for reasons other than gaining an advantage in a civil matter is not prohibited by this rule. The Model Rule drafters did not include a specific provision on this subject in the Model Rules. Rather, they relied on the general "Rights of Third Parties" rule to cover the use of inappropriate threats. MR 4.4. In effect, when a threat would amount to extortion, it is a prohibited threat under Model Rule 4.4.

☛ Watch for fact patterns in which lawyers contact third persons. The key distinctions will be whether the contacted person is or is not represented.

- ☞ Lawyers are prohibited from communicating about the subject matter of a dispute with ***represented persons*** without first obtaining permission from the represented person's lawyer. MR 4.2. Opposing parties, however, may communicate with one another without offending Model Rule 4.2, provided that the lawyer has not instructed the client to do so as a means of circumventing the rule.

- ☞ The rule includes represented persons, even if they are not formally parties to active litigation.

- ☞ No matter how much a particular witness's testimony is expected to favor one side in a dispute, a mere witness is not a represented party. Model Rule 4.2 does not apply to communication with mere witnesses.

- ☞ Organizations speak and function through individuals who are not in and of themselves the organization. When dealing with a represented organization, Model Rule 4.2 prohibits unauthorized communication between an opposing lawyer and employees with managerial responsibilities for the subject of the matter, employees whose acts or omissions may be imputed to the organization with respect to the matter, and employees whose statements may constitute an admission attributable to the organization. MR 4.2 Comment.

- ☞ Whether former employees may be considered as parties for purposes of Model Rule 4.2 has been a controversial question. Both the ABA and the majority of decisions say that former employees are not parties under Model Rule 4.2. Other courts have ruled to the contrary. The better approach is probably to distinguish cases based on the category of employee at issue and that employee's relationship to the matter.
- ☞ Members of a class, once certified, are treated as parties for purposes of Model Rule 4.2.
- ☞ A lawyer may communicate with an opposing party about the subject matter of the representation if the lawyer is "authorized by law or by court order" to so communicate.

☛ In criminal practice, of course, the opposing party of the prosecutor is a criminal defendant. Two different aspects of this special configuration are worthy of note.

- ☞ Fifth and Fourteenth Amendment due process rights and the Sixth Amendment right to counsel protection restrain prosecutors' contact with criminal defendants in ways that go beyond the professional responsibility law constraints of Model Rule 4.2.
- ☞ Prosecutors, especially federal prosecutors invoking not only Model Rule 4.2's "authorized by law" language but also the Supremacy Clause of the United States Constitution, have argued that their crime investigation activities are not restricted by Model Rule 4.2's requirements of consent by an opposing party's lawyer prior to communication.

☛ While not prohibited from communicating with *unrepresented persons* who are involved in a client's matter, lawyers are restricted in what they may say to such a person. MR 4.3.

- ☞ A lawyer is under an affirmative obligation to refrain from stating or implying that the lawyer is disinterested in the matter about which the lawyer is communicating. Any effort to mislead an unrepresented person about the lawyer's interest subjects the lawyer to discipline.
- ☞ When a lawyer "reasonably should know" that an unrepresented person misunderstands the lawyer's interest in the matter, the lawyer is obliged to make reasonable efforts to clarify his role.
- ☞ Lawyers are prohibited from giving legal advice to the unrepresented persons with whom they inevitably come into contact, except to advise unrepresented persons to obtain counsel.
- ☞ Model Rule 4.3 does not prohibit fact gathering provided the lawyer does so without giving advice (other than advice to obtain counsel) to the unrepresented person.

☛ In limited circumstances, a lawyer may have civil liability for wrongful or negligent lawyering activity to those outside the lawyer-client relationship.

- ☞ As a general rule, lawyers do not owe a duty that supports a negligence action to third persons.
- ☞ When a lawyer's work for a client is intended to benefit a third person, the lawyer owes a duty of care to that third person.
- ☞ When a lawyer's work for a client specifically invites the reliance of a third person, the lawyer owes a duty of care to that third person.

- When a lawyer does work for a client who is a fiduciary (such as a trustee of a trust for the benefit of a beneficiary), the lawyer owes a duty to the beneficiary requiring the lawyer to refrain from engaging in acts that assist the client in breaching the client's fiduciary duties.

- Lawyers who know that a client will harm a third person and fail to engage in reasonable steps to prevent the harm may have liability to the third person who is harmed by the client. This duty is highly controversial and not widely accepted.

CHAPTER 8

DUTIES TO THE LEGAL SYSTEM AND SOCIETY

ChapterScope

- This chapter is about a collection of lawyer duties that are neither duties to clients (see Chapters 4 through 6) nor to third parties (see Chapter 7). Rather, these duties are to the legal system or the public generally.

- Many of these duties conflict with duties to clients, and the discussion in this chapter is about rules that set the lines across which client-favoring actions become unacceptably harmful to the legal system or the public.

- Many of these duties, particularly those governing litigation conduct, arise from the notion of the lawyer as *"officer of the court."* A lawyer owes duties to the justice system that create friction with the lawyer's duties to her client.

- Truth-telling inside the court context carries implications not present in out-of-court contexts, such as negotiation. When a lawyer misleads in court, the court itself is misled in addition to the opposing party.

  - Despite the duty of candor to the court, a lawyer is under no general obligation to reveal unfavorable facts to the court. A lawyer must disclose material facts "when disclosure is necessary to avoid assisting a criminal or fraudulent act by the client."

  - A lawyer is prohibited from offering evidence the lawyer knows to be false. MR 3.3(a)(4).

  - Except in representing a criminal defendant, a lawyer "may refuse to offer evidence . . . that the lawyer reasonably believes is false." MR 3.3(a)(3).

  - Lawyers are obligated to disclose to the court controlling, directly *adverse legal authority.* MR 3.3(a)(2). Lawyers have no obligation to disclose adverse authority to opposing parties.

- Lawyers are prohibited generally from requesting or advising a witness to refrain from voluntarily cooperating with another litigant. MR 3.4(f).

- Lawyers are prohibited from bringing actions or taking positions in litigation that are *frivolous.*

- In general, lawyers are obliged to *expedite litigation* to the extent that such activity is consistent with the client's interests. MR 3.2.

- Lawyers are prohibited from expressing *their personal opinion* to jurors about the justness of the client's cause, the credibility of a witness, or the culpability, guilt, or innocence of a party. MR 3.4(e).

- Lawyers are prohibited from undermining the evidence law policies by alluding to matters that are either irrelevant or will not be supported by admissible evidence. MR 3.4(e).

- Lawyers must *obey court orders.* Even when a lawyer knows that a judge is mistaken in making an order or ruling, the lawyer must obey the order, but may make reasonable efforts to preserve the record for later challenge on appeal.

- Although the First Amendment protects most lawyer expression, lawyers are subject to discipline for *intemperate remarks* that serve no useful purpose.

- Lawyers generally and especially prosecutors are limited in what they may say to the media regarding pending litigation and criminal investigations.

- *Ex parte* (without the other party) *communications* seriously undermine the prospect of fair process in the justice system. As such, ex parte communication with decision-makers, both judges and jurors, is strictly regulated.

- The 2002 version of MR 6.1 remains aspirational and not mandatory. A lawyer is not subject to discipline for failing to render *pro bono* service.

I. TRUTH-TELLING INSIDE THE COURT CONTEXT

Truth-telling inside the court context carries implications not present in out-of-court contexts, such as negotiation. When a lawyer misleads in court, the court itself is misled in addition to the opposing party. As in the out-of-court context, each side must be zealous in its in-court representation, and in doing so will attempt to persuade the court that the facts and law are favorable to its side. But the reliability, integrity, and neutrality of the judicial system demand a greater level of candor from its participants than that required in out-of-court contexts.

A. Statements to opposing parties

Lawyers' out-of-court obligations of candor to opposing parties continue in like form in the litigation context. See Chapter 7, §I.

B. Fact statements to the court

A lawyer is prohibited from knowingly making false statements of material fact to the court and from otherwise engaging in acts or omissions that amount to fraud. MR 3.3(a).

1. **Generally:** Lawyers must simultaneously serve the interests of their clients and comply with candor obligations to the court. The rules in this area are an attempted balance between these competing responsibilities.

    a. **False statements of fact:** Lawyers are prohibited from knowingly making false statements of material fact to the court. MR 3.3(a)(1).

    Example: Lawyer represents Criminal Defendant. Criminal Defendant has been convicted of assault and is about to be sentenced. Judge asks Lawyer to comment on Criminal Defendant's sentencing. Lawyer, who knows that Criminal Defendant has two prior convictions for assault from another jurisdiction, says, "Criminal Defendant has a heretofore clean record and should be sentenced with leniency." Lawyer has made a material, false statement of fact to the court and is subject to discipline.

b. **Volunteering adverse facts:** Despite the duty of candor to the court, a lawyer is under no general obligation to reveal unfavorable facts to the court.

Example: Lawyer represents Criminal Defendant. Criminal Defendant has been convicted of assault and is about to be sentenced. Judge is about to sentence Criminal Defendant, and asks Lawyer if she has anything she wishes to say about Criminal Defendant. Lawyer, who knows that Criminal Defendant has two prior convictions for assault from another jurisdiction about which the court is apparently unaware, says, "No, thank you, Your Honor." Lawyer is not subject to discipline. Lawyer is under no duty to volunteer unfavorable facts.

   i. **Mandatory discovery:** Recent amendments to the Federal Rules of Civil Procedure require the parties to voluntarily exchange certain categories of basic information about the pending civil matter. See FRCP 26. These rules operate as a limited exception and require the volunteering of even unfavorable facts when they are responsive to the rule's requirements. A lawyer is ethically obligated to comply with the discovery rules when they require such disclosures.

c. **Disclosing material facts:** Although a lawyer is under no general obligation to reveal unfavorable facts to the court, a lawyer must disclose material facts when disclosure is necessary to avoid assisting a criminal or fraudulent act by the client. MR 3.3 Comment [2].

Example: Lawyer represents Criminal Defendant. Criminal Defendant has been convicted of assault and is about to be sentenced. Judge is about to sentence Criminal Defendant, and asks Lawyer if she has anything she wishes to say about Criminal Defendant. Lawyer knows that Criminal Defendant has two prior convictions for assault from another jurisdiction about which the court is apparently unaware, and that the court is unaware of them because Criminal Defendant has used a false identity. Lawyer must counsel Criminal Defendant to rectify this potential fraud and, if Criminal Defendant refuses to do so, Lawyer must reveal this information.

Example: Lawyer represented Client in a contract dispute with Defendant. Client used a false identity to dupe Defendant into entering into the contractual relationship with her. Lawyer knew of Client's false identity, which continued to be used in the court proceedings. Lawyer is under a duty to reveal Client's fraud to the court. See, e.g., State v. Casby, 348 N.W.2d 736 (Minn. 1984).

Example: Lawyer represented Plaintiff-Client in a personal injury action. While negotiating with Defendant's counsel a settlement agreement that required court approval, Plaintiff-Client died. Lawyer failed to reveal this fact to either opposing counsel or the court and concluded settlement negotiations. Lawyer is subject to discipline for failing to reveal a fact that affects the fundamental validity (not the merits) of the action. Virzi v. Grand Trunk Warehouse and Cold Storage Co., 571 F. Supp. 507 (E.D. Mich. 1983).

2. **Ex parte proceedings:** On those occasions when a lawyer is permitted by law to engage in ex parte communications with the court (see §VI.A), the lawyer must disclose to the court both favorable and unfavorable material facts. MR 3.3(d).

Example: Lawyer in State X approaches Judge ex parte with a Complaint and accompanying Request for a Temporary Restraining Order, which is permitted under the law in State X. Lawyer knows both favorable and unfavorable facts on the critical issue of irreparable harm. Lawyer must reveal both to Judge.

C. Perjury

The perjury problem presents extraordinary difficulties for the lawyer, especially when the person committing the perjury is the lawyer's client. Perjury's affront to the justice system is great, as is the harm that comes to the client when the lawyer reveals the client's perjury.

1. **General duty to refrain from offering false evidence:** A lawyer is prohibited from offering evidence the lawyer knows to be false. MR 3.3(a)(3).

2. **Discretion to refuse to offer some evidence:** Further, a lawyer "may refuse to offer evidence that the lawyer reasonably believes is false." MR 3.3(a)(3). The "reasonably believes" standard is considerably lower than the "knows" standard. A lawyer is given discretion by this rule to decline to present evidence when she "reasonably believes" but does not "know" that the evidence is false. This discretion permits a lawyer to disregard a client's preference for offering such evidence without violating the advocacy duty owed the client.

3. **Perjury by a witness:** Perjury by a witness other than the client is a somewhat easier case. When a lawyer knows that a witness other than the client has offered perjured testimony, the lawyer must promptly reveal the perjury to the court. MR 3.3(a)(3). Even here, however, the lawyer must "know" that the witness's evidence is false.

   Example: Lawyer represents Client. Witness says "X" under oath at a deposition. Later, at trial, Witness says "not-X." Simple contradiction, without more, does not trigger the obligation of the lawyer to reveal a fraud on the court by Witness. People contradict themselves when they are confused, mistaken, remember more at a later date, and so on. Not all contradictions indicate perjury. A lawyer should not disclose this fraud without further indications that the contradictions indeed reflect a fraud on the court.

4. **Perjury by a client:** Unlike the Model Code approach, which explicitly distinguished between client perjury and other witness perjury, the Model Rules' language requires the same answer to both. MR 3.3(a)(3); DR 7-102(B).

   a. **Knowledge of intention to commit perjury:** When the lawyer knows of the client's intention to commit perjury, the lawyer must attempt to dissuade, attempt to withdraw, and, finally, if the perjury occurs, take reasonable remedial measures.

      i. **Dissuade:** The lawyer must attempt to persuade the client to refrain from offering false testimony.

      ii. **Withdraw:** If unsuccessful, the lawyer should request the court's permission to withdraw from the representation. When such a request occurs during or on the eve of trial, courts are unlikely to grant it because of the inevitable delay that will result and the lack of assurance that the same scenario will not simply unfold with the next lawyer to represent the client. The lawyer must attempt to withdraw without breaching a client's confidences.

iii. **Reasonable remedial measures:** If the perjury has occurred despite the lawyer's efforts, the lawyer must take reasonable remedial measures. What constitutes reasonable remedial measures following perjury is the subject of considerable and unresolved debate. Some argue persuasively that the duty a lawyer owes the client should prevent the lawyer from revealing the perjury; others argue persuasively that the lawyer's duty to the court supersedes the duty to the client and that, in any event, lawyers do not owe clients a duty to help them perpetrate frauds on courts. Current case law does not effectively resolve this dispute. In either event, although Model Rule 3.3's language requires a lawyer to engage reasonable remedial measures whether the perjury has come from a client or another witness, what may be reasonable as a remedial measure may well depend on whether the client or another witness has committed the perjury. The February 2002 amendments to MR 3.3(b) make explicit that, whether client or other witness has committed the perjury, reasonable remedial measures include disclosure of the perjury to the court.

b. **Knowledge gained after the perjury:** When the lawyer learns that the client's testimony was perjurious after the perjury occurs but before the proceedings end, the lawyer must first attempt to persuade the client to rectify the matter by revealing the fraud and then testifying truthfully. If that effort fails, the lawyer has only the reasonable remedial measures option and, according to the Model Rules Comment, must reveal the perjury if the lawyer learns of it before the proceedings conclude. If the lawyer does not learn of the perjury until after the conclusion of the proceedings, then the lawyer has no obligation to reveal it. MR 3.3(c).

c. **Duty applies despite confidentiality:** The Model Rule duty to rectify the perjury applies even if doing so would otherwise violate the duty of confidentiality under Model Rule 1.6. MR 3.3(c).

d. **Distinctions between criminal and civil representation:** Perjury issues in criminal representation present special problems because of the criminal defendant's right to testify on his own behalf, the obligation on the state to prove the defendant guilty beyond a reasonable doubt, the privilege against self-incrimination, and the right to counsel. As it must, even without an explicit reference, the Model Rules concede the supremacy of the Constitution. MR 3.3(a)(3).

i. **Sixth Amendment:** The Sixth Amendment right to counsel in criminal cases is not violated when a defense lawyer threatens to withdraw or reveal the perjury if the client persists in a likely presentation of perjured testimony.

Example: Defendant faced trial for murdering Victim. Defendant told Lawyer that, to bolster his claims of self-defense, he would perjure himself on the witness stand. Lawyer assured Defendant that he could successfully claim self-defense without the perjured testimony. Lawyer further told Defendant that he would inform the court of the perjury and withdraw from the representation if Defendant gave false testimony. Defendant did not perjure himself and was convicted. Defendant then moved for a new trial, claiming that Lawyer's advice had deprived him of a fair trial.

The Sixth Amendment right to counsel requires only reasonably effective assistance of counsel. Counsel's duty of loyalty and diligence is limited to legitimate, lawful conduct. The right to counsel includes no right to have a lawyer who will cooperate in planned perjury. Lawyer's first duty when confronted with Defendant's proposal for perjurious testimony was to attempt to dissuade Defendant from the unlawful course of conduct. If Defendant had committed perjury, Lawyer's revelation of that fact to the court and his withdrawal would have been a professionally responsible and acceptable response. An attorney's duty of confidentiality does not extend to a client's announced plans to engage in future criminal conduct. Lawyer's conduct satisfied the Sixth Amendment's "reasonably effective" standard. Nix v. Whiteside, 475 U.S. 157 (1986).

e. **Other suggested options:** Although not accepted in all circles, the following possible options have been suggested for counsel faced with a perjurious client in a criminal case.

   i. **Narrative:** Some have suggested that the lawyer call the client as a witness, ask him to tell his version of the events to the jury, and otherwise participate no further in the client's testimony. Such an approach has the benefits of distancing the lawyer from the active participation in the perjury. It has the shortcomings of signaling to the judge that the lawyer believes the client is committing perjury and of failing to present the client to the jury in a favorable light.

   ii. **Refuse to call the client to testify:** A rather bold approach is to refuse to call the client against the client's wishes. If the client protests in open court, the judge can determine whether the defendant should be permitted to testify. Such an approach distances the lawyer even further from the perjury but threatens client interests to an unacceptable degree.

   iii. **Excuse the criminal defense lawyer from this obligation:** A final suggestion is that criminal defense lawyers be excused from the obligations of Model Rule 3.3(a)(3). Under such an approach, a criminal defense lawyer may call the client as a witness and question the client in the normal fashion. Such an approach advances client interests but makes the lawyer a knowing accomplice to the perjury.

D. Law statements to the court

A lawyer is prohibited from making false statements of law to the court. MR 3.3(a). As an advocate, a lawyer should present the law in the most favorable light for the client. As such, the lawyer need not reveal his objective analysis of the law to the court, but may make any nonfrivolous, client-favoring arguments regarding the law to the court. Because the law is in large measure indeterminate, significant room for interpretation presents itself. Nonetheless, a lawyer may not make false statements about the law to the court.

Example: Lawyer represents Defendant-Client in a personal injury case. Lawyer may make nonfrivolous arguments that favor his client regarding the interpretation of a recent court decision regarding the excited utterance exception to the hearsay rule, even if his objective analysis leads to the conclusion that other, unfavorable interpretations of the authority have greater merit. Lawyer may not, however, tell the court that the state follows the contributory negligence doctrine when Lawyer knows that the legislature has adopted an applicable comparative negligence statute.

E. Disclosing adverse legal authority

Lawyers are obligated to disclose to the court controlling, directly *adverse legal authority.* MR 3.3(a)(2).

1. **To opposing parties:** Lawyers have no obligation to disclose adverse authority to opposing parties. Naturally, when a disclosure of directly adverse, controlling authority is made to a court, it will not ordinarily be done ex parte. See §VI.A. As a result, when the disclosure is made to the court, it will ordinarily and coincidentally also be made to the opposing party. The attendant disclosure to opposing counsel is merely the result of the disclosure to the court. It is not mandated on its own strength.

2. **To the court:** Lawyers are required to disclose controlling, directly adverse authority to the court. Such disclosures may take the form of oral statements in open court during a motion or appellate argument or written statements in briefs or other legal argument papers filed with the court.

    Example: Lawyer failed to cite adverse, controlling precedent in support of his application for a temporary restraining order and preliminary injunction. Lawyer is not redeemed by the fact that opposing counsel subsequently cited the controlling precedent that Lawyer should have disclosed earlier. Lawyer was legitimately entitled to press his own interpretations of precedent, including interpretations that render particular cases inapplicable, but he had a duty to disclose the directly adverse, controlling precedent to the court and is subject to discipline for failing to do so. See similar fact pattern in the context of FRCP 11 sanctions, Jorgenson v. County of Volusia, 846 F.2d 1350 (11th Cir. 1988).

    a. **Controlling:** Only controlling authority, that is, mandatory authority that is controlling on the court currently making the decision, must be disclosed. Thus, when a lawyer is practicing in State X, and he knows of a case from State Y that is precisely on point with his case, he is under no obligation to disclose the case because it is not controlling on the courts of State X.

    b. **Directly adverse:** Only directly adverse authority must be disclosed under this rule. Authority is directly adverse when it is applicable to the present case without extended analogy.

    Example: Plaintiff has filed a claim against Defendant for tortious employment discharge. Lawyer represents Defendant. Lawyer knows of a case from the highest court in the state that establishes that a terminated employee with a specific contract term has a contract-based claim for wrongful discharge. The fact patterns of the decided case and the instant case are similar, except for the presence of the contract term and except for the legal basis of the claim (tort v. contract). Lawyer need not disclose the authority to the court because it is not directly adverse. The contract and the tort claims for wrongful discharge require different elements, and the precedent case was not decided on a point that makes its ruling adverse in the instant case.

    Example: Lawyer is representing Client in a medical malpractice case. Lawyer knows of a veterinary malpractice case decided by his state's highest court that holds contrary to Lawyer's case on the question of what damages are available. Because quite different policies support medical malpractice law from those that support veterinary malpractice law, the veterinary malpractice case is not directly adverse and need not be disclosed. The analogy from veterinary malpractice to medical malpractice is too extended to be deemed direct.

c. **Contesting the disclosed authority:** The requirement of disclosing the controlling, directly adverse authority does not prevent the disclosing lawyer from arguing that the authority does not apply or is wrong and should not be followed.

II. SUPPRESSING EVIDENCE AND WITNESS PAYMENT

A lawyer is limited in the ways in which witnesses may be compensated and in instructing witnesses about whether to make themselves available for testimony or interview by the opposing side. As in all other areas of professional responsibility law, a lawyer may not use a client as an agent to do what the lawyer is prohibited from doing.

A. Suppressing witness availability

Although a witness's testimony may favor one side in litigation over another, witnesses do not belong to particular litigants. As such, lawyers are prohibited generally from requesting or advising a witness to refrain from voluntarily cooperating with another litigant. MR 3.4(f).

1. **Procuring witness unavailability:** Under no circumstances may a lawyer dissuade a witness from appearing at a hearing or persuade a witness to secrete himself so that the witness will be unavailable. MR 3.4(a).

   Example: Lawyer knows that Witness can identify Lawyer's Client, a criminal defendant. Lawyer knows that Witness is hesitant about appearing at trial. Lawyer suggests that if Witness could take an extended vacation to Costa Rica during the trial dates, Witness could avoid the embarrassment that would inevitably come during cross-examination. Lawyer is subject to discipline.

2. **Instructing a witness to cooperate only if subpoenaed:** In general, a lawyer may not instruct a witness to cooperate only if subpoenaed. MR 3.4(f).

   Example: Prosecuting Attorney interviews Eyewitness. Eyewitness tells Prosecuting Attorney that he is nervous about meeting with Defense Counsel. Prosecuting Attorney may offer to be available to accompany Eyewitness anytime Defense Counsel wishes to talk with Eyewitness. However, Prosecuting Attorney must not encourage Eyewitness to refrain from speaking with Defense Lawyer until trial.

3. **Exception:** A lawyer is permitted to request that a witness not cooperate voluntarily if the following two conditions are met. Even when these conditions are met, a lawyer must not request that such a witness avoid orders of court to appear as a witness at trials, hearings, or depositions.

   a. **Relative or employee:** The witness must be a relative, employee, or agent of the client. A client, through his lawyer, may ask his mother, brother, or employee, for example, to refrain from being voluntarily cooperative with the opposing litigant if the lack of cooperation will not harm the witness. MR 3.4(f)(1).

   b. **Witness's interest:** The lawyer must reasonably believe that the request will not harm the witness. MR 3.4(f)(2).

   Example: Lawyer represents Employer-Client. Employer has been named as defendant in a negligence action, and Employee's actions may have caused the Plaintiff's damages. Lawyer could not reasonably conclude that Employee's interest would not be adversely affected by Employee's refusal of cooperation with Plaintiff's counsel. Lawyer must not request that Employee refrain from voluntarily giving information to Plaintiff's counsel.

B. Witness payment rules

Lawyers are restricted in the ways in which they may compensate witnesses. The witnesses should tell what they know at a hearing or trial based on what they know and not based on which side has offered them a higher fee to testify.

1. **Lay witnesses:** Payment of a witness fee to lay witnesses is usually provided for in a state statute. Lawyers may pay nonexpert witnesses only the statutory fee and reasonable expenses incurred by the witness in attending the trial or hearing. MR 3.4 Comment 3.

2. **Expert witnesses:** Expert witnesses may be paid the professional fee that someone in the expert's field charges for his or her time and reasonable expenses incurred by the witness in attending the trial or hearing. However, an expert may not be paid a fee that is contingent on the outcome of the matter. MR 3.4 Comment 3.

   Example: Lawyer hires Expert Witness, a doctor, to examine Personal-Injury-Plaintiff-Client. Lawyer agrees to pay Expert Witness 15% of whatever recovery Lawyer is able to obtain for Client. Lawyer is subject to discipline.

III. LIMITATIONS ON PRESENTATIONS TO A COURT

In a variety of ways, the ethics rules restrict the ways in which lawyers make their presentations in court.

A. Frivolous claims and litigation positions

By both ethics code provisions and litigation sanctions rules, lawyers are prohibited from bringing actions or taking positions in litigation that are frivolous.

1. **Ethics code limits:** In several forms, the Model Rules restrict lawyers' behavior regarding frivolous positions.

   a. **The frivolous claims rule:** Model Rule 3.1, in most respects tracking Federal Rule of Civil Procedure 11, prohibits lawyers from bringing or defending claims on a frivolous basis.

      i. **What is frivolous?** Frivolous claims or positions may be so because they lack legal or factual merit or because they are taken primarily to harass or maliciously injure a third party.

         - **Lacking legal or factual merit**
           A claim or position is not frivolous merely because it loses the day. To be frivolous, an argument must be one that a reasonable lawyer would regard as having no legal or factual merit.

         - **Merely or primarily to harass or injure**
           Under the analogous Model Code provision, a claim was frivolous when it was brought merely to harass or injure. DR 7-102(A)(1). That standard is found in the Model Rules in both MR 4.4 and in the Comment to MR 3.1. Such conduct is subject to discipline.

ii. **Difference between civil and criminal cases:** Criminal cases present a special problem for the frivolous claim rule. In a criminal case, unlike a civil case, a defendant has a due process right to plead "not guilty" and require the government to be put to its proof. By contrast, in civil litigation, when an allegation is made in a pleading that requires response or is made through the discovery device called requests for admissions, a responding party must admit allegations that are true. Model Rule 3.1 is not intended to prevent a lawyer from assisting a criminal defendant in the process of putting the government to its proof. Prosecuting lawyers have special obligations regarding the prosecution of charges that lack merit. See Chapter 9, §I.B.

b. **Discovery and other pretrial conduct:** Frivolous discovery requests and those intended merely to delay are prohibited. MR 3.4(d).

c. **Expediting litigation:** In general, lawyers are obliged to expedite litigation to the extent that such activity is consistent with the client's interests. MR 3.2.

2. **Federal Rule of Civil Procedure 11 and other sanctions:** Beyond the ethics code limitations that create disciplinary liability for filing frivolous claims and taking frivolous positions in litigation, Federal Rule of Civil Procedure 11 and its state law counterparts create sanctions liability for similar conduct. A court may consider a motion for sanctions even though the proceedings have ended. See also Chapter 3, §V.B.

Example: Client, a clothing retailer, brought an antitrust action against Manufacturers A and B, alleging a nationwide conspiracy to fix prices and engage in unfair competition. Firm filed Client's Complaint after phoning clothing retailers in New York City, Philadelphia, Baltimore, and Washington, D.C. From this research, Firm inferred that only one store in each major metropolitan area nationwide sold Manufacturer A's product. Later, Firm voluntarily dismissed the claim, and Manufacturers A and B moved for Rule 11 sanctions. The district court awarded sanctions to the Manufacturers, the appellate court affirmed that ruling, and the district court imposed appellate costs on Firm.

District courts may enforce Rule 11 even after the plaintiff has filed a notice of voluntary dismissal because the harm triggering the Rule's application—needless expense and delay—has already occurred. A Rule 11 violation is complete when the baseless claim is filed. Federal courts may consider many such collateral issues after an action is no longer pending. The court correctly sanctioned Firm, but the imposition of appellate costs is appropriate only when the sanctioned party files a frivolous appeal, not when the appellate court has simply upheld the original award. Cooter & Gell v. Hartmarx Corp., 496 U.S. 384 (1990).

B. **Personal opinion**

Lawyers are prohibited from expressing their personal opinion to jurors about the justness of the client's cause, the credibility of a witness, or the culpability, guilt, or innocence of a party. MR 3.4(e). This rule applies only to personal-opinion statements. It does not prohibit vigorous argument that attempts to persuade the jury about any of the prohibited personal-opinion subject matters.

Example: In his closing argument, Lawyer says at various points, "In my fifteen years of lawyering, I have never seen so clear a case of a witness lying"; "When a witness says one thing one day and another thing the next, that witness is not worthy of belief"; "My client has every reason to tell you the truth about this matter. She has told you everything she knows about this controversy"; and "I wouldn't represent this client if I didn't believe her story. You see me here today, and you know what that means." The first and fourth statements are prohibited. The second and third are appropriate argument.

C. Alluding to matters outside the record

The rules of evidence are designed to regulate the information that the jury receives at a trial. Lawyers are prohibited from undermining evidence law policies by alluding to matters that are either irrelevant or will not be supported by admissible evidence. MR 3.4(e).

1. **Reasonable lawyer standard:** Matters must not be alluded to if a reasonable lawyer would recognize that those matters will not be supported by admissible evidence.

    Example: Lawyer represents Defendant-Client in a personal injury claim. Client has told Lawyer that shortly after the accident, Client overheard Bystander say, "The light was green for Defendant and red for Plaintiff." Lawyer has been unable to discover Bystander's identity and knows of no hearsay exception that would arguably make the statement admissible. Nonetheless, in his opening statement, Lawyer says to the jury, "A Bystander who had a good look at the accident has said that the light was green for Defendant and red for Plaintiff." Lawyer is subject to discipline.

2. **Certainty not required:** The lawyer need not be certain that the evidence will be admitted. If the lawyer reasonably believes that the evidence will be admitted, then the lawyer may freely allude to the evidence. Tactical sense will dictate that the lawyer will want to refer to the evidence in the opening statement only when the lawyer genuinely believes it will be admissible. Otherwise the lawyer's promises of particular pieces of evidence will not be met, and the jury may be left doubting the lawyer's credibility.

3. **Outside the lawyer's control:** If evidence will be admissible only on a condition over which the lawyer in question has no control, the lawyer must not allude to that matter until the evidence is admitted.

    Example: In his opening statement, Prosecutor tells the jury about Defendant's prior convictions that Prosecutor knows will be admissible only if Defendant chooses to testify. Because the Defense and not the Prosecutor will later determine whether Defendant will testify, Prosecutor is subject to discipline.

4. **Matters already ruled inadmissible:** Once the court has ruled a piece of evidence inadmissible, a lawyer is prohibited from referring to it to the jury.

    Example: Lawyer represents Client in an auto accident case. Lawyer offers a witness who would testify that Lawyer's Client is a safe driver. Judge rules that the witness's testimony is inadmissible character-bolstering evidence. Nonetheless, Lawyer tells the jury in closing argument that people who have driven with Client regard her as a safe driver. No such evidence was admitted at the trial. Lawyer is subject to discipline.

D. Obey court orders

Lawyers must obey court orders. Even when a lawyer knows that a judge is mistaken in making an order or ruling, the lawyer must obey the order but may make reasonable efforts to preserve the record for later challenge on appeal. MR 3.4(c).

Example: Lawyer represents Client at trial. Lawyer asks Witness to describe Opposing Party's demeanor at the time of the incident in litigation. Lawyer regards this information as crucial to the case. Opposing Lawyer objects without stating grounds and Judge sustains the objection. Lawyer asks, "Your Honor, may I be heard on this point?" Judge responds, "No, get on to your next question." Lawyer is certain that Judge is wrong. Lawyer tells Witness to answer despite Judge's ruling. Lawyer is subject to discipline and may also be held in contempt of court.

E. **Intemperate remarks**

Although the First Amendment protects most lawyer expression, lawyers are subject to discipline for intemperate remarks that serve no useful purpose.

Example: While representing Defendant, Lawyer was frequently sarcastic, disrespectful, and irrational. He repeatedly accused the Court of cronyism, racism, and incompetence. He demeaned and harassed opposing counsel, publicly charging them with improprieties that had no basis in fact.

He verbally abused witnesses with insults and profanities. Lawyer's conduct exceeded the limits of zealous advocacy. Attorneys must display a courteous and respectful attitude to the Court, opposing counsel, parties, witnesses, court officers, clerks, and any individual involved in the legal process. Such conduct is essential to an orderly system of justice. In re Vincenti, 458 A.2d 1268 (N.J. 1983).

Example: Lawyer, frustrated by Opposing Counsel and by various rulings of Judge, told Opposing Lawyer to "Kiss my ass," and muttered "Ah shit," when Judge overruled Lawyer's objections. Lawyer is guilty of contempt of court. United States v. Ortleib, 274 F.3d 871 (5th Cir. 2001).

IV. OBLIGATION TO IMPROVE THE LEGAL SYSTEM

Lawyers have a responsibility to make efforts to improve the legal system. With the experience of practicing law, lawyers are uniquely capable of spotting needed areas for improvement and of formulating suggested improvements. MR, Preamble; Model Code, Canon 8.

A. **Public office**

Lawyers are encouraged to serve their community in public office.

B. **Support for needed legislation**

Lawyers can support improvements in legislation in a variety of ways.

1. **Drafting committees:** Lawyers should serve on panels and committees of the organized bar and other organizations, such as the American Law Institute and its state-level analogs. Such panels and committees draft summaries of the law and model legislation that often affect the state of the current law, either by legislative adoption or judicial reference to the material generated by the committee or panel.

2. **Legislative advocacy:** Lawyers should seek to use their particular expertise to advocate in legislatures for improvement in the law.

    a. **Representing a client:** A lawyer representing a client's interests in a legislative lobbying effort must disclose the lawyer's interest in the legislation and, if it is not privileged, the client's identity. MR 3.9.

b. Public information: When a lawyer is merely seeking public information for a client, the lawyer need not disclose his interest nor the client's identity.

C. Review of the judiciary

Lawyers have a special responsibility both for protecting the entity of the judiciary and for commenting on its flaws.

1. Defending the entity: As officers of the court and critical members of the justice system, lawyers ought to hold the judiciary as an entity, even if not every particular judge, in high regard.

2. Criticizing judges: Because of their special knowledge, lawyers have an obligation to criticize particular judges, as long as they do so with discretion.

a. Improve the system: If lawyers do not criticize judges and report their wrongful conduct to appropriate disciplinary authorities, the justice system will suffer the consequences of being poorly staffed.

b. Use restraint: Judges are not free to defend themselves in public from every criticism leveled. Lawyers must use discretion when deciding to publicly criticize a judge.

c. Sanctions: When a lawyer's criticism of judges is false, the lawyer may be found in contempt by the judge, the lawyer may be liable to the judge for defamation, and the lawyer will be subject to discipline. MR 8.2(a). Garrison v. Louisiana, 379 U.S. 64 (1964). See §III.E.

d. First Amendment protection: The First Amendment provides limited protection for lawyers' criticism of judges. See In re Sawyer, 360 U.S. 622 (1959).

3. Judicial selection: Lawyers should be active in the judicial selection process to improve the justice system, provided that their level of involvement does not raise questions about the lawyer's self-motivation in supporting one judicial candidate over another.

V. LIMITATIONS ON LITIGATION PUBLICITY

Lawyers generally and especially prosecutors are limited in what they may say to the media regarding pending litigation and criminal investigations. The restrictions are meant to protect the integrity of the adversary system by keeping statements about pending matters inside the courtroom, where they will get directly to the decision-makers, jurors, and judges and can be challenged by an adversary at the time of their making. MR 3.6, MR 3.8(f).

A. Constitutional challenge

The original Model Rule 3.6 was held void for vagueness in Gentile v. State Bar of Nevada, 501 U.S. 1030 (1991). The Court held that the list of permitted statements in former MR 3.6(c) and the rule's invitation to make those statements "without elaboration" gave too little guidance to even the careful lawyer trying to make permitted comment to the media. The rule was amended in 1994 in an effort to remedy the Court's constitutional objections to it.

B. General standard

A lawyer's out-of-court statements can sometimes have a deleterious effect on the quality and integrity of the judicial process, for example, by prejudicing potential witnesses or jurors or by generating public opinion that could affect the potential jurors' objectivity. Because of such statements' possible effects on the judicial process, lawyers are prohibited from making out-of-court statements that a reasonable lawyer would expect to be disseminated by public communication and that the lawyer knows or should know will have a substantial likelihood of materially prejudicing the matter. MR 3.6(a). A number of specific topics for statements are exempted from the rule. MR 3.6(b).

1. **Out of court:** Only statements made out of court are restricted by this rule. If a lawyer makes a statement during a trial or other court proceeding that is picked up by the media present and disseminated, it will not violate MR 3.6.

2. **Likely to be disseminated by public communication:** Only statements that a reasonable statement-maker would expect to be disseminated by means of public communication are restricted by MR 3.6. When the lawyer makes a statement with a microphone in her face, the lawyer should expect its dissemination. By contrast, a wholly private statement made to a clerk in a careful manner that is nonetheless eavesdropped on by a reporter would not subject the lawyer to discipline.

3. **Materially prejudice a matter:** Statements that subject the lawyer to discipline are those that a lawyer knows or reasonably should know will be likely to materially prejudice the matter.

C. Permitted statements

Notwithstanding the general prohibition, the following statements may safely be made without the risk of discipline. MR 3.6(b).

1. **Nature of claim or defense:** Statements regarding the nature of the claim or defense and the identity of the parties (except where the identity is required to be kept secret by law, such as is true in many juvenile matters) may be made. MR 3.6(b)(1).

2. **Public records:** Statements regarding information that is already in a public record may be made. MR 3.6(b)(2).

3. **Investigation in process:** Statements regarding the simple fact that an investigation is in progress may be made. MR 3.6(b)(3).

4. **Scheduling:** The scheduling of the next steps in the process may be stated. MR 3.6(b)(4).

5. **Public assistance:** A request for public assistance in obtaining evidence and information may be made. MR 3.6(b)(5).

6. **Criminal cases:** In criminal cases, the following statements are also permitted.

    a. **Identity, residence, occupation, and family status:** The identity, residence, occupation, and family status of the accused. MR 3.6(b)(7)(i).

    b. **Apprehension:** Information necessary to aid the accused's apprehension, if she has not yet been apprehended. MR 3.6(b)(7)(ii).

    c. **Arrest:** The fact, time, and place of arrest. MR 3.6(b)(7)(iii).

d. Investigation: The identity of investigating and arresting officers, the names of investigating organizations, and the length of the investigation. MR 3.6(b)(7)(iv).

D. Exception for statements that are necessary to protect the client

When a lawyer reasonably believes that making a statement is necessary to counter the effects of a public statement made by the other side in the matter, the lawyer may make such a statement without being subject to discipline. This rule authorizes the age-old children's excuse, "He started it!" MR 3.6(c).

E. Prosecutors' supervision of subordinates' statements

All lawyers have a general obligation to provide reasonable supervision of subordinates in an effort to avoid their breaches of the lawyer's ethics code, but prosecutors have a specially identified duty in the case of extrajudicial statements to exercise reasonable care to prevent violative extrajudicial statements by investigators, police, and others under the supervision of the prosecutor. MR 3.8(f).

VI. EX PARTE CONTACT WITH JUDGES AND JURORS

Our judicial system is built upon the premise that adversaries can make their best arguments to the judge and the judge can then decide the matter. That premise requires that the adversaries' arguments be made in the presence of one another so that each side's response can be heard. ***Ex parte*** (without the other party) ***communications*** seriously undermine the prospect of fair process in the justice system. As such, ex parte communication with decision-makers, both judges and jurors, is strictly regulated.

A. Judges

If lawyers were permitted to have ex parte communications with judges, then litigated matters would be resolved on the basis of a series of one-at-a-time advocacy episodes rather than the give and take of opposing sides presenting evidence in open court and contesting one another's arguments. The justice system would be seriously undermined. As such, except in very limited circumstances, lawyers are prohibited from communicating ex parte with a judge. MR 3.5(b).

1. Subject matter: Some ex parte communications are permitted because of their subject matter.

a. Unrelated matters: Communications between lawyers and judges about matters unrelated to pending or impending litigation are not restricted by the rule. Such communications are not truly "ex parte" because they do not involve other parties at all.

Example: Lawyer has various matters pending in Judge's court. Lawyer goes to Judge's garage sale and discusses the purchase of Judge's used wrought-iron dinette set. This discussion is not an ex parte communication between Judge and Lawyer and is therefore not prohibited.

b. Housekeeping matters: Ex parte communications regarding so-called housekeeping matters that relate to a pending case are permitted. Most such communications will actually occur between the lawyer or her agents and the judge's agents, such as clerks and docket personnel. Housekeeping matters are those that are unrelated to the way in which the judge will ultimately rule on the matter, such as inquiries about available dates for hearings or trial.

Example: Lawyers plans to file an evidentiary motion in Judge's court regarding a pending matter. To schedule the motion hearing efficiently, Lawyers speaks to Judge's Clerk about possible available hearing dates and times without first contacting Opposing Party's Lawyer. As a housekeeping matter, this communication is not prohibited.

2. **No intent requirement:** Even innocently intended ex parte communications are prohibited.

3. **Authorized by law:** When authorized by law, lawyers are permitted to engage in ex parte communications. Such authorizations are typically found in rules governing requests for emergency restraining orders, for example. When such communication is authorized, a lawyer is under heightened candor-to-the-court requirements. See §I.B.2.

4. **Oral or written communications covered:** All forms of communication are covered by this rule. A lawyer who sends a letter to the judge or files a paper with the court without serving a copy on opposing counsel is engaging in prohibited ex parte communications with the judge.

5. **Prohibited even if judge initiates:** A lawyer is placed in a particularly difficult situation when a judge initiates an ex parte communication. Nonetheless, a lawyer is subject to discipline if he engages in even judge-initiated ex parte communication.

Example: Lawyer has a matter pending before Judge. Both are guests at a dinner party. Judge approaches Lawyer to inquire about Lawyer's resolve in pursuing a motion that Lawyer has recently filed in the matter. Lawyer says that he is serious about the motion and that he will indeed pursue it. Lawyer is subject to discipline for engaging in ex parte communications with Judge.

B. Jurors

Lawyers are strictly prohibited from communicating with jurors outside the courtroom before and during jurors' duties. This restriction applies to both grand jurors and trial jurors. Lawyers are prohibited from communicating with jurors after the jurors' duty ends, with some exceptions. Lawyers are prohibited from harassing jurors at any time. MR 3.5(c). See Chapter 7, §II.D.

1. **Before and during proceedings:** Communication outside of open court with jurors during and before their duty is strictly prohibited.

   a. **Rationale:** Any contact between lawyers and jurors may have an effect on the proceedings. The jurors have a sensitive role to play in the justice system, and all of the influences on their decision should come in the form of evidence and argument in open court.

   b. **Any subject:** Even communication about matters other than the current proceedings is prohibited. Lawyers must refrain from even innocent communication with sitting jurors.

   Example: Lawyer finds himself on an elevator with two of the jurors on his case's jury panel. One juror comments on the favorable weather and the outcome of a recent baseball game. Lawyer agrees with the juror about the weather and the game. Lawyer is subject to discipline. See, e.g., Florida Bar v. Peterson, 418 So. 2d 246 (Fla. 1982). Rather than be responsive to the juror, Lawyer should have refrained from communicating. Upon returning to court, Lawyer should inform the judge about the incident and request an instruction that the lawyers are not permitted to talk to jurors outside of open court, and that lawyers' silence during encounters such as occurred in the elevator are attributable not to rudeness but to compliance with ethics rules.

2. **After proceedings end:** Once proceedings have ended, lawyers may have very limited contact with jurors for benign purposes, such as to determine whether the lawyer's presentation manner is effective. Even after proceedings end, however, lawyers must refrain from engaging in harassing contacts with jurors and from conduct that would tend to undermine the jurors' confidence in their verdict and the justice system. The ABA amended Model Rule 3.5 in February 2002. The amended rule permits after-discharge contacts except when the contact is prohibited by law or court order, when the juror has made known a desire not to be contacted, or when the contact involves "misrepresentation, coercion, duress, or harassment." See Chapter 7, §II.D.

3. **Reporting juror misconduct:** A lawyer is under an affirmative obligation to report to the court in which the proceedings are being held juror misconduct or others' misconduct with respect to jurors. Failure to do so subjects the lawyer to discipline.

VII. PRO BONO PUBLICO

The legal profession's history of providing service to the poor is not an entirely happy one. Nonetheless, through organized efforts in bar associations, public agencies, and individual lawyers' efforts, considerable free and reduced-fee legal service is provided. The ethics rules encourage lawyers to engage in pro bono activities. In modest February 2002 amendments to both Model Rule 6.1 and the Preamble, additional encouragement, but no new requirements, were added to the lawyer's duty to provide pro bono services. In a new Comment 11 to Model Rule 6.1, law firms are extolled to encourage lawyers to provide pro bono services. Model Rule 6.1 itself adds the following sentence: "Every lawyer has a professional responsibility to provide legal services to those unable to pay."

A. Organized legal services for the poor

Through the organized bar and public agencies, legal services are provided for a portion of the population that would otherwise be unable to afford to retain a lawyer.

1. **Criminal matters:** Until the decision in Gideon v. Wainwright, 372 U.S. 335 (1963), provision of representation for indigent criminal defendants was a hit-or-miss matter, which some states had and others had not. The Supreme Court, in determining that the Sixth Amendment right to counsel requires that counsel be appointed in criminal matters for indigent defendants, generated the impetus for public defender agencies and court appointment systems for criminal representation in places without a public defender agency.

2. **Civil matters:** No comparable right to counsel exists for most civil cases. As such, states are not required to provide legal service for the poor in most civil matters. Nonetheless, through the federal funding of the Legal Services Corporation and additional funding by states and localities, legal aid or legal services offices exist to serve a portion of the population that would otherwise be unable to afford to retain a lawyer in civil matters. Because the funding is inadequate to the task, the continued unserved public need is substantial.

B. Individual lawyer's duty

Amendments in 1993 and 2002 to Model Rule 6.1 have come as close as the organized bar has to imposing a requirement on individual lawyers to render pro bono service. Nonetheless, even the 1993 version of Model Rule 6.1 remains aspirational and not mandatory. A lawyer is not subject to discipline for failing to render pro bono service.

1. **Setting a goal:** Model Rule 6.1 sets a goal for each lawyer of 50 hours of pro bono service per year.

2. **Appropriate services:** Model Rule 6.1 suggests some of the following as appropriate for pro bono service: providing service at no fee or reduced fee for those of limited means; service to religious, civic, governmental, educational, or charitable organizations at no fee or reduced fee; activities to improve the law, such as participation in bar committees that draft model legislation; and providing financial support for organizations that provide legal service for those of limited means.

3. **Setting priorities:** Model Rule 6.1 encourages lawyers to spend the bulk of their 50 hours per year rendering service at no fee, either directly for those of limited means or to organizations that directly serve those of limited means.

Quiz Yourself on
DUTIES TO THE LEGAL SYSTEM AND SOCIETY

77. Lawyer is defending a man accused of criminal charges stemming from a hit-and-run accident. While trying to put his case together, he learns several facts that may be material to the outcome of the case.

   For example, he learns that there is a very big dent in the defendant's front fender. He also discovers that his client consumed a great deal of alcohol on the night of the incident. Finally, Lawyer interviews a witness who says that shortly before the accident, the client rushed out of a bar upon learning how late it was. Which, if any, of these facts is the lawyer under an obligation to reveal to the court? _____

78. Attorney Richard is working on a large antitrust claim. He is furious because one of his law clerks assigned to do legal research missed a critical, recent case in that area decided by their state's supreme court. The case is highly favorable to his client and signifies a new direction in the law. Richard discovered the omission the day before a motion that he is to argue in court. Richard is scrambling to revise the draft of his motion memorandum to the court that he will submit tomorrow at the motion hearing. Richard is also angry at opposing counsel, Robin, because the case the law clerk missed had been argued by a partner in Robin's firm. Therefore, there is no way that Robin was not aware of this new turn in the law favoring Richard's client. Richard has not yet seen Robin's memorandum to the court; it will also be submitted to the court tomorrow at the motion hearing. But Richard and Robin met a week ago to try to settle the matter. Despite having obviously known about the case, Robin said nothing about it to Richard when they met. Richard asks for your advice on whether he can file for sanctions against her for failure to disclose to him this controlling, directly adverse (to Robin's side) legal authority. _____

79. Attorney Anne is representing an accused drug dealer. Anne has been over her client's story many times and doesn't think that it rings true. There are no glaring inconsistencies, and her investigation has not revealed any directly contrary evidence; she simply thinks that her past experience makes her able to read clients well enough to suspect when one of them is lying. Anne still has no evidence to the contrary, however, and decides that her client's best strategy is to testify. Anne puts her client on the stand to testify. Is Anne subject to discipline? _____

80. Attorney David feels some anxiety about the conflict between his ethical duties to the court and his obligation to his client. He defended the client in a criminal assault charge arising out of an altercation between his client and another man. The jury eventually acquitted David's client, despite the other man's grave injuries, because they apparently believed (on the strength of David's client's testimony) that David's client was a relatively innocent bystander who was unwillingly pulled into the fight. Several days after the verdict, however, David overheard his client laughingly describe how he lured the victim into the fight. David is concerned and asks you whether he must come forward and tell the court that his client committed perjury. _____

81. Attorney represents Plaintiff in a personal injury case resulting from a car accident. Plaintiff's friend is one of the witnesses to the accident, who happened to be walking down the street at the time of the collision. There are other witnesses available to testify about what they saw as well. Plaintiff's friend is painfully shy and would prefer not to testify. If she did testify, her testimony would be against Plaintiff. The discomfort of testifying unfavorably to her friend adds to her misgivings about testifying. Because her testimony would not be the only evidence available of what happened in the accident, Plaintiff's attorney tells the friend that she needn't testify and that she might want to "make herself scarce" during the weeks leading up to the trial. Is the attorney subject to discipline? _____

82. Attorney is preparing a case for trial and determining which witnesses will need to testify. Discussing the matter with Client, they agree that Client's doctor should testify regarding the examination of Client's physical condition, that Client's psychologist should testify regarding Client's mental state during the time in question in the litigation, and that the Client's next-door neighbor should testify regarding Client's character and reputation for truthfulness. Client instructs Attorney to pay each witness $1,000 to compensate them for their time in testifying. May Attorney follow Client's instruction? _____

83. During closing arguments, an attorney makes the following statements:

> It is obvious that my client is innocent. You heard from a witness who testified that she saw my client several miles away from the crime scene at the time in question. Moreover, that witness believes my client is innocent based on a conversation the witness had with a mutual friend. The prosecution's witness gave a very different story, but which one do you think is more believable? It seems to me that the prosecution witness is the one with a reason to lie, and I can tell that the witness did lie.

Evidence of the conversation between the witness and the mutual friend was excluded because it was based on inadmissible hearsay. What ethical problems are there with the lawyer's closing argument? _____

84. Attorney Claire comes to you for advice. While trying a case before Judge Rock, Claire believed that she discovered wrongful conduct on the part of the judge. She made her charges public, but they turned out to be based on misinformation and were false. Judge Rock found her in contempt for making the false charges, and she believes she will also be disciplined by the bar. What arguments can she make in her defense? _____

85. In his opening statements, the prosecutor says the following:

> The accused lives in a house on Maple Street with his wife and children. After this crime was committed, investigators spent several weeks collecting evidence, all of which led to the defendant's arrest. He was questioned on May 7 and arrested shortly thereafter. The accused

has been charged with first-degree murder. Testimony will show that the accused knew the victim and that his romantic relationship with her had recently ended.

A reporter in the courtroom reports all of these statements, and they are widely disseminated in the media. For which of these statements will the prosecutor be subject to discipline for the publicity generated? _____

86. Attorney has an emergency. A family problem has come up, and she is required to leave town quickly. However, she has a motion argument in two days, and she is not even halfway through preparation for it. Without thinking, she grabs the phone and calls the judge at home. She explains her emergency situation and tells the judge that this motion is critically important to the case. He agrees to push the hearing date back by a week. Can the attorney be subject to discipline for this communication? _____

87. Lawyer is at a restaurant, eating lunch during a break from her trial. She is absorbed in her notes, until she looks up to see two jurors standing beside her table. They seem eager to be friendly, and they ask her a couple of questions about where she is from and how she likes the town. Lawyer worries that by not replying, the jurors will be offended and her client will be jeopardized. May she answer these questions, which have nothing to do with trial matters? _____

88. Businessman bought 2 million bottles of salad dressing from a wholesaler. The salad dressing is what is called "shelf stable," meaning that it has no safe-consumption expiration date. But it does have a required "best when purchased by" date on the label. When Businessman buys the salad dressing bottles, the "best when purchased by" date is already six months in the past. In violation of law, he changes the labels, adding a year to the "best" date.

Prosecutor obtains an indictment against Businessman and takes him to trial. Before trial, Prosecutor informs the local media that she is prosecuting Businessman, whom she refers to as the "Salad Killer." She tells reporters that Businessman's dressing is a major public health concern. However, no one has become ill from the salad dressing, and there is no medical evidence that it would be dangerous to consume.

During the trial, Prosecutor refers to the "best when purchased by" date as the "expiration date" in opening statement, questions to witnesses, and closing argument. Is Prosecutor subject to discipline for any of her actions? _____

89. Personal Injury Lawyer interviews a client who presents some symptoms of brain damage following a serious auto accident. Neither the client nor the client's general practitioner physician's report suggests he has such injuries, but the lawyer, being familiar with the effects of such injury, recognizes some possible symptoms. Lawyer suggests that client see a brain injury specialist, and Lawyer pays for the consultation with the specialist, who produces a report indicating the existence of brain damage.

Should Lawyer have made the suggestion to see a specialist or have paid for the visit? Is Lawyer subject to any disciplinary action? _____

90. Jury selection is under way in a capital murder case. Defendant is accused of committing a heinous murder, and Prosecutor is determined to see Defendant is convicted. Judge asks the jurors if they are related to any of the witnesses listed to testify and if any of them have ever been represented by any of the lawyers in the case. The jurors all answer "no" to these two questions. In fact, before their divorce five years ago, Juror Jane was married to the deputy sheriff who will testify for the state in the case. And Prosecutor, when he was formerly in private practice, was her lawyer in the divorce matter.

Prosecutor is concerned that Jane may have bad feelings toward the deputy sheriff, and asked him how he and Jane get along. Once assured that they have a fine relationship, Prosecutor decides to say nothing and the case proceeds.

Did Prosecutor behave properly by not disclosing the relationship between Juror Jane and the deputy sheriff? _____

Answers

77. The lawyer is under no obligation to reveal any of these facts. Generally, there is no obligation to reveal unfavorable facts. The lawyer is, however, prohibited from making false statements about any of these facts. In addition, the lawyer would have to reveal all material information, regardless of how unfavorable, if in an ex parte setting with the judge.

78. No. A lawyer is under a duty to disclose controlling, directly adverse legal authority only to the court. Although this case appears to be controlling and directly adverse, Robin was under no duty to disclose it to Richard. While Richard would find out about the new case when Robin disclosed it to the court, the rule's object is for the benefit of the court, not the individual opposing attorney.

79. No. While a lawyer must not knowingly offer false evidence, Anne's instincts standing alone are insufficient to support the conclusion that she knows her client will commit perjury. Further, a lawyer "may refuse to offer evidence that the lawyer reasonably believes is false." MR 3.3(a)(3). Ordinarily, Anne has discretion to offer evidence that she reasonably believes, but does not know, is false; however, a lawyer may not refuse to let her criminal defendant client testify if she reasonably believes, but does not know, that the client will testify falsely. MR 3.3(a)(3). Allowing her client to testify despite her suspicions, therefore, would not violate the Model Rules.

80. No. After legal proceedings have concluded, a lawyer has no obligation to reveal perjury. MR 3.3(c). This rule applies only when the lawyer does not learn of the perjury until after the proceedings. If David had learned of the perjury before the conclusion of the trial, he would have been obligated to take reasonable remedial measures, including, if necessary, coming forward to reveal the perjury.

81. Yes. Lawyers are prohibited from advising witnesses to avoid the service of a subpoena. MR 3.4(a), MR 3.4(f). Witnesses do not belong to only one side or the other, and Defendant is entitled to have access to the witness without disruption by Plaintiff. The fact that the friend's testimony would not be the only such testimony available is irrelevant. Attorney is subject to discipline.

82. Client's desire to pay each witness for his or her testimony violates witness payment rules. Regarding the next-door neighbor, payment to lay witnesses will be provided for in a state statute. Such a fee will be considerably less than $1,000. Attorney must not follow Client's instruction to pay a lay witness in excess of the statutory fee. For both the doctor and psychologist, if they are testifying as experts rather than mere occurrence witnesses, MR 3.4(b) allows payment of whatever professionals in the field charge for that time period and services, respectively. If they are to be experts, they may be paid as such.

83. First, it violates Model Rule 3.4(e) in alluding to matters not supported by admissible evidence. It was proper for the lawyer to summarize the witness's actual testimony, but improper to allude to a conversation that was not allowed to be heard by the jury. The lawyer could have had no reasonable belief that such evidence was admissible, because the ruling was already made (this is a closing argument). In addition, the lawyer violated Model Rule 3.4(e) by impermissible expression of personal opinion as to the credibility of the prosecution witness. It was proper to point out any possible bias by the witness, but not to argue that the lawyer, personally, did not believe the testimony.

84. Two opposing considerations compete here. There is a need to criticize judges to check the judiciary and attempt to improve the overall legal system. However, lawyers are expected to use discretion when deciding whether to publicly criticize judges. Lawyers do receive some limited First Amendment protection when criticizing judges, so the fact that Claire did not make the charges maliciously but instead believed them to be true will be relevant to her defense.

85. None of them. The rules limiting publicity apply only to out-of-court statements. Because these were all made in opening trial statements, they do not violate the trial publicity rules, regardless of the reporter's story. Had the prosecutor made the statements in a press conference, rather than the courtroom, some would be problematic. It is permissible to state the nature of the crime and the identity of the defendant, information in the public record, the defendant's address and family status, and when he was arrested. The prosecutor could not discuss the defendant's past relationship and history with the victim because this has a substantial likelihood of materially prejudicing the matter.

86. Yes. The attorney's conversation with the judge involved more than a mere housekeeping-type matter. Although scheduling matters such as this are normally considered housekeeping matters that are permitted to be communicated about ex parte, here the lawyer made reference to the critical nature of the motion under the judge's consideration.

87. No, she will be subject to discipline if she responds to such questions. Communications with jurors outside the court are prohibited completely both before and during a trial, regardless of the subject matter. She should not respond, report the incident to the judge, and get an instruction that the lawyer's silence should be interpreted only as compliance with the rules of ethics.

88. Yes, because the Prosecutor has made extrajudicial comments that have a substantial likelihood of heightening public condemnation of the accused. Prosecutor's statements to the media will likely enhance negative opinion against Businessman. In a case like this, it might be necessary to inform the public that there are health risks associated with a certain product, but there is no evidence here that an action like that is needed. The statements here do not fall under the exceptions in Model Rule 3.8(f), which allow prosecutors to make statements that have a substantial likelihood of heightening public condemnation of the accused if those statements are necessary to inform the public of the nature and extent of the prosecutor's action and that serve a legitimate law enforcement purpose.

The Prosecutor is also subject to discipline because she made false statements of material fact to the jury. Under Model Rule 3.3, a lawyer shall not make a false statement of fact or law to a tribunal or fail to correct a false statement of material fact or law previously made to the tribunal by the lawyer. Prosecutor has made false statements to the court and jury by characterizing the "best when purchased by" information as an "expiration date." The false statements are material. The hope of influencing the jury is the very reason Prosecutor made the statements.

89. Lawyer's suggestion to see a specialist and payment for the consultation was appropriate. A lawyer owes a client a duty to do a proper factual investigation of the client's claims, including the engagement of expert advice and diagnosis. It is a lawyer's responsibility, under Model Rule 1.1, to provide competent service. One component of such service is adequate factual investigation. Other laws governing lawyers support this view, including Federal Rule of Civil Procedure 11. Although it

is true that lawyers may not provide financial assistance to clients when litigation is pending or contemplated (MR 1.8(e)), advancing costs of litigation, including costs of medical diagnosis, is permitted. MR 1.8 Comment [10].

90. No. Prosecutor is now subject to discipline because he had a duty to disclose both the juror's false answer to the question and his own knowledge of the relationship between the juror and the witness. This fact pattern follows that of Williams v. Taylor, 181 F. Supp. 2d 604 (E.D. Va. 2002). Any lawyer, especially a prosecutor, and especially in a capital case, has a duty to inform the court of juror misconduct.

Here, Prosecutor must know that he represented the potential juror and she has answered that none of the lawyers ever represented her. His duty is all the more clear because he is the very lawyer involved in her false or mistaken answer, and because he made sure that her relationship with his witness would not prejudice his side.

Exam Tips on
DUTIES TO THE LEGAL SYSTEM AND SOCIETY

- ☞ The courtroom presents a dynamic, exciting setting for exam questions. If your course has emphasized courtroom and advocacy situations, you will have a significant percentage of questions from this chapter.

- ☞ Many of the lawyer's duties to the legal system or the public generally conflict with duties to the client, and the discussion in this chapter is about rules that set the lines across which client favoring actions become unacceptably harmful to the legal system or the public.

- ☞ Truth-telling inside the court context carries implications not present in out-of-court contexts, such as negotiation. When a lawyer misleads in court, the court itself is misled in addition to the opposing party.

- ☞ A lawyer is prohibited from knowingly making false statements of material fact to the court and from otherwise engaging in acts or omissions that amount to fraud. MR 3.3(a).

- ☞ Despite the duty of candor to the court, a lawyer is under no general obligation to reveal unfavorable facts to the court. However, a lawyer must disclose material facts when disclosure is necessary to avoid assisting a criminal or fraudulent act by the client. MR 3.3; MR 1.2(d). The distinction between volunteering adverse facts and making affirmative, false statements is often tested. Notice that a lawyer who does volunteer adverse facts when not required to do so will be subject to discipline for breaching the duty of loyalty to the lawyer's client.

- ☞ On those occasions when a lawyer is permitted by law to engage in ex parte communications with the court, the lawyer must disclose to the court both favorable and unfavorable material facts. MR 3.3(d).

- The perjury problem presents extraordinary difficulties for the lawyer, especially when the person committing the perjury is the lawyer's client. Perjury presents a common essay question topic, but is more difficult to frame as a multiple-choice question.

- A lawyer is prohibited from offering evidence the lawyer knows to be false. MR 3.3(a)(3). A lawyer "may refuse to offer evidence, except the testimony of a criminal defendant, that the lawyer reasonably believes is false." MR 3.3(a)(3). The distinction between evidence the lawyer knows is false from evidence the lawyer reasonably believes is false is subtle and much tested.

- When a lawyer knows that a witness other than the client has offered perjured testimony, the lawyer must promptly reveal the perjury to the court. MR 3.3(a)(3).

- Watch for the timing of the lawyer's knowledge of perjury

    - When the lawyer knows of the client's intention to commit perjury the lawyer must attempt to dissuade, attempt to withdraw, and, finally, if the perjury occurs, take reasonable remedial measures. Reasonable remedial measures include disclosure of the perjury to the court.

    - When the lawyer learns that the client's testimony was perjurious after the perjury occurs but before proceedings end, the lawyer must first attempt to persuade the client to rectify the matter by revealing the fraud and then testifying truthfully. If that effort fails, the lawyer has only the reasonable remedial measures option and according to the Model Rules Comment, must reveal the perjury if the lawyer learns of it before the proceedings conclude.

    - If the lawyer does not learn of the perjury until after the conclusion of the proceedings, then the lawyer has no obligation to reveal it.

- The Model Rule duty to rectify the perjury applies even if doing so would otherwise violate the duty of confidentiality under Model Rule 1.6. MR 3.3(c).

- Perjury issues in criminal representation present special problems because of the criminal defendant's right to testify on his own behalf, the obligation on the state to prove the defendant guilty beyond a reasonable doubt, the privilege against self-incrimination, and the right to counsel. This is a perfect mixture for an essay question.

- A lawyer is prohibited from making false statements of law to the court. MR 3.3(a). As an advocate, the lawyer need not reveal his objective analysis of the law to the court, but rather may make any nonfrivolous, client-favoring arguments regarding the law to the court.

- Lawyers are obligated to disclose to the court controlling, directly adverse legal authority. MR 3.3-(a)(2).

    - Only controlling authority, that is, mandatory authority that is controlling on the court currently making the decision, must be disclosed.

    - Only directly adverse authority must be disclosed under this rule. Authority is directly adverse when it is applicable to the present case without extended analogy.

    - Lawyers have no obligation to disclose adverse authority to opposing parties. Such disclosure occurs incidentally when it is made to the court.

- A lawyer is limited in the ways in which witnesses may be compensated and in instructing witnesses about whether to make themselves available for testimony or interview by the opposing side.

- Lawyers are prohibited generally from requesting or advising a witness to refrain from voluntarily cooperating with another litigant. MR 3.4(f). Under no circumstances may a lawyer dissuade a witness from appearing at a hearing or persuade a witness to secrete himself so that the witness will be unavailable. MR 3.4(a).

- A lawyer is permitted to request that a witness not cooperate voluntarily only if the witness is a relative, employee, or agent of the client and the lawyer reasonably believes that the request will not harm the witness. MR 3.4(f)(2).

- Lawyers may only pay nonexpert witnesses a statutory fee and reasonable expenses incurred by the witness in attending the trial or hearing.

- Expert witnesses may be paid the professional fee that someone in the expert's field charges for his or her time and reasonable expenses incurred by the witness in attending the trial or hearing. However, an expert may not be paid a fee that is contingent on the outcome of the matter.

- Lawyers are prohibited from bringing actions or taking positions in litigation that are frivolous.

- Model Rule 3.1, in most respects tracking Federal Rule of Civil Procedure 11, prohibits lawyers from bringing or defending claims on a frivolous basis. In a frivolous claim situation, always discuss both FRCP 11 and MR 3.1.

- In a criminal case, unlike a civil case, a defendant has a Due Process right to plead "not guilty" and require the government to be put to its proof. Model Rule 3.1 is not intended to prevent a lawyer from assisting a criminal defendant in the process of putting the government to its proof. Prosecuting lawyers have special obligations regarding the prosecution of charges that lack merit. (See Chapter 9 for this connection.)

- Frivolous discovery requests and those intended merely to delay are prohibited. MR 3.4(d).

- In general, lawyers are obliged to expedite litigation to the extent that such activity is consistent with the client's interests. MR 3.2. A violation of Model Rule 3.2 rarely stands alone as the grounds for discipline.

- Lawyers are prohibited from expressing their personal opinion to jurors about the justness of the client's cause, the credibility of a witness, or the culpability, guilt, or innocence of a party. MR 3.4(e).

- Lawyers are prohibited from undermining the evidence law policies by alluding to matters that are either irrelevant or will not be supported by admissible evidence. MR 3.4(e).

    - The lawyer need not be certain that the evidence will be admitted. If the lawyer reasonably believes that the evidence will be admitted, then the lawyer may freely allude to the evidence.

    - If evidence will be admissible only on a condition over which the lawyer in question has no control, the lawyer must not allude to that matter until the evidence is admitted.

    - Once the court has ruled a piece of evidence inadmissible, a lawyer is prohibited from referring to it to the jury.

- Lawyers must obey court orders. Even when a lawyer knows that a judge is mistaken in making an order or ruling, the lawyer must obey the order, but may make reasonable efforts to preserve the record for later challenge on appeal.

- Although the First Amendment protects most lawyer expression, lawyers are subject to discipline for intemperate remarks that serve no useful purpose. Consider the court's contempt power in these situations.

- Lawyers generally and especially prosecutors are limited in what they may say to the media regarding pending litigation and criminal investigations. MR 3.6, 3.8(e) and (g).

    - Because of such statements' possible effects on the judicial process, lawyers are prohibited from making out-of-court statements that a reasonable lawyer would expect to be disseminated by public communication and that the lawyer knows or should know will have a substantial likelihood of materially prejudicing the matter. MR 3.6(a).

    - Only statements made out of court are restricted by this rule.

    - Notwithstanding the general prohibition, statements in several distinct categories may safely be made without the risk of discipline. MR 3.6(b).

    - When a lawyer reasonably believes that making a statement is necessary to counter the effects of a public statement made by the other side in the matter, the lawyer may make such a statement without being subject to discipline. MR 3.6(c).

- *Ex parte* (without the other party) *communications* seriously undermine the prospect of fair process in the justice system. As such, ex parte communication with decision-makers, both judges and jurors, is strictly regulated. Questions often place a lawyer in an innocently intended ex parte communication position. Such an ex parte communication is subject to discipline even though no harm is intended and none results.

    - Except in very limited circumstances, lawyers are prohibited from communicating ex parte with a judge. MR 3.5(b). Some ex parte communications are permitted because of their subject matter. Communications between lawyers and judges about matters unrelated to pending or impending litigation are not restricted by the rule. Such communications are not truly "ex parte" because they do not involve other parties at all. Ex parte communications regarding so-called housekeeping matters that relate to a pending case are permitted.

    - Even innocently intended ex parte communications are prohibited.

    - When authorized by law, lawyers are permitted to engage in ex parte communications. Such authorizations are typically found in rules governing requests for emergency restraining orders, for example. When such communication is authorized, a lawyer is under heightened candor-to-the-court requirements.

    - All forms of communication are covered by this rule. A lawyer who sends a letter to the judge or files a paper with the court without serving a copy on opposing counsel is engaging in prohibited ex parte communications with the judge.

- Lawyers are strictly prohibited from communicating with jurors outside the courtroom before and during jurors' duties. Even communication about matters other than the current proceedings is prohibited. Lawyers must refrain from even innocent communication with sitting jurors.

- Lawyers are prohibited from communicating with jurors after the jurors' duty ends, with some exceptions. Lawyers are prohibited from harassing jurors at any time. MR 3.5. Once proceedings have ended, lawyers may have very limited contact with jurors for benign purposes such as to determine whether the lawyer's presentation manner is effective.

- A lawyer is under an affirmative obligation to report to the court in which the proceedings are being held juror misconduct or others' misconduct with respect to jurors. Failure to do so subjects the lawyer to discipline.

- Amendments in 1993 and 2002 to Model Rule 6.1 have come as close as the organized bar has to imposing a requirement on individual lawyers to render pro bono service. Nonetheless, even the 2002 version of Model Rule 6.1 remains aspirational and not mandatory. A lawyer is not subject to discipline for failing to render pro bono service.

CHAPTER 9
SPECIAL ROLE-RELATED DUTIES

ChapterScope

- Although it may actually be accurate to say that the law governing lawyers is somewhat different for every practice setting (that is, the law of lawyering is slightly different depending on whether the lawyer is in a plaintiff's personal injury practice, a criminal defense practice, an in-house corporate practice, and so on), several special lawyer roles have such clearly defined duties or responsibility adjustments that they warrant separate study.

- The special roles covered in this chapter are those of *prosecutor, supervisory or subordinate lawyer, third-party neutral, and ancillary businessperson.*

- Each of these special roles carries with it special duties and rules governing lawyer conduct.

- Lawyers in these special roles remain subject to all of the general rules that govern lawyer behavior.

- An additional special role, that of judge, is covered in Chapter 11.

- Criminal prosecutors have ethical responsibilities in addition to those of other lawyers. Prosecutors do not represent the crime victim or a complaining witness. Charged with representing the public's interests rather than those of an individual litigant, prosecutors are required to seek justice rather than mere victory in their work.

  - Prosecutors must timely disclose *exculpatory evidence* and mitigating circumstances regarding sentencing.

- Under certain circumstances, *supervising lawyers* will be ethically responsible for the acts of their subordinates, both lawyer and nonlawyer.

  - Subordinate lawyers are not relieved of the duty to follow the rules of professional conduct merely because they are supervised, nor for that matter merely because the misconduct in which they might engage is ordered by the supervising lawyer. MR 5.2.

  - A subordinate lawyer is not subject to discipline when she "acts in accordance with a supervisory lawyer's reasonable resolution of an arguable question of professional duty." MR 5.2(b).

  - Supervisory lawyers are responsible for providing reasonable supervision of lawyer subordinates. MR 5.1.

  - Separate from the acts of lawyer subordinates, supervising lawyers are subject to discipline if they fail to provide adequate supervision.

  - Supervisory lawyers are subject to discipline for the conduct of lawyer subordinates that violates the rules of lawyer conduct when the supervisory lawyer orders the subordinate lawyer to engage in the misconduct, when the supervisory lawyer ratifies the subordinate lawyer's misconduct, or when a lawyer who is either a partner or the subordinate's direct supervisor learns of the misconduct at a time when its effect could be avoided or mitigated and yet fails to take reasonable remedial action.

- Lawyers are subject to the rules of professional conduct for lawyers while providing ancillary services when either of the following two conditions is present: when the services provided are not distinct from the lawyer's legal services (MR 5.7(a)(1)) or when the services are provided by a separate entity either controlled by the lawyer or by the lawyer with others, and the lawyer fails to communicate clearly to the client that the services are not legal services and are not subject to the normal protections in the lawyer-client relationship (MR 5.7(a)(2)).

I. SPECIAL DUTIES OF PROSECUTORS

Criminal prosecutors have ethical responsibilities in addition to those of other lawyers. Prosecutors represent no individual client but rather the government or, viewed another way, the people of their jurisdiction. In particular, prosecutors, as a matter of criminal law, do not represent the crime victim or a complaining witness. Charged with representing the public's interests rather than those of an individual litigant, prosecutors are required to seek justice rather than mere victory in their litigation work.

A. Avoid conflicts with private interests represented

Prosecutors, often part-time prosecutors, also represent private clients. Prosecutors must avoid conflicts between the representation of private clients and the prosecutor's duty to seek justice on behalf of the public.

Example: District Court Judge appointed Lawyer to be a Special Prosecutor to prosecute Contemptee for a contempt charge. In his private capacity, Lawyer/Special Prosecutor represented the opposing party to Contemptee in the action from which the contempt charge arose. District Court may appoint Lawyer to be Special Prosecutor, but Lawyer cannot represent one of the parties to the action. Lawyer's continued duty to be a partisan for one party is incompatible with his prosecutor's duty to seek justice rather than conviction. Young v. United States ex rel. Vuitton el Fils S.A., 481 U.S. 787 (1987).

B. Dismissal of charges not supported by probable cause

Paralleling the general lawyer duty to refrain from bringing claims or taking positions that are frivolous (see MR 3.1), prosecutors are prohibited from prosecuting charges that the prosecutor knows are not supported by probable cause, the usual standard below which judges will not issue warrants and will dismiss charges at preliminary hearings. MR 3.8(a).

Example: Prosecutor has probable cause to believe that Defendant committed Count 1. Prosecutor lacks probable cause to believe that Defendant committed Count 2. Prosecutor charges Count 1 and Count 2 in a criminal charging document. Her plan is to dismiss Count 2 at a later time if necessary, but to attempt to use its dismissal as a bargaining piece in extracting a guilty plea on Count 1 from Defendant. In other words, she will dismiss Count 2 if Defendant will plead guilty to Count 1, and she has no intention of pursuing Count 2 to a conviction. Prosecutor is subject to discipline for charging a crime for which she does not have probable cause. It does not matter that she intends to dismiss it at some future date.

C. Advising defendants of their right to counsel

Prosecutors are charged with the responsibility to make reasonable efforts to assure that defendants are advised of their right to counsel. MR 3.8(b). In some ways, this duty is a heightened form of the general lawyer duty to refrain from giving advice to unrepresented opposing parties except for the advice that the party should obtain counsel. See MR 4.3. The duty is heightened because of the prosecutor's public role in furthering justice rather than merely winning convictions against defendants.

Example: Prosecutor sent Witness to record conversation with Defendant. Prosecutor instructed Witness to tell Defendant that Witness had been subpoenaed and would testify regarding Defendant's illegal acts. Witness was to encourage Defendant to take steps to assure that no documentation of the illegal acts could be found and to report Defendant's statements back to Prosecutor. Prosecutor is subject to discipline for effectively depriving Defendant of his right to counsel by sending Witness to effectively question and communicate with Defendant. For a similar fact pattern focused on the suppression of the Defendant's statements, see United States v. Hammad, 858 F.2d 834 (2d Cir. 1988).

D. Fair treatment of unrepresented accused

Prosecutors have special obligations to protect the unrepresented accused. In particular, prosecutors must not unfairly extract waivers of important pretrial rights, such as right to a jury trial, right to counsel, and privilege against self-incrimination, from the unrepresented accused. MR 3.8(c).

E. Disclosure of exculpatory evidence

Prosecutors must timely disclose exculpatory evidence and mitigating circumstances regarding sentencing. MR 3.8(d). This ethics rule obligation parallels the right of the accused under the Due Process Clause to be provided access to such materials. Brady v. Maryland, 373 U.S. 83 (1963).

Example: Prosecutor is aware that Witness who had initially identified Defendant had later decided that the identification was mistaken. Prosecutor is obligated to provide this information to Defense Counsel. Read v. Virginia State Bar, 357 S.E.2d 544 (Va. 1987).

Example: Defendant made statements to the FBI about his factual guilt and his state of mind at the time of the murder with which Defendant is charged. Prosecutor failed to produce Defendant's statements when requested to do so by Defense Counsel. Prosecutor claimed these documents were FBI police reports and not statements of Defendant. The statements went directly to Defendant's self-defense claim. The failure to provide these statements was fundamentally unfair. Prosecutor is not an adversary in the true sense. Prosecutor's client is the state and his or her objective should be justice, not winning. State v. Harrington, 534 S.W.2d 44 (Mo. 1976).

F. Afford respect to lawyer-client relationships

Prosecutors are required to respect the lawyer-client relationship by refraining from unnecessarily issuing subpoenas that call on lawyers to give evidence about past or present clients. MR 3.8(e).

G. Fairness in investigation

A prosecutor is obliged to pursue investigative leads evenhandedly, without regard to whether they might favor or damage her case.

H. Grand jury fact fairness

All lawyers are obligated to reveal unfavorable facts in ex parte settings, such as hearings on emergency temporary restraining orders. MR 3.3(d). See Chapter 8, §I.B.2. Prosecutors are in such settings regularly in the grand jury context. Thus prosecutors have a regular duty in grand jury settings to present adverse material facts.

II. SPECIAL DUTIES OF SUPERVISING AND SUBORDINATE LAWYERS

More frequently than ever before, lawyers practice in settings that involve employer-employee relationships. Within those relationships, some lawyers supervise the work of other lawyers, and lawyers frequently supervise the work of nonlawyer subordinates. Under certain circumstances, *supervising lawyers* will be ethically responsible for the acts of their subordinates, both lawyer and nonlawyer. Under certain circumstances, subordinate lawyers will be relieved of ethical responsibility for their actions.

A. Lawyers subordinate to other lawyers

1. **General:** Subordinate lawyers are not relieved of the duty to follow the rules of professional conduct merely because they are supervised or, for that matter, merely because the misconduct in which they might engage is ordered by the supervising lawyer. MR 5.2.

   Example: Supervising Lawyer instructs Subordinate Lawyer to impersonate Client and swear out a Complaint in Client's name, thereby saving Client a trip to the courthouse to sign the Complaint himself. If Subordinate Lawyer complies with Supervisor's instruction and commits this fraud, Subordinate Lawyer will be subject to discipline. MR 5.2(a).

   Example: Same facts as example above except that Supervisor threatens to fire Subordinate Lawyer if Subordinate Lawyer refuses to commit the fraud. If Subordinate Lawyer complies with Supervisor's instruction under threat and commits this fraud, Subordinate Lawyer will still be subject to discipline. Threat of job loss does not excuse a subordinate lawyer from complying with the rules of professional conduct.

2. **Exception:** A subordinate lawyer is not subject to discipline when she "acts in accordance with a supervisory lawyer's reasonable resolution of an arguable question of professional duty." MR 5.2(b). When close questions arise about which supervisors and subordinates disagree, someone's view of the matter must ultimately control the actions of the lawyer. Under this provision, subordinate lawyers may safely defer *on close questions and close questions alone* to the judgment of supervisory, usually senior, lawyers.

   Example: Subordinate Lawyer produces a draft Complaint for a client. The Complaint attempts to state a type of claim that State Supreme Court has rejected. Other states' courts have intimated in dicta that they may recognize the claim, but none has as yet. Subordinate Lawyer is concerned about pleading a frivolous claim under Federal Rule of Civil Procedure 11 and Model Rule 3.1. Supervisory Lawyer examines the Complaint and assures Subordinate Lawyer that the Complaint's claim is not frivolous. Supervisory Lawyer's resolution of this arguable question is reasonable. If a court later determines that the Complaint's claim was frivolous and violative of Model Rule 3.1, Supervisory Lawyer and not Subordinate Lawyer will be subject to discipline. Ironically, under the pre-1991 Federal Rule of Civil Procedure 11, in the same situation, Subordinate Lawyer (the pleading's signer) and not Supervisory Lawyer would be liable for the Federal Rule of Civil Procedure 11 monetary sanctions.

   a. **An arguable question:** The exception requires that the ethics question being resolved be an arguable one. There must be reasonable arguments on various sides of the question being resolved.

b. A reasonable resolution: Close questions may often be resolved in a variety of ways. The exception requires that the supervisory lawyer's resolution of the arguable question be a reasonable one. A subordinate lawyer is not protected if he follows a supervisory lawyer's unreasonable resolution of a close question.

B. Lawyers supervising lawyers

Supervisory lawyers are responsible for providing reasonable supervision of lawyer subordinates. MR 5.1.

1. **Providing supervision:** Separate from the acts of lawyer subordinates, supervising lawyers are subject to discipline if they fail to provide adequate supervision.

    a. **Systems:** Law firm partners, or other lawyers with comparable managerial authority, must make reasonable efforts to establish systems that will give reasonable assurance that the firm's lawyers will not engage in conduct that would violate the rules of professional conduct for lawyers. Notice the double use of the word "reasonable." Partners are responsible for taking reasonable efforts to set up systems; if the subordinate lawyers engage in violative conduct despite those systems, the partner is not subject to discipline. MR 5.1(a). Typical systems include file maintenance systems, conflicts-of-interest check procedures, standard forms for fee agreements and engagement letters, and confidentiality requirements systems.

    b. **Direct supervisors:** Supervising lawyers, whether partners or not, who directly supervise other lawyers must make reasonable efforts to ensure that the subordinate lawyers comply with the rules of professional conduct. MR 5.1(b).

    Example: Subordinate Lawyer goes to work for Firm. Firm assigns Supervisory Lawyer to work with Subordinate Lawyer on a complex project. Supervisory Lawyer leaves town for a long weekend, instructing Subordinate Lawyer to file the Complaint on Monday, no matter what. When Subordinate Lawyer asks whether she might have a telephone number where she can reach Supervisory Lawyer over the weekend, Supervisory Lawyer says, "No, I won't be back until Tuesday. I don't expect to hear from anyone here. Just have the Complaint filed before I return." When Subordinate asks whether anyone else in Firm is sufficiently familiar with the matter to answer a question for her while Supervisory Lawyer is away, Supervisory Lawyer says, "Don't you dare ask anyone else. You'll embarrass me. I'm supposed to get this job done, and I'm instructing you to do it." Supervisory Lawyer is subject to discipline for failing to make reasonable efforts to supervise Subordinate Lawyer. "[L]eaving new lawyers to 'sink or swim' will not be tolerated." In re Yacavino, 494 A.2d 801, 803 (N.J. 1985).

2. **Responsibility for lawyer subordinates' misconduct:** Supervisory lawyers are subject to discipline for the conduct of lawyer subordinates that violates the rules of lawyer conduct when any of the following occurs.

    a. **Instruction:** The supervisory lawyer orders the subordinate lawyer to engage in the misconduct. MR 5.1(c)(1).

    Example: Supervising Lawyer instructs Subordinate Lawyer to impersonate Client and swear out a Complaint in Client's name, thereby saving Client a trip to the courthouse to sign the Complaint himself. If Subordinate Lawyer complies with Supervisor's instruction and commits this fraud, Supervisory Lawyer will be subject to discipline.

b. **Ratification:** The supervisory lawyer ratifies the subordinate lawyer's misconduct. MR 5.1(c)(1).

Example: Subordinate Lawyer impersonates Client and swears out a Complaint in Client's name, thereby saving Client a trip to the courthouse to sign the Complaint himself. Supervisory Lawyer learns of Subordinate Lawyer's conduct and says, "Well done. Client will be pleased." Supervisory Lawyer is subject to discipline.

c. **Failure to remedy:** A lawyer who is either a partner or the subordinate's direct supervisor learns of the misconduct at a time when its effect could be avoided or mitigated and yet fails to take reasonable remedial action. MR 5.1(c)(2).

Example: Subordinate Lawyer impersonates Client and swears out a Complaint in Client's name, thereby saving Client a trip to the courthouse to sign the Complaint himself. Supervisory Lawyer and Partner learn of Subordinate Lawyer's conduct on the day of its occurrence, before service of the Complaint on the defendant. Supervisory Lawyer or Partner could easily have instructed Subordinate Lawyer to dismiss the Complaint immediately and avoid further harm. Instead, Supervisory lawyer and Partner do nothing, except enjoy a long lunch together. Supervisory Lawyer and Partner are both subject to discipline.

C. **Lawyers supervising nonlawyers**

Lawyers are responsible for providing reasonable supervision of nonlawyer subordinates.

1. **Providing supervision:** Separate from the acts of nonlawyer subordinates, supervising lawyers are subject to discipline if they fail to provide adequate supervision.

    a. **Systems:** Law firm partners must make reasonable efforts to establish systems that will give reasonable assurance that nonlawyer personnel will not engage in conduct that would violate the rules of professional conduct for lawyers. Again, notice the double use of the word "reasonable." Partners are responsible for taking reasonable efforts to set up systems; if subordinates engage in violative conduct despite those systems, the lawyer is not subject to discipline. MR 5.3(a).

    Example: Law Firm Partner establishes employee rules regarding confidentiality of client matters, including rules that all files are kept on the law firm premises, that breaches of confidentiality are grounds for dismissal from employment, and that all employees sign a pledge statement promising to maintain confidentiality. Paralegal, nonetheless, after drinking to excess, regales a friend with stories of client matters. Partner does not have disciplinary liability for the aberrant behavior of Paralegal.

    b. **Direct supervisors:** Lawyers, whether partners or not, who directly supervise nonlawyer personnel must make reasonable efforts to ensure that the subordinates comply with the lawyer's professional rules. MR 5.3(b).

2. **Responsibility for nonlawyer subordinates' misconduct:** Lawyers are subject to discipline for the conduct of nonlawyer subordinates that violates the rules of lawyer conduct when any of the following occurs.

    a. **Instruction:** The lawyer orders the subordinate to engage in the misconduct. MR 5.3(c)(1).

    b. **Ratification:** The lawyer ratifies the misconduct. MR 5.3(c)(1).

c. **Failure to remedy:** A lawyer who is either a partner or the subordinate's direct supervisor learns of the misconduct at a time when its effect could be avoided or mitigated and yet fails to take reasonable remedial action. MR 5.3(c)(2).

III. LAWYERS AS INTERMEDIARIES

Contrary to the ordinary picture of the lawyer as a partisan, representing one party against the interests of another, lawyers may in limited circumstances act in the role of intermediary. Former MR 2.2. (In February 2002, the ABA deleted the little-used Model Rule 2.2. Nonetheless, its guidance is of value.) As an intermediary, a lawyer attempts to achieve the goals and interests of multiple parties with potentially adverse interests. Such a role is inappropriate when litigation is pending or contemplated. Because the role of intermediary is less commonly engaged in, the lawyer must ensure that all parties understand the nature of the relationship.

A. **Requirements**

To pursue a matter for multiple clients as an intermediary, several requirements must be met.

1. **Consent after consultation:** Each client must consent to the common representation after consultation with the lawyer. Former MR 2.2(a)(1). The consultation must include a discussion of the risks of common representation and its effect on confidentiality.

    Example: Seller asked Attorney to represent her in a real estate transaction. Attorney also agreed to represent Brokers in the same transaction. Attorney did not consult with Seller before agreeing to represent Brokers. Brokers stopped payment on check once a defect in the property was noticed. Attorney had a duty to consult with Seller and Broker regarding the possible risks of common representation. This failure to consult subjects Attorney to discipline. In re Lanza, 322 A.2d 445 (N.J. 1974).

2. **Best interests of clients:** The lawyer must reasonably believe that the clients' best interests will be served by the common representation and that little risk to the clients exists. Former MR 2.2(a)(2).

3. **Impartial representation:** The lawyer must reasonably believe that she can engage in the common representation impartially. Former MR 2.2(a)(3).

B. **Confidentiality**

The evidentiary privilege and the duty of confidentiality do not apply as between the parties commonly represented. See Chapter 5, §I.C.2.b.

Example: Partner 1 and Partner 2 come to Lawyer together to ask Lawyer to act as intermediary and assist them in setting up a partnership. Later, a dispute arises between Partner 1 and Partner 2. Neither of them can assert the evidentiary privilege to prevent testimony by either Lawyer or the other partner regarding communications made in the joint representation.

C. **Withdrawal**

If any of the requirements ceases to be met during the representation, the lawyer must withdraw from the representation of all of the clients. Former MR 2.2(c).

Example: Seller asked Attorney to represent her in a real estate transaction. Attorney also agreed to represent Brokers in the same transaction. Attorney properly consulted with Seller and Brokers before agreeing to represent Brokers. Brokers stopped payment on check once a defect in the property was noticed. Once this actual conflict did arise, Attorney's only response is to withdraw from representing both Seller and Broker. In re Lanza, 322 A.2d 445 (N.J. 1974).

D. Typical situations

The following practice situations are among those that are sometimes thought to be appropriate to the intermediary role. None of these examples, however, is assured of being appropriate to the intermediary role. Each instance of such possible representation must be evaluated based on its own facts.

1. **Buyer and seller in real estate closing.**

2. **Proposed partners setting up a business organization.**

3. **Lender and borrower.**

4. **Spouses:** Divorce cases are typically inappropriate for the intermediary role, except in jurisdictions that authorize such common representation by statute.

   Example: Husband and Wife have been married for six years and have two children. They have no assets and have waived spousal support. Husband and Wife both request Attorney to represent them in this uncontested dissolution. Because there was only the potential for conflict, because the jurisdiction's law permitted such joint representation, and because both parties had consented to representation by Attorney, there is no violation. If at a later time an actual conflict arises, Attorney must withdraw. Klemm v. Superior Court of Fresno County, 75 Cal. App. 3d 893 (1977).

5. **Birth mother and adoptive parents in adoption document drafting.**

   Example: Lawyer represented Biological Mother and Adoptive Parents in their joint endeavor to arrange the adoption of Biological Mother's child by Adoptive Parents. Lawyer is subject to discipline. Regardless of whether there is a potential or real conflict, one attorney may not represent both the adoptive and biological parents in a private adoption proceeding because of the highly emotional nature of the proceedings and the extreme potential for conflict. Informal Opinion 87-1523, ABA Committee on Ethics & Professional Responsibility (1987).

E. Not necessarily a mediator

The role of intermediary is sometimes but not always the equivalent of the role of mediator. A mediator seeks to be a neutral voice that facilitates the voluntary agreement between disputing parties. Lawyers sometimes fill that role. In many other instances, however, a lawyer acting as intermediary is not a neutral in a dispute at all. Rather, the more general intermediary role may involve joint representation of clients who simply want a project, such as a real estate closing or a partnership agreement, to work.

F. A proposed set of standards for mediators

A set of standards for all mediators, including lawyer mediators, has been proposed by a joint group of ABA sections and the American Arbitration Association and is under consideration. These guidelines are not widely accepted as yet. For a lawyer who acts as mediator, the balance between these mediator standards and their general lawyer standards will be delicate and difficult.

One thing, however, is clear. For now, at least, the lawyer standards control where a conflict arises. These proposed standards include requirements that a mediator do the following:

- Recognize that mediation is based on self-determination of the parties
- Conduct the mediation impartially
- Disclose conflicts of interests
- Mediate only if qualified to do so
- Maintain the parties' reasonable expectations regarding confidentiality
- Conduct the mediation fairly and diligently
- Be truthful in advertising and solicitation
- Fully disclose and explain fees
- Improve the practice of mediation

IV. ANCILLARY BUSINESSES

Many lawyers are in some respects business people, managing their own law practice. But some lawyers also maintain ancillary, associated businesses along with their law practice. Rules to govern the lawyer in the ancillary businessperson role have been controversial. MR 5.7. No rule regarding ancillary businesses appeared in the Model Code or the original Model Rules. In 1991, by a close vote, the ABA adopted a restrictive ancillary business rule. Only one year later, the ABA repealed the restrictive rule. In 1994, the ABA adopted the current version of Model Rule 5.7. The Rule has had little effect on the law beyond its expression of the ABA's current position on the matter.

A. General rule

Lawyers are subject to the rules of professional conduct for lawyers while providing ancillary services when either of the following two conditions is present.

1. **Not distinct:** When the services provided are not distinct from the lawyer's legal services. MR 5.7(a)(1).

   Example: Lawyer provides tax law advice and investment counseling to clients. The tax law advice is legal work; the investment counseling is an ancillary business activity. When the lawyer provides the two services to clients as indistinguishable services from one another, the lawyer must comply with the lawyer rules of professional conduct in the giving of investment counseling.

2. **Failure to communicate to client:** When the services are provided by an entity controlled either by the lawyer or by the lawyer with others, and the lawyer fails to communicate clearly to the client that the services are not legal services and are not subject to the normal protections in the lawyer-client relationship. MR 5.7(a)(2).

B. What are ancillary services?

Ancillary or "law-related" services are services that are related to legal services and are not prohibited as unauthorized practice of law when performed by a nonlawyer. MR 5.7(b). Side businesses of lawyers that are entirely unrelated to their law practice are not ancillary businesses.

Example: Lawyer practices law and engages in the gutter cleaning business part-time. Lawyer's gutter cleaning business is not subject to the ancillary business rules.

C. Typical ancillary businesses

Examples of ancillary services are trust management, financial planning, investment banking, and title insurance.

D. The ancillary business problem

The crux of the ancillary business problem is that clients of the ancillary business may expect that, because the businesses are associated with lawyers, lawyer ethics protections, such as confidentiality protection, avoidance of conflicts, and so on, attach to the provision of the ancillary business services as well. The ABA rule attempts to place the burden on the lawyer to either provide the lawyer role protections to the ancillary business client or ensure that the client knows that the protections are not associated with the services. The following example, however, illustrates the difficulty of application of this standard.

Example: Lawyer is acting as both a sports agent and a lawyer in her practice. She approaches potential Client-Athlete to propose that she represent him as his sports agent in his upcoming contract negotiation with his team. The protections of the lawyer-client relationship, such as confidentiality, loyalty and attendant conflict avoidance, competence, diligence, and so on, will attach to their relationship if Lawyer provides the services together (as appears to be the situation here) or if Lawyer fails to communicate to Client-Athlete that these protections do not apply to their relationship (i.e., that she is not acting as his lawyer). But the rule does not resolve the question of whether or not the advertising and solicitation rules apply to Lawyer's client-getting activity. If they do, as they probably should, then Lawyer is subject to discipline for the direct solicitation of Client-Athlete.

V. MULTIDISCIPLINARY PRACTICE

A. Definition

A multidisciplinary practice (MDP) is a partnership or other entity that includes lawyers and nonlawyers and has as one of its purposes the delivery of legal services to client(s) other than the MDP itself or that holds itself out to the public as providing nonlegal as well as legal services. It includes an arrangement by which a law firm joins with one or more professional firms to provide services, including legal services, and there is a direct or indirect sharing of profits as part of the arrangement.

Example: A lawyer, a social worker, and a certified financial planner might form an MDP to provide legal and nonlegal services in connection with counseling older clients about estate planning, nursing home care, and living wills. It also includes an arrangement by which a law firm joins with one or more other professional firms to provide services, including legal services, and there is a direct or indirect sharing of profits as part of the arrangement.

B. Accountants

Associations between lawyers and accountants have been the most controversial. The Big 4 (formerly Big 5) accounting firms, as employers of vast numbers of law-trained individuals, until recently operated as de facto MDPs in which the lawyers were said to provide not legal but "consulting" services to the business's audit clients. Some European countries allow MDPs, while U.S. jurisdictions do not.

C. Lawyers and professional independence

The most frequently raised concern about MDPs relates to the protection of professional independence of lawyers. The provisions of Rule 5.4 are designed to protect the lawyer's professional independence of judgment. Rule 5.4 provides as follows.

1. A lawyer or law firm shall not share legal fees with a nonlawyer (except under limited circumstances).
2. A lawyer shall not form a partnership with a nonlawyer if any of the activities of the partnership consist of the practice of law.
3. A lawyer shall not practice with or in the form of a professional corporation or association authorized to practice law for profit, if a nonlawyer owns an interest therein, or a lawyer is a corporate director thereof, or a nonlawyer has the right to direct or control the professional judgment of a lawyer.

D. Opposing arguments

Those who oppose MDPs argue that practicing law in a multidisciplinary setting has the potential to unduly influence the professional independence of lawyers in the MDP. MDPs would place non lawyers in positions, which could influence the relationship between the lawyer and client. The nonlawyer may not understand or appreciate the role of a lawyer. In an MDP in which lawyers are in the minority, the nonattorney majority could have control over a lawyer's compensation, promotions, and even job security. Thus, a nonlawyer, who may not understand or appreciate the unique role of a lawyer, could exert influence over the lawyer to take a course of action that is financially beneficial to the MDP, at the expense of the client.

E. Pro-MDP arguments

Advocates of multidisciplinary practices argue that in today's world, many lawyers routinely work in practice settings in which they are subject to management oversight by non lawyers. The profession has a history of lawyers working in corporate law departments or government offices. Lawyers also work for organizations that provide legal services to their members or other clients (e.g., union-sponsored and prepaid legal services plans, community legal services organizations). Independence has been maintained in those settings.

Professional independence of judgment is required of all lawyers regardless of the practice setting. Advocates of MDPs propose an added protection, recommending that a lawyer who is supervised by a nonlawyer may not use as a defense to a violation of the rules of professional conduct the fact that the lawyer acted in accordance with the nonlawyer's resolution of a question of professional duty.

F. Other concerns

1. **Confidentiality:** One of the foundations of the legal system is the attorney/client privilege. Model Rule 1.6 provides, a lawyer shall not reveal information relating to representation of a client unless the client consents after consolation. Those who oppose MDPs maintain that it is clear that lawyers working in MDPs will compromise the attorney-client privilege. Attorneys would be allowed to work side by side with nonlawyers who have no or limited privileges. Thus, there would be no privilege for such client communications. Further, the attorney-client

privilege is inconsistent with the rules of other professions. For example, accountants, as auditors of financial information, are required according to accounting standards and Securities and Exchange Commission directives to report certain financial information that they uncover in the course of an audit. This is inconsistent with a lawyer's duty to keep client information confidential. Thus, a single MDP advising clients may have contradictory obligations regarding information which is traditionally protected by the attorney-client privilege. In response to these concerns, advocates of MDPs recommend amendments to the ABA Model Rules of Professional Conduct that would clarify a lawyer's position within the MDP, the lawyer's relationship with the MDP's clients, and the obligations of an MDP to protect client and public interests. They would require the provision of information to clients concerning the lawyer's function as a provider of legal services and the likelihood that the client's communications to nonlawyers in the MDP that are unrelated to the provision of legal services would not be protected by the attorney-client privilege.

2. **Conflicts of interest:** A lawyer's duty of loyalty to his or her clients is critical to the delivery of quality legal services. A lawyer's duty of loyalty is closely related to the concept of independence. If a lawyer's loyalty has been compromised, then that lawyer cannot deliver independent legal services. As previously stated, an MDP inherently may have components that will compromise the independence of a lawyer. These components include management pressures from nonlawyer supervisors or business partners and financial incentives related to the sale of products.

In response to these concerns, advocates of MDPs recommend that in connection with its delivery of legal services, an MDP be governed by the same rules of professional conduct as a law firm with regard to the imputation of conflicts and permissible screening measure. Thus, a lawyer who provides legal services in an MDP would be subject to the rules of lawyer conduct respecting conflicts of interest and disqualification and would be subject to discipline for a violation of those rules. For the purposes of a conflict of interest analysis, the lawyer must treat each and every client of the MDP as the lawyer's client.

3. **Pro bono:** A fundamental aspect of the practice of law is the offering of pro bono services. While offering free services is not unique to the legal profession, lawyers have an honored tradition and are at the forefront of providing professional services for free. However, in the event an attorney is working in an MDP, pro bono service could be de-emphasized. Professionals who are not accustomed to the level of pro bono services provided by attorneys may not appreciate the need to deliver pro bono services to the community. Still, nothing in the MDP would necessarily prevent a lawyer from fulfilling his obligation to fulfill this responsibility.

G. Recent debacles

The collapses of Enron and other corporate entities may be traced in part to the work of accounting giants functioning as de facto MDPs. Regulation in the form of the Sarbanes-Oxley Act and the SEC regulations adopted pursuant to the Act have made these de facto MDPs far more difficult and less profitable. Since 2002, the majority of lawyers working for accounting firms have migrated back into law practice.

Quiz Yourself on
SPECIAL ROLE-RELATED DUTIES

91. You are a prosecutor with the State Attorney's office. In an extremely well-publicized case, a famous actor's girlfriend is murdered. The actor often plays unsavory characters, and this may help explain the public outcry that the actor be arrested. There is a racial element as well, in that the actor is white and his girlfriend was black. People are insisting that justice demands that the actor be arrested. However, you have little or no evidence to tie him to the crime beyond the public opinion polls. To prevent bad publicity and possible racial disturbances, may you bring charges and then drop them if nothing substantial is uncovered in the investigation? _____

92. Bill, a state prosecutor, goes to see Defendant Jay, who will soon be tried for assault. Jay refused his court-appointed attorney in favor of self-representation. Bill knows that Jay makes a very sympathetic witness and is worried about going to trial. Bill would like to advise Jay to forego the jury in favor of a bench trial. What advice can Bill give Jay? _____

93. Prosecutor Steve has a very strong case against Defendant, with excellent evidence and accurate, reliable witnesses. Steve believes his case would be bolstered just a little bit more ("the last nail in the coffin," in Steve's words) with testimony from Defendant's former attorney concerning things that fell outside the attorney-client privilege. May Steve subpoena the defendant's former lawyer? _____

94. Prosecutor Scott is involved in the investigation of a drug smuggler. The investigator reports on several possible leads. Two are promising: a report of the phone calls the Defendant made in the last month and a source that can relate Defendant's recent travels. Other leads look less helpful: Several witnesses intimated that others were involved in the crime and minimized Defendant's role. If Scott directs the investigator to look at the phone records and travel logs, but not follow up on the witness information, has he violated any ethical duty? _____

95. Anne, fresh out of law school, is a new attorney in Barbara's firm. Assigned to work on a case with Barbara, Anne gathers documents to release in response to the opposing party's request for the materials. Barbara praises Anne's diligence, but nevertheless pulls several documents from the stack because "the other side wouldn't be interested." Anne disagrees. Because it's a huge firm, Anne is able to covertly ask several attorneys in the firm hypothetical questions about the exclusion of this type of document in response to a request for documents. All of these attorneys confirm Anne's view that the documents should be included. What are the consequences if Anne says nothing? _____

96. XYZ law firm has a long-standing practice. Although the firm's young attorneys in their first three years of practice are allowed to handle some of their own cases and clients, they must go to their supervisors and discuss each case from the beginning. The supervisors are expected to remain on top of the case and guide the younger attorneys through the unfamiliar terrain. Yvette, a new attorney at XYZ law firm, decides to represent a friend in an action against her friend's landlord. She does not take the case to her supervisor, deciding that she can handle it herself. However, the court rules that the claim is frivolous. Will Yvette's supervisor be subject to discipline? _____

97. Assume the facts are as detailed in the question above. This time, however, a partner from a different division learned of the frivolous claim the day before it was to be filed. He waited, however, until the following week to discuss it with Yvette. Is the partner correct in assuming that because he does not directly supervise Yvette, he has not violated any conduct rules? _____

98. Brenda is buying a house, and Attorney Ann is representing both her and Watson Realty Co., the brokers in the transaction. Ann's role as intermediary is compromised when the deal falls through and Brenda decides to sue Watson for breach of contract. Ann withdraws and is dismayed when Brenda subpoenas her to testify to statements Watson made during the deal. Ann asserts attorney-client privilege. Will she be successful? _____

99. Lynn, a young attorney relatively new to her firm, has just been assigned a secretary. Lynn becomes involved in a contentious case with an older, experienced attorney who succeeds at intimidating her every chance he gets. One day the older attorney phones and begins yelling that his request for production of documents did not yield what he had been looking for. Terrified, Lynn quickly hands the phone to the secretary, instructing her to tell the older attorney that no such documents exist. Actually, Lynn had found the documents past the deadline, and was too afraid to turn them over late. Lynn feels badly for putting her secretary on the spot. Will Lynn be subject to discipline? _____

Answers

91. No. Prosecutors are prohibited from prosecuting charges that the prosecutor knows are not supported by probable cause. Although a public interest is identified here (the avoidance of racial tensions, etc.), bringing charges would subject the lawyer to discipline.

92. Bill cannot advise Jay to give up a jury trial. As an unrepresented accused, Bill has a special duty to protect Jay and to not have Jay waive substantial trial rights. MR 3.8(c).

93. Steve should not subpoena the lawyer in this case. Generally, when such testimony is not a necessity to the case (as here), a prosecutor should if at all possible avoid calling a former attorney to testify. MR 3.8(e).

94. Yes. If Scott pursues all of his favorable leads without looking into possible exculpatory evidence, he will violate an ethical obligation. Prosecutors must investigate leads even-handedly, without regard to the possible help or hindrance they might become in the case.

95. It is likely that Anne has violated an ethical duty. Anne's position as a subordinate does not relieve her of a duty to follow professional conduct rules. One exception is created: Anne could escape disciplinary liability if Barbara's decision is the reasonable resolution of an arguable question of professional duty. MR 5.2(b).

96. Yvette's supervisor should not be subject to discipline for Yvette's actions in this case. Partners and supervisory lawyers are required to make reasonable efforts to establish systems in an attempt to prevent violations of the rules. Here, a system was in place to prevent the filing of frivolous claims, and Yvette's violative conduct went around the system. If her supervisor made reasonable efforts to maintain the supervision, her supervisor will not be subject to discipline.

97. No, the partner may be subject to discipline. Although reasonable systems were in place, both direct supervisors and partners have a responsibility to take steps to avoid or mitigate the effects of any subordinate's misconduct when they learn of it. The partner is not Yvette's supervisor, but his status as a partner means that once he learned that Yvette planned to file a frivolous claim, he had a duty to stop it.

98. No. When representing two parties concurrently, no evidentiary privilege exists as between the commonly represented parties. The two parties should have consented to this after a consultation, thus effectively waiving these privileges.

99. Yes, Lynn is subject to discipline. Model Rule 5.3(c)(1) dictates that an attorney will be subject to discipline for the misconduct of nonlawyer subordinates when, among other things, she orders the subordinate to engage in the misconduct. Lynn's status as an associate rather than a partner is irrelevant; as a supervisor, she is subject to discipline.

Exam Tips on
SPECIAL ROLE-RELATED DUTIES

- When a lawyer in a fact pattern is filling a particular role, special duties and rules will apply.

- Criminal prosecutors have ethical responsibilities in addition to those of other lawyers.

    - Prosecutors do not represent the crime victim or a complaining witness. Charged with representing the public's interests rather than those of an individual litigant, prosecutors are required to seek justice rather than mere victory in their work.

    - Prosecutors are prohibited from prosecuting charges that the prosecutor knows are not supported by probable cause, the usual standard below which judges will not issue warrants and will dismiss charges at preliminary hearings. MR 3.8(a).

    - Prosecutors are charged with the responsibility to make reasonable efforts to assure that defendants are advised of their right to counsel. MR 3.8(b).

    - Prosecutors must not unfairly extract waivers of important pretrial rights, such as jury trial, right to counsel, and self-incrimination, from the unrepresented accused. MR 3.8(c).

    - Prosecutors must timely disclose exculpatory evidence and mitigating circumstances regarding sentencing. MR 3.8(d).

    - Prosecutors are required to respect the lawyer-client relationship by refraining from unnecessarily issuing subpoenas that call on lawyers to give evidence about past or present clients. MR 3.8(f).

    - A prosecutor is obliged to pursue investigative leads even-handedly, without regard to whether they might favor or damage her case.

- Under certain circumstances, supervising lawyers will be ethically responsible for the acts of their subordinates, both lawyer and nonlawyer. Under certain circumstances, subordinate lawyers will be relieved of ethical responsibility for their actions.

    - Subordinate lawyers are not relieved of the duty to follow the rules of professional conduct merely because they are supervised, nor for that matter merely because the misconduct in which they might engage is ordered by the supervising lawyer. MR 5.2.

- ☞ A subordinate lawyer is not subject to discipline when she "acts in accordance with a supervisory lawyer's reasonable resolution of an arguable question of professional duty." MR 5.2(b).

- ☞ The distinction between supervisory lawyers (who may or may not be partners) and law firm partners (who may or may not be supervising the specific subordinate involved) triggers different levels of duty. Watch for this subtle distinction.

- ☞ Separate from the acts of lawyer subordinates, supervising lawyers are subject to discipline if they fail to provide adequate supervision.

- ☞ Supervisory lawyers are subject to discipline for the conduct of lawyer subordinates that violates the rules of lawyer conduct when the supervisory lawyer orders the subordinate lawyer to engage in the misconduct, when the supervisory lawyer ratifies the subordinate lawyer's misconduct, or when a lawyer who is either a partner or the subordinate's direct supervisor learns of the misconduct at a time when its effect could be avoided or mitigated and yet fails to take reasonable remedial action.

- ☞ Lawyers are responsible for providing reasonable supervision of nonlawyer subordinates on the same terms as they are responsible for supervising lawyer subordinates.

☛ Lawyers are subject to the rules of professional conduct for lawyers while providing ancillary services when either of the following two conditions is present: when the services provided are not distinct from the lawyer's legal services, MR 5.7(a)(1), or when the services are provided by a separate entity either controlled by the lawyer or by the lawyer with others, and the lawyer fails to communicate clearly to the client that the services are not legal services and are not subject to the normal protections of the lawyer-client relationship. MR 5.7(a)(2).

CHAPTER 10
ADVERTISING AND SOLICITATION

ChapterScope

- Advertising and solicitation are the two names most frequently given to a lawyer's regulated client-getting activities.

- The term *advertising* has traditionally referred to widely distributed, public statements about the services available from a particular lawyer or law organization.

- The term *solicitation* has traditionally referred to narrower communications directed at one or a small group of identified recipients who are known to need a particular service.

- The organized bar has long regulated lawyers' client-getting activities on the theories that some such activities are inappropriate for a profession, that lawyers trained in the art of persuasion may coerce potential clients, and that client-getting has the ill effect on the justice system of stirring up litigation.

- The bar has also regulated client-getting activities for self-interested suppression-of-competition reasons.

- Although all areas of lawyer regulation are subject to potential constitutional limitation, advertising and solicitation regulation is the area most affected by constitutional limitations because of the status of advertising and solicitation as *commercial speech.* Bates v. Arizona State Bar, 433 U.S. 350 (1977). More than any other area in the Professional Responsibility course, discussion of advertising and solicitation issues resembles Constitutional Law course discussions.

- **Warning:** The Model Code advertising and solicitation provisions are misleading. DR 2-101, 2-102, 2-103, 2-104, 2-105. The Code was amended during the 1970s to reflect some of the earliest constitutional limitations on the regulation of client-getting. E.g., Bates v. Arizona. But because the Model Code has not been updated and amended by the ABA since the Model Rules' adoption in 1983, many of its provisions do not reflect recent court decisions that render enforcement of some of its provisions unconstitutional. E.g., Shapero v. Kentucky Bar Association, 486 U.S. 466 (1988); Peel v. Attorney Registration and Disciplinary Commission of Illinois, 496 U.S. 91 (1990).

- Regulating commercial speech based on its "dignity" or "taste" is constitutionally *impermissible.*

- *Barratry* refers to stirring up controversy and thereby litigation. Its relationship to client-getting activities is the connection between soliciting clients and generating prospective clients' interest in pursuing litigation.

- Lawyers are limited in the ways in which they may *maintain,* that is, support financially, their clients. In terms of client-getting, a lawyer is prohibited from using offers of financial support of a client to induce the client to retain the lawyer.

- *Champerty* law restricts lawyers from acquiring an interest in the subject matter of litigation. In terms of client-getting, champerty law restricts lawyers from buying into client claims for the purpose of attracting the client to retain the lawyer.

- In general, lawyers may not give anything of value to anyone who refers a client to the lawyer.

I. TRADITIONAL DISTINCTIONS BETWEEN ADVERTISING AND SOLICITATION

The ethics rules distinguish between *advertising* and *solicitation*. Categorizing a particular client-getting activity as one or the other is the first step in analyzing whether or not the activity is permitted.

A. Advertising

The term *advertising* has traditionally referred to widely distributed, public statements about the services available from a particular lawyer or law organization. Examples of advertising include Yellow Pages listings, general newspaper advertisements, and television or radio broadcast advertisements.

B. Solicitation

The term *solicitation* has traditionally referred to narrower communications directed at one or a small group of identified recipients who are known to need a particular service. Examples of solicitation include: in-person proposals of professional employment to accident victims (Ohralik v. Ohio State Bar Association, 436 U.S. 447 (1978)), letters proposing professional employment sent to known accident victims or others with specific, known legal needs (In re Von Wiegan, 63 N.Y.2d 163 (1984)), lectures to community groups that are accompanied by proposals of professional employment of the speaker, and in-person solicitation of professional employment on the fourth tee during a round of golf.

Note: The bar's enforcement of restrictions on solicitation has been almost exclusively confined to restricting personal injury lawyers from engaging in in-person solicitation of business. The traditional activity of corporate and banking lawyers' in-person relationship-building and client-getting during "club" activities has never drawn the bar's interest.

C. Blurring of the traditional distinctions

Direct, personal, but form, mail to people known to have particular legal needs partakes of some of the attributes of both advertising and solicitation.

Example: Lawyer sends a letter to people whose homes have recently been foreclosed, proposing that he will assist them with their foreclosure action. Such a letter is treated as advertising rather than as in-person or live telephone solicitation. The absence of a coercive environment and in-person persuasion renders this communication more like advertising than solicitation, even though it is targeted and personal. Advertising is always to some extent targeted. Television ads for certain services are placed to run on television shows that the advertiser thinks will be watched by people who need the service advertised. Shapero v. Kentucky Bar Association, 486 U.S. 466 (1988).

D. Model Rules

The Model Rules treats advertising and solicitation in separate rules (MR 7.2 for advertising and MR 7.3 for solicitation). See §§IV and V. They also create general restrictions that apply to both advertising and solicitation in MR 7.1, 7.4, and 7.5. See §III.

II. CONSTITUTIONAL LIMITATIONS ON DISCIPLINARY AUTHORITY

Advertising and solicitation are speech. As such, some First Amendment protection is provided to these activities, effectively limiting the states' authority to prohibit and regulate them.

A. Commercial speech

Commercial speech, such as advertising, is given some protection under the First Amendment. Virginia Bd. of Pharmacy v. Virginia Citizens Consumer Council, Inc., 425 U.S. 748 (1976). Lawyer client-getting speech is protected commercial speech under the First Amendment. Bates v. State Bar of Arizona, 433 U.S. 350 (1977). The public's right to receive information is a key underpinning of the First Amendment commercial speech analysis. Central Hudson Gas & Electric Co. v. Public Service Commission of New York, 447 U.S. 557, 563 (1980). As such, there are limits on the client-getting restrictions that a bar association and the state may enforce.

B. No broader restrictions than necessary

Restrictions on commercial speech must further a substantial government interest and must be no broader than necessary.

1. **Government interest in truthful advertising:** The government has a substantial interest in protecting the public from being misled or coerced by lawyer communications.

2. **Narrowly drawn:** To pass constitutional muster, restrictions must be focused on substantial government interest and must be narrowly drawn.

3. **No accounting for matters of taste:** Regulating commercial speech based on its "dignity" or "taste" is constitutionally *impermissible.*

C. Permissible regulation

Despite the constitutional limitations on its power to restrict lawyer commercial speech, a state may prohibit lawyer client-getting that is false or misleading, that is coercive, or that promotes transactions that are themselves illegal. In re Primus, 436 U.S. 412 (1978); Zauderer v. Office of Disciplinary Counsel of Supreme Court of Ohio, 471 U.S. 626 (1985); Bates v. State Bar of Arizona, 433 U.S. 350 (1977).

D. Key Supreme Court cases

Following *Bates,* in a line of important cases, the U.S. Supreme Court has elaborated on the constitutionality of various bar enforced commercial speech restrictions. More such case law exists in the client-getting area than in any other area covered in the Professional Responsibility course, and as a result the case law is given special treatment in this chapter.

1. **In re R.M.J.:** In In re R.M.J., 455 U.S. 191 (1982), the Court held that states may not prohibit truthful advertising. In particular, truthful advertising statements that communicate practice concentration are protected speech.

   In this case, Missouri charged one of its lawyers with unprofessional conduct for violating its highly detailed, restrictive (yet typical for the time) advertising rules. The lawyer had, for example, listed in ads that he practiced "personal injury" and "real estate" law instead of using the state-approved language, "tort law" and "property law." He mailed announcement cards to persons other than those on the state-approved list of "other lawyers, clients, former clients, personal friends, and relatives," and he listed the truthful but unapproved information that he was licensed to practice in both Missouri and Illinois. The Court struck down the Missouri discipline of the lawyer, finding no deception in the lawyer's protected, commercial speech. In a mild irony, the Court was understandably "more troubl[ed] [by the lawyer's] listing, in large bold face type, that he was a member of the bar of the Supreme Court of the United States," an almost meaningless claim that might mislead "the general public unfamiliar with" the minimal requirements for admission to the Supreme Court bar. The state had not charged the lawyer with wrongdoing based on this particular statement in his ad.

2. ***Zauderer:*** In Zauderer v. Office of Disciplinary Counsel of Supreme Court of Ohio, 471 U.S. 626 (1985), the Court held that an absolute ban on illustrations in lawyer advertising is too broad and therefore unconstitutional. The Court also held that an advertising statement that no fees are owed unless the client recovers (expressing a contingent-fee arrangement) is misleading and therefore not constitutionally protected because it lacks the information that the client would be liable for other fees and court costs even if there is no recovery.

Zauderer, an Ohio lawyer, placed an advertisement in local newspapers that included a drawing of the Dalkon Shield intrauterine device and the following text:

> The Dalkon Shield Interuterine [sic] Device is alleged to have caused serious pelvic infections resulting in hospitalizations, tubal damage, infertility, and hysterectomies. It is also alleged to have caused unplanned pregnancies ending in abortions, miscarriages, septic abortions, tubal or ectopic pregnancies, and full-term deliveries. If you or a friend has had a similar experience, do not assume it is too late to take legal action against the Shield's manufacturer. Our law firm is presently representing women on such cases. The cases are handled on a contingent fee basis of the amount recovered. If there is no recovery, no legal fees are owed by our clients.

The ad was successful; it netted Zauderer 106 clients. At the time of the ad's placement, Ohio's advertising rules were similar to the ABA Model Code provisions, requiring ads to be presented "in a dignified manner without the use of drawings, illustrations, animations . . . music or pictures," save for minor exceptions. The Court ruled that Ohio's absolute ban on such advertising was too broad and therefore unconstitutional. As long as the advertising is truthful and not deceptive, the speech is protected. With Zauderer's claim that "if there is no recovery, no legal fees are owed by our clients," the Court took exception. Because the claim was likely to mislead a nonlawyer into thinking that no fees or costs would be owed in the event of litigation failure, the Court upheld the state's rule requiring disclosure of liability for costs when a lawyer advertises contingent fees and its discipline of Zauderer for failing to do so.

3. ***Ohralik:*** In Ohralik v. Ohio State Bar Assoc., 436 U.S. 447 (1978), and in In re Primus, 436 U.S. 412 (1978), the Court held that in-person solicitation for pecuniary gain is not protected by the First Amendment because of its possibilities for coercion and overreaching.

In a pair of cases decided the same day, the United States Supreme Court reaffirmed that the First Amendment does not protect in-person solicitation, *for pecuniary gain,* "under circumstances likely to pose dangers the state has a right to prevent." Ohralik v. Ohio State Bar Association, 436 U.S. 447, 449; In re Primus, 436 U.S. 412 (1978). *Ohralik* was a near-classic case of ambulance chasing, involving a lawyer soliciting the business of a casual acquaintance at the acquaintance's hospital bed following an automobile collision. The acquaintance was in traction. In *Primus,* a lawyer was furthering "political and ideological goals" in part by advising a lay person of her legal rights and informing her that the American Civil Liberties Union (with which the lawyer was associated) would provide free legal assistance to vindicate those rights. *Primus* at 415. The Court concluded that the Bar could discipline Ohralik but not Primus, consistent with the First Amendment. The distinction has found its way into Model Rule 7.3. *Primus* notwithstanding, the Bar can discipline a lawyer for actual misconduct in solicitation, such as making false or misleading statements or overreaching the client.

4. *Shapero:* In Shapero v. Kentucky Bar Association, 486 U.S. 466 (1988), the Court held that direct mailings to prospective clients who are known to be in need of the service advertised are protected as are other forms of advertising.

In *Shapero,* the Court recognized that mechanical distractions between "advertising" and "solicitation" are unlikely to produce sound analysis. It had previously been thought by many, with some support in the Rules of the time and the Code, that advertising within limits was permitted, but solicitation for pecuniary gain was absolutely prohibited. Shapero's actions, while not direct solicitation, were more akin to solicitation than to advertising. He sought approval to send a direct mailing to individuals whose homes were being foreclosed that read:

> It has come to my attention that your home is being foreclosed on. If this is true, you may be about to lose your home. Federal law may allow you to keep your home by ORDERING your creditor [sic] to STOP and give you more time to pay them.
>
> You may call my office anytime from 8:30 AM to 5:00 PM for FREE information on how you can keep your home.
>
> Call NOW, don't wait. It may surprise you what I may be able to do for you. Just call and tell me that you got this letter. Remember it is FREE, there is NO charge for calling.

Because it was sent only to individuals identified as needing the service, it had an element of solicitation; because it was in writing rather than in-person contact, it had an element of advertising. The state bar asserted that this was a case of "Ohralik in writing," emphasizing the element of solicitation in the targeted nature of the letter. The Court, however, emphasizing the reasoning behind the solicitation cases (concern that the potential client will be overwhelmed by the lawyer's capacity to persuade, producing overreaching and undue influence), regarded written solicitation to be much less likely to produce overreaching or undue influence and ruled such speech protected.

The Court did not reach the question of whether the letter's use of bold type and puffery was misleading. The Court seemed to contrast the present language and claims from those in other cases as follows:

> To be sure, a letter may be misleading if it unduly emphasizes trivial or "relatively uninformative fact[s]," In re R. M. J., *supra,* at 205 (lawyer's statement, "in large capital letters, that he was a member of the Bar to the Supreme Court of the United States"), or offers overblown assurances of client satisfaction, cf. In re Von Wiegen, 63 N. Y. 2d 163, 179 (1984) (solicitation letter to victims of massive disaster informs them that "it is [the lawyer's] opinion that the liability of the defendants is clear"), *cert. denied,* 472 U.S. 1007 (1985); *Bates, supra,* at 383-384 ("advertising claims as to the quality of legal services . . . may be so likely to be misleading as to warrant restriction"). Respondent does not argue before us that petitioner's letter was misleading in those respects. Nor does respondent contend that the letter is false or misleading in any other respect. Of course, respondent is free to raise, and the Kentucky courts are free to consider, any such argument on remand.

In short, if not false or misleading, written client-getting activities will be protected under the First Amendment. Importantly, Justices O'Connor, Rehnquist, and Scalia dissented; Justices

White and Stevens concurred in part, suggesting that the Court should not express itself on the potential for overreaching of any particular written solicitation such as Shapero's until state courts do. Consequently, only four justices agreed with the full opinion, two of whom are no longer on the Court.

5. *Peel:* In Peel v. Illinois Attorney Registration and Disciplinary Commission, 496 U.S. 91 (1990), the Court held that states may not prohibit all forms of communication about lawyer specialization and certification.

In this specialization case, the Court ruled that a state may not ban statements of certification of specialization by bona fide organizations. An Illinois lawyer had placed text on his letterhead reading, "certified trial specialist by the National Board of Trial Advocacy." The Court suggested that states should consider publishing lists identifying organizations as those whose certifications lawyers may boast of, or should require disclaimers that would ensure that clients understand that the certifying organization is not a state agency. Model Rule 7.4, which generally prohibits lawyers from boasting of specialist status unless they have been certified as such by a state agency, may well be unconstitutional under *Peel.*

6. *Went For It, Inc.:* In Florida Bar v. Went For It, Inc., 115 S. Ct. 2371 (1995), the Court held that a state may place reasonable, narrowly drawn restrictions on direct-mail advertising to prospective clients who are accident victims or victims' family members.

State bar rules prohibited personal injury lawyers from sending targeted direct mail solicitations to victims and their relatives for 30 days following an accident or disaster. Lawyer and his attorney referral service asserted that the mandatory blackout period violated the First and Fourteenth Amendments to the Constitution. Lawyer advertising is commercial speech accorded First Amendment protection. That protection is not absolute, but the government must demonstrate that it has narrowly drawn a regulation that directly and materially furthers a substantial interest. Because this rule promoted the state's interest in regulating the practice of law by forestalling for a brief period the public outrage and irritation with attorneys engendered by means of direct solicitation only days after accidents, it satisfied all constitutional requirements.

III. GENERAL CONSTRAINTS ON ALL COMMUNICATION REGARDING SERVICES

Some restrictions apply equally to all forms of client-getting, whether denominated as advertising or solicitation.

A. False and misleading statements, generally

False or misleading statements in lawyer client-getting communication are subject to discipline. MR 7.1.

Examples: Lawyer advertises that he is "experienced in sports law" when in fact he is a recent law graduate who took a sports law course and was once a college athlete. Such a statement is false and subject to discipline.

Personal Injury Lawyer advertises in the Yellow Pages, "Recovery is Guaranteed! If you don't recover, you don't pay me a fee!" Such a statement is not false, but is misleading and subject to discipline. Although the contingent-fee arrangement that Lawyer proposes in the ad will result in no fee to the lawyer unless there is a recovery from which to draw the fee, the statement implies that the client will have no liability if Lawyer fails to obtain recovery when in fact the client may be liable for litigation costs. *Zauderer.*

Law Firm uses a television advertisement depicting lawyers in a courtroom jury trial scene even though none of the Law Firm's lawyers had tried a case to conclusion before a jury. Such an ad is misleading and subject to discipline. In re Zang, 154 Ariz. 134 (1987).

1. **Testimonials:** Courts in some states have held that lawyer ads that use ***client testimonials*** are inherently misleading by focusing the viewer's attention on selected, favorable client examples and excluding unfavorable examples. In particular, client testimonials may mislead the viewer into thinking that case results are a function of the lawyer and not the merits of the particular claim that a prospective client may have. See e.g., Office of Disc. Counsel v. Shane, 692 N.E.2d 571 (Ohio 1998).

   Example: Lawyer placed a radio ad, narrated by a former Client describing the means by which Lawyer had obtained a huge settlement for Client following a minor traffic accident. Client concluded the ad by stating that he would definitely ask Lawyer to represent him in any future legal matters. In at least some states, such an ad is regarded as misleading advertising. Oring v. State Bar of Cal., 4 Laws. Man. on Prof. Conduct (ABA/BNA) No. 12, at 206 (July 6, 1988). The U.S. Supreme Court heard argument in the *Oring* case (57 U.S.L.W. 3465) but dismissed the writ as improvidently granted (57 U.S.L.W. 3496), and thus never addressed the merits of the case.

   a. **Disclaimer required:** In some states, testimonial advertising is permitted if accompanied by a disclaimer, such as, "the testimonial does not constitute a guaranty, warranty, or prediction regarding the outcome of your legal matter."

2. **Self-laudation:** Self-laudation that is either unverifiable or misleading-but-true is subject to discipline as false or misleading.

   a. **Unverifiable:** Statements that are unverifiable are deemed misleading.

   Examples: Lawyer's newspaper advertisement describes Lawyer as "The County's Best Litigator," "Among the Most Respected Lawyers in the State," and "Serving a Satisfied Clientele." These are not subject to verification and are therefore misleading.

   Immigration Law Attorney placed an advertisement in the Yellow Pages claiming that when other lawyers could not help an individual, he could and that he could help "YOU." This advertisement subjects the lawyer to discipline because it makes claims that are not verifiable. D.C. Op. 249 (1994).

   b. **Misleading but true:** Self-laudation is subject to discipline as being misleading-but-true when, although verifiable and true, the statement misleads the reader or viewer, usually because it appears to be more important than it would be if it could be put into a full context.

   Examples: Lawyer includes in her ad an all-caps, bold, underlined statement "**LICENSED BY THE UNITED STATES SUPREME COURT.**" Because the statement implies that such licensure indicates an important quality measure when in fact licensure by the U.S. Supreme Court requires almost nothing beyond licensure in any state's courts, the statement is misleading and subject to discipline. Zauderer v. Office of Disciplinary Counsel of Supreme Court of Ohio, 471 U.S. 626 (1985).

Lawyer includes in his newspaper ad that he has "Won 90% of his criminal defense cases." Such a statement appears far more impressive than it would if the reader also knew that Lawyer defines "winning" as the entry of a judgment and sentence against his client for anything less than the maximum possible for crimes initially charged and that, by that measure, virtually all criminal defense lawyers "win" more than 90% of their cases.

3. **Firm names:** Firm names may be misleading when they untruthfully imply a relationship to a government or other institution. MR 7.5. Examples of misleading names include "The Ohio Law Firm," "Social Security Legal Services," or "New York Legal Aid" when used by a private law firm.

4. **Information about fees:** Since *Bates,* lawyer statements about fees have been constitutionally protected. Like other advertising statements, they may be restricted only when they are false or misleading.

    Example: "Reasonable and moderate" are adjectives that may be used to describe fees. "The low cost alternative," "Give-away prices," and "below cost" are adjectives that have been held to be misleading. See, e.g., Bishop v. Committee on Professional Ethics and Conduct of the Iowa State Bar Association, 521 F. Supp. 1219 (S.D. Iowa 1981); D.C. Bar Op. 172-9 (1986).

B. **Specialization and certification**

Until the 1970s, state bars were quite restrictive in their regulation of lawyers' indications of practice concentration, specialization, or certification in areas of practice.

1. **Model Code:** The largely outdated Model Code permitted lawyers to identify a specialty only if that specialty was in patent, trademark, or admiralty law. It also permitted lawyers to indicate subject matter areas of practice in which the lawyer engaged only if the lawyer used a prescribed list of words provided by the state bar. DR 2-105.

2. **Model Rules:** More recently, the restrictions on areas of practice, specialty, and certification in a particular area have been constrained by the First Amendment but continue to be real restrictions, all under the rubric of the false and misleading limitation. MR 7.4.

    a. **Areas of practice:** As long as the words used by the lawyer to designate areas in which the lawyer practices fairly communicate those areas, they are protected commercial speech and do not subject the lawyer to discipline. Whether the lawyer chooses to designate areas of practice as "torts" or "personal injury," "contracts" or "commercial litigation," or "property" or "real estate transfers" will not matter for disciplinary purposes. All are permitted. In re R.M.J., 455 U.S. 191 (1982).

    b. **Certification:** Claiming a certification in a particular area presents additional concerns. An unqualified statement of certification may mislead the reader into thinking that the state has certified the lawyer in a particular area. However, a state may not impose a blanket prohibition on statements of certification. Peel v. Illinois Attorney Registration and Disciplinary Commission, 496 U.S. 91 (1990). To make Model Rule 7.4 consistent with Peel v. Attorney Registration and Disciplinary Commission of Illinois, 496 U.S. 91 (1990), the rule was amended in February 2002 to permit statements of certification by clearly identified organizations approved by the ABA or the appropriate state bar. See §II.D.5.

        Examples: In her advertising and communication with the public, Lawyer referred to her status as a licensed CPA and Certified Financial Planner (CFP). The Board that licensed

Lawyer as a CPA reprimanded her for engaging in false, deceptive, and misleading advertising. In particular, the Board disapproved of her including the unapproved "CFP" designation in her ads. Lawyer's advertisements constituted commercial speech. Because she did in fact hold a valid CPA license, her advertisements were truthful in that regard, could not mislead the public, and thus deserved constitutional protection. Without evidence of specific harm resulting from Lawyer's use of the CFP designation, that portion of the advertisements also fell within the First Amendment's safeguards. Ibanez v. Florida Dep't of Business & Professional Regulation, 512 U.S. 136 (1994).

C. Post-event waiting periods

In an effort to guard against the potential for lawyer overreaching of accident victims and their families, some states have imposed waiting periods before any targeted communications may be made.

1. **General applicability:** These restrictions apply to both in-person and live telephone communications as well as direct mail and recorded telephone communications.

2. **Narrowly drawn:** Narrowly drawn waiting-period restrictions are constitutional. Florida Bar v. Went For It, Inc., 115 S. Ct. 2371 (1995).

    Example: Within a few days of a mass disaster, Lawyer mails a letter to survivors and families of deceased victims. Among other things, the letter says "it is Lawyer's opinion that the liability of the defendants is clear." The state bar disciplines Lawyer for violating the state's 30-day waiting period; that discipline is constitutional. In re Von Wiegen, 63 N.Y.2d 163, 179 (1984), *cert. den.* 472 U.S. 1007 (1985).

IV. CONSTRAINTS PARTICULAR TO ADVERTISING

Some restrictions have particular applicability to advertising.

A. Record keeping

To guard against any later dispute over content, a lawyer is required to retain a copy of any advertisement, including the text of any broadcast advertisement, for two years after its last publication. Although still in effect in most states, the language requiring lawyers to maintain a two-year record of advertisements was deleted from Model Rule 7.2 in the February 2002 amendments.

B. Payment for advertising

Lawyers, of course, may pay reasonable costs associated with advertising. MR 7.2(b). This rule states what may seem to be the obvious because, outside of the advertising context, lawyers may not pay others for recommending the lawyer.

C. Name of the lawyer

All advertisements must include the name and address of at least one lawyer or law firm responsible for the advertisement's content. MR 7.2(c).

V. CONSTRAINTS ON IN-PERSON AND LIVE TELEPHONE SOLICITATION

In-person and live telephone solicitation are subject to prophylactic rules that are much more restrictive than the advertising rules.

A. Duress, coercion, and harassment

Although all client-getting communication is subject to discipline if it involves duress or coercion, restrictions on in-person and live telephone client solicitation are meant to protect prospective clients from special dangers of lawyer coercion and duress that attend such communications.

1. **Power of influence:** In theory, at least, lawyers are persuasive individuals with a certain power to influence others.

2. **Difficult to verify content:** Unlike print or broadcast media advertising, the text of an in-person or live telephone client solicitation involves a private discussion with the potential for interaction between the lawyer and the prospective client. As such, keeping a record to verify the content of the solicitation is not a practical way of ensuring that each such communication can be reviewed after the fact. The prophylactic prohibitions on in-person and live telephone client-getting communications are justified in part by the impracticality of preserving the communication for review.

B. Exceptions to the restrictions

1. **Non-live telephone:** Computer, autodial, and recorded telephone solicitations are restricted only by the advertising rules and by the general, false and misleading, and actual duress or coercion limitations.

2. **Relationship with the prospective client:** Subject only to the general limitations on client-getting speech, lawyers may solicit other lawyers or people with whom the lawyer has a family, close personal, or prior professional relationship. MR 7.3(a).

   Example: Lawyer had a conversation with Bank President. Lawyer had formerly done legal work for Bank, and Lawyer and Bank President were social acquaintances. Lawyer told Bank President that Lawyer's cousin, a friend of Bank President, was near death. Lawyer suggested to Bank President that if the Bank was named executor of Cousin's estate and if estate work needed to be done after Cousin's impending death, Lawyer could be retained to do it. Although this act would otherwise be in-person solicitation and subject to discipline, the personal and family relationships in this case fall within the exception to Model Rule 7.3's restriction. Goldwaithe v. Disciplinary Board, 408 So. 2d 504 (Ala. 1982).

3. **Pecuniary gain:** The specific restrictions on in-person and live telephone solicitation apply only when a significant motive for the solicitation is pecuniary gain for the lawyer. MR 7.3(a). See discussions of *Primus* and *Ohralik*, §II.D.3.

VI. OTHER RESTRICTIONS ON SPECIFIC SOLICITATION

There are additional restrictions on solicitation of specific prospective clients or those known to be in need of specific services.

A. "We don't want any!"

Once a prospective client makes known her desire not to be contacted by the lawyer, the lawyer may not contact that prospective client. MR 7.3(b)(1).

B. Disclaimer

Written or recorded communications to those known to be in need of specific services must include the words "Advertising Material" on the outside of any envelope used and at the beginning and end of any recorded communication. MR 7.3(c).

VII. CLIENT-GETTING ON THE INTERNET

An emerging problem relates to the application of the client-getting rules to internet communications regarding lawyer services.

A. General

In general, it seems likely that internet advertising ought to be treated largely as direct mail advertising is treated now. See discussions of *Shapero* and *Went For It*. The recipient of the internet message is as free as the recipient of Shapero's letter to discard it (i.e., press "delete"). As such, internet advertising should be subject to the advertising restrictions, as opposed to the in-person solicitation restrictions, and may also be restricted by narrowly drawn regulations such as those approved in *Went For It*.

B. Territorial difficulties

The Model Code restricts a lawyer's advertising to an area in which the lawyer resides or maintains an office or in which a significant portion of the lawyer's clients resides. DR 2-101(B). The Model Rules has no such territorial restriction. When a message is sent out on the internet, it obviously violates the Model Code provision for any lawyer or firm that does not have a truly global practice. It seems likely that these territorial restrictions will go the way of the states' failed efforts to impose residency requirements for admission to practice. See Chapter 2, §III. Nonetheless, the issue is as yet unresolved. The natural tendency of the bar to inhibit competition will press toward attacks on the internet-advertising lawyer. The real difficulties may eventually present themselves in the form of allegations of unauthorized practice beyond the internet-advertising lawyer's licensed jurisdictions. See Chapter 2, §IV.

VIII. CLIENT-GETTING RELATIONSHIP TO BARRATRY, MAINTENANCE, AND CHAMPERTY

Lawyers have long been restrained by both ethics rules and criminal statutes from engaging in barratry, maintenance, and champerty. All three of these are related to both client-getting and conflicts-of-interest restrictions. See MR 1.8(e), MR 1.8(i); DR 5-103. The client-getting connection involves the traditional ban on the use of special competitive advantages by some lawyers to generate clients and thereby stir up litigation.

A. Barratry

Barratry is a term that refers to stirring up controversy and thereby litigation. Its relationship to client-getting activities is the connection between soliciting clients and generating the prospective clients' interest in pursuing litigation.

B. Maintenance

Lawyers are limited in the ways in which they may maintain, that is, financially support, their clients. In terms of client-getting, a lawyer is prohibited from using offers of financial support of a client to induce the client to retain the lawyer.

C. Champerty

Champerty law restricts lawyers from acquiring an interest in the subject matter of litigation. In terms of client-getting, champerty law restricts lawyers from buying into client claims for the purpose of attracting the client to retain the lawyer. See also Chapter 6, §IV.B.3.

IX. LAWYER AGENTS

As with any other type of lawyer misconduct, a lawyer is not relieved of disciplinary or other liability for the conduct by having an agent do the misconduct on the lawyer's behalf.

A. Runners and cappers

In the client-getting area, such agents are commonly called "runners" or "cappers." Runners and cappers monitor accidents and other events likely to produce legal work and then direct potential clients to the lawyer for whom the runner or capper works.

1. **Discipline:** Lawyers who employ runners or cappers are subject to discipline. MR 5.3(c).

2. **Criminal violation:** In many states, employment of runners or cappers is also a criminal violation.

B. Payment for client referrals

In general, lawyers may not give anything of value to anyone who refers a client to the lawyer.

Example: Lawyer leaves a stack of his business cards with Bartender and agrees to pay Bartender $25 for each client that comes to Lawyer as a result of picking up Lawyer's card in the bar. Lawyer is subject to discipline.

C. Supervise employees

As with other areas of possible misconduct, lawyers must take reasonable efforts to supervise employees and agents to ensure that the agents' conduct complies with the lawyer's rules of professional conduct. MR 5.3.

Quiz Yourself on
ADVERTISING AND SOLICITATION

100. A legal aid lawyer represents a client who is alleging that the housing complex in which he resides has been discriminating on the basis of race in making repairs. The lawyer decides to go door to door in the housing complex to find out if other tenants have had similar experiences and whether they are willing to bring suit. Will the lawyer be subject to discipline for her actions? _____

101. Joe represents the state of Marshall and is defending the state's ethics code sections dealing with lawyer advertising and solicitation against a claim that they violate the constitutional right to free speech of lawyers. What must Joe demonstrate to have the provisions declared constitutional? _____

102. Bob and Sally want to enter private practice in the state of Wythe, specializing in labor law. They want to have a unique name for their firm, so rather than use their last names, they have decided to call themselves Wythe Labor Relations Legal Services. Will they be subject to discipline for the name of their firm? _____

103. Bob is a personal injury attorney, and he knows how hard his clients sometimes struggle to pay all of their expenses until they reach an agreement with the insurance company. Bob wants to offer potential clients a weekly stipend to live on until the case is settled. If the clients win their cases, they will be required to reimburse him. If they lose, he is willing to absorb the cost of the weekly stipends. Bob wants to run an ad clearly and truthfully explaining his policy for his clients. Will Bob be subject to discipline for his ad? _____

104. Allen, a former state trooper, is now an attorney. He plans to run an advertisement stating his background as a former state trooper with the statement, "I can fix your drunk driving problems." Will Allen be subject to discipline for this advertisement? _____

105. Jane decides to place an ad in the local newspaper. In addition to listing her specialties and educational background, she decides to include the phrases, "one of the state's toughest litigators" and "well respected by state and federal judges." She believes the statements to be true and thinks that lawyers are entitled to do a little self-promotion. Will Jane be subject to discipline for the advertisement? _____

106. Peter is planning to send form letters to a select group of individuals that has recently been denied Social Security benefits, proposing that they hire him to represent them at their hearing. Is Peter's letter permissible? _____

107. Joan is an attorney at a law firm that has decided to place an advertisement in the Yellow Pages. Joan is in charge of designing the ad. Because of the large number of distinguished partners in her firm, Joan has decided to only use the firm's name and address in the ad. None of the named partners is currently practicing. Will the firm be subject to discipline for the ad? _____

Answers

100. No. The Supreme Court has ruled that lawyers may solicit clients in person if the lawyer is doing so not for pecuniary gain but rather to further political and ideological goals. In re Primus, 436 U.S. 412 (1978). The lawyer would be subject to discipline, however, for any actual coercion or duress.

101. Joe must demonstrate that the provisions further a substantial government interest and are no broader than are necessary to achieve that interest.

102. Yes. The name of Bob and Sally's firm misleads the public into assuming they are associated with the government or are a nonprofit law firm. Firm names that are false or misleading violate Model Rule 7.5. Firm names may be misleading when they untruthfully imply a relationship to a government or other institution.

103. Yes. A lawyer is prohibited from offering a client financial support to induce the client to retain the lawyer. MR 1.8(e).

104. Yes. Advertisements cannot give rise to unreasonable expectations or refer to illegal activity. Allen's ad implies that Allen will use his connections as a former state trooper to fix his clients' tickets. MR 7.1 Comment 4.

105. Yes. The ad violates the ethics rules because Jane made claims that are not susceptible to verification. Statements that are unverifiable are deemed to be misleading. MR 7.1.

106. Advertising has traditionally referred to widely distributed public statements about services available from a particular lawyer or law organization. Solicitation has traditionally referred to narrower communications directed at one or a small group of identified recipients who are known to need a particular service. As a result of the Court's decision in Shapero v. Kentucky Bar Association, 486 U.S. 466 (1988), Peter's letter would be considered to be advertising and is permissible if it is not false or misleading and if it bears the words ADVERTISING MATERIAL on the envelope.

107. No. Model Rule 7.2(c) requires all advertisements to include the name and address of at least one lawyer or law firm who is responsible for the advertisement's content. Joan's firm's ad complies with this rule.

Exam Tips on
ADVERTISING AND SOLICITATION

- ☞ More than in any other area of Professional Responsibility law, case law is at the center of advertising and solicitation law. Change your exam strategy to take this into account without completely disregarding the Model Rules provisions, which have been fairly effectively amended to keep pace with successful court challenges.

- ☞ **Warning:** The Model Code advertising and solicitation provisions are misleading. DR 2-101, 2-102, 2-103, 2-104, 2-105. The Code was amended during the 1970s to reflect some of the earliest constitutional limitations on the regulation of client-getting. But because the Model Code has not been updated and amended by the ABA since the Model Rules' adoption in 1983, many of its provisions do not reflect recent court decisions that render enforcement of some of its provisions unconstitutional.

- ☛ The ethics rules distinguish between ***advertising*** and ***solicitation.*** Categorizing a particular client-getting activity as one or the other is the first step to analyzing whether or not the activity is permitted.

- ☛ The term ***advertising*** has traditionally referred to widely distributed, public statements about the services available from a particular lawyer or law organization.

- ☛ The term ***solicitation*** has traditionally referred to narrower communications directed at one or a small group of identified recipients who are known to need a particular service.

- ☛ Direct, personal, but form, mail to people known to have particular legal needs partakes of some of the attributes of both advertising and solicitation. Since the *Shapero* case, such communications are treated as advertising by the Model Rules. Written or recorded communications to those known to be in need of specific services must include the words "Advertising Material" on the outside of any envelope used and at the beginning and end of any recorded communication. MR 7.3(c).

- ☛ The Model Rules treat advertising and solicitation in separate rules (Model Rule 7.2 for advertising and Model Rule 7.3 for solicitation). They also create general restrictions that apply to both advertising and solicitation in Model Rules 7.1, 7.4, and 7.5.

- ☛ Advertising and solicitation are speech. As such, some First Amendment protection is provided to these activities, effectively limiting the states' authority to prohibit and regulate them. Commercial speech, such as advertising, is given some protection under the First Amendment.

- ☛ Restrictions on commercial speech must further a substantial government interest and must be no broader than necessary.

- ☛ The government has a substantial interest in protecting the public from being misled or coerced by lawyer communications.

- ☛ Regulating commercial speech based on its "dignity" or "taste" is constitutionally ***impermissible.***

- ☛ Despite the constitutional limitations on its power to restrict lawyer commercial speech, a state may prohibit lawyer client-getting that is false or misleading, that is coercive, or that promotes transactions that are themselves illegal.

- ☛ Some restrictions apply equally to all forms of client-getting, whether denominated as advertising or solicitation.

    - ☞ False or misleading statements in lawyer client-getting communication are subject to discipline. MR 7.1.

    - ☞ ***Self-laudation*** that is either unverifiable or misleading-but-true is subject to discipline as false or misleading. Statements that are unverifiable are deemed misleading. Self-laudation is subject to discipline as being misleading-but-true when, although verifiable and true, the statement misleads the reader or viewer, usually because it appears to be more important than it would be if it could be put into a full context.

    - ☞ Firm names may be misleading when they untruthfully imply a relationship to a government or other institution. MR 7.5.

- ☞ Since *Bates,* lawyers' statements about fees have been constitutionally protected. Like other advertising statements, they may be restricted only when they are false or misleading.

- ☛ Until the 1970s, state bars were quite restrictive in their regulation of lawyers' indications of practice concentration, **specialization,** or certification in areas of practice. As long as the words used by the lawyer to designate areas in which the lawyer practices fairly communicate those areas, they will be protected commercial speech and will not subject the lawyer to discipline. An unqualified statement of certification may mislead the reader into thinking that the state has certified the lawyer in a particular area. However, a state may not impose a blanket prohibition on statements of certification.

- ☛ In an effort to guard against the potential for lawyer overreaching of accident victims and their families, some states have imposed waiting periods before any otherwise protected targeted communications may be made. Narrowly drawn waiting-period restrictions are constitutional.

- ☛ Some restrictions have particular applicability to advertising.

    - ☞ Lawyers, of course, may pay reasonable costs associated with advertising. MR 7.2(b). This rule states what may seem to be the obvious because outside of the advertising context, lawyers may not pay others for recommending the lawyer.

    - ☞ All advertisements must include the name and address of at least one lawyer or law firm responsible for the advertisement's content. MR 7.2(c).

- ☛ In-person and live telephone solicitation are subject to prophylactic rules that are much more restrictive than the advertising rules.

    - ☞ Although all client-getting communication is subject to discipline if it involves duress or coercion, restrictions on in-person and live telephone client solicitation are meant to protect prospective clients from special dangers of lawyer coercion and duress that attend such communications.

    - ☞ Computer, auto-dial, and recorded telephone solicitations are restricted only by the advertising rules and by the general, false, and misleading and actual duress or coercion limitations.

    - ☞ Subject only to the general limitations on client-getting speech, lawyers may solicit people with whom the lawyer has a family or prior professional or close personal relationship. MR 7.3(a).

    - ☞ The specific restrictions on in-person and live telephone solicitation apply only when a significant motive for the solicitation is pecuniary gain for the lawyer. MR 7.3(a).

    - ☞ Once a prospective client makes known her desire not to be contacted by the lawyer, the lawyer may not contact that prospective client. MR 7.3(b)(1).

- ☛ Lawyers have long been restrained by both ethics rules and criminal statutes from engaging in barratry, maintenance, and champerty.

    - ☞ **Barratry** is a term that refers to stirring up controversy and thereby litigation. Its relationship to client-getting activities is the connection between soliciting clients and generating the prospective clients' interest in pursuing litigation.

- ☞ Lawyers are limited in the ways in which they may maintain, that is, support financially, their clients. In terms of client-getting, a lawyer is prohibited from using offers of financial support of a client to induce the client to retain the lawyer.
- ☞ ***Champerty*** law restricts lawyers from acquiring an interest in the subject matter of litigation.
- ☞ In terms of client-getting, champerty law restricts lawyers from buying into client claims for the purpose of attracting the client to retain the lawyer.

☛ Runners and cappers monitor accidents and other events likely to produce legal work, and then direct potential clients to the lawyer for whom the runner or capper works. Lawyers who employ runners or cappers are subject to discipline. MR 5.3(c). In many states, employment of runners or cappers is also a criminal violation.

CHAPTER 11
JUDICIAL CONDUCT

ChapterScope

- Judicial conduct is a part of most Professional Responsibility courses, although it is usually a relatively small part.

- This topic requires a different lens from the rest of the Professional Responsibility course: It is about the role of judge rather than the role of lawyer. The two roles are significantly different, and, as a result, discussion of judicial conduct proceeds from a different set of premises than those from which a discussion of lawyer conduct proceeds. For example, judges are neutrals, not partisans, so the lawyer's duty of loyalty to a client is simply not a part of a judicial conduct discussion. Likewise, judges are not confided in by either of the parties, so the lawyer confidentiality discussion drops out of judicial conduct discussions.

- The law governing judges comes from a wide range of sources. The ABA has adopted a ***Model Code of Judicial Conduct***.

- Conflicts of interest, in the judicial conduct context, are about impairments of a judge's impartiality rather than about impairments of loyalty to a client.

- The limits on what judges may say and do come from a source different from the loyalty to clients that drives the lawyer role limitations. Judges' limitations come largely from the public trust that is placed on judges in their central role in our justice system.

- Even more than lawyers, judges are central to the public's view of the justice system. As such, the avoidance of the appearance of impropriety notion that gets only limited respect in the analysis of lawyer conduct gets much more attention in the judicial conduct area.

I. SOURCES OF JUDICIAL CONDUCT LAW

As is true of the law governing lawyers, the law governing judges comes from a wide range of sources.

A. ABA Model Code of Judicial Conduct

Like its Model Rules of Professional Conduct and Model Code of Professional Responsibility, the ABA has adopted a ***Model Code of Judicial Conduct*** (CJC).

1. **Not directly applicable:** Like its lawyer conduct models, the CJC is not directly applicable to anyone. Rather, it becomes so when adopted by a state's legislature or court system as the applicable rules of judicial conduct for the particular jurisdiction.

2. **Two models:** The 1972 CJC was adopted by 47 states, the District of Columbia, and the United States Judicial Conference. In 1990 and 2007, respectively, the ABA adopted relatively modest revisions of the CJC. States have been switching from the earlier versions of the Model to the 2007 Model since its adoption by the ABA. As of publication, nine states have adopted

the 2007 Model, while seven states have issued committee reports on it. Eighteen states and the District of Columbia have formed committees to review the 2007 Model. References in this outline to the CJC are to the 2007 Model unless otherwise indicated.

B. Federal statutes

A few federal statutes modify the CJC in federal court, particularly as it relates to judicial disqualification procedures and standards. See §V.L.

1. **28 U.S.C. §455:** This statute is the federal analog to the CJC disqualification section.

2. **28 U.S.C. §47:** This statute prohibits an appellate judge from sitting on a case that she decided as a trial judge.

3. **28 U.S.C. §144:** This statute prohibits a judge from hearing a case in which the judge has actual bias against a party.

4. **28 U.S.C. §372:** This statute sets forth the procedure in cases of complaints against federal judges. This statute permits any person to file a complaint with the clerk's office of a federal Court of Appeals alleging that a judge sitting in the appropriate circuit has engaged in conduct that is prejudicial to the administration of justice.

C. Lawyer ethics rules

Most judges are also lawyers, and to the extent they remain relevant to the judge's role, the professional ethics rules governing lawyers apply to judges as well.

1. **General:** Some of the lawyer rules have general applicability, such as those relating to assistance with bar admissions and general licensure rules. These apply to judges who are also lawyers.

2. **Particular rules:** Some of the lawyer rules are really about judges. Model Rule 1.12, for example, governs lawyer conflicts of interest that arise when a judge leaves the bench and moves into practice. See Chapter 6, §VI.A.

D. Other sources

As with lawyer ethics rules, the Constitution, case law, and bar ethics opinions are also important sources of law.

II. WHO IS A JUDGE?

The CJC defines what it means to be a judge and also expressly identifies special rules and exemptions from the rules that apply to various categories of part-time judges. CJC, Application of the CJC.

A. General definition

Judges are officers of judicial systems who perform judicial functions, that is, decide cases. CJC, Application of CJC §I(B).

1. **Need not be a lawyer:** Although most judges are lawyers, in many state court systems, nonlawyers are judges in various lower courts. These judges, despite being nonlawyers, are governed by their states' versions of the CJC. CJC, Application of CJC §I(A).

2. Need not be called "Judge": Some people who perform the judicial function are called magistrate, referee, commissioner, special master, and other names. They are, regardless of name, judges for the purposes of the CJC if they perform judicial functions.

B. Part-time judge categories

Some who perform judicial functions do so part-time. They are subject to a variety of exemptions from the CJC.

1. Retired judge: Some retired judges are subject to recall and are not permitted to practice law. Such judges are not required to comply with Rule 3.8 (Appointments to Fiduciary Positions) at any time, and are not required to comply with Rule 3.9 (Service as Arbitrator or Mediator) except while serving as a judge. CJC, Application of CJC §II.

2. Continuing part-time judge: A continuing part-time judge "serves repeatedly on a part-time basis by election or under a continuing appointment. . . ." CJC, Application of CJC §III. Applicable CJC sections are stated in Application of CJC §III.

3. Periodic part-time judge: A periodic part-time judge serves "repeatedly on a part-time basis, but under a separate appointment for each limited period of service. . . ." CJC, Application of CJC §IV. Applicable CJC sections are stated in Application of CJC §IV.

4. Pro tempore judge: A pro tempore judge serves once or only sporadically on a part-time basis under separate appointments for each service. CJC, Application of CJC §V. Applicable CJC sections are stated in Application of CJC §V.

III. GENERAL JUDICIAL ATTRIBUTES

A. Independence

Our system of justice requires that judges and the judiciary be independent of outside influences, including those of the legislative and executive branches.

Example: Legislature has created a constitutional method for the selection of vacated judicial positions until an election can be held. An independent judicial nominating commission is created. Governor wishes to create uniform rules for these commissions. Although appointment of judicial officers and screening of nominations is an executive function, the state constitution mandates that the commissions be independent of the Governor in rulemaking for the screening of the nominations. In re Advisory Opinion to Governor, 276 So. 2d 25 (Fla. 1973).

B. Integrity

Although a lack of integrity is rarely the sole ground for imposing judicial discipline, a fundamental expectation of judges is that they have integrity. CJC Canon 1.

C. Impartiality

Most of the assumptions underlying our judicial system hinge on the impartiality of judges. See §V.A.

IV. PERSONAL CONDUCT AND ACTIVITY OUTSIDE THE JUDICIAL ROLE

Judges play the central role in our system of justice, and they even more than lawyers must maintain high standards of personal, out-of-role conduct. Public perception of judges has a significant effect on the public confidence in the justice system. As such, the notion of avoiding even the appearance of impropriety has greater force in judicial conduct law than it does in lawyer conduct law. CJC Rule 1.2 Comments.

A. Avoid impropriety and appearance of impropriety

The CJC cautions judges about engaging in conduct that "would create in reasonable minds a perception that the judge violated this Code or engaged in other conduct that reflects adversely on the judge's honesty, impartiality, temperament, or fitness to serve as a judge." CJC Rule 1.2 Comment 5. This standard is an objective one. Because the standard is so vague, clear rules of conduct are difficult to establish.

Example: Judge attended a party hosted by Acquaintance of Long-Standing. Acquaintance of Long-Standing had recently pleaded guilty and been convicted of racketeering. Approximately 200 guests attended the party. Judge was disciplined for failing to avoid the appearance of impropriety in his out-of-role activities. In re Blackman, 591 A.2d 1339 (N.J. 1991).

Example: Judge associated with prostitutes and drug dealers and smoked marijuana. Judge was suspended for one year without pay for these associations and illegal activities because they brought the judicial office into disrepute. In re Whitaker, 463 So. 2d 1291 (La. 1985).

Example: Judge owned notes and bonds issued by City. Judge had purchased these notes and bonds before taking office. A challenge to the control of the notes and bonds was pending in Judge's court. Although Judge did not participate in the decision, there was an appearance of impropriety because Judge continued to purchase City notes and bonds while the decision was pending. Judge's actions violated the Code of Judicial Conduct. Matter of Fuchsberg, 426 N.Y.S.2d 639 (1978).

Example: Judge was a trustee for University, which was negotiating with Hospital for the construction of a new building. Success of the negotiations depended on the decision in a case pending before Judge in which Hospital was being sued. Judge did not know of the conflict until after the case was decided. Actual knowledge of appearance of impropriety is not necessary to sustain violation of the Code. Judge must remedy the conflict as soon as he is aware of the conflict and should have known of the conflict with Hospital and University. Liljeberg v. Health Services Acquisition Corp., 486 U.S. 847 (1988).

Example: Judge, a married man, had a five-year affair with a married woman. Actions outside official capacity will not be grounds for discipline unless the actions exploit the judicial position or are open and inappropriate. Matter of Dalessandro, 397 A.2d 743 (Pa. 1979).

B. Comply with the law

Clearer are cases of judges' misconduct that violates law. Such misconduct violates the "comply with law" standard of the CJC. CJC Rule 1.1.

Example: Defendant was accused of "fixing" trials. Judge testified at trial that Judge had never disposed of a driving while intoxicated (DWI) charge without the presence of prosecution counsel.

Witnesses testified that Judge had conducted ex parte hearings on guilty pleas in DWI cases. Judge was convicted of knowingly making a false material declaration. The CJC states that judges should allow both parties to be heard and should not hold ex parte hearings unless necessary. Judge's statements were material to Judge's claim that no "case fixing" had occurred, and Judge's conviction was sustained. United States v. Anderson, 798 F.2d 919 (7th Cir. 1986).

Example: Judge was accused of conspiracy to conceal stolen goods, conspiracy to prevent prosecution of certain felons, participation in the planning of a burglary, knowingly receiving gifts of stolen merchandise, and procuring false affidavits. The State Bar began proceedings for disbarment. The State Bar found that the charges of conspiracy to conceal stolen goods, participation in the planning of a burglary, and procuring false affidavits were sustained by the evidence. Judge claimed that he was not a practicing attorney, so Judge could not be disbarred until no longer on the bench. Disbarment was ordered because Judge was still a member of the Bar even though currently a judge and subject to judicial discipline. In a later proceeding, Judge was removed from the bench because Judge no longer met the state's requirement that all judges be attorneys. In re Stice, 339 P.2d 29 (Kan. 1959).

1. **No conviction necessary:** A judge's contrary to law conduct need not result in a conviction before judicial discipline is imposed.

   Example: Judge admitted to substance abuse problem and voluntarily began treatment. Commission removed Judge for misconduct after considering all evidence of misconduct as a whole. The Code supports this punishment for any judge who voluntarily engages in illegal drug activity. Starnes v. Judicial Retirement Commission, 680 S.W.2d 922 (Ky. 1984).

2. **Intentional or bad faith refusal to follow precedent and other mandatory authority:** A judge can be subject to discipline for repeatedly failing to follow the law in his own decisions. In re Hague, 315 N.W.2d 524 (Mich. 1982).

C. **Preserving the prestige of the judicial office**

Judges are prohibited from lending the prestige of their offices to private interests. Using court stationery either for personal business or to advance private interests, for example, violates this principle.

Example: Judge is engaged in a dispute with Video Planet (VP) over VP's claim that the Judge forgot to return a copy of "To Kill a Mockingbird" that Judge rented and therefore owes VP $69.95. Judge writes a letter to VP on court stationery arguing that he did in fact return the tape on time. Judge's conduct violates CJC Rule 1.3(E) Comment 1.

D. **Judges as witnesses**

Because of the judge's potentially excessive influence on a fact finder, there are some limitations on the use of judges as witnesses. The limitations in fact, however, are minimal.

1. **As fact witness:** As long as the judge is not presiding over the proceeding, a judge may be called as a fact witness. In other words, the fact that a percipient witness is a judge does not affect his or her availability as a witness. The mere fact that a judge may be an influential witness is insufficient reason to excuse the judge-witness from the obligation to testify when called as a fact witness.

2. **As character witness:** A judge is prohibited from testifying as a character witness except when duly summoned. CJC Rule 3.3. A judge must be subpoenaed to obtain her presence and

testimony as a character witness. Consistent with the CJC, a judge may testify as a character witness when subpoenaed. Indeed, a judge must obey the subpoena.

E. Organizational membership

A judge is not permitted to be a member of an organization that "practices invidious discrimination on the basis of race, sex, gender, religion, national origin, ethnicity, or sexual orientation." CJC Rule 3.6(A).

F. Speaking, writing, and teaching

Within certain constraints, judges are permitted to teach, speak, and write about the law, the legal profession, and the justice system. CJC Rule 3.1 Comment 1.

1. **Pending cases:** Judges are required to be cautious in their discussion of pending cases. They must refrain from making either public or nonpublic comments that risk the fairness of the proceedings.

2. **Judicial duties take precedence:** Speaking, teaching, and writing activities must be secondary in importance to the judge's judicial responsibilities.

3. **Appearance of bias:** A judge must be careful to avoid creation of an appearance that the judge would not enforce the law or decide cases fairly.

    Example: Judge wrote editorial letters opposing the death penalty in a state that has the death penalty. Doing so may give the impression that the judge will not impose the death penalty when the law calls for its imposition in his court.

G. Government activities

Judges are permitted to engage in legislative and public hearings and to consult about legal matters with the executive or legislative branches.

H. Civic and charitable activities

"Subject to the requirements of Rule 3.1, a judge may participate in activities sponsored by . . ." not-for-profit organizations unless the organization is likely to come before the judge's court or will regularly be involved in litigation in any court. CJC Rule 3.7(A).

1. **Fundraising:** Judges may not engage in direct fundraising for such organizations, unless it is soliciting donations "from members of the judge's family, or from judges over whom the judge does not exercise supervisory or appellate authority." CJC Rule 3.7(A)(2).

I. Financial activities

Except for closely held family businesses, judges may not be director, officer, manager, partner, advisor, or employee of a business. CJC Rule 3.11(B)(1).

Example: Judge was acting in a management capacity for Real Estate Inc. In this capacity, Judge was hired as Real Estate Inc.'s lawyer, executed contracts on behalf of Real Estate Inc., and executed deeds on behalf of Real Estate Inc. For this and other misconduct, Judge was removed from office. See In re Intemann, 540 N.E.2d 236 (N.Y. 1989).

J. Fiduciary activities

Except for such services performed for family members, a judge is prohibited from serving as executor, administrator, trustee, guardian, or other fiduciary. CJC Rule 3.8(A).

Example: Judge holds a power of attorney to execute contracts and other documents on behalf of Green, who is not a member of Judge's family. Judge is subject to discipline for serving as Green's fiduciary. Georgia Ethics Advisory Opinion 80 (1986).

K. Practicing law

Full-time judges are not permitted to practice law, except for serving interests of herself or her family members, as long as she does not serve as "the family member's lawyer in any forum." CJC Rule 3.10.

L. Outside income limitations and reporting requirements

When judges are permitted to earn outside income (from teaching, writing, speaking, etc.), such income must be limited to reasonable amounts for the services rendered and must not appear to compromise the judge's integrity and impartiality.

Example: Judge is paid a $20,000 honorarium for making a speech at the annual meeting of the State Association of Wine Producers (SAWP). Ordinarily, SAWP pays a $1,000 honorarium. Judge has violated the CJC by accepting this out-of-proportion income.

1. **Gifts and favors:** Judges may not accept gifts or favors from a person whose interests are or are likely to be before the judge. Gifts that are appropriate to special occasions (wedding or anniversary, for example) are permitted.

2. **Reporting of income:** Judges must file annually as a public document a statement of the nature and amount of compensation received. CJC Rule 3.15(A).

V. JUDICIAL DUTIES

The defining characteristic of the judge is the performance of judicial duties, that is, deciding cases.

A. Impartiality

Perhaps the most central attribute of the judge's role in our justice system is impartiality. All of the other rules and assumptions flow from this central notion. See, for example, ex parte communication rules in §V.G and disqualification rules in §V.L.

Example: Traffic Judge's compensation is fixed by reference to the amount of fines that are levied against defendants (that is, the more money defendants pay in fines, the more money Traffic Judge is paid). Such an arrangement violates fundamental principles of impartiality upon which the judicial function operates. Tumey v. Ohio, 273 U.S. 510 (1927).

B. Diligence

The old saying is, "Justice delayed is justice denied." Judges are required to be diligent in the discharge of their duties. Thus, judges must process and resolve cases and motions filed in their court without unnecessary delay. CJC Rule 2.5(A).

Example: Judge was frequently absent from court, was late when attending, and was unavailable when court was not in session. Judge was removed from office for gross dereliction of duties. Starnes v. Judicial Retirement Commission, 680 S.W.2d 922 (Kan. 1984).

C. Competence

Judges must also have and maintain competence in the law and in decision-making. CJC Rule 2.5(A). In some jurisdictions, this requirement has been interpreted to require judges to attend continuing judicial education classes.

Example: In various cases, Judge did the following. Judge instructed jury at the end of a criminal trial to find the defendant guilty. (Judge claimed that this was proper if there was no contradictory evidence.) Judge ordered a DWI case to proceed even though Counsel for Defendant was unavailable for trial, and Defendant was not in the courtroom. Judge failed to advise Defendant of his right to appeal following conviction for misdemeanor. All of these actions were fundamental errors of a most egregious nature. Judge is subject to discipline for incompetence. McCullough v. Commission on Judicial Performance, 776 P.2d 259 (Cal. 1989).

D. Maintain courtroom decorum

Judges are authorized and required to maintain courtroom decorum. CJC Rule 2.8(A). This means that judges have power (the contempt power) to discipline those in their courtrooms for disruptive behavior. For example, lawyers may be removed for failure to follow a judge's rulings. The power must not, however, be abused. Judges may not, for example, remove lawyers from court simply because the judge is unhappy with the lawyer's arguments.

E. Patience

Even while maintaining courtroom decorum and disposing of the court's business diligently, a judge must exhibit patience. CJC Rule 2.8(B).

F. Avoid bias and prejudice

To remain impartial, a judge must avoid bias and prejudice. CJC Rule 2.3(A). Judges have been disciplined for a wide variety of slurs against women, Kennick v. Comm. on Judicial Performance, 787 P.2d 591 (Cal. 1990); Italian-Americans, In re Carr, 593 So. 2d 1044 (Fla. 1992); Mexican-Americans, Gonzalaes v. Comm. on Judicial Performance, 657 P.2d 372 (Cal. 1983); African-Americans, Id.; Jews, Id.; and Arabs, In the Matter of Ain, New York Comm. on Judicial Conduct, (Sept. 21, 1992). Claims by judges that they were "joking" have not been treated as a defense. Gonzalaes v. Comm. on Judicial Performance, 657 P.2d 372 (Cal. 1983).

1. **In judicial functions:** In addition to racial, gender, and ethnic biases, judges must avoid bias in favor of friends and associates and against particular causes or groups of lawyers.

    Example: Judge continued the case of a personal friend for two years and then dismissed the case without explanation. Judge is subject to discipline. McCullough v. Commission on Judicial Performance, 776 P.2d 259 (Cal. 1989).

    Example: Judge showed bias against Legal Services attorneys and criticized tenant-oriented laws. During one case, in an effort to cut off legitimate argument and presentation of evidence, Judge stated that attorney for tenant should take a look at others in the crowded courtroom and "take all the time you want." In the same case Judge said, "I resent bitterly [law school clinical students] coming in with the same defense day in and day out." Judge's actions were improper and violated the Code of Judicial Conduct. Matter of Albano, 384 A.2d 144 (N.J. 1978).

2. **Restraining lawyer bias:** In maintaining courtroom decorum and conduct, judges are required to restrain lawyer bias, although not to the extent of prohibiting legitimate argument. CJC Rule 2.3(C).

Example: To establish Witness's possible bias in favor of Defendant, Lawyer questions Witness about his and Defendant's common membership in the Aryan Nation, a white supremacist group. Lawyer also questions Witness about the tenets of the organization that dictate that its members will steal, lie, and kill for one another. If Lawyer's questioning (and later argument to the jury) on this matter is permitted by the evidence rules, Judge should not restrain Lawyer's conduct on the ground that it expresses Lawyer's prejudice against the Aryan Nation and its members.

G. Ex parte communications

An ex parte communication is a communication, whether written or oral, that involves less than all of the parties or their counsel to a matter, that is about a pending or impending matter, and that is made by or to the judge presiding in the matter. Canon 3A(4), 1972 CJC. Except in limited circumstances, judges may not engage in ex parte communications. See Chapter 8, §VI.A.

1. **Rationale:** Our adversarial justice system operates on the premise that all parties have an opportunity to be heard on all matters relevant to a case. Ex parte communications undermine the premise by affording some parties opportunities to influence the judge's decision-making in the absence of other parties.

2. **Good faith is no excuse:** Even when a judge engages in ex parte communications for good but not authorized-by-law reasons, the judge is subject to discipline.

   Example: Domestic Relations Judge engages in ex parte communications with parties' lawyers in a divorce matter because he believes that the welfare of the children will benefit from his separate one-on-one intercessions with the parties. Despite his good-faith reason for doing so, Judge is subject to discipline for violating the ex parte communication rule. In re Sturgis, 529 So. 2d 281 (Fla. 1988); In re Yaccarino, 502 A.2d 3 (N.J. 1985).

3. **Pending matter discussion presumed:** In the absence of evidence to the contrary, a private communication between a judge and a lawyer with a matter pending before the judge will be presumed to have been about the pending matter. Kennick v. Commission on Judicial Performance, 787 P.2d 591 (Cal. 1990).

4. **Timing:** A case continues to be a pending matter until its final disposition. As such, even after a trial judge has ruled, the judge is not permitted to have ex parte communications with counsel while appeals are pending.

5. **Exceptions:** The CJC permits ex parte communications in a few distinct situations.

   a. **Housekeeping matters:** Communications for scheduling or administrative purposes do not violate the ex parte communication rules, provided the judge "reasonably believes that no party will gain . . . [an] advantage [from the communication] . . . and the judge makes provision promptly to notify all other parties . . . and gives the parties an opportunity to respond." CJC Rule 2.9(A)(1).

   Example: Lawyer is attempting to schedule a motion hearing at Judge's court. Lawyer calls on the telephone, expecting to get the scheduling clerk, but Judge answers the telephone. Without referring to the subject matter of the motion or the case in general,

Lawyer asks Judge when the next possible motion hearings may be scheduled. Judge gives Lawyer three possible dates and times, and Lawyer proceeds to schedule and notice the hearing. This communication regarding a housekeeping matter does not violate the rule prohibiting ex parte communications.

Example: Judge has reached a decision on a matter that was heard as a bench trial two weeks prior. Judge calls Winning Lawyer and asks that she prepare Findings of Fact and Conclusions of Law. This communication is not a housekeeping matter, and the Judge's communication makes her subject to discipline.

b. **Disinterested experts:** Judges may consult with other judges and with disinterested experts on the law if before the consultation, the judge identifies the person to the parties and affords the parties an opportunity to respond. CJC Rule 2.9(A)(2).

Example: Judge is presiding over a case in which a thorny professional responsibility issue arises. Judge calls her former Professional Responsibility professor, outlines the issue, and asks for Professor's opinion regarding the law of Professional Responsibility. If Judge notifies the parties, informs them of Professor's name and of Professor's advice, and gives the parties an opportunity to be heard, then Judge will have obtained excellent legal advice without violating the ex parte communication rules.

c. **Court clerks:** Central to a judicial clerk's job is the giving of advice to the judge. Judges may consult with clerks about the law in the absence of the parties without restriction. Even judicial clerks, however, may not do independent fact investigation and then communicate the results to the judge. CJC Rule 2.9(A)(3).

Example: Judge's clerk went to Plaintiff's factory and observed the operation of machines that were the subject of a fact dispute between the parties. The clerk reported the results to Judge. The clerk's communication to Judge violates the ex parte communication rules. Price Bros. Co. v. Philadelphia Gear Corp., 629 F.2d 444 (6th Cir. 1980).

d. **Authorized by law:** Other law authorizes ex parte communications in various limited circumstances, such as requests for emergency temporary restraining orders (including those in spousal and child abuse cases), applications for wire taps, and when a party has been given notice of a hearing but fails to appear.

H. Public comments

Judges are prohibited from making public or private comments regarding pending matters that risk the fair outcome of the matter. CJC Rule 2.10(A).

I. Criticism of jurors

Aside from expressing appreciation of jurors' service, judges may neither compliment nor criticize jurors' decisions. CJC Rule 2.8(C).

J. Making appointments

Judges are required to make appointments that their office permits on the basis of merit and not based on nepotism or favoritism. CJC Rule 2.13(A).

K. Reporting others' misconduct

Judges have duties to report misconduct of other judges and of lawyers under certain circumstances. CJC Rule 2.15.

1. Other judges: In a duty that is roughly analogous to the lawyer's misconduct reporting duty under Model Rule 8.3, judges have obligations to report other judges' misconduct under certain circumstances. CJC Rule 2.15(A) & (C). Judges have not been particularly diligent about compliance with this mandate.

a. Permissive reporting: Judges "shall take appropriate action" (which may in the judge's discretion mean reporting misconduct) when a judge receives information that raises a "substantial likelihood that another judge" has violated the CJC. CJC Rule 2.15(C).

Example: Judge was upset about a court reorganization plan. As a form of protest, Judge distributed "Don't Give a Damn" fliers. Chief Judge became aware of Judge's behavior. This conduct may, but need not, be reported because it does not affect the administration of justice. See In re Vorhees, 739 S.W.2d 178 (Mo. 1987).

b. Mandatory reporting: A judge "shall inform the appropriate authority" when the judge has "knowledge" that another judge has committed misconduct "that raises a substantial question" about that judge's fitness for office. CJC Rule 2.15(A).

Example: Judge is presiding over pretrial matters in a criminal case. Other Judge, in a private communication, requests Judge to release the Defendant in the matter. Judge does not report this ex parte request by Other Judge. Judge is subject to discipline. See In re Gassman, determination (NY Commission on Judicial Conduct, Mar. 25, 1986).

2. Lawyers: Although judges have historically ignored this requirement, they are required to report certain lawyer misconduct as well. CJC Rule 2.15(B) & (D).

a. Permissive reporting: Judges "should take appropriate action" (which may, in the judge's discretion, mean reporting misconduct) when a judge receives information that raises a "substantial likelihood that a lawyer" has violated her state's professional ethics rules. CJC Rule 2.15(D).

b. Mandatory reporting: A judge "shall inform the appropriate authority" when the judge has "knowledge" that a lawyer has committed misconduct "that raises a substantial question" about the lawyer's honesty, trustworthiness, or fitness as a lawyer in other respects. CJC Rule 2.15(B).

Example: Lawyer offers Judge a bribe in exchange for favorable treatment in a pending case. Judge does not accept the bribe but does not report Lawyer's misconduct. Judge is subject to discipline. See In re Laurie, 84-CC#5 (Ill. Courts Commission 1985).

3. Privilege: A judge's report of misconduct is absolutely privileged from civil actions for damages.

L. Disqualification and waiver

Largely because of the motivation of the litigants, disqualification is among the most important and most litigated areas of judicial conduct. Both CJC Rule 2.11 and federal statutes govern this topic. A judge who voluntarily removes herself from hearing a matter is said to have *recused* herself. 28 U.S.C. §§47, 144, 455.

1. **Objective and subjective test:** The basic standard for judicial disqualification is an objective one. "A judge shall disqualify himself or herself [when] . . . the judge's impartiality might reasonably be questioned. . . ." CJC Rule 2.11(A). The central federal statute is similar. 28 U.S.C. §455. A judge must also, however, be subjectively free from bias.

2. **Rule of necessity:** Occasionally, an issue arises that would disqualify every judge that is sitting on a court with jurisdiction to resolve the issue. When this phenomenon occurs, the "rule of necessity" says that judges are not disqualified.

   Example: State Legislature passed changes to the state employee retirement program. The changes had a financial effect on every state court judge. A challenge was brought to the changes. State Court Judge is not disqualified from hearing the case because every state court judge would be similarly disqualified. Hughes v. Oregon, 838 P.2d 1018 (Or. 1992).

3. **Grounds for disqualification:** Beyond the general standard, a wide variety of specific categories of reasons may cause a reasonable person to question a judge's impartiality.

   a. **Bias in general:** Naturally, a judge's bias may be reason to question her impartiality. Bias, however, will be grounds for disqualification only when the bias is against a party, as opposed to the legal rules governing the case, and when the bias against a party arises from a source outside the present litigation.

      i. **Bias against what?** A judge's bias regarding the governing legal rules is insufficient to warrant disqualification. Only bias for or against a party is disqualifying.

         Example: Judge has made public statements that criticize strikes by public employees. Later, when Town Teacher's Union goes on strike, a case is filed in Judge's court that requests the teachers be ordered back to work. Judge is not disqualified in such a case by virtue of his fixed and preexisting views regarding teacher strikes. Papa v. New Haven Federation of Teachers, 444 A.2d 196 (Conn. 1982).

      ii. **Source of the bias:** When a judge becomes biased during judicial proceedings based on what happens inside the judicial proceedings, that bias is not disqualifying. Only a bias that has its source outside the judicial proceeding in question is disqualifying.

         Example: Judge becomes incensed during the proceedings at the disruptive conduct of Party and at the outrageously frivolous positions taken by Party's Lawyer. The strong dislike that Judge develops during the proceeding toward Party and Party's Lawyer is not disqualifying.

   b. **Judge's relationship to party, witness, or lawyer:** A wide variety of personal and professional relationships may cause a question to be raised regarding the judge's impartiality.

      i. **Family:** A judge is disqualified when the judge's spouse or a "person within the third degree of relationship" is a party, a lawyer, or a material witness in a matter. CJC Rule 2.11(A)(2). A "person within the third degree of relationship" is a great-grandparent, grandparent, parent, uncle, aunt, brother, sister, child, grandchild, great-grandchild, nephew, or niece. CJC, Terminology.

         Example: Construction Company agreed to binding arbitration with District Union over delinquent contributions. Arbitrator was the son of the Vice-President of International Union. The father-son relationship between Arbitrator and Vice-President denied

Construction Company impartiality. Morelite Construction Corp. v. New York City District Counsel Carpenters Benefits Fund, 748 F.2d 79 (2d Cir. 1984).

ii. **Law clerks:** Except in unusual circumstances, a judge is not disqualified when a judge's former law clerk or intern represents a party. When the former clerk was a clerk during the early stages of the same matter before the court and later undertook representation of a party in the matter, or when the clerk or intern was simultaneously working for the court and in practice with a firm representing a party in a matter pending before the court, disqualification should result. Fredonia Broadcasting Corp. v. RCA, 569 F.2d 251 (5th Cir. 1978); Simonson v. General Motors, 425 F. Supp. 574 (E.D. Pa. 1976).

iii. **Campaign supporters:** A judge is not per se disqualified when an ordinary judicial election campaign contributor of the judge is a party or a lawyer in a matter, although the contributions are relevant to the disqualification analysis. Nathanson v. Korvick, 577 So. 2d 943 (Fla. 1991). This analysis focuses on the size of the contribution compared to "the total amount of money contributed to the campaign, the total amount spent in the election, and the apparent effect such contribution had on the outcome of the election," with particular attention given to the timing of the contribution, the judge's election, and the pendency of the case. If a contribution appears to create a serious risk of actual bias, the judge must recuse himself, regardless of whether or not actual bias is proven. Caperton v. Massey Coal Co., No. 08-22, 2009 U.S. LEXIS 4157 (2009). The judge is automatically disqualified, however, when the judge's campaign coordinator or a campaign committee member is a party or lawyer in a matter. MacKenzie v. Super Kids Bargain Store, 565 So. 2d 1332 (Fla. 1990).

iv. **Social relationships:** Only rather close social relationships between judge and party, lawyer, or material witness are disqualifying. Ordinarily, a judge can be expected to put all but the closest social relationships aside when exercising the judicial function.

v. **Former practice associates:** Ordinarily, judges may hear cases in which one of the parties is represented by the judge's former law partners and other associates in practice. When the judge was associated with the lawyer during the pendency of the action, however, the judge is disqualified. See §c.ii.

c. **Judge's prior relationship to the matter:** Judges may have prior relationships to the matter before them as well as to the parties and lawyers.

i. **Judge was the lawyer:** When the judge was formerly a lawyer on the same or a substantially related matter, the judge is disqualified. Sharp v. Howard County, 607 A.2d 545 (Md. App. 1992).

ii. **Judge formerly associated with the lawyer:** When the judge was associated with one of the lawyers while the lawyer was representing the party in the same or a substantially related matter, the judge is disqualified. CJC Rule 2.11(A)(6)(a).

iii. **Judge is a material witness:** When a judge has been a material witness in a matter, the judge is disqualified. CJC Rule 2.11(A)(6)(c).

iv. **Prior personal knowledge of disputed facts:** When a judge has prior personal knowledge of disputed evidentiary facts regarding the matter, the judge is disqualified. CJC Rule 2.11(A)(1).

d. Economic interest: A judge is disqualified from hearing the matter when she has more than a de minimis (very small) economic interest in the outcome of the matter.

Example: Plaintiff filed case for bad-faith denial of insurance claim. After several appeals, the State Supreme Court affirmed (5-4) the granting of punitive damages even though a partial payment had been made. The State Supreme Court decision was authored by Judge, who had filed as plaintiff two other cases that were similar to the case filed by Plaintiff. The change in the law instituted by the State Supreme Court affected the decisions in the cases filed by Judge. Judge's interest was direct, personal, substantial, and economic, and Judge had, in essence, acted as a judge in his or her own case. Aetna Life Insurance Co. v. Lavoie, 475 U.S. 813 (1986).

   i. **Type of interest:** The disqualifying interest under this rule must be economic; it may be in either the subject matter of the controversy or a party to the proceeding. CJC Rule 2.11(A)(3).

   Example: Judge owns a one-third interest in Corporation. Corporation is a party to a matter in Judge's court. Judge has more than a de minimis economic interest in one of the parties and is therefore disqualified.

   Example: Judge is presiding over a case in which the legal issue involves the legality of subdividing a piece of property. Judge owns a similar piece of property that he would like to subdivide. Judge's ruling will create a precedent for the treatment of his own property. Judge owns more than a de minimis economic interest in the subject matter of the case and is therefore disqualified. See In re Zoarski, Memorandum of decision (Conn. Judicial Review Council, Apr. 17, 1991).

   ii. **By whom and in what capacity held:** The disqualifying interest may be held by the judge personally or as a fiduciary, by a member of the judge's family residing in the judge's household, or by the judge's spouse or a person within the third degree of relationship to the judge.

   iii. **How affected:** The interest must be one that "could be substantially affected by the proceeding." However large the interest might be, minor or highly speculative effects on it are not disqualifying. CJC Rule 2.11(A)(2)(c).

   Example: Judge owns a substantial number of stocks in Steel Manufacturing Corp. (SMC). SMC makes steel for numerous purposes and customers, one of which is Bus Manufacturing Corp. (BMC). BMC sells buses to local transit authorities across the country, including Local Transit Authority (LTA). Pending in Judge's court is a negligence action filed against LTA by Passenger. If Passenger prevails, LTA will be required to pay a large judgment to Passenger. Paying a large judgment to Passenger will make it less likely that LTA will go forward with plans to buy new buses from BMC this year, which will in turn mean that BMC will buy slightly less steel from SMC this year, and might conceivably have a small effect on the value of Judge's stock in SMC. This sort of speculative, small effect on Judge's interest in the proceeding is not disqualifying.

   iv. **Magnitude of interest:** A de minimis (very small) interest in the subject matter or a party to the proceeding is not disqualifying. CJC Rule 2.11(A)(2)(c).

Example: Judge owns one share of common stock worth $30 in Corporate Party. Corporate Party is a defendant in a proceeding in Judge's court. The Judge's interest in Corporate Party is de minimis and therefore not disqualifying.

v. Knowledge: Only those interests that are known to the judge are disqualifying, but a judge has a duty to keep informed about the judge's and his or her spouse's and minor children's economic interests. When an otherwise disqualifying interest is divested immediately upon discovery, a judge is permitted to continue to preside. CJC Rule 2.11(A)(3), Rule 2.11(B), Rule 2.11(C). The judge also has a duty to make reasonable efforts to be informed of the economic interests of family members.

Example: Judge presided over a case for three years. After issuing a declaratory judgment, Judge discovered that he owned stock in the parent company of Defendant. Judge immediately divested himself of the stock. If interest is divested upon discovery, Judge may continue to preside over the matter. Kidder, Peabody & Co., Inc. v. Maxus Energy Corp., 925 F.2d 556 (2d Cir. 1991).

4. Remittal (waiver) of disqualification: Most sources of disqualification can be waived by the parties, permitting the judge to continue in the matter, provided the appropriate procedures are followed. CJC Rule 2.11(C); 28 U.C.S. §455.

a. CJC: Under the CJC, parties may not waive the judge's personal bias regarding a party. They may waive any other form of disqualification.

b. Federal law: Under 28 U.S.C §455, the parties may waive disqualification only when it follows from the general standard, that is, when the judge's "impartiality might reasonably be questioned." They may not waive any of the more specific reasons for disqualification, including personal bias regarding a party, personal knowledge of disputed facts, prior service as a lawyer in the matter, financial interest, or family interests. Thus, disqualification is less waivable under federal law than under the CJC.

c. Procedure: For the waiver to be effective, the judge must disclose the nature of the disqualifying interest on the record, and the parties must all agree, without the participation of the judge, that the judge should continue in the matter. If the judge is willing to continue under those circumstances, then she may do so after incorporating the parties' agreement into the record. CJC Rule 2.11(C).

VI. POLITICAL ACTIVITIES

Judges must maintain a separation from the give and take of politics. As a result, a variety of restrictions on the political activities of judges and judicial candidates exist. CJC Canon 4.

A. In general

Because states have so many varied systems for selecting judges, including a variety of appointive and elective systems, the CJC drafters suggest that jurisdictions choose from among the CJC provisions as may be appropriate to the particular jurisdiction's systems. As a result, the CJC provisions are in some respects internally inconsistent. Some general points may be made nonetheless.

B. Restrictions on judges and candidates of all types

Both judges and candidates are prohibited from the following activities.

1. **Political leadership:** Lead, hold office in, or make speeches for political organizations.

2. **Public endorsement or opposition:** Publicly endorse or oppose candidates for office.

3. **Solicitation of funds:** Solicit funds for or contribute to political organizations.

C. Restrictions on judges

A judge is required to resign from judicial office when the judge becomes a candidate for a nonjudicial office.

D. Restrictions on candidates

Candidates must maintain the dignity of the judicial office they seek and refrain from making promises or pledges other than to faithfully and impartially discharge the judicial function. This provision's constitutional status is in doubt. Although not specifically addressing the "pledges and promises" clause, the Supreme Court, in Republican Party of Minnesota v. White, 122 S. Ct. 2528 (2002), held that Minnesota's CJC violated the First Amendment by prohibiting judicial candidates from speaking publicly about their views on legal and political issues.

VII. LIABILITY FOR CIVIL WRONGS COMMITTED

When judges engage in the core judicial function of deciding cases, they are absolutely immune from civil damage suits. This immunity is needed to protect judges from fear of retaliation for difficult decisions. If a judge could be sued for judicial decisions, there might be no end to the cases in which judges would be required to fully defend, and the judicial function would be damaged.

A. Immunity for judicial action

Even when a judge errs in judicial decision-making, the judge is immune from damage actions. Pierson v. Ray, 386 U.S. 547 (1967). The immunity does not extend beyond the judicial function. For example, judges may be liable for negligence in driving their automobiles, for breach of contract when they fail to make the installment payments on their CD players, and so on.

B. Administrative actions

Administrative actions by judges also fall outside the protection of absolute judicial immunity.

Example: Judge appointed Probation Officer. Two years later, Judge promoted Officer. A year later, Judge fired Officer. Officer charged that the firing was based on gender discrimination in violation of Title VII. Judge claimed absolute immunity for decisions. Although there is immunity for judicial decisions, decisions of an administrative nature do not receive the same protection. The decision to fire Officer was an administrative one, and Judge does not have absolute immunity from tort suit for this decision. Forrester v. White, 484 U.S. 219 (1988).

Quiz Yourself on
JUDICIAL CONDUCT

108. Judge is accused of trying to bribe someone in a matter wholly unrelated to his judicial functions. An abundance of evidence substantiates the charge. Nonetheless, no criminal charges are brought against Judge. Is judge correct in his belief that because no criminal charges were brought, he will not lose his position on the bench? _____

109. Alice's neighbor, Bob, is a judge. One evening, someone breaks into Alice's house. Bob remembers seeing someone suspicious on the street earlier in the evening. Bob volunteers to testify to the approximate time he spotted the shady character, as well as to the prowler's appearance. Does Bob's conduct violate the CJC? _____

110. Judge Smith's docket is getting a little bit backed up. In fact, he has cases that are three months behind where they should be. Judge Smith realizes that part of the reason he's behind is that he has had to end his court sessions early three days a week to be on time for a course he teaches at the nearby university. He prefers teaching to being a judge, but realizes it's important to maintain his status as a judge, because the university gives special consideration to this status and pays him two and a half times the average teaching salary. What, if any, rules have been violated? _____

111. Attorney Carl is trying a case in Judge Douglas's court. Carl and Judge Douglas run into each other one evening while each is dining alone. Carl does not join the judge's table, but he does stop by and talk for approximately 20 minutes. A party on the opposite side of the case is present at the restaurant and witnesses the discussion. If neither Carl nor Judge Douglas is willing to testify that he was not discussing the case, will the judge be considered to have violated a rule of conduct? _____

112. Judge Amy and Judge Brenda are friends who both belong to the local country club. Amy has lately heard some disturbing rumors around the club about Brenda, specifically, that Brenda took a bribe to acquit a wealthy white-collar criminal defendant. The rumors come from very reliable sources. Amy has no direct evidence, but she does notice that Brenda has been avoiding her and suddenly began living in a fairly ostentatious manner several months ago. Amy knows their judges' salaries would not support such a lifestyle. What are her duties in terms of reporting Brenda? _____

113. While a judge's chambers are being redecorated, he is forced to use the public restrooms down the hall. One day, he accidentally overhears a last-minute emergency meeting between the attorney and criminal defendant presently before his court. The judge hears the attorney discussing his participation with the client in an attempt to bribe and/or coerce members of his client's jury. What are the judge's reporting requirements? _____

114. Judge has an old friend from childhood who is charged with criminal conduct in a case pending in Judge's court. Judge and his friend see each other often, keep in frequent contact, and consider themselves close. Judge honestly believes, however, that despite this friendship, he can remain neutral. His higher duty, he understands, is to uphold the law. Is the Judge correct in deciding that he need not disqualify himself? _____

115. Local Democratic party leaders approach Judge about running for the state senate. It is a fairly small state, and Judge's popularity assures that she will have to invest only a small amount of time and effort on the campaign. For almost the entire timetable of the campaign, she foresees no effect on her judicial duties. For how long may she remain on the bench? _____

116. Judge presides over a complex civil suit that takes several weeks to try. The issues are very difficult, and although her law clerks work overtime to keep her current and knowledgeable, she is struggling with this unfamiliar area of the law. In the end, she applies an incorrect legal standard, wrongly causing B to prevail over A. The appeals court overturns the judge's decision, noting the judge's error. What action can A bring against the judge to recover the costs of the appeal? _____

117. Judge owns stock in BIG Manufacturing Corp (BMC). The value of his shares is approximately $500, and BMC is a large Fortune 500 company. BMC is sued in tort by a plaintiff who claims to have been injured while visiting one of BMC's job sites. The plaintiff is asking for $34,000 in damages. Should the judge be disqualified for hearing the case? _____

118. Judge has in the past made statements condemning the current laws that offer too little protection for abortion clinics from their vigorous protestors. Now, several abortion protest defendants are to appear in Judge's court. Should Judge be disqualified? _____

119. Judge is presiding over a case against BCD Corporation. The case involves a sexual harassment claim against BCD and several of its former high-level managers. While the judge was still in private practice, one of his fellow attorneys at a law firm litigated a matter against BCD in a completely unrelated labor dispute over wages. BCD argues that the judge should be disqualified because of his former associations. Are they correct? _____

120. Prosecutor, using proper procedures through the clerk's office, rescheduled a matter pending before Volatile Judge. The rescheduling upset Judge because Judge had made other plans for the newly scheduled date. Volatile Judge left a vulgar message on Prosecutor's voice mail expressing anger over the rescheduling. The judge's message, in part: "I did not appreciate that one f***ing bit. And if I find out you ever did that again to me or any other members of the county court bench, I'll shove it up your a** so far it will make your throat hurt." _____

Answers

108. No. No conviction or criminal charge is necessary to support judicial discipline. There is sufficient evidence that the judge's conduct was contrary to law. There would be special concern about the judge's fitness for office because the charges are directly related to the judge's integrity and honesty.

109. No. A judge is permitted to be a fact witness, as long as the judge is not presiding in the matter. Had the testimony concerned Alice's character, Bob could not have testified voluntarily, but instead would have to be induced by a subpoena.

110. Several rules are implicated here. CJC Rule 2.5(A) requires diligence in judicial proceedings. Judges are also limited to only a "reasonable amount" of outside income, and the judge's large outside salary may be problematic with this standard. Finally, judicial duties must take precedence over other commitments that a judge undertakes. CJC Rule 2.1.

111. Yes. CJC Rule 2.9(A) prohibits judges from engaging in ex parte communications. Moreover, absent evidence to the contrary, their conversation will be presumed to be about the pending matter.

112. Amy should be held to a permissive reporting standard. That is, she "should" take appropriate action, which allows her discretion in whether to report or not. Because this involves permissive and not mandatory reporting, Amy could take other forms of action, such as confronting Brenda in an effort to resolve the matter.

113. The judge has a mandatory requirement to report the attorney's conduct. CJC Rule 2.15(B). The judge "shall" inform the disciplinary authorities when he has knowledge that a lawyer committed misconduct that raises a "substantial question" about the lawyer's honesty, trustworthiness, or fitness as a lawyer.

114. No. Under CJC Rule 2.11(A)(1), the standard in this case has both an objective and a subjective element. Therefore, regardless of the judge's individual belief in his neutrality, he must disqualify himself when his impartiality might reasonably be questioned by an objective observer.

115. The judge may not remain on the bench for any length of time. The judge is required to resign when she becomes a candidate for any nonjudicial office.

116. A cannot bring any action against the judge. Judges are absolutely immune from civil damage suits when engaging in their core judicial functions. The immunity covers the judge even when there is an error in decision-making.

117. The judge probably does not need to be disqualified. His interest in the company is small, and any possible harm to the value of his shares is both speculative and negligible in amount.

118. No. The judge's statements in the past concerned the general legal rule, and not the parties themselves. Bias is grounds for disqualification only when directed at a specific party, as opposed to the legal rules governing the case.

119. No. Normally, a judge is disqualified for personal representation of or against a party in his courtroom. CJC Rule 2.11(A)(6)(a). However, the prior representation must have taken place in the same or a substantially related matter. Here, the two matters are wholly unrelated, causing no conflict.

120. Judges are often said to rule over their fiefdoms, but this foulness goes far beyond propriety. Volatile Judge is subject to discipline for his outburst. The matter is made clearer still because it happened in a phone message. Judge had time to contemplate his communication and still went far beyond abusiveness.

Exam Tips on JUDICIAL CONDUCT

- The Multistate Professional Responsibility Exam typically devotes 10 to 15% of its questions to judicial conduct. Some Professional Responsibility teachers attempt to mirror this ratio.

- Disqualification and waiver are the prime topics for judicial conduct questions.

- Judicial conduct law is fundamentally different from lawyer conduct law because the judge and lawyer roles are fundamentally different. For example, judges are neutrals, not partisans, so the

- lawyer's duty of loyalty to a client is simply not a part of a judicial conduct discussion. Likewise, judges are not confided in by either of the parties, so the lawyer confidentiality discussion drops out of judicial conduct discussions.

- The law governing judges comes from a wide range of sources.

  - The ABA has adopted a *Model Code of Judicial Conduct* (CJC). Like its lawyer conduct models, the CJC is not directly applicable to anyone. Rather, it becomes so when adopted by a state's legislature or court system as the applicable rules of judicial conduct for the particular jurisdiction.

  - Most judges are also lawyers and to the extent they remain relevant to the judge's role, the professional ethics rules governing lawyers apply to judges as well.

- Although a lack of integrity is rarely the sole ground for imposing judicial discipline, a fundamental expectation of judges is that they have integrity. CJC Canon 1.

- Most of the assumptions underlying our judicial system hinge on the impartiality of judges.

- Public perception of judges has a significant effect on the public confidence in the justice system. As such, the notion of avoiding even the *appearance of impropriety* has greater force in judicial conduct law than it does in lawyer conduct law. CJC Rule 1.2 Comments.

- Judges' misconduct that violates law violates the "comply with law" standard of the CJC. CJC Rule 1.1.

- A judge's contrary to law conduct need not result in a conviction before judicial discipline is imposed.

- A judge can be subject to discipline for repeatedly failing to follow the law in his own decisions.

- Judges are prohibited from lending the prestige of their offices to private interests.

- Because of the judge's potentially excessive influence on a fact finder, there are some limitations on the use of judges as witnesses. The limitations, in fact, however, are minimal. As long as the judge is not presiding over the proceeding, a judge may be called as a fact witness. A judge is prohibited from voluntarily testifying as a character witness. CJC Rule 3.3. A judge must be subpoenaed to obtain her presence and testimony as a character witness.

- A judge is not permitted to be a member of an organization that "practices invidious discrimination on the basis of race, sex, religion or national origin." CJC Rule 3.6(A).

- Within certain constraints, judges are permitted to teach, speak, and write about the law, the legal profession, and the justice system. CJC Rule 3.1 Comment 1.

- Judges are required to be cautious in their discussion of pending cases. They must refrain from making either public or nonpublic comments that risk the fairness of the proceedings.

- "Subject to the requirements of Rule 3.1, a judge may participate in activities sponsored by . . ." not-for-profit organizations unless the organization would be likely to come before the judge's court or will regularly be involved in litigation in any court. CJC Rule 3.7(A)(2). Judges may not engage in direct fundraising for such organizations, unless it is soliciting donations "from members of the judge's family, or from judges over whom the judge does not exercise supervisory or appellate authority." CJC Rule 3.7(A)(2).

- Except for such services performed for family members, a judge is prohibited from serving as executor, administrator, trustee, guardian, or other fiduciary. CJC Rule 3.8(A).

- Full-time judges are not permitted to practice law, except for serving interests of herself or her family members, as long as she does not serve as "the family member's lawyer in any forum." CJC Rule 3.10.

- When judges are permitted to earn outside income (teaching, writing, speaking, etc.), such income must be limited to reasonable amounts for the services rendered and must not appear to compromise the judge's integrity and impartiality.

- Judges may not accept gifts or favors from a person whose interests are or are likely to be before the judge. Gifts that are appropriate to special occasions (wedding or anniversary, for example) are permitted.

- Perhaps the most central attribute of the judge's role in our justice system is impartiality. All of the other rules and assumptions flow from this central notion.

- Judges are required to be diligent in the discharge of their duties. CJC Rule 2.5(A).

- Judges must also have and maintain competence in the law and decision-making. CJC Rule 2.5(A).

- Judges are authorized and required to maintain courtroom decorum. CJC Rule 2.8(A). Watch for fact patterns with out-of-control lawyers. In maintaining courtroom decorum and conduct, judges are required to restrain lawyer bias, though not to the extent of prohibiting legitimate argument. CJC Rule 2.3(C).

- To remain impartial, a judge must avoid bias and prejudice. CJC Rule 2.3(A).

- Except in limited circumstances, judges may not engage in ex parte communications. When ex parte communications occur, discuss both the lawyer's and judge's misconduct.

    - In the absence of evidence to the contrary, a private communication between a judge and a lawyer with a matter pending before the judge will be presumed to have been about the pending matter.

    - A case continues to be a pending matter until its final disposition. As such, even after a trial judge has ruled, the judge is not permitted to have ex parte communications with counsel while appeals are pending.

    - The CJC permits ex parte communications in a few distinct situations.

        - Communications for scheduling or administrative purposes do not violate the ex parte communication rules provided the judge "reasonably believes that no party will gain . . . [an] advantage [from the communication] . . . and the judge makes provision promptly to notify all other parties . . . and gives the parties an opportunity to respond." CJC Rule 2.9(A)(1).

        - Judges may consult with other judges and with disinterested experts on the law if, before the consultation, the judge identifies the person to the parties and affords the parties an opportunity to respond. CJC Rule 2.9(A)(2).

        - Judges may consult with clerks about the law in the absence of the parties without restriction. Even judicial clerks, however, may not do independent fact investigation and then communicate the results to the judge. CJC Rule 2.9(A)(3).

- ☞ Other law authorizes ex parte communications in various, limited circumstances, such as requests for emergency temporary restraining orders.

☛ Judges are prohibited from making public or private comments regarding pending matters that risk the fair outcome of the matter. CJC Rule 2.10(A).

☛ Aside from expressing appreciation of jurors' service, judges may neither compliment nor criticize jurors' decisions. CJC Rule 2.8(C).

☛ Judges have an obligation to report other judges' misconduct under certain circumstances. CJC Rule 2.15(A) & (C).

- ☞ Judges "should take appropriate action" (which may in the judge's discretion mean reporting misconduct) when a judge receives information that raises a "substantial likelihood that another judge" has violated the CJC. CJC Rule 2.15(C).

- ☞ A judge "shall inform the appropriate authority" when the judge "has knowledge" that another judge has committed misconduct "that raises a substantial question" about that judge's fitness for office. CJC Rule 2.15(A).

☛ Judges are required to report certain lawyer misconduct as well. CJC Rule 2.15(B) & (D).

- ☞ Judges "should take appropriate action" (which may in the judge's discretion mean reporting misconduct) when a judge receives information that raises a "substantial likelihood that a lawyer" has violated her state's professional ethics rules.

- ☞ A judge "shall inform the appropriate authority" when the judge "has knowledge" that a lawyer has committed misconduct "that raises a substantial question" about the lawyer's honesty, trustworthiness, or fitness as a lawyer in other respects.

- ☞ A judge's report of misconduct is absolutely privileged from civil actions for damages.

☛ Disqualification is among the most important and most litigated areas of judicial conduct. Both CJC Rule 2.11 and federal statutes govern this topic. A judge who voluntarily removes herself from hearing a matter is said to have **recused** herself. 28 U.S.C. §§47, 144, 455.

- ☞ The basic standard for judicial disqualification is an objective one. "A judge shall disqualify himself or herself [when] the judge's impartiality might reasonably be questioned. . . ." CJC Rule 2.11(A). The central federal statute is similar. 28 U.S.C. §455. However, a judge also must be subjectively free from bias.

- ☞ Occasionally, an issue arises that would disqualify every judge that is sitting on a court with jurisdiction to resolve the issue. When this phenomenon occurs, the ***"rule of necessity"*** says that judges are not disqualified.

- ☞ Naturally, a judge's bias may be reason to question her impartiality. Bias, however, will be grounds for disqualification only when the bias is against a party as opposed to the legal rules governing the case, and when the bias against a party arises from a source outside the present litigation.

- ☞ A wide variety of personal and professional relationships may cause a question to be raised regarding the judge's impartiality.

- ☞ When the judge was formerly a lawyer on the same or a substantially related matter, the judge is disqualified.

- When the judge was associated with one of the lawyers while the lawyer was representing the party in the same or a substantially related matter, the judge is disqualified. CJC Rule 2.11(A)(6)(a).

  - When a judge has been a material witness in a matter, the judge is disqualified. CJC Rule 2.11(A)(6)(c).

  - When a judge has prior personal knowledge of disputed evidentiary facts regarding the matter, the judge is disqualified. CJC Rule 2.11(A)(1).

  - A judge is disqualified from hearing the matter when she has more than a de minimis (very small) economic interest in the outcome of the matter.

  - The disqualifying interest under this rule must be economic; it may be in either the subject matter of the controversy or in a party to the proceeding. CJC Rule 2.11(A)(3).

  - The disqualifying interest may be held by the judge personally or as a fiduciary or by a member of the judge's family residing in the judge's household or by the judge's spouse or a person within the third degree of relationship to the judge.

  - The interest must be one that "could be substantially affected by the proceeding."

  - However large the interest might be, minor or highly speculative effects on it are not disqualifying. CJC Rule 2.11(A)(2)(c).

  - A de minimis (very small) interest in the subject matter or a party to the proceeding is not disqualifying. CJC Rule 2.11(A)(2)(c).

  - Only those interests that are known to the judge are disqualifying, but a judge has a duty to keep informed about the judge's and the judge's spouse and minor children's economic interests. CJC Rule 2.11(A)(3), 2.11(B), 2.11(C). The judge also has a duty to make reasonable efforts to be informed of the economic interests of family members.

- Most sources of disqualification can be waived by the parties and the judge permitted to continue in the matter, provided the appropriate procedures are followed. CJC Rule 2.11(C); 28 U.C.S. §455.

  - Under the CJC, parties may not waive the judge's personal bias regarding a party. They may waive any other form of disqualification.

  - Under 28 U.S.C. §455, the parties may waive disqualification when it follows only from the general standard, that is, when the judge's "impartiality might reasonably be questioned." They may not waive any of the more specific reasons for disqualification. For the waiver to be effective, the judge must disclose the nature of the disqualifying interest on the record, and the parties must all agree on the record, without the participation of the judge, that the judge should continue in the matter. CJC Rule 2.11(C).

☛ When judges engage in the core judicial function of deciding cases, they are absolutely immune from civil damage suits. Even when a judge errs in judicial decision-making, the judge is immune from damage actions. The immunity does not extend beyond the judicial function. Administrative actions by judges also fall outside the protection of absolute judicial immunity.

Essay Exam Questions

QUESTION 1: Several employees of Microchips Incorporated filed a class-action suit against Microchips for gender discrimination. Darlene DeLesio, an attorney in Microchip's in-house legal department, began to work on the defense of the suit. In the course of her preparation, DeLesio obtained information from Microchips about its personnel practices. As DeLesio explained later, "I obtained specific information from the personnel department concerning salaries and hiring practices.... I participated in a conference with outside consultants hired by the corporation to prepare statistical information regarding employment. I obtained intraoffice memoranda . . . regarding the case."

DeLesio decided not only that the plaintiffs had a good case against Microchips, but also that she herself had been the victim of gender discrimination by Microchips. She elected to join the very class-action suit against Microchips that she had been preparing to defend. Accordingly, DeLesio asked the plaintiffs' counsel to represent her, and she resigned from her position at Microchips.

Plaintiffs' counsel agreed to represent DeLesio, and she joined the litigation as a plaintiff. Microchips' new counsel then moved the court to disqualify plaintiffs' counsel, alleging a conflict of interest. Should the motion be granted? Explain. Is DeLesio subject to discipline for her conduct?

For a discussion of the issues raised, see Hull v. Celanese Corp., 375 F. Supp. 922 (S.D.N.Y. 1974), *aff'd,* 513 F.2d 568 (2d Or. 1974).

QUESTION 2: During a recess from trial, Defense Counsel (DC) finds Potential Witness (PW) in the courthouse lobby. PW is a friend of Defendant, who has said that he witnessed the crime and that Defendant was not present and therefore could not have committed the crime. PW says to DC, "When it's my turn, I know what to do. I'll stick with the story just the way I told it to you." DC responds, "You must tell the truth." A discussion ensues, during which DC comes to believe that PW's favorable story for Defendant is false and that PW intends to commit perjury. DC says, "You're not doing your friend any favors. I won't call you as a witness."

Unnoticed by DC, Prosecutor has overheard her last comments to PW. Prosecutor, misinterpreting the comments, now believes that PW would testify to a version of the events that favors the government and that DC was berating PW in an effort to persuade PW to testify falsely for the Defendant.

Trial is resumed moments later, and Prosecutor calls PW as his witness. Much to Prosecutor's chagrin, PW testifies to the Defendant-favoring version of the events that DC believes is false. DC does not cross-examine PW, and PW is excused. Trial continues to a conclusion with no more mention of PW.

Is Prosecutor subject to discipline? Is Defense Counsel subject to discipline? Both? Neither?

QUESTION 3: Defendant has been convicted of capital murder and his direct appeals have been completed. Now his new lawyers are preparing to file a habeas petition. As part of the lawyers' investigation, they seek to interview jurors from the trial. Defendant's lawyers are careful to tell the jurors who they are and whom they represent. Trial Prosecutor learns that Defendant's lawyers are contacting the trial jurors and sends each juror a letter telling the jurors not to cooperate with Defendant's lawyers, but instead to contact Trial Prosecutor's office to report any attempts at contact made by Defendant's lawyers.

Are any of the attorneys involved subject to discipline?

Essay Exam Answers

SAMPLE ANSWER TO QUESTION 1:

Because of her work as a lawyer for Microchips, Ms. DeLesio has both a continuing duty of loyalty to Microchips and confidential information of Microchips, her former client. These two realities drive the analysis of her possible discipline and the disqualification of her new lawyer.

When a court considers a motion to disqualify, it will consider a range of interests beyond the usual policies of the conflicts rules. For example, the equities of the motion's timing, the interest of the opposing party in having counsel of choice, and judicial economy will be factors. Here, the equities probably favor Microchips. It does not appear that Microchips has delayed the motion to gain a litigation advantage, the case is at a relatively early stage, so substituting new Plaintiff's counsel is unlikely to result in substantial delay, and there is no indication that Plaintiff's counsel somehow screened Ms. DeLesio. (As a plaintiff rather than a new lawyer, screening her may have been impossible in any event.)

In some sense, Ms. D is like a lawyer switching sides. It is as if she has represented one side in litigation and then switched to represent the other side. If she is viewed this way, she would clearly be disqualified from representing Plaintiffs herself. Her association with Plaintiffs' counsel could result in her disqualification imputing to Plaintiffs' counsel, thus disqualifying them as well. Such a gross conflict (a lawyer switching sides in the same litigation) would not be waivable. Even though some respect should be paid to client autonomy, allowing clients to waive most conflicts by giving informed consent, some gross conflicts such as this one are not waivable. Even if this conflict were waivable, waiver in this instance is beyond imagining. The affected client is Microchips. Far from being amenable to giving a waiver, Microchips is moving to have Plaintiffs' counsel disqualified (i.e., have the effects of the conflict enforced).

It is true that she is not really switching sides as a lawyer, but rather, has gone from being a lawyer for one side to being a party on the other side. The lawyer-implicated result is much the same, however. The confidences of her former client will presumably be revealed to the other side in the litigation. The key question (discussed below) may be whether she is permitted to reveal Microchips' confidences. If so, then she will not be subject to discipline for revealing confidences and the conflicts implications will be much reduced.

She might argue that she is not revealing confidences of Microchips in her role as lawyer, but rather, as a private person. That argument is unavailing. She gained the confidences as a lawyer. She had access to the information only because of her work for Microchips as its lawyer. A lawyer's duty of confidentiality does not stop when the lawyer is not acting as a lawyer. Rather, it stays with the lawyer when the lawyer goes out to dinner with friends or makes business decisions. A lawyer may not use confidences of a client to disadvantage the client. MR 1.8(b). That duty applies even after the lawyer-client relationship has ended. This prohibition would, for example, keep a lawyer from using confidences of a client to buy property adjacent to property the client plans to buy and develop. Again, the client can waive this prohibition, but surely Microchips is not inclined to waive in these circumstances. Here, Ms. D is using Microchips' confidences to disadvantage Microchips and advantage herself.

A better argument for Ms. D might be an analogy to the duty of confidentiality exception for self-defense and fee collection. A lawyer may reveal a client's confidences to the extent reasonably necessary to collect the lawyer's fee, or to self-defend against charges (criminal, disciplinary, or civil) against the lawyer. Here, Ms. D is using Microchips' confidences not to collect her fee, but to enforce employment rights against Microchips. Ms. D was not only Microchips' lawyer, but also its employee. She is entitled to pursue lawful claims against her former employer as any other employee would. The only way for her to pursue those lawful claims is to use her former client's confidences. The policies favoring her are essentially the same as in the case of the lawyer using confidences to collect her fee or self-defend. A client's wrongdoing (failing to pay a fee or bringing wrongful claims against a lawyer) ought not to be advantaged by protection of confidences that might undo the wrongful conduct. Here, Ms. D believes she was the target of gender discrimination by Microchips. Microchips ought not to be advantaged in defending against such charges by being able to enforce the confidentiality rules against the victim (Ms. D) of its misconduct.

The self-defense exception ought to apply to allow Ms. D to pursue her claim. This exception, however, permits only so much revelation of confidences as reasonably necessary to self-defend. As such, Ms. D could not use Microchips' confidences to assist the other plaintiffs. If she has revealed to Plaintiffs' counsel broader information than necessary to pursue her own case, then she is subject to discipline. As well, because of the extreme difficulties of determining or monitoring the measure of information she has or would in the future reveal to Plaintiffs' counsel, she should not be permitted to join the plaintiffs' case, and Plaintiffs' counsel should be disqualified from continuing in the matter. Ms. D may retain her own counsel and pursue her claim using only such information as necessary to pursue her own claim. Cooperation with Plaintiffs' counsel, revealing Microchips' confidences to them, would subject her to discipline.

SAMPLE ANSWER TO QUESTION 2:

The central issues here involve the possibility that PW has committed perjury. Neither DC nor Prosecutor has knowingly offered false testimony. DC may have a duty to report PW's suspected perjury, but that responsibility is diminished because DC neither called nor examined PW. DC was careless in allowing her conversation with PW to be overheard, but that error in judgment is insufficient to subject her to discipline. DC acted properly in handling PW and was under no obligation to consult with her client before deciding not to call PW as a witness. Finally, Prosecutor's mistaken but perhaps reasonable belief that DC was suborning perjury may create a duty for Prosecutor to report DC's "misconduct."

Perjury, especially in a criminal matter by a defendant or a defense witness, presents a serious challenge for lawyers and the justice system. Perjury is an especially significant affront to the court, and lawyers are expected to take some responsibility for the integrity of judicial proceedings. Revealing perjury, especially a client's perjury, is an especially grave breach of trust and confidentiality.

Lawyers are prohibited from knowingly offering false testimony. MR 3.3(a)(3). Here, DC did not offer this evidence and, indeed, did not cross-examine PW when PW was called by Prosecutor. Had DC taken advantage of the situation by asking PW questions that further elaborated on what DC believed was a false story, the situation would be strikingly different. But under the circumstances in the fact pattern, DC has not offered false evidence, and neither has Prosecutor. Although Prosecutor called PW as his witness, Prosecutor did so expecting truthful, government-favoring testimony to result. Prosecutor was mistaken. While Prosecutor may have offered false evidence, he has not done so knowingly.

Lawyers have discretion to decline to offer evidence they reasonably believe, but do not know, to be false. This discretion does not extend to a decision to decline to call a criminal defendant client, but PW is not the defendant. Some might argue that this narrowing of discretion should apply to defense witnesses. The rationale for the narrowing of discretion is based on the defendant's right to testify on his own behalf, but a defendant also has a right to the use of compulsory process (i.e., calling witnesses on defendant's behalf). Based on the compulsory process right, a reasonable argument exists for taking from defense counsel the discretion to decline to offer defense witnesses. Nonetheless, DC operated in compliance with MR 3.3(a)(3) and handled PW properly in this respect. DC is not subject to discipline for declining to call PW as a witness.

Once called by Prosecutor, DC arguably had a duty to inform the court of her expectation that PW was about to perjure himself. However, DC could not know what PW would do, having been called as a witness by Prosecutor. When a lawyer has not offered the false evidence, the duty to report exists only when the lawyer "knows" that the evidence will be or has been false. DC could not be said to have known PW's testimony would be false in advance, once PW was called by Prosecutor. What DC should have done after the testimony is a somewhat closer question. At this point, PW has testified to what DC came to believe was a false version of the events. Still, she may not know that PW's testimony is false. Unless DC has more powerful indications than her sense of her conversation with PW, it seems more accurate to say that she believes but does not know that PW has testified falsely. Remembering that she did not cross-examine PW, and because the question says that the trial ended without further mention of PW, I assume that DC did not argue PW's version of the facts to the jury, she had no duty to reveal PW's perjury to the court. (The duty to reveal perjury of which a lawyer knows continues to the conclusion of the proceeding, which means until the final judgment has either been affirmed on appeal or the time to appeal has passed. MR 3.3 Comment 13.)

Arguably, because DC did not know that PW's testimony was false, because DC represents a criminal defendant, and because PW was called not by DC but by Prosecutor, DC had a duty to her client to argue a reasonable defense theory based on PW's testimony. Such choices, however, if they are reasonable tactical choices, are within the discretion of the lawyer. Lawyers must defer to their clients about the goals of representation, but have discretion to make reasonable tactical choices. Likewise, DC was not obliged to consult with her client regarding her decision to decline to call PW as a witness.

DC should not have engaged in the conversation with PW in a place where they could be overheard. That sort of error, if it had resulted in damage to a client, might support a malpractice action by a client against a lawyer. But such an error is not so grave as to subject DC to discipline for lack of competence. MR 1.1.

Prosecutor believed that DC was suborning perjury. Prosecutor was mistaken, but his belief was based on his personal knowledge (the conversation he overheard) and the belief, although mistaken, was his. Lawyers have a duty to report the misconduct of other lawyers when that conduct raises substantial questions about the honesty, trustworthiness, or fitness of the lawyer. Further, the reporting lawyer must know of the misconduct for the duty to report to arise. Suborning perjury is the sort of serious misconduct that must be reported. Prosecutor would have a duty to report DC's conduct if it can be said that Prosecutor knows of it. Here, once PW has testified, Prosecutor must surely be left unsure of what had happened in the lobby between PW and DC. As such, it seems that Prosecutor's knowledge of any misconduct probably falls short of the rule's requirements. If Prosecutor did report the conduct, thus mistakenly reporting DC to the bar discipline authorities, Prosecutor could successfully assert a claim of privilege to any defamation claim brought by DC.

Neither Prosecutor nor DC is subject to discipline.

SAMPLE ANSWER TO QUESTION 3:

Defendant's lawyers are not subject to discipline for contacting jurors after the trial. As long as lawyers do not harass former jurors or violate some other rule of professional conduct, they are not subject to discipline. Under MR 3.5, a lawyer is prohibited from communicating with a juror after trial only when the court prohibits the communication, the juror has made his or her desire not to communicate known, or the communication involves harassment.

In this case, the court has not issued an order prohibiting the jurors from speaking about the case, and the jurors have not made it known that they choose not to communicate. Defendant's lawyers are trying to prepare an appeal for their client, and have not conducted themselves in a harassing manner. The jurors in this situation are potential fact witnesses in a proceeding to review a conviction. They do not belong to anyone, and can be contacted by Defendant's lawyers as long as the lawyers act within their ethical guidelines, which they appear to be doing in this situation.

However, the Prosecutor is subject to discipline for dissuading witnesses from cooperating with opposing counsel. A lawyer may not dissuade a witness from cooperating with opposing counsel except in very limited circumstances, none of which is present here. MR 3.4(f).

Multistate-Style Exam Questions

1. Attorney Smith represents a commercial fisherman who was being prosecuted for violating a statute prohibiting salmon fishing at a particular time of year. In preparing for trial, Smith hoped that the government agent who had cited the Defendant could not identify him. He decided to test the witness's identification.

   Next to him at counsel table, Smith placed Mr. Jones, who resembled the Defendant, and had Jones dressed in outdoor clothing consisting of denims, heavy shoes, a plaid shirt, and a jacket-vest. Defendant wore a business suit and large round glasses and sat behind the rail in a row normally reserved for the press. Smith neither asked the court's permission for, nor notified the court or government counsel of, the substitution.

   On Smith's motion at the start of the trial, the court ordered all witnesses excluded from the courtroom. Jones remained at counsel table.

   Throughout the trial, Smith acted as if Jones was the Defendant. He gestured to Jones as though he were his client, gave Jones a yellow legal pad on which to take notes, and referred to Jones as "my client." The two conferred. Smith did not correct the court when it expressly referred to Jones as the Defendant and caused the record to show identification of Jones as Defendant.

   During trial, two government witnesses misidentified Jones as Defendant. Following the government's case, Smith called Jones as a witness, Jones testified that he was not Defendant, and Smith disclosed the substitution.

   Is Attorney Smith subject to discipline?

   (A) Yes, because a client is entitled to zealous advocacy.

   (B) Yes, because the attorney disclosed the misrepresentations before the trial ended.

   (C) Yes, because a lawyer may not make a false statement of material fact to a tribunal.

   (D) Yes, but only if the court first finds the attorney to be in contempt.

2. During the trial of a civil case, Attorney Jones was examining a witness for his client when opposing counsel objected to a question on the ground of hearsay. The trial judge sustained the objection, and Attorney Jones asked if he might approach the bench. A conference was held, during which Attorney Jones cogently explained why the judge's ruling was erroneous. Attorney Jones was correct; the trial judge's ruling was erroneous. Not persuaded, the trial judge reiterated his ruling sustaining the objection. Attorney Jones, still out of the jury's hearing, said, "Judge, I mean no disrespect but you are wrong. This information is vital to my client's case and the jury must have it." At this point, Attorney Jones approached the witness and quietly told the witness to answer the question. The witness answered the question, and opposing counsel again objected and moved that the answer be stricken. The trial judge granted the motion to strike and instructed the jury to disregard the answer. The trial judge later in private berated Attorney Jones. The trial continued without further incident.

   Is Attorney Jones subject to discipline?

   (A) Yes, because a lawyer may not advise a client to disregard a ruling of the court.

   (B) No, because a lawyer may not fail to seek the client's lawful objectives.

   (C) No, because a lawyer may advance a position that is supported by existing law.

   (D) No, because a lawyer may take reasonable steps in good faith to test the validity of a court's ruling.

3. An indigent client came to see Attorney Jones for advice and counsel regarding a dispute with his landlord. After examining the circumstances, Attorney Jones advised the client to give notice to the landlord and move out. Attorney Jones reasonably anticipated that no litigation would ensue. Because the client did not have the funds, Attorney Jones loaned him $250 to make a deposit on a new apartment.

Is Attorney Jones subject to discipline?

(A) Yes, because an attorney may not loan money to a client.

(B) No, because the attorney was not to take unfair advantage of the client.

(C) No, because no attorney-client relationship was formed.

(D) Yes, if the attorney failed to obtain the client's informed consent in writing to this business transaction.

4. Attorney Smith is an accomplished trial lawyer and writer. She has been approached by a murder defendant who wants her representation. Smith says that she will represent the defendant if the defendant grants Smith publication rights to the defendant's story. The defendant agrees and is effectively represented by Smith.

Is Smith subject to discipline?

(A) No, because the representation was effective.

(B) Yes, because the attorney failed to make full disclosure to the defendant before obtaining defendant's consent.

(C) Yes, because a lawyer is prohibited from acquiring an interest in publication rights with respect to the subject matter of a client's representation.

(D) Yes, because a lawyer is prohibited from acquiring an interest in publication rights with respect to the subject matter of a client's representation until the representation is completed.

5. Attorney Jones is one of only three individuals in town who are experienced criminal defense lawyers. He is approached by Daryl Thompson, who has been charged with breaking into the home of Irving Trumbull, the president of the "Only Bank in Town." The Bank is one of Jones's only repeat customers, and Jones has dealt with Mr. Trumbull regarding much of the Bank's collection business for the last four years. Thompson is a man of modest means, but is not indigent. Attorney Jones told Mr. Thompson that he would not represent him because of Jones's representation of the Bank.

Is Attorney Jones subject to discipline?

(A) Yes, because the financial hardship to Jones is insufficient to excuse his duty to represent Mr. Thompson.

(B) No, because representing Mr. Thompson would have created a conflict of interest.

(C) Yes, because Jones failed to seek Mr. Thompson's informed consent.

(D) No, because, with few exceptions, none of which is present here, a lawyer is under no duty to represent every prospective client.

6. In which of the following situations would the information received by the attorney be covered by *both* the attorney-client privilege and the ethical duty to preserve the client's confidential information?

I. Lawyer L is representing Client C in a personal injury claim. L and C attend the same church. At a church social, while walking through the buffet lunch line, C tells L that injuries are much less serious than he had previously thought.

II. L is representing C in a boundary line dispute with C's neighbor. When combing through the county land records, L discovers that C's grantor apparently had no legal title to the land he purported to grant to C.

III. L is defending C in a first degree murder case. In the course of her investigation, L talks to a taxi driver who tells L that he remembers that on the night in question, C rode in his taxi to an address near the scene of the murder.

IV. L represents C in an action for breach of an oral contract. When preparing the case for trial, L stumbles across an old newspaper clipping reporting C's conviction of a felony in a distant state 15 years ago.

(A) All of the above.

(B) II, III, and IV only.

(C) I only.

(D) None of the above.

7. Edgar was charged with a felony after the police found marijuana plants growing in his vegetable garden. The police search was of doubtful legality. Edgar implored his friend and neighbor, Attorney Joyce, to defend him in the case. Joyce warned Edgar that her regular practice was limited to worker's compensation law, that she had never handled a criminal case before, and that she had little time to prepare herself to handle his defense. Edgar said he understood all that, and Joyce reluctantly agreed to represent him. At the time, she intended to do the necessary research on criminal procedure, but the pressure of her regular work prevented her from doing it. A reasonably prudent criminal defense lawyer would have moved to suppress the evidence resulting from the police search. Because of her ignorance of criminal procedure, Joyce did not make a motion to suppress. The evidence was admitted at Edgar's trial, and he was convicted.

Which of the following is most nearly correct?

(A) Joyce is not subject to discipline because it is uncertain whether a motion to suppress would have been granted.

(B) Joyce is not subject to discipline because she duly warned Edgar of her lack of time and her lack of experience in criminal defense work.

(C) Joyce is subject to discipline because a motion to suppress might have been granted.

(D) Joyce is liable to Edgar for malpractice because she failed to do the research needed to handle the case competently.

8. Lawyer represented Client in a lawsuit completed over a decade ago. Lawyer has not represented Client since. Plaintiff, who was not involved in the prior litigation with Client, seeks to retain Lawyer to sue Client in another matter that, although distinct from the prior litigation, is ancillary to it and involves in part the same facts and circumstances, some of which are confidential.

It is proper for Lawyer to:

(A) Decline to represent Plaintiff.

(B) Refer the matter to his law partner, who was not involved in the prior litigation and who became associated with Lawyer only a year ago.

(C) Accept the representation after notifying Plaintiff and Client.

(D) Refer the matter to Smith, a lawyer in another firm, in exchange for 10% of the fee that Smith will charge Plaintiff.

9. John Doe requested that Attorney defend him in a murder charge. Attorney told Doe that he restricted his practice to civil matters, so he gave Doe the names of three good criminal defense lawyers. As Doe was leaving, Doe told Attorney the facts leading to his arrest, including an admission that he shot the victim. Doe then asked Attorney what his reactions were. Attorney briefly discussed temporary insanity as a defense. Doe subsequently hired another lawyer. Attorney did not charge Doe any fee. The prosecutor learned of Doe's conversation with Attorney and has subpoenaed Attorney to appear as a witness in Doe's trial.

Is it proper for Attorney to testify that Doe admitted shooting the deceased?

(A) Yes, because an attorney-client relationship was never formed between Doe and Attorney.

(B) Yes, because Attorney did not charge Doe any fee.

(C) No, because the lawyer-client evidentiary privilege extends to prospective clients, and a lawyer may not disclose the confidences or secrets of a prospective client.

(D) No, because Attorney told Doe that Attorney did not handle criminal matters.

10. Attorney Jones is the majority shareholder of Collection Agency, Inc. If Collection Agency's collection efforts are not successful, Jones has authorized Collection Agency's Manager, who has graduated from law school but not been admitted to the bar, to write a letter which, in Manager's best judgment, is appropriate. The letter is on Jones's legal letterhead. The letter may, if Manager so decides, contain a statement that the matter has been referred to Attorney Jones and that suit will be filed in five days if payment is not received. Manager is authorized to sign Attorney Jones' name to the letter. Jones does not personally review each letter before it is sent.

Is Attorney Jones subject to discipline?

(A) Yes, because Attorney may not threaten suit to gain advantage in a civil case.

(B) Yes, because the letter is a threat.

(C) Yes, because Collection Agency, through Manager, is engaging in the unauthorized practice of law.

(D) No, because Manager is authorized to act as Jones's agent.

11. Lawyer Smith represents Client Jones in a personal injury case. During negotiations with the defendant's counsel, Smith said, "Mr. Jones just can't accept anything less than $50,000 to settle this claim." In fact, Smith had been authorized by Jones to accept as little as $35,000.

Is Smith subject to discipline?

(A) Yes, because a lawyer is prohibited from making a false statement of fact.

(B) Yes, because he has failed to carry out his client's directive.

(C) No, because such statements in negotiations are not generally regarded as statements of fact.

(D) No, because the statement was made in good faith.

12. Lawyer Green was contacted by criminal defendant Junior. Junior asked Green to represent him and told Green that Junior's father would be paying Green's fee. Green contacted the father, who confirmed that he would pay the fee. Green proceeded to represent Junior.

Is Green subject to discipline?

(A) No, because the father agreed to pay Green's fee.

(B) No, because Junior knew that his father was paying the fee.

(C) Yes, because a lawyer is prohibited from accepting payment for legal services from a third party.

(D) Yes, because Green failed to obtain Junior's informed consent to the arrangement.

13. Lawyer Black believes that he can earn a good living by serving, in an efficient manner, scores of black lung victims. Black sends a tasteful, direct-mail advertisement of his services to all 25-year veterans of coal mining in Black's home state.

Is Black subject to discipline?

(A) No, because the First Amendment protects lawyer advertising to the same extent as it protects any other speech.

(B) No, because the advertisement is tasteful.

(C) Yes, because this activity amounts to direct solicitation in writing.

(D) No, because the First Amendment protection of lawyer advertising as commercial speech is sufficient to prohibit the state's blanket prohibition on direct mail advertising.

14. Attorney Youngblood is a public defender representing an armed robbery defendant. The case was called for trial after several previous postponements. The district attorney advised the judge that a key prosecution witness was missing and asked for another postponement. The judge was greatly upset about the effect of this further postponement on the administration of justice and on his calendar, and gave the prosecution a one-day postponement to find the witness. The judge said that if the witness was not produced and the prosecutor was not ready to go forward the next day, the indictment would be dismissed. No one said anything to Youngblood, and she said nothing, other than announcing that she was ready for trial.

The next day the D.A. announced to the judge that the police had found the witness by checking his forwarding address at the post office. In talking to the witness, the D.A. had learned that since moving, he had been in touch with the public defender's office and that, in fact, Youngblood knew where he was.

Is Youngblood subject to discipline?

(A) Yes, because a lawyer may not fail to disclose that which the lawyer is required by law to reveal.

(B) No, because a criminal defendant is entitled to zealous advocacy.

(C) Yes, because a lawyer may not interfere with the discovery of evidence by an opponent.

(D) No, because a lawyer is under no duty to assist an opponent's effort to locate evidence.

15. Lawyer Lawrence was contacted by Client Clarence. Clarence told Lawrence about an emergency situation in which Clarence was involved that would warrant Lawrence's filing an application for a temporary restraining order to be issued against Clarence's adversary. Clarence tells Lawrence of material facts that are adverse to Clarence's position. When Lawrence approached the local judge with his ex parte application for the temporary restraining order, he did not disclose these adverse facts to the court.

Is Lawrence subject to discipline?

(A) No, because a lawyer is under no duty to disclose facts that are adverse to the lawyer's client.

(B) No, because a lawyer cannot be compelled to testify against the lawyer's client.

(C) Yes, because a lawyer is prohibited from making false statements of fact to a tribunal.

(D) Yes, because a lawyer must disclose material adverse facts to a court when making an ex parte presentation.

16. Attorney Jones worked for two years for the Veterans Administration (VA). While there, his main function was to investigate claims filed by veterans. During the course of his employment, he once investigated a claim filed by Charles, a Korean War veteran. After Jones left the VA, the agency denied Charles's claim. Charles comes to Jones, who is now engaged in private practice, and asks him to represent him in a suit against the VA for the benefits to which Charles believes he is

entitled. Is Jones subject to discipline if he accepts Charles's case?

(A) No, because Jones has left the VA.

(B) No, if Jones was not privy to confidential information regarding Charles arising from his employment at the VA.

(C) Yes, because Charles's case was pending while Jones was employed at the VA.

(D) Yes, if Jones had substantial and personal responsibility for Charles's VA claim while in his VA employment.

17. Attorney Jones represents Porter in a civil law suit. Attorney Smith represents the opposing party. Smith notices that Jones has been unduly contentious during the discovery phase of the case and has offended the judge to whom the case is assigned for trial. Also, she believes that Jones has made several questionable tactical decisions. She honestly believes that Porter stands a good chance of being hurt by Jones's conduct. May Smith discuss this matter with Porter?

(A) No, because Porter is represented by Jones.

(B) No, unless she believes Jones's conduct amounts to a disciplinary violation.

(C) Yes, if it will not hurt Smith's client.

(D) Yes, if Smith gets the informed consent of her own client first.

18. Bob is a financial planner. He is not licensed to practice law. He has recently been helping his clients prepare their wills as part of his estate-planning service. Has Bob committed unauthorized practice of law?

(A) No, because will preparation is an integral part of financial planning and Bob is an expert in this field.

(B) Yes, because preparing legal documents is considered to be practicing law.

(C) Yes, because financial planning is best done by a tax lawyer.

(D) No, because Bob is careful to ensure that all his clients know he is not an attorney.

19. The state of Wythe has decided to limit those it admits to the practice of law in its state to only those that either reside in the state or maintain an office in the state. Will the state's requirement withstand a constitutional challenge by a nonresident who does not wish to maintain an office in the state?

(A) Yes, because it is within the authority of the state to determine who it will permit to practice law in its courts.

(B) No, because this requirement violates the Constitution's Privileges and Immunities Clause.

(C) No, because this requirement violates the equal protection guarantee of the Fourteenth Amendment.

(D) Yes, because the state has a substantial interest in ensuring that its lawyers know the local rules, are available for court appearances, and do their share of volunteer and pro bono work in the state.

20. Sally is an attorney who wishes to defend her client against charges that have been brought against him in a state in which she is not licensed to practice. Which of the following are true?

I. The only way for Sally to represent her client is for her to receive a license to practice in the state.

II. Sally may represent her client if her pro hac vice application is granted.

III. Sally may be required to associate with a local attorney for the purposes of the case.

(A) I, II, and III.

(B) II and III.

(C) I and III.

(D) None of the above.

21. The state of Wythe has recently decided to make membership and annual dues to the state bar mandatory. Joan doesn't feel that she should be forced to belong to the bar and required to send them annual dues if she wants to practice law in the state. She brings suit arguing that the requirements are unconstitutional. Will Joan prevail?

(A) No, it is within the authority of the state to require membership in and dues payment to the state bar.

(B) Yes, requiring Joan to join the bar to gain her license is a violation of her First Amendment rights.

(C) Yes, this type of requirement is prohibited by the Supreme Court's 1990 decision in Keller v. State Bar of California.

(D) No, the Model Rules permits the states to require bar membership.

22. Lawyer represents Client in a civil matter. Representation is completed, and three years later, Client dies. Following Client's death, in conjunction with a criminal investigation of Grand Jury Target, Prosecutor requests Lawyer's files on Client's matter. If Lawyer resists Prosecutor's request, will Lawyer be successful?

(A) Yes, because Client is not the subject of Prosecutor's investigation.

(B) Yes, because the lawyer-client evidentiary privilege extends even beyond the client's death.

(C) No, because former clients receive a diminished lawyer-client evidentiary privilege.

(D) No, if Prosecutor's need for the material is great.

23. Beth and Dave are opposing counsel in a civil trial. During depositions, Beth's client gets caught in an inconsistency. When questioned further on the matter, Beth's client alleges that Beth told him to change his story if he wanted to reduce his liability. A friend of Dave's works for the same firm as Beth. Dave's friend told him that he knows that Beth has allowed her clients to perjure themselves on the stand. If Dave believes Beth has committed attorney misconduct, must he do anything about it?

(A) He does not have to report Beth because he does not have direct knowledge of her misconduct.

(B) He does not have to report Beth because her actions, even if true, do not raise a substantial question as to the lawyer's honesty, trustworthiness, or fitness as an attorney.

(C) He must report her misconduct or he will be in violation of the ethics rules.

(D) He should report her misconduct because it will give him an advantage in the litigation.

24. Bob, a CEO of a large corporation, meets with the corporation's legal counsel. Bob's executive assistant is present during the entire meeting. During the meeting, the CEO discusses the corporation's strategy in a recently filed lawsuit as well as the status of his divorce, in which he is represented by other counsel. Is the information Bob told the attorney regarding his divorce protected?

(A) The information is protected by the attorney-client evidentiary privilege and the duty of confidentiality.

(B) The information is protected by the duty of confidentiality, but not the attorney-client privilege, because the presence of the executive assistant during the discussion of Bob's divorce precluded the creation of the attorney-client privilege.

(C) The information is protected by the evidentiary privilege only.

(D) The information is not protected.

25. Sally talked to the neighbor of her client and learned where her client was on the night the crime for which he was arrested was committed. Her client refused to tell Sally where he was that night. Is the lawyer's knowledge of the location subject to the attorney-client privilege?

(A) No, because the evidentiary privilege was never established.

(B) No, but Sally may still be subject to discipline for violating the duty of confidentiality if the court orders her to testify and she does so.

(C) Yes, the information is covered by the attorney-client privilege and the court may not override this evidentiary privilege.

(D) Yes, but the Judge can order the client to reveal the information.

26. Stan's client confesses to him that he stole a large amount of cash from his employer and hid it on his property. Stan goes to his client's property and locates the money. If Stan does not want to reveal the location of the money and does not want to violate any ethics rules, what should he do?

(A) Put the money in a safety deposit box.

(B) Take the money to his office, count it, write down the serial numbers, and return it to where he found it.

(C) Leave the money where it is.

(D) Turn the money over to the police and refuse to tell the police how or where he found it.

27. Bart feels he is being treated unfairly at work. He goes to his lawyer's office and tells him that he owns a gun and he's going to shoot his boss. Bart leaves the office and his lawyer calls the boss to warn him. On the way to his boss's office, Bart calms down and changes his mind. The boss is understandably distressed and fires Bart. Bart reports his lawyer to the bar for violating the duty of confidentiality. Will the lawyer be subject to discipline?

(A) Yes, because Bart is the only person with the right to waive the duty of confidentiality.

(B) No, because the lawyer was required by law to warn the boss.

(C) No, because the future-crimes exception to the duty of confidentiality permits the lawyer to reveal information the lawyer reasonably believes necessary to prevent reasonably certain death or substantial bodily harm.

(D) Yes, because the lawyer was not reasonable in his belief that Bart was going to shoot his boss.

28. Jill has represented Jack's construction company for a number of years. In the course of that representation, she has prepared a number of contracts for him. Jill has learned that Jack is using the contracts that she has prepared for him to defraud his customers, by adding clauses to the contracts that permit him to carry out his fraudulent scheme. Jack has recently requested that Jill prepare several more agreements between him and his clients. Jack's company accounts for over half of Jill's business. Can she continue to represent him?

(A) Jill can continue representing Jack because the Constitution guarantees the right to legal representation.

(B) Jill must withdraw because Jack is using her services to further his fraud.

(C) Jill can continue to represent Jack as long as she does not directly commit a crime or fraud.

(D) Jill must withdraw only if she will directly profit from Jack's fraud.

29. Which of the following conflicts are NOT waivable?

   (A) Third-party fee payment.

   (B) Conflict between two current clients.

   (C) Lending clients money when litigation is pending or contemplated, other than advancing litigation costs.

   (D) Conflict between a current and a former client.

30. Lawyer Adam and Client Bill wish to enter a joint business venture. To achieve this and satisfy the conflict rules, Adam puts everything in writing—both Bill's consent and the transaction itself, which Adam also takes care to put into terms that Bill can understand. On these facts alone, which statement is true about the transaction?

   (A) It satisfies the conflict rules because everything is in writing.

   (B) It satisfies the conflict rules because the language is that which Bill can understand.

   (C) It fails to satisfy the conflict rules, because it must also be objectively reasonable and because Bill must be advised that it would be desirable and have the opportunity to seek independent legal counsel.

   (D) Both A and B.

31. Corporation C hired Firm in 1995 to assist with a corporate restructuring. Firm also helped to draft several employment contracts for high-ranking executives. Firm's representation of Corporation C ceased. In 2002, a Client approaches Firm, wishing to be represented in a personal injury matter against Corporation C. Which statement is true?

   (A) The Firm cannot represent the Client against Corporation C because it owes the Corporation a duty of loyalty.

   (B) The Firm can represent the Client if both Client and Corporation give informed consent.

   (C) The Firm can represent the Client because his interests are not directly adverse to the former Corporation client.

   (D) The Firm can represent the Client because there is not a substantial relationship between the two representations.

32. Assume the same facts as those found in Question 31, but assume that Client's proposed representation arises from the employment contract drafted by Lawyer D at Firm. May Lawyer F, also with Firm, represent Client?

   (A) Yes, because the matters are not substantially related.

   (B) Yes, because the interests are not directly adverse.

   (C) No, because Lawyer F and all the lawyers at Firm are disqualified based on Lawyer D's prior representation in a substantially related matter.

   (D) Yes, if Lawyer F is in a different practice section of the law firm.

33. When may a former judge engage in private representation in a matter in which he was involved while formerly on the bench?

   (A) When the judge was not involved personally and substantially.

   (B) When the parties consent after consultation.

   (C) When the parties settled the matter during proceedings so that the judge was prevented from ruling on the merits.

   (D) Both A and B.

34. An investigator working on a prosecutor's rape case uncovers information about another possible suspect. As the investigation continues, the probability increases that the new suspect, rather than the man arrested for the crime, is the guilty party. What is the prosecutor's ethical obligation?

   (A) Immediately request a hearing with the judge assigned to the case.

   (B) Immediately request an ex parte meeting with the judge assigned to the case.

   (C) Turn the information over to the defense attorney in a timely manner.

   (D) Continue to investigate the new suspect until he is sure that the new suspect is the guilty party before revealing the information to the defense.

35. Partner in a law firm discovers that a secretary in a different section of the firm is continuously leaking confidential client information. The firm has each new employee watch a video on client confidentiality and sign an agreement to abide by the confidentiality rules. Does the Partner violate any rules by not stopping Secretary's conduct?

   (A) Yes, because as a partner he has a duty to take reasonable remedial action to stop further breaches once he learns of them.

   (B) Yes, because the firm's systems to prevent such conduct were not reasonable.

   (C) No, because the partner is not the secretary's direct supervisor.

   (D) No, because the firm has reasonable systems in place to prevent such confidentiality breaches.

36. You are a divorce attorney, and Nathan and Lynn come to your office seeking a divorce. They believe they've worked out an amicable preliminary settlement and need you only for the technicalities. Your state allows such representation, and you agree. The next day, Lynn calls and discusses a family heirloom that she and Nathan both want, and she muses about her chances of prevailing in a lawsuit. What action should you take?

   (A) Explain to Lynn that if things progress to litigation, you will be forced to withdraw from representing either side.

   (B) Withdraw as counsel for both.

   (C) Withdraw as counsel for Nathan only.

   (D) Withdraw as counsel for Lynn only.

37. Lawyer places an advertisement containing the statement, "Most experienced criminal lawyer in the state—I produce results." This statement:

   (A) is permitted because it is mere puffery.

   (B) will subject the lawyer to discipline because it is unverifiable and therefore misleading.

   (C) false and will subject the attorney to discipline.

   (D) refers to an illegal activity and will subject the attorney to discipline.

38. A private law firm chooses the name Immigration Legal Services of California. This name:

   (A) will subject the attorneys to discipline because it does not contain the name of at least one of the attorneys in the firm.

   (B) is permitted because it is protected commercial speech under the First Amendment.

   (C) will subject the attorneys to discipline as misleading because it untruthfully implies a relationship to the government or other institutions.

   (D) is permitted because neither the Model Code nor the Model Rules addresses permissible firm names.

39. As a result of the Supreme Court's decision in In re Primus, 436 U.S. 412 (1988), which of the following is true?

(A) Lawyers have no First Amendment right to solicit clients in person.

(B) States may not ban advertisements containing true claims of certification of specialization by a bona fide organization.

(C) A lawyer may solicit clients in person if it is to further political or ideological goals and not for pecuniary gain.

(D) States may prohibit lawyers from contacting accident victims for 30 days after the accident.

40. A lawyer wants to include information about his fees in his advertisement. Such information:

    (A) is permitted as long as it is not false or misleading.

    (B) receives no constitutional protection after the Court's decision in Bates v. Arizona State Bar, 433 U.S. 350 (1977).

    (C) may be prohibited by the states because it is inappropriate for the profession.

    (D) is permissible only if the fees are described in general terms such as "reasonable and moderate" rather than in actual dollar figures.

41. Form letters written to a specific group of clients identified as being in need of certain legal services are:

    (A) treated essentially as advertisements as a result of the Supreme Court's decision in Shapero v. Kentucky Bar Ass'n in 1988.

    (B) not protected speech because of concerns for the potential for overreaching and undue influence.

    (C) prohibited by the Court's decision in Ohralik v. Ohio State Bar Ass'n in 1988, which reaffirmed that the First Amendment does not protect in-person solicitation.

    (D) considered to be the equivalent of in-person solicitation and permitted, provided the letters are not false or misleading.

42. Judge is the treasurer of a local charitable organization. He is shamefully removed from this position on suspicion of embezzlement, although he is never formally charged. Can Judge be removed from his position on the bench?

    (A) No, because the problem was in the context of Judge's personal involvement in the organization, rather than any official functions.

    (B) Yes, because it is inappropriate for a judge to hold office in the organization.

    (C) No, because Judge was neither charged nor convicted.

    (D) Yes, because the episode bears on his integrity.

43. Judge is involved in a discussion with Attorney Camille. Judge recently ruled on a case in which Camille represented one of the parties, and now Camille is asking advice regarding the appeal. Judge believes that justice will be served by giving Camille the advice, and his personal role in the case is over. Is this ex parte communication proper?

    (A) Yes, the case is no longer pending before the judge's court.

    (B) Yes, the judge has a good-faith motivation in discussing the case.

    (C) Yes, the discussion is only on housekeeping matters.

    (D) No, the ex parte communication is not proper.

44. Judge is the treasurer for a local charitable organization. During the charity's annual fund-raising drive, judge asks some of his friends and associates to buy tickets to a dinner dance. He is careful to avoid using the auspices of his office to pressure anyone into

contributing; in fact, no one with whom he speaks is connected to his judicial role. Has any judicial conduct rule been violated?

(A) Yes, Judge violated the rule prohibiting him from being an officer in an organization.

(B) Yes, Judge is prohibited from directly fundraising for an organization.

(C) Yes, Judge is not permitted to have a membership in a local organization.

(D) No judicial conduct rule was violated.

45. Mike's house is broken into and some of his valuables are stolen. When Mike, a lawyer, files a claim with his insurance company, he overstates the value of the stolen property and includes property that was not stolen. Mike receives a payment from the insurance company for several thousand dollars more than the true value of his stolen property. Can Mike's actions subject him to discipline by his state's bar?

(A) No, even though Mike was not honest with the insurance company, dishonest acts outside the lawyer's role will not subject a lawyer to discipline.

(B) Yes, Mike has acted fraudulently, and his conduct will subject him to discipline.

(C) No, only criminal conduct committed when acting as an attorney will subject Mike to discipline.

(D) No, Mike's act says nothing about his fitness as a lawyer.

46. Julie has observed Beth, her opposing counsel, engage in behavior that clearly violates an ethics rule and raises a substantial question about Beth's fitness as a lawyer. Julie feels she is obligated to report Beth to the disciplinary authorities. What should Julie do first to start disciplinary proceedings against Beth?

(A) File suit in state court.

(B) Report Beth to the judge hearing their case.

(C) File a complaint with the bar disciplinary committee.

(D) File suit in federal court if their case is in federal court.

47. Sam filed a bar disciplinary complaint against his former attorney, James, because Sam felt that he lost his case as a result of James's lack of due care. The disciplinary proceedings were recently dismissed. Sam does not feel that the Bar adequately considered all the relevant evidence. How can Sam appeal the decision by the Bar?

(A) Sam cannot appeal the bar decision, but he may bring a malpractice suit against James.

(B) Sam may appeal the decision to the state trial court.

(C) Sam may appeal the decision to the state court of last resort.

(D) Sam may appeal the decision in federal court.

48. Disciplinary proceedings have been started against Alex. Alex feels that his actions did not amount to disciplinary violation, and feels that his best course of action would be to have a jury trial. Will his timely request for a jury trial be granted?

(A) Yes. He has a constitutional right to a jury.

(B) No. There is no right to a jury trial in a disciplinary proceeding.

(C) Yes. All state bars guarantee a right to a jury.

(D) It depends. It is within the discretion of the bar committee whether to grant his request, but there is no constitutional right to jury trial in disciplinary cases.

49. Bill and Abby are solo practitioners on the same floor of a small office building. Al-

though they specialize in different areas, they often consult one another about the legal issues on which they are working. A client comes to Bill with a legal problem that Bill knows is within Abby's area of specialization. Bill obtains the client's permission to consult with Abby about the matter. After the client leaves, Bill talks to Abby about the client's problem, and Bill and Abby agree that Abby will do the substantive legal work for Bill for an agreed-upon hourly rate. Bill will continue to serve as the client's counsel. Will the arrangement between Bill and Abby subject them to discipline?

(A) No, fee splitting is permitted by lawyers that work together.

(B) No, provided the client agrees in writing and the fee is reasonable.

(C) Yes, the bar permits fee sharing only if the lawyers are members of the same firm.

(D) Yes, because Bill is not competent in the area of the law raised by the client's problem.

50. Joe is starting a biotech firm and goes to see Beth, a lawyer and an old friend, for legal advice regarding patents, corporate trademarks, and taxes. Beth has spent the 20 years since law school writing wills and working on domestic-relations issues. Can Beth represent Joe?

(A) No. A lawyer has a duty to decline representation when she lacks competence.

(B) Yes. Joe approached Beth and asked for her services.

(C) Yes, as long as Beth can achieve the requisite level of expertise in the new field by reasonable preparation.

(D) No. Because Beth has been friends with Joe for over 20 years, she will have a conflict of interest in representing him.

51. Larry has been a key member of the defense litigation team representing Priceler Corporation, a major auto company, in a series of class-action matters. These matters have involved claimed defects in the auto heating/cooling systems. In this context, Larry has become quite familiar with the class-action defense strategies devised by Priceler management and the defense team. Larry later leaves the law firm to establish his own practice. About a year into his own practice, a prospective client approaches Larry about representation against Priceler. The client was driving a Priceler minivan when it was hit from the rear by another vehicle. This contact caused the rear van hatch door to open, and the client's child was severely injured. A class action is pending against Priceler regarding the rear-door latch defect. Larry accepts this client's case and proceeds to file a civil complaint, joining the class-action matter against Priceler. Is it permissible for Larry to represent the prospective client in the class-action suit against Priceler?

(A) Yes, it is permissible because Larry has ended his representation of Priceler.

(B) No, because representation against a former client is never permissible.

(C) No, because mere knowledge of the former client's business or mindset makes representation against the former client impermissible.

(D) No, because it is not permissible for a lawyer to represent a client against a former client on matters that are substantially related.

52. Prospective Client asks Young Lawyer for representation in a divorce matter, but suggests he has only enough money to pay half the lawyer's usual fee. Young Lawyer undertakes the representation at this reduced rate, hoping that doing a good job will bring more clients down the road. The next day, Client's mother calls Young Lawyer and says she is quite happy that Young Lawyer is representing her son in the divorce matter and says she hopes any issues regarding

custody of Client's minor child will be resolved in favor of Client. Client's mother suggests that she will pay the remaining amount of Young Lawyer's usual fee and asks that her son, who is proud and stupid, not be told of their arrangement. May Young Lawyer accept Client's mother's offer?

(A) Yes, Young Lawyer has no duty to inform Client and may accept Client's mother's offer without Client's knowledge.

(B) Yes, Young Lawyer may accept Client's mother's offer, but only if Young Lawyer discusses the matter with Client and Client gives informed consent.

(C) No, Young Lawyer is prohibited from receiving funds for Client's case from anyone other than Client.

(D) No, Young Lawyer is prohibited from involving other family members in a divorce matter.

53. Lawyer practices law in a small beach community, and although she greatly desires one, she does not yet own a beach house. Client approaches Lawyer for advice about a serious financial problem. The state is threatening to foreclose on Client's beautiful beach house because Client has been unable to pay back taxes. Client's prospects are improving, but if events run their course, he will lose the house to foreclosure before he is able to obtain the funds needed to pay the tax debt. Client asks Lawyer various legal questions regarding his circumstances (foreclosure procedures, tax questions, etc.). Lawyer sees only one way out for Client: Pay the tax debt. Although Lawyer would dearly love to own Client's beach house and considers offering to buy it, Lawyer has a fit of generosity and offers to loan the client money to pay the tax debt on very generous terms, at an interest rate far below the market rate. Client gratefully accepts Lawyer's generosity. Has Lawyer breached any lawyer ethics duties?

(A) Yes, because Lawyer can never provide financial assistance to her client.

(B) Yes, because Lawyer is providing legal judgment in this transaction and therefore may not provide financial assistance.

(C) No, because Lawyer is allowed to loan money to a client within ethical guidelines.

(D) No, because Lawyer's generosity should be rewarded.

54. The legislature in Lawyer's jurisdiction has recently passed a "Plain English" law, requiring all consumer contracts to be drafted in terms that are understandable to nonlawyers. Fast Eddy's Payday Consumer Friendly Finance (FEPCFF) drafts a new form loan agreement that will comply with the new law. Consumer Joe comes to Lawyer complaining that FEPCFF is not so friendly after all, and that its form contract is indecipherable. He tells Lawyer his story of being taken advantage of by FEPCFF and reveals considerable confidential information about Joe's finances. Consumer Joe asks Lawyer to represent him against FEPCFF.

Lawyer decides not to represent Joe. May Lawyer defend FEPCFF when it contacts him to ask for representation?

(A) No, because Lawyer owes Joe a duty of confidentiality as a prospective client, and Lawyer would have to abuse the confidences of Joe in order to represent FEPCFF in this matter.

(B) No, because Lawyer has knowledge that FEPCFF has acted unethically and may not represent the company.

(C) No, because Lawyer could never represent FEPCFF after any contact with Joe, a potential opposing party.

(D) Yes, because Lawyer has not received funds from Joe and therefore owes him no duty of confidentiality regarding the information Joe told to Lawyer.

Multistate-Style Exam Answers

1. C	12. D	23. C	34. C	45. B
2. A	13. D	24. B	35. A	46. C
3. D	14. D	25. A	36. B	47. A
4. D	15. D	26. C	37. B	48. D
5. D	16. D	27. C	38. C	49. B
6. D	17. A	28. B	39. C	50. C
7. D	18. B	29. C	40. A	51. D
8. A	19. B	30. C	41. A	52. B
9. C	20. B	31. D	42. D	53. C
10. C	21. A	32. C	43. D	54. A
11. C	22. B	33. D	44. B	

Table of Cases

Advisory Opinion to Governor, In re 219
Aetna Life Ins. Co. v. Lavoie 230
Ain, Matter of 224
Albano, Matter of 224
Amarin Plastics v. Maryland Cup Corp. 142
Amendments to the Rules Regulating the
    Florida Bar, In re 50
American Cable Productions, Inc., In re 124
Anderson, United States v. 221
Armstrong v. McAlpin 121, 123
Austern, In re 34

Balla v. Gambro, Inc. 52
Bates v. Arizona
    State Bar 199, 201, 203, 206, 214
Beiter Co., In re 82
Belge, People v. 85
Bigos, United States v. 78
Bishop v. Committee on Professional Ethics and
    Conduct of the Iowa State Bar Ass'n. 206
Blackman, In re 220
Brady v. Maryland 185
Brown v. Board of County Comm. 49

Caperton v. Massey Coal Co. 229
Caplin & Drysdale v. United States 56
Carr, In re 224
Casby, State v. 157
Central Hudson Gas & Electric Co. v. Public
    Service Comm. of New York 201
Cinema 5 Ltd. v. Cinerama, Inc. 112
Clark v. Virginia Board of Bar Examiners 16
Colin, In re 33
Cone v. State Bar of Florida 57
Connecticut, People ex rel. v. Randolph 49
Cooter & Gell v. Hartmarx Corp. 164
Crews v. Buckman Laboratories Int'l. 52
Cuyler v. Sullivan 114

Dalessandro, Matter of 220
DeBartolo, In re 17
Dixon v. State Bar of California 84
Dodd, In re 60

Fentress, People v. 77, 80
Fisher v. United States 79
Florida Bar v. Ball 85
Florida Bar v. Brumbaugh 23
Florida Bar v. Neale 32
Florida Bar v. Peterson 170
Florida Bar v. Went For It, Inc. 204, 207
Forrester v. White 232
Fredonia Broadcasting Corp. v. RCA 229
Fuchsberg, Matter of 220

Garrison v. Louisiana 167
Gassman, In re 227
Gentile v. State Bar of Nevada 14, 167
Gideon v. Wainwright 171
Goldfarb v. Virginia State Bar 15, 55, 71
Goldman v. Kane 109
Goldstone v. State Bar 52
Goldwaithe v. Disciplinary Board 208
Gonzaleas v. Comm. on Judicial
    Performance 224
Grand Jury Subpoena Duces Tecum, In re 5, 81
Greene v. Greene 103, 109
G.W.L., In re 16

Haagen-Dazs Co. v. Perche No!
    Gelato, Inc. 115, 118
Hague, In re 221
Hammad, United States v. 185
Hanson, In re 140
Harrington, State v. 185
Hebenstreit, In re 60
Himmel, In re 24, 27
Hishon v. King & Spaulding 15
Howell v. State Bar of Texas 34
Hughes v. Oregon 228

Ibanez v. Florida Dep't. of Business &
    Professional Regulation 207
In re. *See name of party*
Intemann, In re 222
International Telemeter Corp. v.
    Teleprompter Corp 62

Iowa State Bar Ass'n Committee on Professional Ethics & Conduct v. Bitter 111
Iowa State Bar Ass'n Committee on Professional Ethics & Conduct v. Hill 33
Iowa State Bar Ass'n Committee on Professional Ethics & Conduct v. Nadler 59

Jamil, United States v. 141
Jones v. Barnes 62
Jorgenson v. County of Volusia 161

Keller v. State Bar of California 11, 27
Kennick v. Commission on Judicial Performance 224, 225
Kidder, Peabody & Co., Inc. v. Maxus Energy Corp. 231
Klemm v. Superior Court of Fresno County 190
Knight, In re 139
Kriegsman v. Kriegsman 66
Kutner, In re 52

Lanza, In re 189, 190
Laurie, In re 227
Law Students Civil Rights Research Council, Inc. v Wadmond 17
Leis v. Flynt 18
Liljeberg v. Health Services Acquisition Corp. 220
Lopez, United States v. 144
LSC v. Valazquez 6

MacKenzie v. Super Kids Bargain Store 229
Mallard v. U.S. District Court 50
Marietta, In re 141
Matter of. *See name of party*
Maxwell v. Superior Court 110
McCullough v. Commission on Judicial Performance 224
Meredith, People v. 79
Meyerhofer v. Empire Fire & Marine Ins. Co. 84
Monsanto, United States v. 56
Moran v. Harris 54
Morelite Construction Corp. v. New York City Dist. Counsel Carpenters Benefits Fund 229
Mourad v. Automobile Club Ins. Ass'n. 52

Nathanson v. Korvick 229
Neisig v. Team I 142
Nix v. Whiteside 160

Office of Disc. Counsel v. Shane 205
Ohralik v. Ohio State Bar Ass'n. 200, 202, 203, 208
Oring v. State Bar of California 205
Ortleib, United States v. 166
Orwell, State v. 79

Papa v. New Haven Federation of Teachers 228
Parsons v. Continental Nat'l. Am. Group 107
Peel v. Illinois Attorney Registration and Disciplinary Comm'n 199, 204, 206
People v. *See name of opposing party*
Pfeifer v. Sentry Ins. 108
Pierson v. Ray 232
Price Bros. Co. v. Philadelphia Gear Corp. 226
Primus, In re 201, 202, 212
Professional Adjusters, Inc. v. Tandon 22
Public Services Electric and Gas Co. v. Associated Electric and Gas Ins. Services Ltd. 142-143

Ranta v. McCarney 19
Read v. Virginia State Bar 185
Republican Party of Minnesota v. White 232
R.M.J., In re 201, 203, 206
Rosenberg v. Levin 68
Ruffalo, In re 35
Ryder, In re 79

Sawyer, In re 167
Schiessle v. Stephens 112
Schwimmer; United States v. 144
SEC v. National Student Marketing Corp. 89
Shapero v. Kentucky Bar Ass'n. 199, 200, 203, 212
Sharp v. Howard County 229
Simonson v. General Motors 229
Simpson v. Motorists Mutual Ins. Co. 78
Snyder, In re 34
Spaulding v. Zimmerman 4, 136
Starnes v. Judicial Retirement Comm'n. 221, 223
State Farm Mut. Auto. Ins. Co. v. K.A.W. 113
State v. *See name of opposing party*
Stice, In re 221
Sturgis, In re 225
Supreme Court of New Hampshire v. Piper 14
Supreme Court of Virginia v. Friedman 14
Sutton, United States v. 144
Swidler and Berlin v. United States 80
SWS Financial Fund A v. Salomon Bros., Inc. 119

Tarasoff v. Regents of the Univ. of California 146
Taylor v. Hayes 39
Togstad v. Vesely, Otto, Miller & Keefe 36, 51
Tumey v. Ohio 223

United States v. *See name of opposing party*
Upjohn v. United States 6, 81, 143

Vincenti, In re 166
Virginia Bd. of Pharmacy v. Virginia Citizens Consumer Council, Inc. 201
Virzi v. Grand Trunk Warehouse and Cold Storage Co. 157
Von Wiegen, In re 200, 203, 207
Vorhees, In re 227

Warhaftig, In re 32, 58

Washington Legal Foundation v. Legal Foundation of Washington 57
Washington Legal Foundation v. Texas Equal Access to Justice Foundation 57
Weber v. Cueto 23, 24
Westlake v. Abrams 4
Whitaker, In re 220
Wieder v. Skala 52

Yacavino, In re 187
Yaccarino, In re 225
Young v. United States ex rel. Vuitton et Fils S.A. 184

Zang, In re 205
Zauderer v. Office of Disciplinary Counsel of Supreme Court of Ohio 201, 202, 205
Zoarski, M., In re 230

Table of Statutes, Rules, and Opinions

Constitution

Amend. I 13, 14, 16, 34, 156, 166, 167, 176,
180, 201–204, 206-207, 213
Amend. V 56, 57, 93, 144, 152
Amend. VI 56, 110, 114, 144, 152, 159-160, 171
Amend. XIV 17, 144, 152

United States Code

12 U.S.C. §§1961-1968 56
21 U.S.C. §§848-853 55
28 U.S.C. §47 .... 218, 227, 238
28 U.S.C. §144 .... 218, 227, 238
28 U.S.C. §372 218
28 U.S.C. §455 .... 218, 227, 228, 238, 239
28 U.S.C. §530B 143
28 U.S.C. §1915(d) 50
28 U.S.C. §1927 41

Federal Rules of Civil Procedure

FRCP 11 .... 40-41, 45, 161, 163, 164, 176, 179, 186
FRCP 26 157

Federal Rules of Evidence

FRE 502 150
FRE 801(d)(2)(D) 142, 143

Code of Federal Regulations

17 CFR §§205.1-205.7 116
28 CFR §77.1 et seq. 143

Model Code of Professional Responsibility Canons

Canon 6 58
Canon 7 58
Canon 8 166

Model Rules of Professional Conduct

MR, Preamble 166

MR 1.0 Comment 6 105
MR 1.0(d) 136
MR 1.0(e) 105
MR 1.0(f) 23
MR 1.0(l) 23
MR 1.1 .... 47, 50, 58, 58, 59, 72, 176
MR 1.1 Comment 72
MR 1.2 .... 60, 72
MR 1.2(a) Comment 48, 61, 72
MR 1.2(b) 63
MR 1.2(d) 38, 45, 63, 72, 139, 177
MR 1.3 .... 48, 58, 60, 72
MR 1.4 .... 60, 61, 72
MR 1.4(a) 61
MR 1.4(b) 61
MR 1.5 .... 47, 52, 71
MR 1.5(a) 47, 52, 71
MR 1.5(a)(1) 52
MR 1.5(a)(2) 53
MR 1.5(a)(3) 53
MR 1.5(a)(4) 53
MR 1.5(a)(5) 53
MR 1.5(a)(6) 53
MR 1.5(a)(7) 53
MR 1.5(a)(8) 53
MR 1.5(c) 54, 71
MR 1.5(d)(1) 54
MR 1.5(d)(2) 54
MR 1.5(e) 47, 55
MR 1.5(e)(1) 55
MR 1.5(e)(2) 55
MR 1.5(e)(3) 55
MR 1.6 .... 9, 23, 29, 75, 86, 87, 88, 89, 90,
96, 116, 146, 159, 178, 193
MR 1.6(a) 75, 76, 77, 82, 83, 94, 96
MR 1.6(b)(1) 75, 85, 86, 93, 95
MR 1.6(b)(3) 83, 93
MR 1.6 Comment 6 86
MR 1.6 Comment 8 84
MR 1.6 Comment 10 88
MR 1.6 Comment 11 88
MR 1.6 Comment 14 86
MR 1.7 .... 101, 112, 117, 129
MR 1.7(a) 99, 112, 127

MR 1.7(a)(1)	102
MR 1.7(a)(2)	102, 105, 108, 110, 130
MR 1.7(b)	99, 101, 102, 108, 127, 129, 130
MR 1.7 Comment 18	105
MR 1.7 Comment 24	117
MR 1.8	102
MR 1.8 Comment 10	177
MR 1.8(a)	105, 108, 109, 128, 129, 130
MR 1.8(b)	90, 93, 111, 130
MR 1.8(c)	110, 127, 130
MR 1.8(d)	103, 109, 130
MR 1.8(e)	103, 111, 129, 130, 177, 209, 212
MR 1.8(f)	5, 105, 130
MR 1.8(g)	113
MR 1.8(h)	38, 110, 130
MR 1.8(i)	103, 111, 130, 209
MR 1.8(j)	130
MR 1.9	102, 114, 131
MR 1.9(b)	102
MR 1.9(c)	102
MR 1.9(c)(1)	89
MR 1.9(c)(2)	90
MR 1.10	100, 102, 118, 131, 132
MR 1.11	5, 102, 118, 121, 123, 132
MR 1.11(a)	102
MR 1.11(b)	102
MR 1.11(c)	122, 133
MR 1.11(e)	122
MR 1.12	102, 118, 119, 120, 127, 132, 218
MR 1.12(b)	121, 132
MR 1.12(c)	102, 121, 132
MR 1.13	6, 90, 100, 101, 102, 106, 115, 116, 117, 128, 131
MR 1.13 Comment 3	81
MR 1.13 Comment 5	90
MR 1.13 Comment 6	81
MR 1.13(b)	115
MR 1.13(c)	115
MR 1.13(d)	116
MR 1.13(e)	116
MR 1.14(a)	63, 64
MR 1.14(b)	64
MR 1.15	27, 57
MR 1.15(a)	57, 58, 72
MR 1.15(b)	57
MR 1.15(c)	57
MR 1.15(d)	58
MR 1.15(e)	57
MR 1.16	70
MR 1.16(a)	50, 64, 71, 73
MR 1.16(a)(1)	50, 64, 73
MR 1.16(a)(2)	50, 65, 73
MR 1.16(a)(3)	65, 73
MR 1.16(b)	73
MR 1.16(b)(1)	65, 73
MR 1.16(b)(2)	65, 73
MR 1.16(b)(3)	65, 73
MR 1.16(b)(4)	66, 73
MR 1.16(b)(5)	66, 73
MR 1.16(b)(6)	66, 73
MR 1.16(b)(7)	66, 73
MR 1.16(c)	66, 67, 73
MR 1.16(d)	67, 73
MR 1.18	101, 102, 114
MR 2.2	88, 189
MR 2.2(a)(1)	189
MR 2.2(a)(2)	189
MR 2.2(a)(3)	189
MR 2.2(c)	189
MR 2.3	88
MR 2.3(c)	90
MR 2.4	88
MR 3.1	40, 50, 163, 164, 179, 184, 186
MR 3.1 Comment	163
MR 3.2	60, 155, 164, 179
MR 3.3	33, 86, 88, 176, 177
MR 3.3(a)	156, 160, 177, 178
MR 3.3(a)(1)	156
MR 3.3(a)(2)	155, 160, 178
MR 3.3(a)(3)	6, 155, 158, 159, 160, 175, 178
MR 3.3(a)(4)	155
MR 3.3(b)	159
MR 3.3(c)	88, 159, 175, 178
MR 3.3 Comment 2	157
MR 3.3(d)	157, 177, 185
MR 3.4	33
MR 3.4(a)	162, 175, 179
MR 3.4(b)	175
MR 3.4(c)	165
MR 3.4 Comment 3	163
MR 3.4(d)	164, 179
MR 3.4(e)	155, 164, 165, 175, 176, 179
MR 3.4(f)	155, 162, 175, 179
MR 3.4(f)(1)	162
MR 3.4(f)(2)	162, 179
MR 3.5	149, 171, 180
MR 3.5(b)	169, 180
MR 3.5(c)	170
MR 3.6	5, 167, 168, 180
MR 3.6(a)	168, 180
MR 3.6(b)	168, 180
MR 3.6(b)(1)	168

Rule	Pages
MR 3.6(b)(2)	168
MR 3.6(b)(3)	168
MR 3.6(b)(4)	168
MR 3.6(b)(5)	168
MR 3.6(b)(7)(i)	168
MR 3.6(b)(7)(ii)	168
MR 3.6(b)(7)(iii)	168
MR 3.6(b)(7)(iv)	169
MR 3.6(c)	167, 169, 180
MR 3.7	123, 133
MR 3.7(a)(1)	124
MR 3.7(a)(2)	124
MR 3.7(a)(3)	124
MR 3.8	5
MR 3.8(a)	184, 197
MR 3.8(b)	184, 197
MR 3.8(c)	185, 196, 197
MR 3.8(d)	185, 197
MR 3.8(e)	180, 185
MR 3.8(f)	167, 169, 176, 197
MR 3.8(g)	180
MR 3.9	166
MR 4.1	33, 90, 136, 148
MR 4.1 Comment	137
MR 4.2	135, 141, 142, 143, 144, 149, 151, 152
MR 4.2 Comment 7	142
MR 4.3	135, 142, 144, 145, 152, 185
MR 4.4	135, 149, 151, 163
MR 4.4(a)	139, 140
MR 4.4(b)	150
MR 5.1	183, 187
MR 5.1(a)	187
MR 5.1(b)	187
MR 5.1(c)(1)	187, 188
MR 5.1(c)(2)	188
MR 5.2	183, 186, 197
MR 5.2(a)	186
MR 5.2(b)	183, 186, 196, 198
MR 5.3	210
MR 5.3(a)	188
MR 5.3(b)	188
MR 5.3(c)	141, 210, 215
MR 5.3(c)(1)	188, 197
MR 5.3(c)(2)	189
MR 5.4	193
MR 5.4(a)	70
MR 5.5	20-22
MR 5.5(a)	20
MR 5.5(b)	20
MR 5.5(c)(1)	20
MR 5.5(c)(2)	21
MR 5.5(c)(3)	21
MR 5.5(c)(4)	21
MR 5.5(d)	20
MR 5.5(d)(1)	21-22
MR 5.5(d)(2)	22
MR 5.7	191
MR 5.7(a)(1)	184, 191, 198
MR 5.7(a)(2)	184, 191, 198
MR 5.7(b)	191
MR 6.1	48, 156, 171, 172, 181
MR 6.2	49
MR 6.2(a)	49
MR 6.2(b)	49
MR 6.2(c)	49
MR 6.3	106
MR 7.1	200, 204, 212, 213
MR 7.1 Comment 4	212
MR 7.2	200, 207, 213
MR 7.2(b)	207, 214
MR 7.2(c)	207, 212, 214
MR 7.3	200, 203, 208, 213
MR 7.3(a)	208, 214
MR 7.3(b)(1)	209, 214
MR 7.3(c)	209, 213
MR 7.4	200, 204, 206, 213
MR 7.5	200, 206, 212, 213
MR 8.1	17, 28
MR 8.1(a)	27
MR 8.1(b)	9, 17, 26, 28
MR 8.2(a)	167
MR 8.3	9, 23, 24, 27, 29, 52, 90, 227
MR 8.3(a)	9, 23, 26, 27, 29
MR 8.3(c)	9, 23, 29, 90
MR 8.4	32, 33, 43
MR 8.4(a)	141
MR 8.4(c)	33
MR 8.4(d)	34, 144

Model Code of Professional Responsibility Disciplinary Rules

Rule	Pages
DR 1-102(A)	59
DR 1-102(A)(3)	32
DR 2-101	199, 212
DR 2-101(B)	209
DR 2-102	199, 212
DR 2-103	199, 212
DR 2-104	199, 212
DR 2-105	199, 206, 212
DR 2-106	52
DR 2-106(A)	52

DR 4-101	76, 94
DR 4-101(B)(2)	90, 93
DR 4-101(B)(3)	90, 93
DR 4-101(C)(3)	75, 85, 95
DR 5-101	104
DR 5-103	209
DR 6-101	58, 59
DR 6-102	38, 59
DR 7-101	58
DR 7-102	58
DR 7-102(A)(1)	163
DR 7-102(B)	158
DR 7-105	151

Model Code of Judicial Conduct

Canon 1	219, 236
Rule 1.1	220, 236
Rule 1.2, Comment 5	220
Rule 1.2, Comments	220, 236
Rules 1.3(E)	221
Rule 2.1	234
Rule 2.3(A)	224, 237
Rule 2.3(C)	225, 237
Rule 2.5(A)	223, 224, 234, 237
Rule 2.8(A)	224, 237
Rule 2.8(B)	224
Rule 2.8(C)	226, 238
Rule 2.9(A)	225, 234
Rule 2.9(A)(1)	237
Rule 2.9(A)(2)	226, 237
Rule 2.9(A)(3)	226, 237
Rule 2.10(A)	226, 238
Rule 2.11	227, 238
Rule 2.11(A)	228, 238
Rule 2.11(A)(1)	229, 235, 239
Rule 2.11(A)(2)	228
Rule 2.11(A)(2)(c)	230, 239
Rule 2.11(A)(3)	230, 231, 239
Rule 2.11(A)(6)(a)	229, 235, 239
Rule 2.11(A)(6)(c)	229, 239
Rule 2.11(B)	231, 239
Rule 2.11(C)	231, 239
Rule 2.13(A)	226
Rule 2.15	227
Rule 2.15(A)	227, 238
Rule 2.15(B)	227, 235, 238
Rule 2.15(C)	227, 238
Rule 2.15(D)	227, 238
Rule 3.1	222, 236
Rule 3.1, Comment 1	222, 236
Rule 3.3	221, 236
Rule 3.6(A)	222, 236
Rule 3.7(A)	222
Rule 3.7(A)(2)	222, 236
Rule 3.8	219
Rule 3.8(A)	222, 237
Rule 3.9	219
Rule 3.10	223, 237
Rule 3.11(B)(1)	222
Rule 3.15(A)	223

Public Laws

107-204	116

ABA Opinions

ABA Formal Op. 85-352 (1985)	89
ABA Formal Op. 91-359 (1991)	142
ABA Formal Op. 336 (1974)	33
ABA Informal Op. 86-1518 (1986)	138
ABA Informal Op. 87-1523 (1987)	190
ABA Op. 314 (1965)	85

State Rules

Florida Rule 1.3(a)	50
Florida Rule 1.6	87
Illinois Rule 1.6	87
Iowa DR 5-101	110
Michigan Rule 1.6	87, 88
Minnesota Rule 1.6	87, 88
Minnesota Rule 1.8(e)(3)	111
Texas Rule 1.05	87, 88
Virginia DR Rule 4-101	87

State Ethics Opinions

D.C. Bar Op. 172-9 (1986)	206
D.C. Op. 249 (1994)	205
Florida Bar Op. 89-3 (1989)	140
Georgia Ethics Advisory Op. 80 (1986)	223
Maryland Ethics Op. 89-46 (1989)	24
New Jersey Ethics Op. 595 (1986)	140

Restatement of the Law Governing Lawyers

§122	104, 105

Index

ABA. *See* American Bar Association
Accountants and lawyers, 192-193
"Administration of justice" rules, 34
Admission pro hac vice, 18
Admission to practice, 15-18
Advancing funds to clients, 111
Adverse legal authority, 160-162
Advertising and solicitation, 199-210
    barratry/maintenance/champerty, 209-210
    client rejection, 209
    difference between, 200
    disclaimer, 209
    false/misleading statements, 204-206
    firm names, 206
    in-person/live telephone solicitation, 208
    Internet advertising, 209
    lawyer agents, 210
    name of lawyer, 207
    payment for advertising, 207
    post-event waiting periods, 207
    record keeping, 207
    runners/cappers, 210
    self-laudation, 205-206
    specialization/certification, 206-207
    Supreme Court cases, 201-204
    testimonials, 205
Aggregate settlements, 113-114
Alluding to matters outside the record, 165
American Bar Association (ABA), 10, 11-12
American College of Trial Lawyers, 10
Amorous relations with clients, 110
Ancillary services/businesses, 191-192
Asian Bar Association, 10
Associations of lawyers, 10-11
Association of Trial Lawyers of America, 10
Attorney-client privilege, 76-80, 82-83, 143. *See also* Confidentiality
Attorneys. *See* Lawyers
Attorneys' fees. *See* Fees

Barratry, 110-111, 210
Business transactions with clients, 108-110

Canons of Ethics, 11-12
Cappers, 210
Case authority, 13

Certification/specialization, 206-207
Champerty, 110-111, 210
Character, 16-17
Chinese Wall defense, 39, 118
Christian Legal Society, 10
Civil liability to third persons, 145-146
Client testimonials, 205
Client trust accounts, 57
Client's conduct, liability for, 38
Commercial speech, 13, 201. *See also* Advertising and solicitation
Commingling funds, 58
Communication
    client, with, 60-64
    ex parte, 169-171, 225-226
    represented (opposing) parties, with, 141-144
    unrepresented persons, with, 144-145
Competence, 58-60
Confidentiality, 75-91, 101, 189
    consent and, 83
    evidentiary privilege, 76-80, 82-83
    exceptions, 83-89
    future crimes/frauds, harms, 85-88
    government agency client, 81
    implied authorization, and, 83
    multidisciplinary practice lawyers, 192-194
    misconduct reporting, 23-24
    organizational clients, 81
    other professional duties subject to, 89-90
    self-defense type situations, 83-85
    use of information for lawyer's benefit, 90-91
    to what does duty apply, 82-83
    to whom duty owed, 80-82
Conflict of interests, 39-40, 99-124
    advancing funds to clients, 111
    business transactions with clients, 108-110
    corporate lawyers, Sarbanes-Oxley restrictions on, 116-117
    disqualification for, 39-40
    former government lawyer, 121-123
    former judges, 120-121
    general principles, 101
    imputed conflicts, 118-119
    insurance defense, 106-108
    lawyer as witness, 123-124
    lawyer-client conflicts, 108-111

legal services practice, 106
multidisciplinary practice lawyers, 194
model rule organization, 101-102
multiple-client conflicts, 111-117
organizations, lawyers for, 106, 115-116
positional, 117
screening procedures, 118-119
special role-related rules, 120-124
third-party interference, 105-108
waiver, 102-105, 108
Constitutional constraints, 13-14
Contempt of court, 38-39
Contingent fees, 53-54, 67-68
Continuing part-time judge, 219
Controls on lawyer conduct, 31-41
   contempt of court, 38-39
   discipline, 32- 36. *See also* Discipline
   disqualification motions, 39-41
   liability for client conduct, 38
   malpractice, 36-38
Conversion of funds, 58
Corporate lawyers, 6. *See also* Organizations, lawyers for
Sarbanes-Oxley restrictions, 116-117
Counseling crimes/frauds, 63, 139
Court appointments, 49-50
Criminal conduct, 33, 65
Criminal defense lawyers, 5-6
Criticizing judges, 167
Customs Bar, 10

Deceit, 33-34
Decision-making authority, 61-64
Defamation privilege, 24
Diligence, 58-60
Disability, client under, 63-64
Disbarment, 34
Discipline, 32-36
  disbarment, 34
  grounds, 32-34
  malpractice, contrasted, 32
  mitigation, 35-36
  procedure, 34-36
  reprimand, 34
  suspension, 34
Disclosure. *See also* Confidentiality
  adverse legal authority, 160-162
  material facts, of, 157
  self-defense type situations, 83-85
Dishonesty, 33-34

Disqualification motions, 39-41, 118-119
  judicial disqualification, 227-231
Do-it-yourself forms, 19
Drafting committees, 166
Duties
  confidentiality. *See* Confidentiality
  fiduciary, 37, 56-58
  improve legal system, 166-167
  judicial, 223-231
  legal system and society, to, 155-172
  reject representation, 50-51
  report of misconduct, 23-24
  third parties, 135-146

Ethics 2000 Commission, 12, 13
Ethics codes, 11-13
Ethics opinions, 13
Evidence, suppressing, 162-163
Ex parte communications, 169-171, 225-226
Ex parte proceedings, 157-158
Expediting matters, 60, 164
Expert witnesses, 37, 163
Extraterritorial practice, 19

Fact statements to court, 156-158
False statements of material law or fact, 136, 156
Federal Bar Association, 10
Fee forfeiture, 55-56
Fee splitting, 54-55
Fees, 52-56, 67-68, 206
Fiduciary duties, 37, 56-58
Former government lawyer, 121-123
Former judges, 120-121
Forwarding fee, 54
Fraud, 33-34
Fraudulent statements/silences, 136-137
Frivolous claims, 40-41, 50, 163-164
Future crimes/frauds, 85-88

Government lawyers, 5
  former (conflicts of interest), 121-123
Gross conflict exception, 102-103

Handling of clients' money, 56-58
Harassment rules, 138-140
Housekeeping matters, 169-170, 225-226

Imputed disqualification rule, 118-119
Indirect contempt, 39
Information generally known, 89
Informed consent, 104-105

In-person/live telephone solicitation, 208
Insurance defense, 106-108
Integrated bar, 11
Intemperate remarks, 166
Interest-other-than-the-client's exception, 103-104
Intermediary role, 189-191
Internet advertising, 209
IOLTA programs, 57

Joint representation (criminal cases), 114
Judges, 217-232
    attributes, 219
    bias, 224-225, 228
    conduct outside judicial role, 220-223
    criticism of, 167
    disqualification, 227-231
    duties, 223-231
    ex parte communication, 169-170, 225-226
    financial activities, 222
    former (conflicts of interest), 120-121
    honorariums/outside income, 223
    liability for civil wrongs committed, 232
    political activities, 231-232
    reporting others' misconduct, 227
    sources of judicial conduct law, 217-218
    speaking/writing/teaching, 222
    types, 218-219
    witnesses, as, 221-222
Judicial disqualification, 227-231
Judicial selection, 167
Jurors
    ex parte communications, 170-171
    lawyer-juror relationship, 140
    misconduct reporting, 171

Law statements to court, 160
Lawyer-client relationship, 47-68
    communication/shared decision-making, 60-64
    competence and diligence, 58-60
    conflicts of interest, 108-111
    court appointments, 49-50
    fees, 52-56, 67-68
    fiduciary duties, 56-58
    sexual relations with client, 110
    termination of relationship, 64-68
    undertaking representation, 48-52
    when begun, 51
    wrongful discharge, 51-52
Lawyers
    intermediaries, as, 189-191
    law governing, 2
    role, 3-6
    supervisory, 186-189
    witnesses, as, 123-124
Legal aid lawyers, 6
Legislative advocacy, 166-167
Liability for client conduct, 38
Liability to third persons, 38, 145-146
Literary rights, 109-110
Litigation publicity, 167-169
Live telephone solicitation, 208
Loyalty, 101

Maintenance, 110-111, 210
Malpractice, 32, 36-38, 59
Mandatory withdrawal, 64-65
Media rights, 109-110
Mediators, 190-191
Minimum fee schedules, 55
Misappropriation of funds, 58
Model Code of Judicial Conduct, 217-218
Model Code of Professional Responsibility, 12
Model Rules of Professional Conduct, 12-13
Moral philosophy, 1
Moral turpitude, 16, 33
Morally activist lawyer, 4
Multidisciplinary practice (MDP), 192-194
Multijurisdictional practice, 19-22
Multiple-client conflicts, 111-117

National Association of Women Lawyers, 10
National Bar Association, 10
National Conference of Black Attorneys, 10
National Lawyers Guild, 10
National Lesbian and Gay Bar Association, 10
Negotiation setting, 137-138
Noisy withdrawal, 86-87

Obey court orders, 165-166
Opposing party, communication with, 139, 141-144
Order to continue, 66-67
Organization of the bar, 10-11
Organizations, lawyers for
    conflicts of interest, 106, 115-116
    duty of confidentiality, 80-82
    third-party interference conflicts, 105-108

Part-time judge, 219
Periodic part-time judge, 219
Perjury, 158-160
Permissive withdrawal, 65-66

Personal opinion, 164-165
Plea bargains, 144
Positional conflict of interest, 117
Post-event waiting periods, 207
Practice setting, 5-6
Presentations to court, 163-166
Preventing client harm to third person, 146
Pro bono work, 48, 171-172
    multidisciplinary practice lawyers, 194
Pro tempore judge, 219
Prosecutorial communication with opposite party, 141, 143-144
Prosecutorial duties, 5, 143-144, 169, 184-185
Prosecutorial threats, 140-141
Prospective clients, 77, 114
Public office, 166
Publicity, 167-169

Quantum meruit, 67

Recusal (judicial), 227-231
Reducing agreements to writing, 138
Referral fee, 54, 210
Report of juror misconduct, 171
Report of misconduct, 23-24, 227
Reprimand, 34
Residency requirements, 14
Restatement of the Law Governing Lawyers, 13
Retired judge, 219
Right and wrong, 2
Role morality, 2-3
Runners, 210

Same side multiple client representation, 113-114
Screening procedures, 118-119
Self-defense permitted disclosure, 83-85
Self-governance, 23-24
Self-laudation, 205-206
Settlement, 62, 113-114
Sexual relations with client, 110
Shared decision-making, 61-64
Solicitation, 200. *See also* Advertising and solicitation

Sources of law governing lawyers, 11-15
Specialization/certification, 206-207
Speech rights of lawyers, 13-14
State bar associations, 11
Statements to court, 156-158, 160, 161
Subordinate lawyers, 186-189
Substantial relationship test, 114-115
Supervision of nonlawyers, 188-189
Supervisory lawyers, 186-189
Suppressing witness availability, 162-163
Suspension, 34

Telephone solicitation, 208
Termination of lawyer-client relationship, 64-68
Test cases, 63
Testimonials, 205
Third party,
    duties to, 135-146
    interference conflicts, 105-108
Third persons, liability to, 38, 145-146
Threats of criminal prosecution, 140-141
Trust accounts, 57
Truth-tellng
    inside of court context, 156-162
    outside of court context, 136-138

Unauthorized practice, 19-23
Undercover agents, 144
Undertaking representation, 48-52
Unlicensed, practice by, 22-23

Waiting periods, 207
Withdrawal from representation, 64-68, 86-87, 160, 189-190
Witnesses
    harassing, 140
    judges as, 221-222
    lawyer as, 123-124
    lawyer-witness relationship, 140
    payment rules, 163
    suppression of availability, 162-163
Work product doctrine, 97
Wrongful discharge, 51-52